Democratic Politics and Party Competition

This new book addresses central issues in the comparative study of democracy, principally those issues that can be illuminated through the work of the Comparative Manifestos Project (CMP).

Applying the Comparative Manifestos' approach, the contributors to this volume outline the intellectual challenges that it faces and indicate some of the ways that the comparative study of democracy may be carried forward. Addressing a wide range of issues within the broader area of political science, the volume:

- Provides an up-to-date account of the achievements of the CMP.
- Illustrates some of the ways that the comparative study of democracy may be carried forward into the future, focusing on potential extensions of the CMP research programme.
- Presents a wide range of opinions and uses of the CMP's methodology and discusses a number of challenges to this particular approach.

Honouring the lifetime achievement of Professor Ian Budge, who has provided distinguished intellectual leadership for the Comparative Manifestos Project over the last 25 years, this innovative study will appeal to researchers of comparative politics, government and democratic theory.

Judith Bara is a Lecturer in Politics, at Queen Mary, University of London and a Research Fellow in Government at the University of Essex, UK. **Albert Weale** is Professor of Government at the University of Essex, UK. He is also co-editor of the *British Journal of Political Science* and Fellow of the British Academy.

Routledge/ECPR studies in European political science
Edited by Thomas Poguntke
University of Birmingham, UK, on behalf of the European Consortium for Political Research

ecpr

The Routledge/ECPR studies in European political science series is published in association with the European Consortium for Political Research – the leading organisation concerned with the growth and development of political science in Europe. The series presents high-quality edited volumes on topics at the leading edge of current interest in political science and related fields, with contributions from European scholars and others who have presented work at ECPR workshops or research groups.

Also available from Routledge in association with the ECPR:
Sex Equality Policy in Western Europe, *Edited by Frances Gardiner*; **Democracy and Green Poltical Thought**, *Edited by Brian Doherty and Marius de Geus*; **The New Politics of Unemployment**, *Edited by Hugh Compston*; **Citizenship, Democracy and Justice in the New Europe**, *Edited by Percy B. Lehning and Albert Weale*; **Private Groups and Public Life**, *Edited by Jan W. van Deth*; **The Political Context of Collective Action**, *Edited by Ricca Edmondson*; **Theories of Secession**, *Edited by Percy Lehning*; **Regionalism Across the North/South Divide**, *Edited by Jean Grugel and Wil Hout.*

Democratic Politics and Party Competition

Essays in honour of Ian Budge

Edited by Judith Bara and Albert Weale

 Routledge
Taylor & Francis Group

LONDON AND NEW YORK

First published 2006
by Routledge
2 Park Square, Milton Park, Abingdon, Oxon OX14 4RN

Simultaneously published in the USA and Canada
by Routledge
270 Madison Ave, New York, NY 10016

Routledge is an imprint of the Taylor & Francis Group, an informa business

Typeset in Baskerville by Wearset Ltd, Boldon, Tyne and Wear
Printed and bound in Great Britain by TJI Digital, Padstow, Cornwall

British Library Cataloguing in Publication Data
A catalogue record for this book is available from the British Library

Library of Congress Cataloging in Publication Data
A catalog record for this book has been requested

ISBN10: 0–415–38505–9 (hbk)
ISBN10: 0–203–96577–9 (ebk)

ISBN13: 978–0–415–38505–3 (hbk)
ISBN13: 978–0–203–96577–1 (ebk)

To Ian Budge

Political scientist, colleague, friend

Contents

Figures

Tables

Contributors

Judith Bara is Lecturer in Politics at Queen Mary, University of London and Research Fellow in Government at the University of Essex.

John Bartle is Senior Lecturer in Government at the University of Essex.

Pamela Johnston Conover is Professor of Political Science at the University of North Carolina.

Ivor Crewe is Professor of Government and Vice-Chancellor of the University of Essex.

Hans Keman is Professor of Comparative Political Science at the Free University of Amsterdam.

Michael Laver is Professor in the Department of Politics, New York University.

Michael D. McDonald is Professor of Political Science at Binghamton University.

Iain McLean is Official Fellow in Politics and Professor of Politics at Nuffield College, Oxford.

Ken Newton is Professor of Comparative Politics at the University of Southampton.

Jack H. Nagel is Professor of Political Science at the University of Pennsylvania.

David Robertson is Professor of Politics and Tutor in Politics at St Hugh's College, Oxford.

Donald D. Searing is Burton Craige Professor of Political Science at the University of North Carolina.

Andrea Volkens is Research Fellow at the Wissenschaftszentrum Berlin.

Hugh Ward is Professor of Government at the University of Essex.

Albert Weale is Professor of Government at the University of Essex.

Paul Whiteley is Professor of Government at the University of Essex.

Preface

The academic world is a 'small world' as David Lodge entitled one of his sharp and witty novels. It is therefore not exceptionally surprising that a former PhD student of Ian Budge should happen to be the Series Editor of the Routledge/ECPR Studies in European Political Science where this volume in honour of his work is published. Having read Ken Newton's excellent and highly entertaining account of the Budgean modus operandi I cannot resist the temptation to add a few details from the perspective of someone who wrote his PhD thesis under Ian's supervision at the EUI.

What comes to mind when thinking back to the Florentine years? Ken mentions the illegible handwriting, and I clearly remember that the first serious challenge on my way to completing a PhD thesis was the task of deciphering Ian's comments on the margins of my outlines and first chapter drafts. Our first meeting, however, made a far more lasting impression on me. Roaming the corridors of the medieval Badia Fiesolana in search for the appropriate supervisor who was to guide one's work over the next three (or so) years, I met Ian Budge and presented some very preliminary ideas about how one might be able to explain the phenomenon of the emerging of Green parties in many Western European countries. He listened patiently and then told me that he was not really convinced by the approach I wanted to follow. 'But if you argue your case well, it will be alright with me', he continued, and I think this simple sentence should be the basic law of PhD supervision. We proceeded on that basis without any problems towards the completion of my thesis and one of the great mysteries of our times is how he could read entire chapter drafts in sometimes little more than half an hour and always spot the weak points that I had tried to carefully hide from his attention.

It is fitting that a volume in honour of Ian Budge's work should be published in the ECPR book series since he has played such an influential role in building up the ECPR. Furthermore, Ian Budge's work has always embodied one of the central missions of the Consortium, that is, the commitment to systematic comparative research. Bringing junior and senior researchers together in Joint Sessions and Research Sessions has provided the launch pad for many large comparative projects; and the Comparative Manifestos Project, in which Ian Budge has played such a central role, is certainly one of the most important endeavours in empirical political science. It starts from the simple assumption that analysts should, in the first instance, take the programmatic statements of political parties seriously and see whether or not they keep faith to their ideological roots and, eventually, carry out their election promises.

Anyone who wants to answer these questions for more than very few parties over a relatively short period of time needs to convert manifesto prose into quantitative data, and this was the initial mission of the Comparative Manifestos Project. By now, the data set includes more than 50 countries and the data on some parties covers more than five decades – a unique data base for answering the questions sketched out above and many more. What is more, some of the findings from the Manifesto Project can be read as an antidote to political cynicism: parties tend to keep faith to their basic ideological commitments when writing their election manifestos and, within the given political and economic constraints, parties do make a difference to policy outputs.

This volume revisits some of these themes and pushes them further. As the editors point out in their introduction, the contributions centre around three broad themes, including the 'empirical validity of the generalisations that emerge from Ian Budge's account of democracy', related methodological problems, and wider theoretical and methodological implications. It assembles contributions from leading experts in the field, among them many long-standing collaborators of Ian Budge. As such, it is far more than an acknowledgement to his work. It pushes back the boundaries of our understanding of how party competition and democratic government function – and it is precisely this forward-looking nature which makes it such a appropriate tribute to Ian Budge's achievements.

Thomas Poguntke, Series Editor

Acknowledgements

There are few occasions on which personal moments intersect with the right time to assess professional developments in political science, but this volume records one such occasion. In the last 25 years political scientists have made great strides in understanding the workings and processes of democracy. Ideas of party competition, electoral choice and government formation have been elaborated. Data gathering to test these ideas has been refined and developed. Central to this process has been the work of the Comparative Manifestos Project, possibly the largest network of political scientists in the world. One testament to work of this group is the 2003 Best Data Set Award by the Comparative Politics Section of the American Political Science Association. So, when the occasion came for Ian Budge to retire, it seemed a good idea to mark the occasion in the way that he wanted, namely with a conference devoted to the examination of these professional questions. The present volume is the fruit of those efforts.

The conference itself was held at the University of Essex between 26 and 28 May 2004. It is a mark of the professional and personal respect in which Ian is held that participants were willing to travel from Germany, the Netherlands, Ireland and the United States, as well as the UK, to attend the event, and one participant from Australia routed his journey so as to be there. Altogether there were 19 papers presented. Inevitably, it did not make sense to include all of these in a single volume, and in some cases other commitments pressed upon busy authors. Moreover, some papers had to be extensively rewritten or revised in order to make a coherent volume. The editors and organisers are grateful to all participants in the conference for their contributions, including those (Sarah Birch, Anthony King, Hans-Dieter Klingemann, David McKay and David Sanders) whose papers are not included here. We should also like to thank Ken Newton who undertook the biographical sketch of Ian Budge included in this volume.

The conference itself was proof of the old adage that if you want a job done, find a busy person to do it. In particular, Jackie Pells and Linda Day of the Essex Department of Government, did an excellent job. We are also grateful to the Department of Government and the University of Essex for financial support for the conference itself and to the University Librarian, Robert Butler, and his colleagues Nigel Cochrane and Sandy Macmillan, for facilitating the exhibition which demonstrated Ian Budge's pioneering contribution to the Essex Summer School as well as to the Comparative Manifestos Project. Many of the participants in the conference have also contributed to the former as both students and faculty. We also owe a huge debt to Julie Snell for managing, with her usual skill, the task of turning disparate typescripts into an intelligible sequence.

It is one thing to have an interesting set of papers, another to have a coherent volume. We are grateful to three anonymous referees on the project whose advice has proved helpful in this task. Thomas Poguntke, in his role as Series Editor of the Routledge ECPR Studies in European Political Science, expedited the project, and Heidi Bagtazo and Harriet Brinton at Routledge have been a model of efficiency. We are grateful to them all.

Above all, however, we should like to express our gratitude to Ian Budge, the inspirer of this project and the dedicatee of this volume. He has been a political scientist who has taught us much. More importantly, he has been a colleague and friend who has generously shared his talents and enthusiasms with many people. We hope he finds evidence of his beneficent effect in these papers.

Judith Bara
Albert Weale

Introduction

Judith Bara and Albert Weale

The modern theory of political democracy is built upon the practice of party competition. Political parties campaign for support. Individual electors vote for parties. These votes are aggregated to produce an outcome. Elected parties enter the legislature. If there is an outright winner among the parties, then the winner forms the government. If there is no outright winner, then parties normally have to bargain over the formation of a governing coalition. The prospect of future elections keeps parties in the government and legislature accountable to the electorate, whose interests they are supposed to be serving.

Although simple to describe in outline, political democracy through competitive elections is complex to understand in detail. On what basis do political parties campaign? Do they stand on an ideological orientation or on specific policy promises? How do voters decide upon their vote choice? To what extent do they calculate or to what extent do they choose on the basis of habitual identifications? What are the bases and dynamics of coalition negotiation? Do parties in government behave in ways that are responsive to the expressed preferences of voters? If so, what happens when such responsiveness is at odds with historic or principled commitments? Such questions and many more besides are the staples of political science. Moreover, the answers that are given have implications for our evaluation of how well representative democracies perform when judged by democratic principles and values.

Over many years, Ian Budge has written and thought about these questions extensively. The research that he has conducted, both in his own right and in collaboration with others, constitutes an impressive intellectual achievement in providing evidence and arguments by which some of the fundamental questions of political democracy are addressed. Historically informed, comparative in method, innovative in approach and driven by a passion for the development of democracy, the research that Ian Budge has conducted marks a signal contribution to our collective political science understanding. As importantly, he has not only pursued an individual research agenda, he has contributed uniquely to the development of political science in Europe and internationally. Among his achievements are the Essex Summer School in Data Analysis, the director-ship of the European Consortium of Political Research in its formative years and the role that he has played in the Manifesto Research Group, latterly the Comparative Manifestos Project (CMP). The Comparative Manifestos Project is regarded as a landmark in empirical political science, not only in its own right but because of its rich and publicly available data set, a data set that incidentally won a prize from the Comparative Politics section of the American Political Science Association in 2003.

In the next chapter Ken Newton narrates Ian Budge's life in political science, touching on all these achievements and the personal qualities on which they have depended. In the remainder of this chapter we lay out the central themes and issues that inform this collection of chapters, originally presented at a conference at the University of Essex in May 2004 and now offered in honour of Ian's work.

The elements of political democracy

Democracy is about making political choices and Ian Budge has sought to understand the processes by which these choices are made. Although his work has a number of dimensions, one central strand has been the way that he has animated and drawn upon the work of the Manifesto Research Group, latterly the Comparative Manifestos Project. By building upon a comprehensive analysis of the contents of some 780 parties across 54 countries over a period that stretches back more than 50 years, the research groups have provided a rich body of empirical evidence in terms of which the workings of political democracy can be understood. Anyone who has worked with such data will know how painstaking they are to collect and how complex they can be in detail. It is a mark of the intellec-tual quality that Ian Budge has brought to this work that we now under-stand the basic dynamics in terms of which representative democracy operates. We also understand how these basic elements are related to some of the central values of democracy.

To say that political parties and party competition are central to demo-cracy is to pose a challenge to a number of long-standing traditions of political thought. For many traditional theorists within the democratic canon have been suspicious of parties or factions presuming that they undermine the sense of civic virtue and public interest that are central to the political culture of a democracy. For example, Rousseau was notori-ously critical of forms of political organisation that were, in his terms, 'partial', seeing only unalloyed commitment to the general will as the basis for a free and democratic political order. Such scepticism about sec-tional interests fed into the French republican tradition enhancing its dis-trust of secondary associations. To take a rather different example, although Madison was critical of those to whom he referred as 'theoretic politicians' (and since he was talking about the problem of political scale, it is difficult to believe that he did not have Rousseau in mind), he also argued that, though it was not possible to eliminate factions, it was necessary to tame them. Similarly, within the utilitarian tradition, Bentham and his followers also were cautious about partial interests, to whom they attached the epithet 'sinister'.

How, against this background, is it possible to craft a conception of legitimate political democracy in which political parties, a form of partial association par excellence, play a fundamental and positive role? One answer to this question is that we need to think about party competition as a system, and not just about political parties as agents. It is through the competition for votes and the processes of coalition bargaining that an outcome may emerge that can embody some sense of the popular will. In this regard, there is an analogy with economic theories of competition, in which the selfish pursuit of profit by firms is central in producing an efficient equilibrium. Perhaps, just as in economic markets under certain conditions, competition may produce outcomes that are beneficial for consumers, so political competition might produce outcomes that are beneficial to citizens. Yet, in economics, firms may not be intending to serve consumer interests when they compete with one another: the efficient market equilibrium is a product of human action but not of human design. Can we extend the analogy between economic and political competition, such that we can conclude that citizen representation works independently of the intentions of political parties?

In this connection, one central conclusion arising from the work of the Comparative Manifestos Project is important, namely that, although political parties are office-seekers, they are not purely office-seekers. In this respect the analogy between political parties and firms breaks down. Parties in general have an attachment to ideological principles in the broad sense, and they construct their party programmes in ways that are consistent with ideological commitments. For example, in a pure office-seeking model, there is no reason why parties should not leapfrog one another in ideological space, with one party sometimes to the left of its main competitor and sometimes to the right. If chasing down a winning share of the popular vote is all that matters to parties, then they have to go to where the votes are. However, in practice, parties do not leapfrog in this way. Over time they generally maintain their ideological positions relative to their main rivals, and even in the United States – often regarded as an ideology-free zone by commentators and journalists – the Democrats have consistently been to the left of the Republicans, although each party has adjusted its policy position within broad ideological limits. Hence, when we are discussing the party systems of modern representative democracies, we are not referring to a pure spoils system in which securing the fruits of office entirely determines how parties behave. Instead we also have to look at the role of ideological principles in shaping the competitive behaviour of political parties.

Already we have anticipated another finding of Budge's empirical account of democracy, namely that there is a dominant ideological cleavage across political systems, which can be characterised in terms of a contest between left and right. One central argument here (see Budge and Keman, 1990: 36) is that the scale of reforms that are implied by the demands of socialist or progressive parties is so great that all parties need to take up an attitude in relation to the socialist–bourgeois confrontation. A logically distinct, but nonetheless complementary, argument is that variations in manifesto positions on different aspects of public policy are well explained, in a statistical sense, by one principal component, which can be interpreted as a left–right dimension. For example, although there is no logical compulsion for the position that a party takes on defence to be associated with its position on the running of the economy, in practice the two sets of opinions do co-vary. Statistical inference thus reinforces the everyday vocabulary of journalism, commentary and common sense.

This argument about the dominance of the left–right cleavage is not incompatible with other sources of allegiance playing a significant role in forming partisanship, including religion, region or language, as posited in the Lipset–Rokkan model for Europe. Rather the argument is one about the general saliency of the left–right cleavage and therefore the important role it normally plays in democratic politics. Parties might conceivably be divided by their attitudes to transubstantiation or the Schleswig-Holstein question (as historically some have been). It is simply that, as a matter of fact, they are not. In practice, ideological commitments take their colouring from the attitudes that parties take up towards the large issues of managing the economy and the distribution of income, wealth and property.

There are two important implications of the role of ideology in general and the role of the left–right cleavage in particular that bear upon the place of party competition in securing the conditions for democracy. The first of these concerns the role of ideological connectedness in coalition bargaining. Unlike pure office-seeking theories of coalition formation, the Budge view emphasises the place of ideological compatibility in the formation of coalitions. Because parties are ideologically committed to their manifestos, they will not willingly give up an element of their programme in order to achieve office. Rather they will use bargaining over the content of the coalition programme as an opportunity to secure the programmatic concerns that are most important to them. Surplus coalitions, in which the governing team is of more than minimum winning size, are not an embarrassment for this theory. Moreover, parties in a governing coalition will seek to occupy ministries that are particularly important to them and to their constituents.

In respect of party competition and coalition formation, there is one important result that Ian Budge has proposed about the relationship between governments and the electorate. This is that viable governments typically include representatives of the median voter in ideological space

(McDonald *et al.*, 2004). The median party in the coalition, when scaled by the left–right metric, is the party that coincides with the left–right position of the median voter. If majority rule with more than two alternatives means that the median voter is decisive, and if the governing coalition typically includes representatives of the median voter, then there is a sense in which in their workings elections bestow a 'median mandate' upon governments. In this way party competition, in the circumstances in which parties have ideological commitments, secures responsiveness between popular preferences and political outcomes. Perhaps, rather intriguingly, this result obtains both across proportional representation/multiparty systems and across first past the post/dominant two-party systems, although deviations from the median mandate occur more frequently in simply plurality systems than in PR systems. Overall, however, democratic responsiveness is not such a rare flower after all.

None of this would carry much by way of implication if governments then did what they liked, but here again Ian Budge's analysis offers some strong claims. In particular, he has argued that, contrary to much journalistic and popular cynicism, political parties in office generally implement their manifestos, at least in the sense that they move public expenditure in the direction that is implied by their ideological stance (Budge and Hofferbert, 1990; Hofferbert and Budge, 1992). If they are on the left, they seek to move public expenditure upwards, whereas if they are on the right, they seek to move it downwards. In this way, at least, party competition contributes to responsive and accountable government, central values in the theory of democracy.

One way of bringing out the central place of political parties in a democracy is to ask what, if any, their role would be if the population at large determined the broad content of public policy rather then representative assemblies. Ian Budge has addressed this issue in *The New Challenge of Direct Democracy* (Budge, 1996). In the projected political system described in that work, Ian Budge imagines the electorate deciding on policy measures through referendums using electronic and information technology. The technology means that one of the central traditional objections to direct democracy, namely its lack of feasibility in a large-scale society, loses its force. And Ian Budge adduces that where devices of direct democracy have been used, they have performed as well as the institutions of representative government. It might be thought that in such a system, there would be no role for political parties. If they are not to occupy the offices of legislation, what are they to do? The answer is that they play an important role in defining the agenda, packaging measures to be put to the populace and forwarding political programmes. In short, detach democracy from representative government, and you would still need political parties.

Bringing these ideas together, we can see that there are a number of elements at work in Ian Budge's synthesis of the modern theory of

political democracy. They include: ideologically informed parties, electoral competition, an account of the structure of ideological space over
which competition takes place and the motivation of parties in pursuing
their programmes both in relation to the electorate and in relation to
government. It is an important part of this research programme that it
rests upon claims about party behaviour that are rigorously tested against
empirical evidence. It is this combination – a clear theoretical articulation
together with a grounding in cross-national, comparative empirical evidence – that marks out Ian Budge's work.

Theories come at various levels of generality in political science. At the
lowest level, what is sometimes called a theory is little more than an empirically derived generalisation about political behaviour to be found in one
political system, for example the old French adage that voters have their
hearts on the left and their pocket books on the right. Other empirical
generalisations aspire to record behaviour that is common across a
number of political systems, for example the claim that political parties
never fully converge in the ideological alternatives they present to voters.
Ian Budge's account of democracy rests upon empirical claims that are
supposed to be true at a high level of generality, pertaining not just to
particular political systems but applicable to competitive systems as such.
Of course, the limits of application are implicit in the claim that the
propositions are empirical claims about *democracy*, so that party behaviour
in non-competitive systems – whether they be the Roman Senate, Florentine factions or the eighteenth century House of Commons – may well
follow a different logic. Yet, these limits are broad, and examining such
claims to empirical generality provides a rich challenge to research.

The chapters in this volume look at different aspects of these claims. In
particular, they examine three sorts of questions. What evidence is there
for the empirical validity of the generalisations that emerge from Ian
Budge's account of democracy? What are the methodological problems
associated with his account, particularly in respect of the claim that the
left–right cleavage is dominant? And what possible implications, either
theoretical or normative, might there be of the account and how far can
the approach be extended? In the rest of this introduction, we look at
these three sets of issues in turn.

Empirical generalisability

The quantity of evidence generated by the work of the Comparative Manifestos Project is considerable, covering as it does over 50 years and 780
political parties in 54 countries. However, even with that extensive scope,
the data are still drawn from a specific period and a limited set of places.
For most of that period, the international system associated with the Cold
War was still in place, with implications for the range and character of
political parties within different countries. Political authority was, in

historical terms, concentrated at the level of the nation state, so that party competition at national level was closely tied to the public policy choices that could be made. Issues concerned with the management and control of the economy were generally salient, so that voters could be mobilised around different accounts of how economic policy was best conducted. Electoral rules remained stable. Given these relatively invariable features, there is clearly a possibility that the empirical generalisations upon which Ian Budge's theory of democracy rests reflects the temper of the times rather than any more permanent characteristics of democratic party competition.

As we have already noted, a central theoretical claim of the Budge school of political democracy is a claim that political parties are not simply office-seekers, but they are also organisations that take policy positions, positions to which they have long-standing and deep commitments. In specific terms, Ian Budge and Hans Keman worked out and tested the implications of this view in their study of party government in 20 countries (Budge and Keman, 1990). Yet, as Hans Keman points out in his chapter, the empirical data in terms of which they were able to test their approach were drawn from the period of the Cold War, and in Europe in particular there have been substantial changes in party systems during the 1990s and beyond. Traditionally dominant parties like the Christian Democrats in Italy have lost their electoral hold. New parties like the Greens have entered into governing coalitions, as in Germany. And electoral landslides have taken place in a number of countries, including the Netherlands, France, Italy and Scandinavia. Thus, one natural way of testing the robustness of the theoretical approach is to examine whether it is still supported from data drawn from the period 1990–2005.

The specific propositions about party government that Budge and Keman advanced were stated in terms of a general logic of government formation in political democracies. In particular, this logic assumes that the government is formed by that party or combination of parties that can win a legislative vote of confidence, and that the rules of combination followed a hierarchical pattern. Thus, the most important goal of all democratic parties was to counter threats to the democratic system; where there were no threats, the socialist–bourgeois cleavage predominated; and where neither of these two conditions held, parties pursued their own group-related preferences. In these claims, we see instantiated the core claims that parties are more than office-seekers and that they perform a representative function by their being linked to significant social interests.

Keman shows that, despite the many significant changes that have taken place in European party systems over the 15 year period he studies, the empirical evidence gives fundamental support to these propositions. For example, it is an implication of the theory that we should expect surplus coalitions, that is to say coalitions containing more parties than are strictly necessary to form a government with a parliamentary majority.

Without such surplus coalitions, governing to achieve the ends that parties favour would become more difficult in many cases. And indeed we find that in some 28 per cent of cases, governing coalitions are surplus and such coalitions tend to last the longest. In the same vein, Keman finds evidence to support the claim that parties seek to control those ministries that are most important to themselves in ideological and policy terms, as the original theory predicted. Finally, we should expect to see numerically dominant parties seeking to control the overall direction of government through their occupancy of the chief executive post of prime minister, and this we also find, with Social Democrats and Christian Democrats being prominent in this regard. In short, the empirical evidence is consistent with and generally supportive of a theory of party government that derives from the general model of party competition in a democracy.

We all owe Andrea Volkens a huge debt for acting as de facto grower and guardian of the CMP data sets. In addition to this her chapter in this volume develops the use of the material in new directions. Like Keman's chapter, it also focuses on a European dimension but, unlike Keman, who compares the behaviour of parties in European party systems, Volkens focuses directly on party groupings in the European Parliament. The inception of the Manifesto Research Group (MRG) took place in 1979, the same year that direct elections to the European Parliament were introduced, so this is a timely review of certain forms of behaviour over the whole period of its life as a representative institution.

This work is indeed the first scholarly examination of *programmatic* convergence, both within and between these developing party groups – largely, but not entirely, created along traditional party family lines – on the basis of policy distance. Indeed, as Volkens rightly points out, parties are the main examples of collective actors working within their national environments and beyond, and as such face increasing pressure to cooperate transnationally. The European Parliament represents an appropriate arena to test how successfully they are adapting to such challenges.

Volkens avers that although parties within the European Parliament do not need to operate on the basis of government or opposition, they do need to build alliances to create majorities so that decisions can be effected. It is unlikely that any single party grouping will dominate to be able to ensure this on its own so we are indeed looking at a rather different form of coalition building. Understanding how parties within groupings position themselves in terms of specific policies in relation to each other gives us a basis for understanding the complexion of likely 'coalitions' between groups which are needed to arrive at majorities on specific decisions.

Measures seeking to identify and compare party positions, saliencies and traditional CMP left–right scores for six party groupings across each parliamentary period from 1979 to 2004 were used to compare party behaviour along left–right and European integration dimensions. This allows for a degree of triangulation so that both face validity and correlational validity can be tested. Overall, these measures yielded both expected and unexpected results.

Volkens finds that, since 1979, distances between parties and party groupings have decreased unambiguously across both the left–right and the European integration measures, despite a series of enlargements which have brought in parties from very different regional and cultural backgrounds. However, her research also finds that left–right convergence has not necessarily taken place in a straightforward manner and is complicated by contradictory moves, 'sometimes to the right, at other times to the left'. The only real exception here is the Party of European Socialists (PES) which has consistently moved rightwards since 1979. On the other hand, in terms of European integration, parties have grown more incompatible over time – again with the exception of the PES – suggesting greater internal strife within groupings along this issue. Overall, Volkens concludes that saliency of issues/policies for both individual parties is a good indicator that it is likely that they will try and work for a 'joint' position, both within and between party groupings, and the CMP data thus is a useful indicator of such behaviour.

The left–right positioning of parties is also at the heart of Michael McDonald's contribution to the volume. Like Keman, he focuses on a series of national party systems and he clearly roots his discussion of how parties shape policy agendas within the purview of Budge's interpretation of how democratic theory applies to political parties in terms of both how they influence policy agendas and how they attempt to maximise their vote shares. The chapter also captures Budge's energy and zeal in developing and applying his particular concepts and infusing similar enthusiasm in others.

McDonald asserts in the chapter that an important role of parties in democracy is indeed to set the policy agenda, but in such a way that the electorate is presented with choices it can use to direct the policy decisions of government. The CMP data show that party policy positions, along a left–right continuum, need to be characterised in terms of two prominent features. They are distinctly different *and* volatile. Using these features as empirical background information, McDonald makes two important points that we need to understand about party policy position offerings to electors. First, it is precisely this combination of distinctiveness and volatility that proves sufficient to create accurate representation in party democracies. By offering varied choices at least one party will usually be positioned in the vicinity of the median voter, and that leaves it to electors to make the choice on the basis of party policy packages on offer. Second, he argues that distinctiveness and volatility are inherent consequences of the operation of democracy inside parties. Party distinctiveness comes from left- and right-leaning candidates sorting themselves according to parties' general policy tendencies when they enter politics, and party volatility comes from alternation in factional control inside parties. Indeed it is often the unpredictable and unexpected which explain the reality of the political world in which we live and voters as well as parties often behave in ways that we would not necessarily have foreseen.

The last chapter in Part I by Judith Bara picks up on this theme by developing two areas which have developed from this project. These are the investigation of how party policy programmes relate to public concerns and whether it is possible to use computerised coding techniques as an alternative to manual coding. The chapter develops both of these by discussing how a new computerised dictionary, based on responses to standard 'most important problem' type of questions in opinion surveys, was applied to a sample of the general election manifestos of the three major parties in Britain. The data obtained was then mapped against general estimates of public concerns during periods leading up to each election concerned and validated against a reconstituted set of original MRG codes for the relevant election programmes.

The proposition under investigation is that parties, whilst reflecting major public opinion in general, will tend to develop policy priorities which are closer to those of their rivals than to the main concerns of the public. This is shown to be the case in the main and the estimates produced by the computerised coding technique are also shown to be good reflections of the MRG estimates. The principal reasons for this are that parties and public are concerned with different types of issue. Whilst both could be said to favour bread and butter, domestic issues, as demonstrated clearly by both manifesto content and responses to public opinion polling, parties are more concerned with a medium-term policy agenda which can help then achieve power, carry out legislative programmes and be re-elected as a 'responsible' rather than 'responsive' government. The public's concerns on the other hand are with more immediate problems or moral dilemmas, neither of which are necessarily the kind of thing that parties consider a basis for good manifesto content.

We are far from pretending that the chapters in Part I are a comprehensive vindication of the approach that Ian Budge has pioneered over the years. However, they do extend that approach outside of the political context in which the theory was originally developed and for this reason they offer some test of the robustness of that approach. If party competition involves ideologically informed parties seeking to form governments to implement programmes, in which there is vigorous internal competition and with a willingness to carry over their political visions to the European level, we seem to have the elements of an approach to democracy that is not only theoretically coherent but also empirically informed.

Left and right? Some methodological issues

As we have seen, one of the central results that Ian Budge sees as coming out of the work of the CMP is the dominance of the left–right dimension in our understanding of democratic politics. This result is important, as McLean and Nagel point out in their chapters, in both empirical and normative terms. Empirically it is important because, if it is plausible, our explanations of party competition become straightforward. We can understand the movement of parties towards the centre ground as a simple consequence of their search for office informed by their understanding of the underlying disposition to vote given by the ideological preferences of voters understood in one-dimensional left–right terms. Conversely, significant departures from this convergence towards the median will be explained as departures from pure office-seeking, whether that is inadequate information, the internal balance of forces in the party as discussed by McDonald or some other factor. To be sure, the CMP analysis implies that parties will not completely converge, but the pressure of centrism is such in a one-dimensional world of party competition that it characterises the basic logic of party competition parsimoniously and straightforwardly. Moreover, if this is the pattern of behaviour empirically, it offers the basis for an understanding of democratic government in normative terms. If we are majoritarians, then correspondence of governing party position and policy preference of the median elector suggests that party competition is sufficient to achieve majority rule.

The contrary view depends upon a series of results in formal social choice theory, together with an understanding of real-world political competition. It states that all politics is irreducibly multidimensional. This is the view taken by William Riker in his later works, even though at one stage in his career he favoured the view that politics was intrinsically bipolar and one-dimensional (compare McLean, 2002 and Weale, 1984). The social choice results establish that while, under a certain set of assumptions there will be an equilibrium in one dimension of party competition in which parties will converge upon the median voter, there is typically no such equilibrium in a multidimensional policy space, even if all the other conditions of median convergence are in place. If, in practice, there is a multiplicity of issues upon which voters can be mobilised, then it should always be possible, according to Riker, for losing parties to find a combination of policy positions that will defeat current winners or incumbents. There is no winning position in multidimensional policy space that can be guaranteed to be secure against some other position. Democratic politics is not the steady convergence to something like a stable equilibrium but contains the potential for constant chaos, as losing parties seek to raise the salience of issues with which they think they can win. If this is so, concludes Riker, the idea of majoritarian democracy becomes strictly meaningless and the moral case for majority rule is . The moral imperative depends on the existence of a popular will discovered by voting. As Riker once put it, 'If the people speak in meaningless tongues, they cannot utter the law that makes them free.' (Riker, 1982: 239).

In the context of this debate about the feasibility of majoritarian democracy, the CMP results are significant. If they can be sustained, they provide the basis for a critique of the Rikerian chaos view of democracy. How plausible is it to think that the approach adopted by the CMP is right and that we can understand party in terms of one dominant ideological dimension? Can we use party manifestos as the basis for inferring the character of party competition? Iain McLean suggests that there are two possible sceptical responses to these questions. The first is an extremely strong claim; the second rather more modest. The strong form of scepticism is to deny the value of content analysis as a way of determining party positions and ideological stances. The trouble with this position, as McLean forcefully and correctly points out, is that it posits an unsatisfactory alternative, namely the unsystematic and therefore unrepresentative selection of texts by researchers. The virtue of the CMP approach is to take a mass of data, the content of which no one person could possibly understand, and to distil these data into a manageable form. If there is a problem in the CMP approach, it is not with the ambition of constructing dimensional scales inferred from manifesto statements, but in the specific way in which the task is undertaken.

The particular problem on which McLean focuses is the procedure by which political positions are inferred from salient terms. The coding frame for the CMP assigns positions depending upon the occurrence of key terms. For example, within the CMP approach, to stress militarism, freedom, human rights, constitutionalism and free trade is to take a position on the right. To stress nationalisation, protectionism, economic planning and a positive mention of labour groups is to take a position on the left. Yet, there are classical liberals who would wish to dispute the association with social control and militarism (Brittan, 1988, is a particularly clear example) and libertarian socialists who would want to dissociate themselves from a centralised political control of the economy. The particular policy example that McLean has in mind is that of free trade, which though often thought of as being a right-wing position has both a history and a rationale in terms of left-wing values.

These methodological doubts are supplemented by analytical considerations advanced by Nagel, who argues that there are severe problems of explanation in inferring too much from the fact that a single principal component explains a great deal of the variance in policy positions across different sectors of public policy. Even if we take correspondence with the median voter as a normative standard for evaluating the performance of democracies, there are considerable problems in supposing that explanations of party competition can be premised on the assumption that the issue space is one-dimensional. If we do so, we risk missing much of what is crucial about political behaviour. Voters may resort to more than one dimension when competition is close; voters who care about non-dominant dimensions may turn out to be pivotal in some circumstances; analysts will miss the way in which the saliency of different issues will move some voters on some occasions; the dynamics of party support will be misunderstood; and large changes in the bases of party competition will be missed.

In part, the issues that Nagel raises touch upon one of the central analytical debates of political science, namely the choice between a generalising approach to the understanding of behaviour and an idiographic approach. Another way of putting the same contrast is to say that there are two competing accounts of how explanations in political science are best couched. On the one side are those who think that to explain is to bring particular instances under a general law, whilst on the other side are those who look at the particularities of cases as constituting the bases of understanding. The temptation, which should not always be resisted, is to say that both sides have some portion of the truth, and that judgement is needed as to when general and specific *explanantia* are cited.

Robertson, however, suggests that the resolution is not purely an empirical matter but involves conceptual clarification of the notion of a dimension. He also seeks to offer reasons connected with the logic of institutions why we should in general expect political and legal stances to be one-dimensional. One important fact is that decisions taken in one domain of public policy have implications for other domains. This is true, for example, in any political system in which there is a constraint on the overall volume of public expenditure, since increasing the money spent on one item will mean less money for other items. Moreover, institutional procedures may make choices sequential in a lexicographic way, as in Robertson's example of the South African Constitutional Court, where the judges first have to decide whether they have jurisdiction before they decide upon the merits of any particular case. The two sets of decisions involved quite distinct considerations, but their distinctiveness does not cause problems because they are invoked at different stages of the process.

Robertson also wishes to argue that, in addition to these institutional constraints, there are constraints of what we can call political culture. Only a pure office-seeking Downsian party could operate in a world in which all aspects of public policy were treated as equally salient, a point that echoes Nagel's criticism of the CMP approach in its treatment of saliency theory. Moreover, according to Robertson, taking a position on what matters carries implications for the position one adopts on other issues. There is a logic of reflection limiting the freedom to take positions. And even where it may seem that political competition is two dimensional, with actors performing heresthetical manoeuvres to take advantage of potential disequilibrium, the dimensionality may be being wrongly identified, since dimensionality is necessarily a scaling concept not just the need to answer a question posed by a situation. In short, whatever the methodological difficulties associated with the CMP conclusion that political competition is characteristically one-dimensional, there are general reasons for thinking that this is a productive way of thinking.

Within the CMP approach the operational definition of an ideology is a summary of the policy positions offered by political parties. Thus, when voters vote for parties, they are implicitly identifying those parties with their overall policy positions and their choices are to be explained in terms of the relative closeness of parties to voters in the ideological/policy summary space. This is a version of the classic Downsian position. Voters vote for those parties that are closest to them in ideological space. Suppose, however, that policy positions of the left–right variety are poor predictors of how voters vote. Then the democratic credentials of the electoral system are called into question. What exactly is the electoral connection if it does not connect the ideological preferences of citizens to the parties for whom they vote? Can there be another basis for the electoral connection?

It is this possibility that Michael Laver explores. Using a unique data set from the Irish general election of 2002, in which for one constituency electronic voting records were published on the preference orderings of voters, he is able to examine the relationship between policy preferences and party preferences. He finds that policy preferences are a poor predictor of the electorate's choice. However, he takes up an idea originally pioneered by Budge and Farlie (1977) of party-defined spaces. The key insight here is that we can measure voters' attachments to parties by their propensity to vote for those parties. For example, in the choice between party A and party B, a firm adherent to party A is 100 per cent likely to vote for that party, a undecided voter is as likely to vote for A as for B, and a voter inclined towards B may be twice as likely to vote for B as to vote for A.

Laver is able to show that using this approach it is possible to define the character of the electoral contest in terms of the relative attachment of voters to different parties. In particular, in the Irish context, he is able to show that the primary division is between pro and anti Fianna Fáil voters, thus confirming a widely held view about the form of divisions in the Irish electorate. Among those voters who oppose Fianna Fáil there is a further division over the nationalist question. Yet the main point is that the conflicts are defined in terms of voters' attachments to parties rather than to policy positions, where these have been aggregated into some left–right metric.

As Laver notes, the discussion by Budge and Farlie was framed in terms of the Michigan voting theory, according to which voters are assumed to have a partisan identification formed through early socialisation, reinforced or reduced in the light of subsequent changes in the life course. The key point is that a preference for party comes first, and the rationalisation that is offered for parties in terms of their policy positions are not part of the explanatory scheme. This model is usually offered as the standard alternative to conventional spatial theory, though interestingly

Downs himself sought to reconcile the two approaches by seeking to show that partisan attachment would be a rational strategy by voters who wished to economise on the search for information in a situation of uncertainty.

Putting these points together, what conclusions should we come to about the role of ideological dimensions in party competition? The account that we gain from Budge and the CMP is a more stable and constrained view than is offered by Riker. In Riker's account parties are opportunistic free agents who seek to disrupt existing winning coalitions by trying out new dimensions of political difference. In the CMP world, parties do compete by ideological movement, but they do so in a world more constrained by institutional procedures, ideological traditions and the attachments that social groups historically have to political parties. In the Riker world, the material of political competition is virtually wholly endogenous to the competitive process itself, revealed in the heresthetical and rhetorical skills of leading actors. In the Budge world, there is less autonomy of political competition. But the competition that does take place, by that very fact, allows for a meaningful sense in which popular preferences are translated into public policies. However one evaluates these competing research programmes, one cannot deny that Ian Budge's framework emerges as progressive in the sense that it is capable of generating fruitful and empirically significant findings and results.

Implications and extensions

The modern practice of democracy is a complex interplay between actions and decisions at the individual level, as citizens decide whether or not to turn out and how to cast their votes, and aggregate procedures and process, as representative parties are elected and governments emerge. In normative terms, a fundamental element in the justification of democracy is that the aggregate processes provide the best outcome possible for individual voters, each of whom has his or her own concerns, attitudes and point of view. The CMP account of representative democracy is essentially a view that focuses on the aggregate picture. It looks at how systems of party competition fare in producing democratically justifiable outcomes. Yet, such an account will carry implications for how individuals relate to the democratic process, and this is one question that pervades the chapters in the final part of this collection.

In developing the use of the CMP data to new areas of enquiry, John Bartle acknowledges the context of the relation between the individual and the aggregate. He points out that there are two contrasting traditions of voting behaviour, each corresponding to a focus either on the individual or the collective. Both traditions acknowledge the interplay of partisan attachment and ideological predisposition, but do so in different ways. On the one hand, those who study voters at the individual level have found it difficult empirically to find much room for the role of ideology in explaining vote choice. Just as Laver showed that position in policy space was a poor predictor of vote choice in the Irish electorate, so John Bartle reminds us that, though accounts of politics in terms of ideology are intuitively appealing, most researchers at the individual level have struggled to find a role for strong ideological effects. To some extent, as he shows, the difficulties here reflect the frame of theoretical reference that analysts have brought to the problem, with researchers in the Michigan tradition stressing the role of socialised habit rather than reflective political choice. When those working in this tradition have seen a role for ideology, its place is set in the context of partisanship.

Aggregate level models, by contrast, have given a prominent place to party ideology in explaining election results and Bartle points to the role that summary ideological positions may have in simplifying the way in which complex issues are presented. It is, of course, in this tradition that the CMP analysis operates. But this is not to say that the CMP data supports any particular aggregate level interpretation. As Bartle points out, the story of how Labour improved its vote share by moving closer to the centre between 1987 and 1992 – a typical piece of aggregate level folk wisdom – runs up against the awkward problem that the CMP data show Labour to be moving slightly leftwards at this time. Yet, if policy mood is also important, so that Labour's leftwards shift coincides with public opinion moving to the left at this time, then we have a more complete explanation.

In an analysis conducted at both the individual and the aggregate levels, Bartle shows that for the 2001 UK election the relationships between party positions, ideology and partisanship are complex. At both levels it is difficult to identify ideological influences in the absence of partisanship, although the exact interrelationships cannot be unpacked with the available data. Perhaps, although this is not a conclusion that Bartle himself draws, it is partisanship that helps to translate the noise of voters' unstable preferences into a relatively clear aggregate signal.

Another problem in relating the individual and the aggregate in the theory of democracy is raised by the issue of turnout, a theme that Paul Whiteley takes up in his chapter. Theories of democracy like those advocated by the CMP give a central role to the tendency of parliaments and governments to reflect the preferences of the median voter. Yet a convergence by parties to the median voter has one potentially detrimental effect, namely that of reducing the incentive for voters to turn out to vote. Since the practice and institutions of democracy require citizens to participate in elections if they are to retain their legitimacy, an inbuilt tendency of party competition to reduce turnout would amount to an internal contradiction of political democracy. Whiteley shows that this internal contradiction exists in theory. How far is it a problem in practice?

Like Bartle, Whiteley examines data at both the individual level, drawing upon data from the British Election Study, and at the aggregate level, using the data generated by the CMP. At the aggregate cross-national level Whiteley finds prima facie evidence, using the CMP data, that dispersion in party positions is associated with turnout. The closer parties are in their left–right positions, the lower the level of turnout and vice versa. But do these results reflect the aggregated effects of motives that operate at the individual level? By drawing upon the British Election Study for 2001, a year in which the strong likelihood that Labour would be re-elected could be expected to reduce the incentive to turn out, Whiteley sees how much explanatory power considerations of party distance from voters add to existing, well-validated models of turnout. He finds some evidence that the proximity of voters to the position of parties, as measured by attitudes to the balance between spending and taxation, does affect turnout, although there is no effect from left–right self-placement (a result that reflects a finding of Bartle's). However, as Whiteley also points out, it is important to place these effects in the context of more general incentives for voting, including sense of efficacy, political knowledge and social norms. In short, the disposition to vote is not simply determined politically, but takes its impetus from social context.

So far, we have only considered accounts of party competition in political democracies in which parties respond to the preferences of the electorate. This is in line with the dominant tradition of thinking about democracy that defines a democracy as a political system in which parties and governments are responsive to the preferences of citizens. However, although a dominant tradition of thinking, this cannot be the sole way in which democracies operate, as Hugh Ward reminds us. The power that political parties have at their disposal means that they will want to shape the preferences of citizens as well as respond to those preferences, and there is prima facie evidence that these processes are at work. Yet, although this possibility has been adopted by commentators and political actors – indeed Mrs Thatcher's attempt to end what she saw as the hegemony of socialism in the UK is a paradigm instance – the possibility has not been extensively explored by political scientists, despite the innovative treatment of the subject by Dunleavy and Ward (1981) some 25 years ago.

Suppose then that we augment the standard assumption that, in a democracy, political parties are responsive to the preferences of the electorate with the assumption that voters may respond to the announced positions of political parties. Is it possible to test whether there is empirical support for holding to both of these claims? In particular, as Ward puts it, can we find evidence that the position of the median voter is made more favourable to a party as a result of its adopting a political programme? Part of the problem is that empirical testing of the relevant propositions is demanding of data, but Ward employs the CMP data together with monthly Gallup data from 1979 in the UK to investigate these possibilities. He finds that there is some evidence that the Conservative party during this period was able to shift public opinion in its favour, whereas the Labour party was more responsive. He supplements this empirical analysis with a formal model showing that it is possible to state a consistent set of assumptions in which there is an advantage in preference shaping given to the more powerful political party. It is an implication of this model that influential parties may well choose, quite rationally, to adopt relatively extreme positions, in order to shift the balance of public opinion in their direction. The non-convergence of policy positions that the CMP data reveal may thus after all be consistent with forms of sophisticated, long-term office-seeking.

Another implication of Ward's paper is that democracy in practice should not be conceived simply as a mechanism of response to the preferences of citizens. There are reciprocal patterns of interaction between parties and the public. There is a natural tendency to think that the possibility of parties influencing public opinion must be malign, because democracies should be systems of popular government. However, it may be that mutual influence is part of the essence of democracy, if we think that democracy is not just a process of preference aggregation but also a process in which preference formation is a matter of discussion and deliberation between parties and the body of citizens at large. It is this possibility that Weale explores, asking how far democracy through party competition corresponds to the norms of deliberative democracy.

It is possible to see the norms of deliberative democracy as simply imposing a requirement that preferences be reflected upon and debated before being voted upon. However, Weale argues that deliberation taken seriously implies a distinct notion of decision making from that of voting, namely decision by discussion on merits. If this is so, then median correspondence will not be sufficient to define a democracy, and there will be an argument in favour of super-majoritarian conceptions of democracy. Similarly, although party competition will simplify political choices for voters, lowering the burdens of judgement, it will also sometimes over-simplify issues, thus avoiding the engagement with reasons and evidence that deliberative democracy advocates. Finally, the CMP analysis of party competition, according to which parties do not engage with the concerns of one another, but rather seek to own certain issues, is at odds with the aspiration of deliberative democrats to see the public forum as one of quality, not cheap, talk. There is no easy reconciliation between the practices of aggregative democracy and the norms of deliberative democracy.

These wider issues of political culture and party competition are explored by Searing, Crewe and Conover in their chapter. In the analysis offered by Budge and Keman of party competition and government formation, it is assumed that defending the democratic system is the prime objective of political actors. This presupposes that the normal practices of democracy are bounded by a concern to maintain the integrity of the rules of the democratic game. However, the conditions that need to be in place in order for this maintenance to occur are not clear. In particular, serious issues arise about the toleration of extreme groups, who are not prepared to abide by these rules. In what processes then is such toleration rooted?

In a careful empirical analysis of respondents from the US and Britain, Searing, Crewe and Conover show that differences of response are partly located in patterns of community, and partly located in differences of national political culture. In particular, the political culture of the US favours an interpretation of toleration, in which reference is commonly made to the requirements of the constitution with the implication that extreme or undemocratic parties should be entitled to certain civil and political freedoms. Such freedoms cannot be justified as serving the role of contributing to the intelligent formation of preferences, as deliberative democrats suppose, but express some culture of respect that underlies any notion of democracy. And yet democracy also asserts that the preferences of the community should prevail, and it is this aspect of a democratic political culture that is picked up by the British citizens to whom Searing and his colleagues talked. As with the tension between aggregative and deliberative components of democracy, there is no reason to believe that these two elements of democratic political culture are easily reconciled with one another.

Conclusions

We began by noting that, although the workings of political democracy were simple in basic conception, they were also complex in practice. Exactly how competitive party elections enable democracy to flourish involves detailed assessments of these complex processes. The approach that Ian Budge has favoured is not uncontroversial, no research paradigm in political science could be. However, it does rest upon the weight not only of coherent argument in the realm of theory building but also serious empirical investigation upon a comparative basis. Compared to many other current approaches to democracy, therefore, it is methodologically far superior. Moreover, if it can be vindicated, it carries substantial implications for normative theory, implications that are supportive of an extension and deeper democratisation of public life. All the contributors to this volume have drawn inspiration from the support, contributions and achievements of Ian Budge, a friend of democracy as well as a colleague and friend of those involved in this project. For that reason, we hope that he will find in these chapters an acknowledgement of the deep respect in which he is held.

Bibliography

Brittan, S. (1988) *A Restatement of Economic Liberalism* (Houndmills and London: Macmillan).

Budge, I. (1996) *The New Challenge of Direct Democracy* (Cambridge: Polity Press).

Budge, I. and D. Farlie (1977) *Voting and Party Competition* (London: Wiley).

Budge, I. and R.I. Hofferbert (1990) 'Mandates and Policy Outputs: U.S. Party Platforms and Federal Expenditures', *American Political Science Review* 84:1, 111–131.

Budge, I. and H. Keman (1990) *Parties and Democracy. Coalition Formation and Government Functioning in Twenty States* (Oxford: Oxford University Press).

Budge, I. H.D. Klingemann, A. Volkens, J. Bara and E. Tanenbaum (2001) *Mapping Policy Preferences: Estimates for Parties, Electors, and Governments 1945–1998* (Oxford: Oxford University Press).

Dunleavy, P. and H. Ward (1981) 'Exogenous Voter Preferences and Parties with State Power: Some Internal Problems of Economic Models of Party Competition', *British Journal of Political Science* 11: 351–380.

Hofferbert, R.I. and I. Budge (1992) 'The Party Mandate and the Westminster Model: Election Programmes and Government Spending in Britain, 1948–85', *British Journal of Political Science* 22:2, 151–182.

McDonald, M., S.M. Mendes and I. Budge (2004) 'What are Elections for? Conferring the Mmedian Mandate', *British Journal of Political Science* 34: 1–26.

McLean, I. (2002) 'William H. Riker and the Invention of Heresthetic(s)' *British Journal of Political Science* 32:3, 535–558.

Riker, W.H. (1982) *Liberalism against Populism* (San Francisco: Freeman and Co.).

Weale, A. (1984) 'Social Choice versus Populism? An Interpretation of Riker's Political Theory', *British Journal of Political Science* 14:3, 369–385.

1   Ian Budge

A life of writing and organising, walking and talking

Ken Newton

Introduction

How can we best celebrate the professional life and times of the man who has been (almost) everywhere and done (almost) everything? In one way, his career is a dead straight line from school and first degree in Edinburgh to a stretch of no less than 40 years in the Government Department at the University of Essex. In that time he only ever lived in two houses in Colchester. Simple and boring, you might say. Seen another way, his career takes in many of the most illustrious centres of political science in the north, south, east and west, covers the founding years of some of the most important professional organisations in European political science, a clutch of path-breaking research projects, and no less than 19 books, plus seventy articles and chapters in prestigious books and journals on both sides of the Atlantic.

It is difficult to know how to do justice to such prodigious energy and achievement in the space of a few thousand words. But since the man himself would have done it – no doubt by knocking off a delightful little essay one Saturday morning when it was too wet to work in the garden in Colchester – I must do my best.

On writing

Ian Budge was born in 1936 in Leeds, but spent his youth from the age of five in Edinburgh, going on to take an MA in history (first class, of course) at its university in 1959. This was followed by a Masters in Political Science (with distinction, of course) at Yale. The first trip to Yale was in the best traditions of young intellectuals who travel and study abroad to avoid conscription into the army, and because universities are prepared to pay the best and brightest to hang around libraries and coffee shops reading, writing and arguing. This they rightly call 'education'. Yale paid the most, so he went there. The British army's loss (Ian would surely have risen to the rank of Private – first class, of course) is political science's gain.

He intended to stay in New Haven for only a year, but it had the best politics department in the USA (the world?) at the time, and the young, ex-historian was hooked by Harold Lasswell and Robert Dahl. He had given up on history because, he says, it failed to complete explanations and left things hanging in the air. Yale did the *real* science of politics, so he returned to do a PhD with Robert Dahl, interviewing Members of Parliament and electors in London to test Dahl's theory that democratic stability rests on a consensus among competing elites about the rules of the democratic game.

Here is what Robert Dahl has to say about his graduate student at Yale:

> You were an ideal student: ready, even eager, to discuss the subject with a thoughtfulness, originality, and firmness tempered by a ready wit and a capacity to learn from the views of others.
>
> From a student you moved on to become a colleague in political science, one whose extraordinary scholarly contributions allowed your previous teachers like me to take pride, in the largely unwarranted fashion as we all do, in having in some small way contributed to your development as a scholar.

Perhaps it would have been the end of his lifelong interest in democracy and democratic stability if Ian had found that Dahl's theory fitted the facts. But it did not do so particularly well, as we can see in the book of his PhD, *Agreement and the Stability of Democracy*, 1970. So he persisted with his attempt to uncover the origins of democratic stability with a comparison of Glasgow and Belfast (*Political Stratification and Democracy*, 1972 and *Belfast: Approach to Crisis*, 1973). The two cities were similar in many ways, except in respect of democratic stability. Once again general theory did not fare too well. There were no more cross-cutting cleavages in Glasgow than Belfast, and politics in Glasgow happened to owe a lot to the particular circumstances of how the Progressive Party responded to the destabilising influence of the Protestant Action party back in the 1930s.

With three books published (in three years) on democratic theory and stability, but all of them leaving some important things 'hanging in the air', he turned to voting and elections, which are, as he puts it, 'a more satisfactory field for general explanation'. This yielded another three volumes (*Party Identification and Beyond*, 1976, *Voting and Party Competition*, 1977 and *Explaining and Predicting Elections*, 1983). Anybody else would have been well satisfied with this output, not least because *Voting and Party Competition* was one of the most important books in its field. But Ian was still dissatisfied. He complains that he and his mathematician co-author, Dennis Fairlie had to run simulations rather than completely determinate theories, and that they were still dependent upon judgements about what were the main campaign issues. Hence he abandoned (for the time being) voting and elections and moved on to the next phase of his research in the form of the Manifestos Project.

This is not the place to go into the Manifestos Project, which is covered in other chapters in this book, but it should be said that it involved a huge amount of data gathering and coding, a great deal of coordination, and some serious international collaboration with many political scientists around the world. It was Ian's idea and creation, and he organised and drove it on from its inception in 1979, until 1996, by which time it was no longer a research project but a global social movement that had created a whole sub-field of political science and produced a whole literature to go with it. It is an extraordinary intellectual and organisational achievement, and was awarded a prize by the Comparative Politics group of the American Political Science Association in 2003.

In terms of Ian's intellectual career built around his interest in democratic processes and stability, the manifesto books produced a positive result for the saliency theory of party behaviour, which must have been very satisfying indeed, but less positive results for testing general coalition theories (*Parties and Democracy: Coalition Formation and Government Functioning in 22 Democracies*, 1990 and *Party Policy and Government Coalitions*, 1992. The measly 22 countries became 48 in *Party Governments in 48 Democracies*, 2000).

The Manifestos Project continues unabated (see *Mapping Policy Preferences. Estimates for Parties, Governments and Electors 1945–1998*, 2001), but with Ian as its godfather not its director after 1996. By then he had moved onto a new phase of work. The concern was still with the subject that fascinated the young research student at Yale 45 years ago, but it now took a more elaborate and comprehensive shape, involving a synthesis of much that has gone before and revolving around median mandate theory, voting, elections, parties and democracy. Such a comprehensive project produces a more complete explanation and leaves less hanging in the air. The first books in this latest phase of his work are *Elections, Parties, Democracy: Conferring the Median Mandate* (2005, with Michael McDonald) and *Organising Democratic Choice: Theoretical Synthesis and Comparative Simulations* (2006).

In between writing monographs, and editing research volumes, there have been occasional distractions in the way of general volumes and textbooks, but only half a dozen or so of these have appeared in print. The early textbook on British politics, *The New British Political System* (1983) transformed itself into *The Changing British Political System* (1987) and then into *The Developing British Political System* (1993). It took on a completely different all-singing, all-dancing, technicolour existence with *The New British Politics* in 1998, and is now going into its fourth edition. For good measure there was a textbook on European politics (*The Politics of the New Europe*, 1997) and a few other books on Scottish Politics, Democratic Government, Ideologies and Party Strategies, Direct Democracy, and an edited Festschrift for Jean Blondel.

Looking through Ian's CV makes one thing clear: here is a man perfectly happy to write books and articles on his own, and perfectly happy to write books and articles with others. In fact he has written a lot with many others – Derek Urwin, Cornelius O'Leary, Dennis Fairlie, David McKay, David Robertson, Hans Keman, Jaap Woldendorp, Hans-Dieter Klingemann, Rick Hofferbert, Ivor Crewe, Andrea Volkens, Judith Bara and even Ken Newton. All of them, without a doubt, are struck by how metronomic he is about producing high quality material to deadlines. One of his Essex colleagues once observed 'Isn't it strange – X is always late to a meeting by varying amounts, but Ian is always late by two minutes and 14 seconds.' Well, I can tell you, he might have been late for meetings, but he was never yet late for a deadline that I know of. No wonder we are all more than happy to collaborate with him.

Before we leave the subject of Ian Budge's writing, I cannot resist a personal note. In 1977 he published an article with Dennis Fairlie in the *British Journal of Political Science* on my own modest contribution to our understanding of the world. It was titled 'Newtonian mechanics and predictive election theory: a point by point comparison'.

On organising

Ian Budge's first full-time job was at the University of Strathclyde (1963–66) where he took part in the development of the new Politics Department. He soon moved to Essex (1966) where he played an even bigger role in developing the fledgling Government Department, alongside Jean Blondel and Tony King. At Essex he also served as the Founder and Director of the Summer Schools in Quantitative Social Science Data Analysis (1968–73), as Chair of the Department, 1974–77 and Executive Director of the ECPR, 1979–83. Not surprisingly he rose from the lowly rank of Assistant Lecturer in 1963 to full Professor in 1976.

His time as Executive Director of the ECPR was crucial. Not only did he follow in the footsteps of Jean Blondel, no enviable task in itself, but he ensured that the rapid growth of the Consortium continued in terms of numbers and activities. He managed the Central Services with a sure hand, and the oligarchs of the Executive Committee with calm assurance. More than 25 years later, it is tempting to assume that the ECPR was set on its pre-ordained, path-dependent way to become the enormously successful and enterprising institution it now is, but that would be wrong. Though growing fast and building up its wide repertoire of innovative activities, the ECPR was still an infant organisation in 1979. It had 90 members, it is true, compared with 310 today, but its finances were still shaky, and it could easily have succumbed to some disabling disease of youth. Ian helped to nurture it and turn it into a stable and permanent institution, as he did the Summer School and Government Department.

I remember turning up at the ECPR's Joint Sessions in Florence, which were taking place in a specially designed conference centre. With only a couple of hours or so to the opening event of the Sessions, the moveable interior walls of the high-tech building were still organised around the needs of the departing shoe exhibition. The electricians and scene shifters were hanging around in their blue overalls, talking, laughing and smoking, but there was not a seminar room in sight, nor anything that looked even vaguely like ever becoming one. There sat Ian calmly drinking coffee next to a frantic Valerie Stewart who was sick with worry. 'Don't worry, Valerie', he said. 'It'll be fine.' And it was, of course.

Some years later I, too, was worried sick about the impending disaster of a Joint Sessions whose local organisers did not seem to have anything under control. I turned to Ian for advice. 'Don't worry, Ken', he said. 'It'll be fine.' And it was, of course. I have learned many things from Ian, but perhaps the most important is the lesson 'Don't worry. It'll be fine.' I tried to practise this calm assurance myself in the ECPR, and tried to pass it off as part of my own unflappable personality but, in truth, it was Ian's example.

That experience of 'just in time' organisation at the Florence Joint Sessions may well have stood him in good stead because he returned to the city and to the European University Institute in 1982 as an ordinary spear-carrying professor, if there is such a thing. Perhaps he was trying to escape the heavy administrative load at Essex – a 'greedy institution' if ever there was one – but in Florence he was quickly drawn into the major administrative role of running the politics group and sorting out a few messy organisational, financial and personality tangles. He did so, and returned to Essex in 1985. Florence was lucky to have him.

Between 1968, when he propelled the Essex Summer School into existence, and 1985, when he finished at Florence, he carried one crushing organisational burden after the other, pretty much without pause for the entire 19 year period – the Summer School, the Department of Government, the ECPR and the EUI politics department. In the same years he was involved in the writing of eight books – one of which (the early British politics textbooks) went through three major revisions – plus 23 articles and chapters.

For those who don't know the inside story, the Executive Director of the ECPR had a contract with the Essex Government Department in those days that divided his time into two equal parts. One involved teaching and administration in the Department and University, the other running the Central Services for the ECPR – a full-time job all on its own. It was assumed that the third half was to be given to research and publications of a quantity and quality expected of any professor at Essex.

This would keep any ordinary mortal busy for 18 hours a day, but in his spare time in these years Ian also served on the Executive Committee of the Political Studies Association of the UK and as Academic Director of its 1978 Annual Conference, as founder and Director of the Manifestos Research Group, as Graduate Director of the Essex Department, as Director of the EUI Summer School on Parties, as Director of three ECPR workshops and participant in many others, and in various capacities on committees and boards of the British Social Science Research Council/Economic and Social Research Council (SSRC/ESRC). Rarely can any single person have delivered as many public goods for the political science profession.

All these jobs were (still are) important, time consuming, onerous and largely thankless chores that only people with initiative, diplomatic skill, energy, enthusiasm and too many other things to do, are asked to shoulder. The motto of the Executive Director of the ECPR is 'If you want something done, ask a busy person', so naturally Ian was one of those in the early years at Essex who was asked to do the most important things. Here is what Jean Blondel writes about his role as the Founder and Director of the Essex Summer School.

> *You* were the creator of the Summer School. It began in 1968 thanks to you, on the basis of the Unesco grant which Allen Potter succeeded in attracting to us: you got Michigan to help – I have to mention Lutz Erbring and his dedication in this respect – and you ran the operation. Yet the crunch was to be the following year. We then had no grant: everyone else would have given up. You did not. You had the courage and vision to agree to run the school on a shoestring and this was critical. That decision established the fact that the school was to be a permanent fixture

Jean fails to mention the attraction of the fabled Essex towers and the blinding beauty of the University's neo-brutalist architecture as the main foundation of the Summer School's success, but it is certainly true that Ian's courage, vision, organising skills and sheer indomitable spirit helped as well. The Summer School is one of the truly important institutions of European political science, and if European political scientists in their hundreds look back on it with a strong mixture of pleasure and appreciation (as they do), it is thanks to Ian Budge. So also do a not much smaller number of Essex graduate students (there are about 70 MA and 80 PhD students registered in any one year), who owe a lot to Ian when he was three times Director of the Graduate School (1972–76, 1985–88, and 1992–94). So also do the approximately 20 PhD students he has supervised at Essex and Florence – enough to populate a decent sized department of politics with well trained and highly motivated professors. Like Robert Dahl, Ian can take largely warranted pride in having contributed in some crucial way to their development as scholars.

On walking and talking

PhD students, (and their supervisors) can learn a few lessons from Ian about how to turn out printed words to deadlines. Here's how it's done –

Budge fashion. First avoid all machines. Not just computers and word processors, but things as advanced and complicated as typewriters, including the most primitive manual ones. If you are a proper scientist, who has relied all his life on computers to analyse large data sets covering voting, elections, manifestos, parties and government formation, and if you have written a book about electronic democracy into the bargain, then you have no need of writing machines or electronic gadgets. For productive efficiency take several large, lined writing pads and a quiet room in your house overlooking the garden. That way you'll get through the work in double quick time, so that you can get down to the real business of gardening or walking later in the day.

Then, with laser-intense concentration, start to scrawl words on the pad, filling page after page with large and completely illegible handwriting. After a few hours of scribbling you will have a good part of a chapter or an article drafted, which can then be typed by one of the two people in the world who can read your writing. Of course, there will be a liberal sprinkling of typing errors in the transcript (Armenia appeared as America in one of our joint books, recondite as Aroldite and Parti Communista as Party Carouser) but this is of little account. But don't worry. It'll be fine. You can correct later – if you've a mind to.

One of my colleagues rightly says that you can judge a person by what secretaries say about them. You would have thought that secretaries would hate Ian for his endless supply of manuscripts in illegible scrawl. But none of it – they love him. He talks to them, treats them generously, tells them about the play he saw last night and brings them cuttings of plants from his garden. And they, for their part, convert the scrawl into orderly typescripts as magicians shape smoke into black cats. The moral of the story is: do not turn yourself into a secretary; concentrate on the writing. Don't worry. It'll be fine.

But this is not the whole story of how to write more than 19 books and 70 articles. Your aversion to typewriters and word processors must extend to all other machines. Do not even trust the phone – speak into them so loudly that the person listening at the other end puts their phone down, goes to the window, and listens to you directly. Above all leave the black arts of driving the family motor car to your wife and when she is not there to chauffeur, walk or take the bus.

Walk, especially, but not in any old fashion. First, you must develop a bustling and slightly idiosyncratic gait, slightly lopsided but energetic and very fast. Second, you must know every single footpath for a radius of 50 miles around your home, and be sure to cover them all at least once a year to check that some wicked farmer has not ploughed them under. In that case, you must set out across the field reclaiming your right of way, irrespective of the shotguns pointing at you and the murderous farm dogs charging you down. Third, you must take friends and colleagues, whether or not they actually like walking, on rambles of ten, 15 or 20 miles around the most beautiful bits of countryside in Essex and Suffolk. If your colleagues protest that they actually hate walking, you say firmly, 'Don't worry. It'll be fine.', and then take them on one of the most arduous, foot-slogging treks of the year.

So, you see, writing and walking are inextricably linked in the Budgean universe. At this point I must confess that I played a crucial part in the life of the Budge family for some time. When we were colleagues I was under Judy Budge's strict orders to go walking with Ian to keep him out of the house for not less than ten hours, come what may. My reward, when we returned, was the most truly delicious dinner cooked by Judy. The orders were so strict, and my devotion to the dinners so great, that on one occasion I kept Ian out for the full ten hours, not come what may, but come hell and high water. Our riverside path (just outside Manningtree, it was) was flooded by at least two and a half feet of freezing water but, undismayed, Ian announced firmly, 'Don't worry. It'll be fine.', and set off wading. I followed, thinking of the reward to come.

Once I put it to Ian that we might take a bus to some distant village, spend the day in the pub, and then ring for Judy to collect us in the car. He rejected the suggestion with contempt, and took me on the longest, hardest and most muddy walk in the world to teach me the lesson of the inextricable link between walking and writing.

Writing and walking is not the whole story. There is talking as well. To write you must walk, and to walk you must talk. I'm not sure about the exact causal sequence here, but I do know that to talk well in the Budge style, you must have a few crucial qualities: an astonishing memory for names, facts and figures; an insatiable curiosity about the world; a huge experience of living in foreign parts; a few languages; a great liking for your fellow human beings; and a knowledge of many things. Put them together and you have the basic ingredients of the Budge Walking and Talking Experience.

Take the languages first. A well educated Edinburgh lad o'parts has Latin and French, of course, and a bit of Gaelic and German, and quite possibly enough English English to show willing. Add conversational Italian, and some Spanish and Dutch, all in an Edinburgh accent, and you are well set. Dutch? Once on a walk one lovely summer's day by the River Colne, I bet him our lunchtime beer that he could not tell me the Dutch for 'My key is in my overcoat pocket', and he came back with something sounding rather like the Dutch (in an Edinburgh accent) for 'Mein Schlussel in meine Manteltasche ist', which I know is roughly the equivalent in German. I had to concede that he knew a bit of Dutch, and paid for drinks in the pub.

Trying to get my own back some time later I told him I knew the German for porcupine. This time he challenged me, rejecting my claim that it was 'Stachelschwein', and saying it was 'Igel', which is actually the German for hedgehog. Now, hedgehogs and porcupines are not to be confused, least of all in German, and I am still surprised that Ian did not have total mastery of this essential conceptual equipment of modern political scientists. I was delighted to win the bet. It is the only time I ever did. He paid for the drinks that day.

The languages are simply a way to get you around the world talking to people whether they are Italian, Dutch, French, Spanish, American, German, Latin or even English. That way if you live in Madison (at the University of Wisconsin, 1969–70), Florence (the European University Institute, 1982–85), California (Irvine, 1989, 2000), Berlin (WZB, 1990), Barcelona (the Autonoma, 1991), the Netherlands (NIASS, 1995–96) and Canberra (ANU, 2001) you can get about freely, talk to the locals, do business, and learn first-hand about local history, culture, food, politics, topography, art and, of course, the best local walks. This hand-gathered knowledge is then shared with your walking companions back in Essex. It makes for fascinating conversation about anything and everything from Strauss opera and Gaelic folklore, to Italian politics and building coracles. If you do not believe the bit about building coracles, then ask Ian to show you his. He built it himself. But resist the kind and generous invitation to try it out for yourself on the River Colne.

So there you have it. All you need is the walking and talking, the languages, the unfailing memory, prodigious energy, huge enthusiasm, a distaste for computers and cars, an insatiable curiosity about the world, the experience of living and working in half a dozen or so other countries, the illegible handwriting and the affection of secretaries, the garden, a delight in the company of your fellow human beings, a capacity to cooperate extremely effectively with others or to do it all on your own, high intelligence, an uncanny knack for designing the architecture of your next chapter or article, and an ability to focus with singular attention on the writing pad in front of you for hours at a time.

Oh, and yes, perhaps you should also ask the Good Lord to make 36 hours a day available to you, because with a mere 24 you do not have a significant probability (one tailed test, significant at 0.001) of making the grade. Last of all – and this is absolutely essential – you must get yourself a Judy Budge. Without one you cannot possibly succeed. With nothing more than these you too can write large amounts of path-breaking research and build institutions that will be a great boon to generations of political scientists to come. No wonder I have failed to achieve even half as much as he. But then precious few have.

Part I

Empirical developments and applications

2 Party government formation and policy preferences

An encompassing approach?[1]

Hans Keman

Introduction

Up to the 1990s it appears (with hindsight) that party politics and party government in Western Europe were characterised by stable patterns. Bartolini and Mair (1990), for instance, demonstrated that patterns of electoral competition were more or less established, whereas Budge and Keman (1990) developed a 'general' theory of party government that reflected structural tendencies regarding party cooperation. Together with the ending of the Cold War, the accomplishment of the welfare state and, generally, a relatively high level of prosperity, all seemed well for everybody.

Yet, this picture seems wrong and is falsified by political developments in many of the European democracies: since the early nineties one can observe electoral 'turmoil' and governmental 'turnover' that is more dramatic than before. Recall the institutional changes in Belgium completed in the early 1990s, or the complete overhaul of the Italian party system, also in the early nineties. These examples appear perhaps as 'exceptions to the rule'. But they are not: electoral landslides occurred in the Netherlands (1994 and 2003), France (1993), Italy (1994) and Scandinavia (throughout the 1990s) and new parties emerged almost everywhere – in particular Greens and far right ones (Mair, 2002). These changes are documented in Table 2.1.

Even at first glance, one can observe that voters turn out less – the cross-national average between 1985 and 2000 is 8 per cent and electoral volatility is around 12.4 per cent, which is 5 per cent more than between 1960 and 1980 (Mair, 2002: 131). At the same time the growth of successful 'new' parties is remarkable. Except for Ireland, and Spain, these parties not only emerged, but also gained a substantial share of the vote – on average 14.1 per cent, twice as much as compared with the early eighties. At the same time the established parties were in jeopardy. Both Christian Democrats and Social Democrats lost not only electoral support – on average their share of the vote was down by 7.0 per cent (Keman and Pennings, 2004), but also their position as 'pivot parties' directing, in fact, governmental composition and policy direction (see Keman, 1997).

Table 2.1 Electoral & Governmental Change in Western Europe (1985–2000)

Country	Turnout	ChangeTO	Volatility	ChangeEV	VotesNP	ChangeNP	Innovation	Alternation
Austria	84.3	−12.2	9.4	7.7	34.1	17.1	22.7	1.88
Belgium	*91.9*	*−3.0*	*10.8*	*5.5*	*24.2*	*13.1*	*22.0*	*1.25*
Denmark	84.4	−2.4	12.4	−3.1	10.1	2.4	39.2	0.48
Finland	70.4	−10.4	11.0	3.1	7.3	4.6	91.7	1.25
France	68.9	−13.4	15.4	6.6	21.2	15.0	13.5	0.25
Germany	79.5	−6.2	9.0	4.0	11.8	3.5	11.8	2.50
Greece	*80.5*	*−8.1*	*7.8*	*−3.5*	*4.2*	*2.8*	*10.0*	*0.54*
Ireland	67.6	−7.9	11.7	6.0	0.0	0.0	62.6	0.47
Italy	86.1	−6.5	22.9	13.0	32.8	15.7	41.5	0.13
Netherlands	77.9	−7.7	19.1	6.8	10.8	8.7	37.1	1.43
Norway	80.6	−6.0	18.8	22.0	25.0	21.0	24.3	0.54
Portugal	67.1	−11.5	11.3	0.7	13.1	−3.3	0.0	3.00
Spain	74.3	−9.2	7.5	−4.6	0.0	0.0	66.7	1.00
Sweden	85.7	−8.5	13.8	7.5	6.2	4.0	29.6	0.37
Switzerland	44.4	−5.6	8.0	3.6	11.3	−2.7	0.0	0.00
Average	76.2	−7.9	12.6	5.0	14.1	6.8	31.5	1.01

Sources: Mair, 2002; Siaroff, 2000; Armingeon *et al.*, 2002; Woldendorp *et al.*, 2000.

Notes
all in per cents; Average = cross-national average (N = 15). Turnout (TO) = electoral participation (italics = compulsary voting, partly in Greece, and until 1994 in Italy); Volatility (EV) = electoral volatility; (NP) = new parties; Innovation: entrance and duration of a new party in government; Alternation: frequency and extent of government composition (0 = no change; high value is less change, low values much and encompassing change). Level = 2000; Change = absolute differences 1985–2000.

Peter Mair has suggested that governmental composition can be patterned on the basis of 'alternation' and 'innovation'. The former is the extent to which the party composition changes more or less completely. The latter measure indicates the entrance of a new *partner* (not to be confused with new *parties* per se!). Both indicators of a change in party composition are considerable. Table 2.1 shows that the actual rate of innovation is 31.5 per cent. This means that during the nineties, in three out of ten of all governments there have been *new* partners participating. Conversely, in some countries the established parties were ousted for the very first time. In Belgium, Italy and the Netherlands this concerned the Christian Democrats (for the first time since the Second World War!). And in Scandinavia the Social Democratic parties gradually lost their dominant position as party of government. This development can also be seen from the rate of alternation: apart from Switzerland – where the 'magic formula' allows for no change – most countries show frequent changes in government composition. Except for Germany and Portugal, the other European democracies have experienced quite some alternations and concomitant entrance of 'new' parties in government (see also: Mair, 2005) during the last decade of the twentieth century.

These observations of change between 1985 and 2002 imply in my view that the existing parameters of government composition have changed too. Second, that this is – at least in part – an effect of new patterns of party competition. Third, that apparently policy considerations appear to play a less, or different, role in the process of government formation. These observations obviously lead to the question of whether or not existing and accepted theories of government formation and composition are still valid. For, if electoral competition has changed, and the dynamics of party systems are in flux, one may well wonder whether or not party governments are still formed by the same institutional 'logic' as before and whether the 'old' parties are still in control or not. Therefore, this chapter aims at replicating the Budge and Keman approach, on the one hand, and at an examination of recent data (covering the period 1985–2000) in order to explore possible new patterns of government formation, on the other hand. This problematic is the issue that I wish to investigate in this chapter.

As a benchmark for exploring this question I shall make use of the 'General Theory of Party Government' developed and tested by Ian Budge and Hans Keman (1990). This theory was empirically developed during the 1980s and, of course, based on a number of exogenous factors that reflected post-war parliamentary democracy. In addition, this approach not only combined *office*-seeking elements with *policy*-seeking assumptions, but also integrated party government in the overall process of policy making and related performance (see also Keman, 2002; Budge *et al.*, 2002). In this chapter I shall focus explicitly on two crucial elements embedded in this approach:

1   policy preferences as reflected in the composition of party govern-
    ment, and
2   distribution of ministries between party families within coalition gov-
    ernments.

The first element is directly relevant for examining whether or not the
'power' distribution of parties within governments has changed in the
1990s as a function of changing electoral competition and increasing rates
of innovation (see Table 2.2) and that indirectly may well affect the policy
control of parties in government. The second element is considered as
crucial for the 'policy making' capacities of party government. For it refers
to the directions of policy as represented by the parties relative to their
positioning in terms of various programmatic dimensions (like left versus
right, but also regarding international politics, economics and welfare).

   This analysis is thus intended to understand to what extent and in what
way the original theory of Party Government is still valid and robust, on
the one hand. On the other hand, the analysis will demonstrate whether
or not policy considerations are (still) vital for the understanding of party
government composition. Before presenting the data analysis, a short
résumé of the general theory of party government will be given.

The general theory of party government

This approach departs from a series of assumptions that reflect the institutional devices of parliamentary democracy. These assumptions can be
found in Table 2.2 and have a logical and hierarchical ordering.

   Although the rule of majority is in general adhered to, it is *not* con-

Table 2.2 General assumptions of an integrated theory of democratic party govern-
         ment

1	In parliamentary democracies the party or combination of parties that can win a legislative vote of confidence forms the government.
2	Parties seek to form that government capable of surviving legislative votes of confidence, which will most effectively carry through their declared policy preferences under existing conditions.
3.1	The chief preference of all democratic parties is to counter threats to the democratic system.
3.2	Where no such threats exist, but socialist–bourgeois (or left versus right) differences are important, the preference of all parties is to carry through policies related to these differences.
3.2	Where neither of the preceding conditions holds, parties pursue their own group (or constituency) related preferences.

Source: Taken from Budge and Keman, 1990: 34 (Table 2.1).

Note
Assumption 4 included in the original table will not be analysed in this chapter.

sidered as a condition *sine qua non* (but a preferred situation). Hence, contrary to the ideas within the strict rational choice theory that employs office-seeking behaviour, it is considered important to develop a theory that seeks to answer the question of how different parties do form a *viable* government. These parties are considered to be more or less coalescent in terms of left and right preferences. Parties which are seen as non-congruent are therefore not suitable for stable government. Rule 3.1 may seem strange at present, but it is not. Although originally this rule applied mostly to Communist parties and the like – and thus is hardly relevant after 1989 – it is relevant again with the rise of populism and right-wing extremist parties during the 1990s (Mény and Surel, 2002; Capoccia, 2002). Some of these have sometimes entered party government: the LPF in the Netherlands, the KrF in Denmark, and the FPÖ in Austria for example (see also Pennings and Keman, 2003). Hence, Rule 3.2 is certainly still an important feature of the process of forming a coalition government. In my view the left versus right distinction remains a central dimension of the relationship between office-seeking and policy-seeking behaviour of most parties with respect to the formation and the functioning of party government. This contention spills over into Rule 3.3: policy preferences of parties are pursued according to their own programme and are related to their constituencies (or electorate see: Schmidt, 1996; Keman, 2002).

The process of government formation and related consequences of composition in terms of distributing ministries, on the one hand, and thereby defining the policy direction of party government, on the other hand, was elaborated in Table 2.4 in Budge and Keman (1990: 50–52). The approach consisted of the whole process of *government formation – policy pursuit – turnover of personnel – durability and termination of governments – continuity*. In this chapter I shall confine the analysis to the first part, which is adapted in Table 2.3.

The specifications presented here as a part of an *encompassing* approach are meant to generalise existing practices as can be found across contemporary European parliamentary systems. Although some of the assumptions mentioned in Table 2.3 may well appear as almost self-evident, it should be noted that most literature on coalition governments is more often than not characterised by stressing idiosyncrasies and case-specific features (see for instance Dodd, 1976; Pridham, 1986; Laver and Shepsle, 1996; Müller and Strøm, 1999). As such these studies are not wrong, but they do not help much to develop empirically-based theories that transcend case-based analyses. Such an ambition, however, underlies the Budge and Keman approach. Hence, in this theory of Party Government it is assumed that:

- There is a reward for the major party in government as well as for another party that is necessary to form a coalition (I); in addition, all

Table 2.3 Major implications of the general assumptions of the integrated theory of democratic party government

---

Distribution of government ministries between parties in a coalition:

I   The largest party in a coalition will take the Premiership. Subsequently the second largest party will take the Deputy Premiership.

II   Subject to overall proportionality, each party will seek control of ministries in their own areas of policy concern: for instance, Labour parties will tend to seek Ministries of Social Affairs, Health, and Labour Relations etc. (i.e. focus on the 'Welfare State'); Conservative and Liberal parties will be inclined to seek Ministries of Internal and External Security, Justice, Foreign Affairs etc. (i.e. the 'traditional' core of the state apparatus).

III   Where a particular type of party does not exist, the most ideologically similar of the existing parties will seek ministries in the area of policy concern that is close to their programme and electoral constituency.

IV   These tendencies are least evident when governments are formed to counter anti-democratic threats and less evident when governments are formed in a situation of socialist–bourgeois hostility (i.e. if and when party systems are highly polarised then this feature dominates the composition of a coalition).

V   A small party in a government, which could be formed by a large party on its own, will not necessarily get a proportionate share of ministries (this assumption can go into different directions: more or less than proportionate).

Source: Taken from Budge and Keman, 1990: 50 (Table 2.4).

     participating parties get a fair (i.e. proportional) share of ministries (II and V).

*   All parties seek office that corresponds with their policy preferences (II and III) or at least as close as possible depending on a party's size (V).

*   Given the rates of Innovation and Alternation (see Table 2.1) the parameters of party system organisation will have an impact on coalition formation and concomitant distribution of ministries among parties (III and IV).

These points of departure appear still valid and relate directly to the general assumptions as mentioned in Table 2.2. However, the caveat here is twofold: (i) I expect that the emergence and entrance of new parties and concomitant change of a party system may well lead to new patterns of policy preferences. Hence, if correct it implies that distributional patterns found before the 1990s may have changed. (ii) the decline of dominant parties (like Social Democratic and Christian Democratic parties; see Keman and Pennings, 2004) has been conducive to programmatic convergence between these contenders for governmental office. If this is indeed the case then this will change the process of government formation.

     For instance, the participation of Green parties has had an impact on the distribution of ministries due to the overall change of policy preferences. The German coalition since 1997 may serve as an example here. In addition high levels of electoral volatility have been conducive to new patterns of party composition and distributing ministries. This has been the case in the Netherlands since 2002. Finally, due to electoral losses, 'pivot parties' have been redirecting their programmatic profile. This has resulted in new priorities in terms of policy pursuit – the Third Way development of Labour highlights this process (Merkel, 2001).

If the above argument is correct, then it may well be that the assumption under II in Table 2.3 ought to be relaxed. Both the general assumptions with regard to socio-economic differences (II and III) and regarding specific priorities in relation to a party's constituency (IV) may well have changed or is considered as less prominent. Yet, although the circumstances have changed during the nineties, and some of the assumptions may be less self-evident than before, I still contend that the original theory is: '*more* plausible than office-seeking theories. [...] The policy-commitment fits existing evidence better than earlier formulation, since it is compatible with all types of government which actually form' (Budge and Keman, 1990: 61, italics added).

This claim will be empirically examined in the remainder of this chapter for the period 1985–2000. To this end I shall present data on parties and governments formed in 15 parliamentary democracies (see Table 2.1). Second, recent data derived from the MRG-data set (Budge *et al.*, 2001) will be used to underpin the policy-seeking behaviour of parties. This type of data – not available in this format in the late 1980s – will enable me to perform a directional analysis of the relationship between policy positions of parties seeking office. In other words, the analysis performed here allows for examining the structural quality of our original theory.

Variations in party government

In this chapter the West European countries will figure that are listed in Table 2.1. They have not only in common that they are parliamentary democracies, but also that most are characterised by multiparty systems with (more often than not) three or more competitive party families. Hence, this selection is ideally suited for examining the robustness and plausiblity of the general theory of party government. To this end the information on governments formed after 1985 (the last year included in the Budge and Keman data collection) have been employed (*n* = 86). Table 2.4 presents the main features of the party systems and the coalition governments formed.

First of all it can be noted that on average the complexion of party governments tends toward the 'centre of gravity' – 2.6 indicates the median position on a scale of five. The left versus right distribution of the policy-seeking indicator used reinforces this observation. Governments are on

Table 2.4 Party system and party government (1986–2000)

Variable	Mean	S.D.	Range	n
Type of government	3.02	1.22	5.0	86
Duration of government	638.3	441.55	1241.0	85
Size of government	18.14	6.27	26.0	85
Complexion of government	2.60	0.89	4.0	84
Parliamentary Support (%)	63.12	11.00	31.5	86
Left v. Right Party System	−4.91	22.67	111.3	470
Left v. Right Parties in Gov.	−1.74	20.28	96.6	232
Effective N. of Parties	5.05	1.71	7.29	86

Sources: All taken or derived from Woldendorp *et al.*, 2000: 16–19; Budge *et al.*, 2001.

Notes
Type of government = scale from One-PG-MWC-Surplus-Minority [one-PG and multi-PG]: 1–5; Duration = Days; Complexion of Government = scale of ideological dominance: from right-dominant-balanced-left-dominant (1–3–5). Parliamentary support = of government by parties in parliament; Left v. right = scale developed by Pennings and Keman (2003) measured for all parties and parties in government only; Effective number of parties, see Armingeon *et al.*, 2002.
S.D. = Standard Deviation: N = number of valid cases (86 for governments; 232 and 470 for parties).

average only two points away from the arithmetic middle-point of the scale (that runs from −100 to +100; see Budge *et al.*, 2001: 228). For party systems as whole this is slightly more (to the left). This apparent 'centre of gravity' is also visible in most coalition governments formed. They tend to be of a 'surplus' nature (i.e. three on the scale of one to five) with an average cross-national majority around 63.0 %. Hence many governments formed have a parliamentary support that is not only sufficient but also indicates a tendency towards oversized or 'surplus' coalitions. Hence, in office-seeking behaviour coalition governments are not only more often a majority government, but also look for stability by including more parties than would be expected by using the MWC criterion. As is well known, this contradicts the office-seeking type of coalition theory (see also Lijphart, 1999). In fact Table 2.5 makes this clear by reporting the distribution of types of government between 1985 and 2000.

Obviously 'minimal winning' coalitions (MWCs) are often occurring but only for approximately one-third of all governments under review here. Almost 28 per cent of the coalition governments formed are of a 'surplus' nature, whereas – perhaps surprising – minority governments concern 27 per cent of all the cases (see Figure 2.1). From this distribution of types of government one can draw the conclusion that the policy commitment of parties in governments seems still quite tenable for the 1990s; for the combination of a strong parliamentary backing and including more partners than strictly necessary not only contradicts the 'minimal winning' claim of office-seeking approaches, but also supports the idea that a viable government is one that is capable of policy making (see also

Table 2.5 Types of party government

Distribution	%	n
Single party governance	5.8	5
Minimal Winning Coalition	36.1	31
Surplus coalition government	27.9	24
Single party minority government	16.2	14
Multi party minority government	11.6	10
Caretaker government	2.4	2
Total	100.0	85

Table 2.2 – assumptions 1 and 2). This contention is further enhanced if one correlates the sus-type and minority governments with their duration. Excluding the two caretaker governments, it appears that almost 80 per cent of these governments last at least one year or longer (whereas the average across all types is just under two years!). It appears that indeed most governments in European parliamentary democracies are formed with the intention to *make* policy and this idea is reinforced by the duration of government; for policy formation and implementation is – amongst many other things – predominantly a matter of time (Keman, 2002; Budge *et al.*, 2002).

This conclusion brings us to one of the major assumptions of the General Theory of Party Government: if there is no major or direct threat to the democratic order then the partisan approach (i.e. party differences do matter) is an important variable for understanding the formation of government in relation to the policies pursued (see Assumption 1). In Table 2.4 two indicators of the socialist–bourgeois divide, or the left versus right distribution across party systems and government parties has been presented. In addition I have used a measure that is meant to indicate the

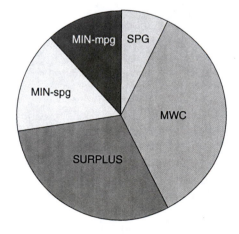

Figure 2.1 Distribution of type of government.

Table 2.6 Left versus right across parties in government and the party system

Country	Complexion of government	Left v. right		Difference government and party system
		Government	Party System	
Austria (n=4)	3.3	3.8	3.3	0.5
		(15.2)	(21.7)	
Belgium (n=5)	2.4	−1.1	−0.4	−0.7
		(21.2)	(6.1)	
Denmark (n=5)	2.8	−0.9	−7.3	6.4
		(33.4)	(9.3)	
Finland (n=6)	2.6	−22.6	−22.5	−0.1
		(28)	(17.4)	
France (n=7)	2.1	2.4	−4.7	7.1
		(52.8)	(15.8)	
Germany (n=4)	1.9	9.9	−7.5	17.5
		(18.7)	(10.8)	
Greece (n=2)	2.9	−6.2	−8.0	1.8
		(0)	(3.5)	
Ireland (n=5)	1.5	−7.6	−16.8	9.2
		(20.9)	(14.3)	
Italy (n=7)	1.6	19.2	10.4	8.8
		(14.2)	(5)	
Netherlands (n=4)	2.0	−2.9	−8.0	5.1
		(17.9)	(9.9)	
Norway (n=3)	3.3	−14.1	−11.4	−2.7
		(5.7)	(6.5)	
Sweden (n=2)	3.7	−11.8	−4.8	−7.0
		(18.0)	(15.3)	
Switzerland (n=4)	1.9	−3.4	−3.0	−0.4
		(5.9)	(2.4)	
Averages (n=58)	2.4	−0.7	−5.6	4.9
	(2.2)	(58.8)	(46.2)	

Sources: Budge *et al.*, 2001; Woldendorp *et al.*, *2000*.

Notes
One party governments are excluded. Figures in parentheses are ranges. Left–Right scores are calculated according to Pennings and Keman 2003; see also Appendix 2.a.1. Negative outcomes indicate a more leftist policy position and vice versa more rightist. Differences are absolute.

'complexion of party government' (Woldendorp *et al.*, 2000: 19). This measure denotes the relationship between the different party families in government and their relative strength in parliament. Together with the left versus right measure based on the MRG-data set this will highlight how the policy-making dimension is distributed across the universe of discourse as well as the distance between parties in government and the party system as a whole.

The complexion of government reflects the basic tendencies of governmental design in relation to parliament. In five countries (Austria,

Denmark, Greece, Norway, Sweden) it is tilted to the left. In France, Germany, Ireland, Italy and Switzerland the opposite design is apparent. This division, however, cannot directly be derived from the policy positions of the government of the day and party systems. On average the positions taken by parties in both parliament and government are towards the left. Only in Austria and Italy both government and parliament are right-wing oriented, whereas in France and Germany there is a situation of 'divided governance'. Looking at the gap between government and parliament it is obvious that about half of the government/party system relationship is more or less close (i.e. less than half of the cross-national average) and the other cases – in particular Germany, Ireland, Italy and Sweden – show a difference. What does this mean? It signifies by and large that 'policy' seems to matter and that the differences between party government and the direction of party systems can be observed. Hence, party differences in terms of policy-seeking are important parameters for understanding the formation and design of party government in Europe. From this I conclude that party government:

- tends to be formed by means of policy-seeking behaviour;
- tends to rely often on a majority in parliament, but not necessarily so;
- tends to be equally characterised by 'surplus' and 'minority' types, on the one hand, as by minimal-winning coalition government, on the other;
- is in general quite enduring, regardless of the type of government;
- tends to be tilted towards a centre-left policy direction;
- varies as to their positions on left versus right in Government vis-à-vis parliament.

In summary, therefore, by and large the analysis confirms for the recent period what Budge and Keman (1990: 23) proposed as a 'core' theory of government coalitions (see Table 2.2). In addition, and more precisely, the results of this section invites an examination of the Assumptions put forward in Table 2.3 specifying the General Theory of Party Government.

Forming a coalition: distributing ministries across different parties

Although the policy-seeking approach is plausible and viable, it involves office-seeking behaviour by necessity. If a party wishes to pursue its policy preferences in a parliamentary democracy where coalitions are the predominant type of government, then a party ought to:

1 gain access to party government,
2 strive for obtaining the office of Prime Minister or Deputy Prime Minister and
3 secure at least as many ministries as proportionally is justified.

All these (strategic) rules are in fact part of an office-seeking game when forming a coalition. At the same time they are also pursued within a policy-seeking context. Pure and simple: without representation in government a party is deemed to remain in opposition and pursue politics from parliament. Yet, without controlling the policy sectors that matter the policy pursuit is still absent. Hence, a party in a multiparty environment must therefore seek power through office and if feasible take overall control (i.e. premiership) and certain ministries in the preferred policy sectors. First I shall examine to what extent office-seeking behaviour can indeed be observed.

Evidently office-seeking behaviour is important as regards the formation of coalition governments ($n = 68$). In fact the rule of proportionality (as suggested by Budge and Keman, 1990: 130) appears to work quite well as demonstrated by the correlations between seats in parliament and government. All participants appear to get a 'pay-off' that is indeed proportional to their parliamentary size. Only if the largest party is very sizeable is this effect diminishing. In effect, Table 2.7 demonstrates that the smaller partners in a coalition are proportionally well off. Table 2.7 also confirms the (almost) self-evident assumption that, as a rule, the largest party takes the premiership. The role of deputy PM is not available in all countries (only in 58 per cent of all governments), but if it is for the taking, the second largest party almost always gets it.

Although the range within each party category is high, it is safe to contend that the policy-making capacity of each party below the second largest is decreasing. On average they control roughly 35 per cent of a coalition, whereas the largest party secures – in addition to taking the premiership – more than half. Hence, one can conclude from this analysis that although 'power-*sharing*' is the name of the coalition formation game, the principal players see to it that they get the ministries they wish. The question is then: is this also true for their assumed policy-seeking motives?

Party government formation and shaping policy preferences

An often overlooked element in the literature on party government remains the relationship between the overall complexion of party government and the *qualitative* distribution of ministries (but see Blondel and Thiébault, 1991; Laver and Shepsle, 1996; Müller and Strøm, 1999; Keman, 2003). This relationship is important because it enables us to inspect whether or not parties are capable of *directing* policy making by means of controlling certain policy sectors. In general, before the elections, a party has made public what type of policies it prefers, and endeavours to communicate them by means of an electoral manifesto. Hence, it follows that such a party is assumed to play a 'nested' game: its strategy involves office-seeking as a means to further its programmatic preferences

Table 2.7 Office-seeking behaviour: distribution of seats in parliament and ministries in government

Parties in Coalition Government	Mean	Max.	Min.
Largest: ($n=68$)			
% seats in parliament	33.7	49.3	11.5
% seats in government	52.0	93.3	14.3
% having the PM-ship	84.0		
Correlation: seats/ministers = *0.71**			
Second largest: ($n=68$)			
% seats in parliament	16.9	42.7	1.6
% Seats in government	28.3	53.3	6.1
% having the Deputy PM	66.0		
Correlations: seats/ministers = *0.82**			
with largest size party 1 = *0.58*			
Third largest: ($n=46$)			
% Seats in parliament	8.8	22.5	1.6
% Seats in government	16.6	33.3	3.7
Correlations: seats/ministers = *0.66**			
with largest size party = *0.30*			
Fourth largest: ($n=24$)			
% Seats in seats in parliament	8.5	27.0	1.2
% Seats in government	14.6	28.6	3.9
Correlations: seats/ministers = *0.89**			
with largest size party = *−0.14*			
Fifth largest: ($n=9$)			
% parliament	3.4	7.6	1.8
% government	5.4	10.0	3.3
Correlations: seats/ministers = *0.45*			
with largest size party = *0.17*			

Source: Woldendorp *et al.*, 2000.

Notes
Parties are ordered by size in parliament. Correlations are Pearson
Product-Moment Coefficients (* significant at 0.01). Single party governments are
excluded. All figures are percentages of total seats in parliament and government.

by gaining control of certain ministries within a coalition. In other words, a party will attempt to get not only as many ministers as possible in government, but also to strive for an optimal distribution in terms of policy sectors. This idea can be found in the General Theory of Party Government (Tables 2.2 and 2.3).

The Dutch government formation game may serve here as an illustration (Keman, 2003). On several occasions parties first draw up a 'policy agreement', that is, basically a translation of the party platforms into one government agreement (Andeweg and Timmerman, 2005). Only then do parties start to negotiate who gets what ministry. Quite often this leads to a stalemate (e.g. in 1977, 1981, 1994). More recently, in 2003, the PvdA (Labour) and the CDA (Christian Democracy) had reached a policy agreement, but at the end of the day (or rather, night) they could not agree on which policy sectors were to be dominated by what party (i.e. which party got the ministry or not). The final result has been that, by including Democrats 66, CDA and VVD could instead develop a distribution of ministries that satisfied all.[2]

This story tells us that indeed office- and policy-seeking behaviour is a *nested* game. It also tells us that the *relative* strength of the first and second party (see Table 2.7) is an important feature of how the game will develop. Third, although party differences do matter, so I argue, it equally matters to what extent policy sectors are contested during the formation game in view of policy preferences of *all* parties involved. This line of argument is reflected in the Assumptions listed in Table 2.3. In this section I shall therefore analyse to what extent these ideas can be empirically substantiated. This analysis will be done differently, however, from the original exercise as reported in Budge and Keman (1990: Chapter 4).

Central to the argument has been the given distribution of party families within each country under review (Budge and Keman, 1990: 92–97). In addition each party family was assigned a ranking of ministries they would prefer most. In fact, this has been a hazardous procedure: first, although 'party family' is a comparative concept that can 'travel' it is a quite heroic assumption that *policy* preferences also travel likewise (they are not the same as ideological principles); second, an ordering as given in the original study is essentially *static* and does not take into account *circumstances* (socio-economic developments and socio-cultural issues, unique events, international pressures etc.). Nevertheless, these 'exogenous' factors do play a role with regard to the shaping of policy preferences. Third, recent research has shown that policy positions tend to converge over time in many multiparty systems (Keman and Pennings, 2004) implying that parties *either* compete more vigorously over the distribution of ministries (as was highlighted in the Dutch case) *or* consider this rather as a quid-pro-quo process. Finally, as put forward in the introductory section, times are changing, and so has party politics during the 1990s. New parties have emerged, and some of these have entered government (like the Greens in Finland, Germany and Belgium; Populists in Austria and the Netherlands; new Christian parties in Scandinavia; and the 'new Right' in Italy). In summary, although ideological differences may well remain to define party families per se, it does not signify a static set of policy preferences. On the contrary (see Klingemann and Volkens 2002).

Table 2.6 demonstrated where programmatic saliency has been presented in terms of left versus right for each country. These differences have been expressed on the level of the party system and party government. In addition I have pointed to the relationship *between* parliament and government by means of the variable 'complexion of government'. Both variables can be seen as indicators of government viability as regards its policy-seeking capacities: the more coherent a coalition is, the more one can expect that policy positions have converged. In order to analyse this I have developed four clusters that reflect this.

Cluster 1 concerns those polities where cabinets are dominant and the ideological complexion is tilted to the right: France, Germany and Ireland. Furthermore these systems are characterised by 'divided government' (see also: Müller and Strøm, 1999: 145–146). Cluster 2 are polities where cabinet governments are not very different from the party system in terms of policy positions, nor are these considered to be dominant (see: Woldendorp *et al.*, 2000: 56–57). Cluster 3 is conversely characterised by a dominant government and a clear left-wing orientation of government (exceeding the party system). Finally, Cluster 4 consists of Finland and Italy. Both polities are characterized by high scores on policy (respectively left wing and right wing) without a dominant government. Each of the clusters represents an own dynamic as regards translating policy preferences into the agreement between parties in government (see also Keman, 1997; Siaroff, 2000).

This relationship has been reported in Table 2.8. In addition to the left versus right distinction (see also Table 2.6) three policy domains have been analysed:

1 regulation of the economy,
2 provision of welfare and
3 internal and external security.

I consider these policy domains as central concerns of every political party and of any government. They represent the type of policy preferences as referred to in Table 2.3. I expect that the variation across the clusters will reflect the interdependent relationship between party system and party government.

First of all it can be noted that indeed the party composition of government by and large reflects the policy preferences of the party system. Hence, there is a relationship between office-seeking and policy-seeking behaviour across all coalition governments. Second, it is obvious that one policy domain does vary across the four clusters: the provision of welfare. Clusters 1 and 4 show a difference between government and parliament of two points. This difference is negative for government in Cluster 1 and positive in Cluster 4. This is according to the underlying rationale for the clustering as such: 1 is right-wing and dominating parliament whereas 4 is left-wing oriented but more dependent on parliament.

In Clusters 2 and 3 government and parliament (reflecting the party system) are closely linked as regards the preferred policy course (the dif-

Table 2.8 Policy preference of all parties and parties in government by clusters (1986–98)

Preferences	Cluster 1	Cluster 2	Cluster 3	Cluster 4	Total
Right–left	–8.7	–1.9	–9.2	–3.3	–5.6
(party system)	(21)	(16)	(6)	(12)	(55)
Right–left	0.7	–0.8	–12.1	1.8	–0.7
(government)	(21)	(16)	(5)	(12)	(54)
Difference	*9.4*	*1.1*	*2.9*	*5.1*	*4.9*
Economic regulation	3.3	2.3	1.8	5.4	3.3
(party system)	(21)	(16)	(6)	(12)	(55)
Economic regulation	3.0	2.3	1.6	5.9	3.3
(government)	(21)	(16)	(5)	(12)	(54)
Difference	*0.3*	*0.0*	*0.2*	*0.4*	*0.0*
Welfare state	11.6	9.5	11.2	10.6	10.7
(party system)	(21)	(16)	(6)	(12)	(55)
Welfare state	9.5	9.8	11.6	12.6	10.5
(government)	(21)	(16)	(5)	(12)	(54)
Difference	*2.1*	*0.3*	*0.4*	*2.0*	*0.3*
Security policies	2.3	1.4	1.4	1.9	1.9
(party system)	(21)	(16)	(6)	(12)	(55)
Security policies	1.4	1.2	1.5	0.9	1.3
(government)	(21)	(16)	(5)	(12)	(54)
Difference	*0.8*	*0.2*	*0.1*	*1.0*	*0.6*

Source: Data taken from Budge *et al.*, 2001: 233–243.

Notes
Reported scores are arithmetic means. Party system = all parties in party system; government = parties in government. Number in parentheses. Clusters mentioned in text.

ferences are 0.4 at most). This is an important finding: in parliamentary systems with coalition governance office-seeking and policy-seeking behaviour is strongly interrelated. Only if the executive–legislative relations are tilted towards government (Cluster 1) or where the party system is highly polarised (Cluster 4) is the relationship weaker.

Finally, as regards the variation across clusters and policy domains it can be surmised that Clusters 1 and 4 have higher scores on economic regulation implying stronger preferences in this policy domain. Conversely, Cluster 3 has the lowest scores in this respect, but is among the highest on welfare.

In summary, Table 2.8 has demonstrated a strong link between office-seeking and policy-seeking behaviour. Second, the relationship between parliament and government makes a difference in how this relationship is shaped. Third, it is striking how small the differences between parliament and coalition governments is, if the left versus right distinction is disaggregated into policy domains (see also Klingemann *et al.*, 1994; Budge *et al.*, 2002). Hence, our theory of party government seems to be still plausible in view of the robustness of the empirical results with respect to policy-seeking behaviour. If this conclusion really holds, then it would also imply that office-seeking motives prevail to serve the policy-seeking behaviour.

Seeking office to control policy making

Table 2.3 states clearly that the distribution of ministries is crucial for understanding how coalition government is formed. Equally important is to have a strong role in coordinating government as a whole. In this section I therefore shall examine the relationship between party families and ministerial control over policy domains (see for this also Laver and Shepsle, 1996; Blondel and Thiébault, 1991; Müller and Strøm, 1999). Central here is how parties interact with each other with regard to transforming policy preferences into control over policy domains. I expect that in party systems where the 'centre of gravity' is more or less crowded and the range of party differences is small the distribution of ministries will be according to the relative strength in parliament. Conversely, where there is no genuine pivot party (i.e. one party that is dominant and central; see Keman, 1997) that the policy preferences are guiding the distributional struggle. Therefore I have divided the countries under review into three categories:

- *Cluster 1* are polities, those where there are pivot parties (family) and the policy distances are small: Austria, Belgium, Finland, Greece, Switzerland (and Portugal).
- *Cluster 2* are the cases in between Clusters 1 and 3 (see below).
- *Cluster 3* are, finally, party systems without a pivot party and with a more polarised division of parties: Germany, Ireland, Norway.

Table 2.9 reports the outcomes of the distribution of ministries across party families and policy domains. First of all, it is obvious that both the dominance and centrality of a party family matters. This is not only the overwhelming case with the acquisition of the premiership, but also as regards the control of policy domains. The scores for the Social Democrats demonstrate this: this is the only electorally strong party that is prevalent in every country under review here (Liberal parties also, but these are hardly ever in a strong parliamentary position). This explains why the Social Democratic parties dominate in all policy sectors (over 40 per cent except for the security sector). The role of the other party families seems to be dependent on whether or not they are the second or third largest party (see also Table 2.7) and, of course, as is the number of parties within a government coalition. In most instances the Conservatives

Table 2.9 Allocation of ministries by policy domain to party families

Policy domain	Party families					
	SD	CD	Lib	Cons	Other	New
1 Overall coordination (PM)	**42.3**	*28.2*	1.4	23.9	0.0	0.0
Cluster 1	**43.3**	*23.3*	3.3	*23.3*	6.7	0.0
Cluster 2	**52.2**	*30.4*	0.0	13.0	4.3	0.0
Cluster 3	27.8	*33.3*	0.0	**38.9**	0.0	0.0
NB: in 83.1% of all cases the largest party takes PM-ship						
2. Economic regulation						
Finance	**49.2**	16.9	5.1	*28.8*	0.0	0.0
Cluster 1	**56.5**	4.3	4.3	*34.8*	0.0	0.0
Cluster 2	**55.6**	*27.8*	11.1	5.6	0.0	0.0
Cluster 3	*33.3*	22.2	0.0	**44.4**	0.0	0.0
Economic affairs	19.4	22.2	**41.7**	13.9	0.0	2.8
Cluster 1	22.2	**27.8**	22.2	**27.8**	0.0	0.0
Cluster 2	18.2	*27.3*	**54.5**	0.0	0.0	0.0
Cluster 3	*14.3*	0.0	**71.4**	0.0	0.0	14.3
Labour	46.9	23.4	1.6	25.0	2.6	0.0
Cluster 1	**41.7**	20.0	0.0	*37.5*	0.0	0.0
Cluster 2	**60.0**	*20.0*	0.0	12.0	8.0	0.0
Cluster 3	**33.3**	**33.3**	6.7	22.2	0.0	0.0
3 Welfare state						
Social affairs	**52.8**	*15.1*	2.6	14.3	3.9	1.3
Cluster 1	**52.9**	0.0	0.0	*35.3*	11.8	0.0
Cluster 2	**61.9**	*19.0*	9.5	0.0	4.8	4.8
Cluster 3	**40.0**	26.7	0.0	*33.3*	0.0	0.0
Health care	**43.6**	21.8	9.1	20.0	5.5	0.0
Cluster 1	**66.7**	0.0	0.0	*20.0*	13.3	0.0
Cluster 2	**40.0**	*28.0*	20.0	8.0	4.0	0.0
Cluster 3	26.7	*33.3*	0.0	**40.0**	0.0	0.0
Education	**48.9**	19.1	6.4	*21.3*	0.0	4.3
Cluster 1	**60.0**	0.0	0.0	*40.0*	0.0	0.0
Cluster 2	**47.1**	*29.4*	17.6	0.0	0.0	5.9
Cluster 3	**40.0**	*26.7*	0.0	*26.7*	0.0	6.7
4. Internal and external security						
Foreign affairs	**38.9**	*27.8*	13.9	13.9	4.2	1.4
Cluster 1	**44.8**	*31.0*	0.0	17.2	6.9	0.0
Cluster 2	**36.0**	*26.0*	24.0	0.0	4.0	0.0
Cluster 3	**33.3**	11.1	22.2	*27.8*	0.0	5.6
– Defense	**30.1**	*21.9*	17.8	20.5	8.2	1.4
Cluster 1	20.0	23.3	16.7	23.3	16.7	0.0
Cluster 2	**46.2**	11.5	*30.8*	3.8	3.8	3.8
Cluster 3	23.5	*35.3*	0.0	**41.2**	0.0	0.0
– Interior	**46.6**	*24.1*	8.6	10.3	10.3	0.0
Cluster 1	**68.8**	12.5	0.0	0.0	*18.8*	0.0
Cluster 2	**41.7**	*37.5*	16.7	0.0	4.2	0.0
Cluster 3	**33.3**	*16.7*	5.6	33.3	11.1	0.0

Source: derived from Woldendorp *et al.*, 2000.

Notes
Party Family: SD = Social Democracy; CD = Christian Democracy; Lib = Liberal; Cons = Conservative; Other = Not mentioned in Budge *et al.*, 2001; New = Not in Government before 1986. *n* = 1026. See Text for contents of Clusters 1 – 2 – 3. Bold = largest proportion; *Italics* = second largest proportion.

and Christian Democratic party family come second in the distribution. Again, this is in part explained by the presence or not of these parties in a country. The Liberal party is only represented in the economic sector and the security sector. The 'other' and 'new' members are only marginally involved and almost always as a 'smaller' participant. All in all, these results are not surprising and demonstrate the viability of the original approach as developed by Budge and Keman (see Table 2.3). Yet, the policy-seeking dimension, which seems not to be prolific on the general level, becomes more important if the results are analysed on the level of the three clusters. Recall that these clusters were formed on the basis of party distances within countries and the existence of 'pivotal' parties.

The *first* cluster represents the party systems with small(er) policy distances and a pivot party contains 23 governments. Here the distribution tends to oscillate between the centre-left and centre-right, where the Christian Democratic parties are literally in between: they do not dominate, but they are almost always 'around' (but second). However, it is obvious that Social Democratic parties claim most ministries and do so more often than others. Hence, a coalescent party system clearly pays off (see also Kitschelt, 1997; Pennings and Keman, 2003). Only economic regulation and defence are less accessible for Social Democratic party control (which support Budge and Keman, 1990: 97).

The *second* cluster, with competing pivot parties within a moderately organised party system, it appears that Social Democracy is benefiting from the medium distances between the main parties as well as of the possibility to form minority governments (in this cluster are also Denmark and Italy). Hence, the type of government appears here to be a 'window of opportunity' for Social Democracy. This is particularly visible in the control over the economy as well as the welfare state.

The *third* cluster is characterised by open competition and no stable direction in terms of left and right. This is confirmed but the results: although Social Democracy often prevails, it appears that Christian Democracy and other right-wing (or Conservative) parties do participate often and are represented in all domains. This is not the case for 'other' parties (more often than not 'new' Liberals or 'Greens') and 'new' parties. These are obviously minor partners in coalitions and apparently act as supposed in Rule V in Table 2.3. Yet it should be noted that their main domain of control is Security.

All in all it can be concluded that all the main parties do get much of what they wish in terms of ministries. However, this process is much less distinctive than is often put forward in the literature. In all cases the left versus right dimension seems to play a role, but not an overriding one. Second, in most cases, power must be 'shared' within a policy domain and this seems not to lead to fixed patterns of allocation of ministries. Obviously Social Democracy is strongly represented (since it is strong and prevalent everywhere). However, nowhere it is really dominating any of the policy domains. In fact no party seems to dominate any policy domain. Hence I conclude that although policy preferences do influence the distribution of ministries across policy sectors the golden rule of forming and maintaining a multiparty government is to give and take rather than to dominate other parties unnecessary. This is one of the lessons various parties had to learn the hard way when their electoral fortunes dwindled during the last decade (see Müller and Strøm, 1999).

Conclusions

In this chapter I have set out to examine to what extent the relationship between parties and government under conditions of multiparty system dynamics has changed. I used as a frame of reference the theory of Party Government developed by Ian Budge and Hans Keman (1990). The main conclusion must be that, although electoral politics is in flux and other (often 'new') parties have emerged after 1990, that 'our' theory still stands up and is capable of explaining government composition. This conclusion is justified in view of the following findings reported in this chapter:

- Electoral change, the emergence of new parties and new directions within party systems during the nineties have *not* been translated in drastically *different* patterns of government formation and composition.
- This does not mean there is no change, but if it comes to forming a government, the grip of the *established parties* – in particular if they are central and dominant – on the proceeding and outcome is still quite firm. This is certainly true for Social Democracy and Christian Democracy.
- Contrary to the emphasis in the original General Theory of Party Government the *differences* within party systems – operationalised as between party families – are *less directive and decisive* than was assumed. Only if disaggregated into clusters, party differences and policy positions seem to matter.
- It can be concluded that although *electoral competition* is changing, the competition for *governmental office* remains *consensus* orientated towards the parliamentary arena and concomitant party system.
- This conclusion appears tenable in view of the distribution of *types* of governments as well as that policy domains are allocated across *all* party families (flexibility).
- There seems to be a tendency of the 'established' parties, in particular under the present challenge of other 'innovative' parties, towards '*colonising*' policy domains (see Keman, 1991; but also Katz and Mair, 2002).
- Office-seeking *and* policy-seeking remain strongly interdependent features for party behaviour and our understanding thereof with respect to participation in coalition government.

Hence, I would like to conclude that the approach of Budge and Keman still stands and has indeed withstood the test of time! As far as amendments to this approach are concerned, I would suggest that the institutional context needs more attention (see also Laver and Budge, 1992). In addition, the role of policy preferences can be refined further and substantiated by investigating the policy performance (Keman, 2002). Finally, one aspect of electoral change is, in my view, that party *competition* is more and more differently structured as regards social and economic constituencies. Policy concerns and related preferences are becoming different from the 'old days' and 'innovative' if not 'alternative' coalitions of parties in parliament will emerge. This will no doubt affect the patterned composition of party government. Yet, despite all of this I think that the *process* of government formation and related policy pursuit will, by and large, remain to follow the ideas set out in the general theory of party government.

Appendix

Table 2.A.1 Operationalisation of left versus right scale

Anti-imperialism = 103	Military: positive = 104
Peace = 106	Individual rights = 201
Internationalism: positive = 107	Constitutionalism: positive = 203
Democracy = 202	Governmental and Adm. efficiency = 303
Protectionism: positive = 408	Free enterprise = 401
Controlled economy = 412	Protectionism: negative = 407
Anti-growth economy = 416	Economic orthodoxy = 414
Welfare state: expansion = 504	Welfare state limitation = 505
Social justice = 503	Law and order = 605
Pro-labour = 701	Social harmony = 606

Notes
Sum of the left minus the right scores is the actual outcome for each party. The values (proportions of programme emphases) indicate, if *negative*, inclination to the left and, if *positive*, a tendency towards the right. The numbers regarding the issues mentioned correspond with the variable numbers in Budge *et al.*, 2001: 220–228 (see also: Pennings and Keman, 2002).

Notes

1 The author is grateful for the assistance of Onno Bosch, Sabine Luursema and Arjan Schakel.
2 And, ironically, based on a government agreement which resembled almost perfectly the one already struck between PvdA and CDA!

Bibliography

Andeweg, R.B. and A. Timmermans, (2005) 'Conflict Management in Coalition Government', in K. Strøm, W.C. Müller and T. Bergman (eds) *Coalition Governance in Parliamentary Democracies* (Oxford: Oxford University Press).

Armingeon, K., M. Beyeler, M. Freitag and M. Senti (2002) *Comparative Political Dataset 1960–2000* (Bern: Institut für Politikwissenschaft (Universität Bern)).

Bartolini, S. and P. Mair (1990) *Identity, Competition and Electoral Availability: The Stabilisation of European Electorates 1885–1985* (Cambridge: Cambridge University Press).

Blondel, J. and J.-L. Thiébault (eds) (1991) *The Profession of Minister* (London: MacMillan Press).

Budge, I. and H. Keman (1990) *Parties and Democracies. Coalition Formation and Government Functioning in 20 States* (Oxford: Oxford University Press) (paperback edition: 1993).

Budge, I., H.D. Klingemann, A. Volkens, J. Bara and E. Tanenbaum (2001) *Mapping Policy Preferences: Parties Electors and Governments, 1945–1998* (Oxford: Oxford University Press).

Budge, I., R. Hofferbert, H. Keman, M. McDonald and P. Pennings (2002) 'Comparative Government and Democracy', in Hans Keman (ed.) *Comparative Democratic Politics. A guide to Contemporary Theory and Research* (London: Sage), pp. 65–98.

Capoccia, G. (2002) 'Anti-system Parties – A Conceptual Reassessment', *Journal of Theoretical Politics* 14:1, 9–35.

Dodd, L.C. (1976) *Coalitions in Parliamentary Government* (Princeton: Princeton University Press).

Gunther, R., J.R. Montera and J.J. Linz (eds) (2002) *Political Parties. Old Concepts and New Challenges* (Oxford: Oxford University Press).

Katz, D. and P. Mair (2002) 'The Ascendancy of the Party in Public Office. Party Organisational Change In Twentieth-Century Democracies', in R. Gunther, J.R. Montera and J.J. Linz (eds) *Political Parties. Old Concepts and New Challenge* (Oxford: Oxford University Press), pp. 113–135.

Keman, H. (1991) 'Party Control of Ministers and Ministries in Western Europe', in J. Blondel and J.-L. Thiébault (eds) *The Profession of Minister* (London: MacMillan Press), pp. 99–118.

Keman, H. (1997) 'Centre-Space Politics: Party Behaviour in Multi-Party Systems', in H. Keman (ed.) *The Politics of Problem-Solving in Postwar Democracies* (Houndmills, Basingstoke: Macmillan), pp. 162–186.

Keman, H. (2002) 'Policy-making Capacities of European Party Government', in K.R. Luther and F. Müller-Rommel (eds) *Political Parties in the New Europe* (Oxford: Oxford University Press), pp. 207–245.

Keman, H. (2003) 'Regierung durch Koalitionen in Belgien und den Niederlanden: die veränderten Profile der Beneluxländer', in S. Kropp, S. Schuttemayer and R. Sturm [Hrsg.], *Koalitionen in West- und Ostregierungen* (München: Leske + Budrich), pp. 107–136.

Keman, H. and P. Pennings (2004) 'The Development of Christian and Social Democracy Across Europe: Changing Positions and Political Consequences', in D. Th. Tsatsos, E.V. Venizelos, X.I. Contiades (eds), *Political Parties in the 21st Century* (Berlin and Brussels: Wissenschafts Verlag/Emile Bruylant).

Kitschelt, H. (1997) 'European Party Systems: Continuity and Change', in M. Rhodes, P. Heywood, V. Wright (eds) *Developments in West European Politics* (Houndmills, Basingstoke: Macmillan).

Klingemann, H.-D. and A. Volkens (2002) 'Parties, Ideologies and Issues. Stability and Change in Fifteen European Party Systems, 1945–1998', in K.R. Luther and F. Müller-Rommel (eds) *Political Parties in the New Europe* (Oxford: Oxford University Press), pp. 171–206.

Klingemann, H.-D., R.I. Hofferbert and I. Budge (1994) *Parties, Policies and Democracy* (Boulder, CO: Westview Press).

Laver, M. and I. Budge (1992) *Party Policy and Government Coalition* (Basingstoke: MacMillan).

Laver, M. and K.E. Shepsle (1996) *Making and Breaking Governments* (Cambridge: Cambridge University Press).

Lijphart, A. (1999) *Patterns of Democracy: Government Form and Performance in Thirty-Six Countries* (New Haven: Yale University Press).

Mair, P. (1997) *Party System Change: Approaches and Interpretations* (Oxford: Clarendon Press).

Mair, P. (2002) 'In the Aggregate: Mass Electoral Behaviour in Western Europe, 1950–2000', in Hans Keman (ed.) *Comparative Democratic Politics. A guide to Contemporary Theory and Research* (London: Sage), pp. 122–140.

Mair, P. (2005) 'Party Systems and Alternation in Government', unpublished paper.

Mény, Y. and Y. Surel (eds) (2002) *Democracies and the Populist Challenge* (New York: Palgrave).

Merkel, W. (2001) 'The Third Ways of Social Democracy', in R. Cuperus, K. Duffek and J. Kandel (eds) *Multiple Third Ways. European Social Democracy Facing the Twin Revolution of Globalisation and the Knowledge Society* (Amsterdam/Berlin/Vienna: Friedrich-Ebert-Stiftung/Wiardi Beckman Stichting/ Renner Institut), pp. 27–62.

Müller, W.C. and K. Strøm (eds) (1999) *Coalition Governments in Western Europe* (Oxford: Oxford University Press).

Pennings, P. and H. Keman (2002) 'Towards a New Methodology of Estimating Party Policy Positions', *Quality & Quantity* 38: 55–79.

Pennings, P. and H. Keman (2003) 'The Dutch Parliamentary Elections in 2002 and 2003: The Rise and Decline of the Fortuyn Movement', *Acta Politica* 38:1, pp. 51–68.

Pridham, G. (ed.) (1986) *Coalitional Behaviour in Theory and Practice: An Inductive Model for Western Europe* (Cambridge: Cambridge University Press).

Schmidt, M.G. (1996) 'When Parties Matter', *European Journal of Political Research* 30: 155–183.

Siaroff, A. (2000) *Comparative European Party Systems. An Analysis of Parliamentary Elections Since 1945* (New York, London: Garland Publishing).

Taggart, P. (2000) *Populism* (Buckingham: Open University Press).

Woldendorp, J., H. Keman and I. Budge (2000) *Party Government in 48 Democracies (1945–1998). Composition – Duration – Personnel* (Dordrecht: Kluwer Academic Publishers).

3 Policy changes of parties in European Parliament party groups

Andrea Volkens

Introduction

During the 25 years of their existence, the focus of the Manifesto Research Group (MRG) and its successor, the Comparative Manifesto Project (CMP) was on parties. Initiated by Ian Budge in 1979 with the aim of estimating policy positions of parties on the basis of programmes issued for national elections, the MRG/CMP analysed programmatic convergences and divergences of parties across countries for party families, often focusing on the left–right dimension (Budge, 2002).

Today, globalization compels national parties to cooperate internationally. The European Parliament (EP) is a special case where representatives of national parties join party groups created along the lines of party families. National parties are the major actors in EP party groups that in turn dominate the EP. This chapter provides a first attempt at estimating programmatic convergences and divergences between and within EP party groups along left–right and European integration dimensions for the six legislative terms of the EP since 1979. Based on the MRG/CMP data, it tests hypotheses on party competition in the European context.

Policy distances between EP party groups are relevant because majorities across party groups have to be built to take binding decisions. As with national government coalitions, decreasing policy distances between EP party groups can contribute to cooperation between them. Distances between national member parties within EP party groups are important because ideological homogeneity of EP party groups is assumed to be a prerequisite for group unity. The more compatible the programmes of national parties in EP party groups are, the easier it is for them to agree on joint policy positions.

The following section of the chapter develops hypotheses on changes in programmatic stances of parties and their influence on EP party groups. Methodological assumptions and procedures for measuring policy stances of national parties and EP party groups by means of content analyses of election programmes are discussed, policy distances within EP party groups are estimated by examining variations of member parties' positions around EP party group means and policy distances between EP party groups are estimated by comparing EP party group means. The chapter concludes with a discussion of the implications of these results for the functioning of EP party groups.

Theories of party policy change and the functioning of EP party groups

Many theories assume that policy positions of parties are converging. In the 1960s, Kirchheimer (1966) diagnosed a transformation of cleavage-based mass parties into catch-all parties at the same time that Bell (1962) declared an 'end of ideology'. Today, Katz and Mair (1995) talk about cartel parties, and rational choice theory predicts parties to adjust to the position of voters in the centre of the policy spectrum for vote-seeking reasons (Downs, 1957). These approaches imply that parties in national party systems are becoming more similar with respect to their policy positions so that parties no longer offer distinct policy packages for voters to choose between as is suggested in normative theories of representative party democracy.

In opposition to these dominant theories of convergence, modifications to spatial theory assumptions for party competition can explain why parties may still offer distinct policy packages. The assumption of complete information, on the part of the voters as well as on the part of the parties, that underlies many convergence theories is often criticized. Enelow and Hinich (1984) suggest that leeway for party policy changes is restricted; at most, parties can change their policy positions only gradually in the long run. Budge (1994) argues that parties may be well informed about voters' preferences through public opinion polls, but cannot be certain about how preferences will affect voting decisions, so in the face of such uncertainty, parties rely on ideologies. By doing so, they keep up their separate identities and, at the same time, serve the interests of party activists who are more strident proponents of ideology than voters.

The mobilization theory (Iversen, 1994a, b) expands rational choice considerations into a model of representational policy leadership in which 'voters are attracted to parties presenting relatively "intense" policy positions, and some party elites appear to be actively engaged in public opinion formation' (Iversen, 1994b: 155). According to the directional theory of voting, 'centrist parties will generally have a shaky and unstable support base in multiparty systems' (Rabinowitz and Macdonald, 1989: 110). This line of argument was further extended by incorporating motivations for voting decisions beyond policy preferences. Adams (2001) and Adams and Merrill (1999) include retrospective economic evaluations, partisanship and socio-demographic characteristics in their models. All these modifications of rational choice theories can claim empirical evidence: cleavages and social–psychological attachments to class, religion and ethnicity seem to be retained although some core groups of parties fade; lingering differences between social groups to which parties attend seem to limit convergent tendencies.

The saliency theory of party competition (Robertson, 1976; Budge and Farlie, 1977, 1983) offers additional arguments as to why parties may still differ. In contrast to theories that assume parties compete by taking opposite stands, saliency theory argues that 'the key difference between parties is the varying extent to which they mention one-position issues' (Budge, 2001: 52). This proposition develops the general distinction between position and valence issues of spatial theories (Stokes, 1963). While parties can take opposing positions on some issues, such as being favourable or opposed to European integration, there are many valence issues such as environmental protection to which no direct counter-position is feasible. Because valence issues are to some degree favoured by all voters, it would be electoral suicide to argue against these goals. In addition, parties 'own' certain positions on which they are judged as being competent so that they 'gloss over areas which might favour their rivals while emphasizing those on which they feel they have an advantage' (Budge, 1987: 24). Therefore, the MRG/CMP approach to measuring left–right positions of parties has always been a combination of position and saliency, defined as the 'relative intensities with which issues are addressed' (Janda *et al.*, 1995: 178), although others argue that 'position and salience are two distinct components of the policy of a given actor' (Laver, 2001: 66). Saliency theory assumes that parties will take action if they can agree on a joint position and if this position is of some importance to the party. In coalition governments, unimportant positions can easily be traded for more important goals.

Empirical studies on left–right policy changes based on MRG/CMP measures (Budge *et al.*, 1987) indicate that parties avoid a certain lower threshold of convergence with political competitors; as a rule they stick to a certain space (Budge, 1993) and keep a distance between them (Volkens, 2004). The left–right dimension places parties on a spatial continuum between specifically defined left and right poles. Left–right positions of parties, as estimated by content-analyses of election programmes, have been shown to capture the basic cleavages of industrialized societies (Budge *et al.*, 2001). A recent study on left–right changes of parties in the 15 European Union member states between 1945 and 1998 detected a cyclical pattern with decreasing distances between the 1940s and the 1960s, increasing distances between the 1970s and the 1980s, and again decreasing distances between the 1980s and the 1990s (Volkens and Klingemann, 2002). Parties moved along the left–right continuum quite frequently so that periods of convergence are followed by periods of divergence. Although they hardly ever 'leapfrog', many parties alternate priorities in different directions within their own ideological space (Budge, 1994).

At a European level, the left–right dimension seems to be growing in importance. Empirical tests of the dimensionality of the manifestos of party federations written prior to European elections between 1979 and 1999 indicate that EU political space is increasingly one-dimensional and similar to the national left–right dimension (Gabel and Hix, 2002). Roll-call analysis and surveys of members of the EP (MEPs) have also confirmed that the behaviour of party groups as well as the preferences of MEPs are ordered according to the left–right dimension (Hix and Lord, 1997). Since EP party groups are created along the lines of party families and since parties often change their priorities from one election to the next, left–right policy distances between EP party groups can be expected to fluctuate between legislative periods. When the first EP legislative period is compared with the sixth, however, programmatic left–right positions of EP party groups may have become more similar because left–right distances were decreasing between party families during the 1980s and 1990s.

There are four rival models of EU policy space (Marks and Steenbergen, 2002) based on different assumptions about the importance of policy dimensions and their relationships (Gabel and Hix, 2002). These four models are combinations of the left–right dimension and the European integration dimension. Based on content analyses of policy positions of the Socialist, Christian Democrat, Liberal and Green party leaders between 1976 and 1994, Hix concludes that 'the EU political space is essentially two-dimensional: an Integration–Independence dimension, arising from different identities and interests of national and territorial groups; and a (summary) Left–Right dimension, arising from the different interests of (trans-national) socio-economic groups (i.e. classes)' (1999: 92). This two-dimensional result is consistent with a study of citizen attitudes on EU issues (Gabel and Anderson, 2002).

Experts do not only judge that European integration issues are becoming more important for European parties, they also see that parties are increasingly favourable towards European integration (Ray, 1999).

> One of the striking features of national party responses to the European Union is the manner in which most parties of EU member states are or else have become pro-European Union. [. . .] By the 1990s, only a handful of communist and extreme right-wing parties remained uncompromisingly anti-EU.
>
> (Gaffney, 1996: 19)

Hix explained convergence towards a pro-European position as a function of Socialists moving from a moderately anti-integration position at the end of the 1970s to a pro-European position at the end of the 1980s (Hix, 1999: 87). Therefore, EP party groups' programmatic positions could also be expected to become more similar.

Because of institutional shifts in EU power relations which favour the EP, its formal structures now provide significant scope for EP party group influence if members can act as a united group (Bowler and Farrell, 1999).

Up to now, the capacity of party groups to act in concert has been studied by measuring voting cohesion and MEP attitudes. Almost all of these studies reveal a high degree of intra-group cohesion, defined as the ability of party groups to achieve internal unity (Hix and Lord, 1997). In these studies, ideological homogeneity of the members of party groups is usually considered to be decisive for EP party group unity. Bardi (1994) argues that in the middle of the 1990s most EP party groups had reached a high level of ideological homogeneity with only a few deviating parties. The impact of party families is amply shown in a recent study by Hooghe *et al.* (2002). Almost two-thirds of the variance in issue positions of national parties can be explained by party families. In the party family approach, parties are primarily seen as differing in terms of ideologies based upon the same major and enduring conflicts in national societies. Nonetheless, there are reasons to expect differences between parties with the same party family origin. Brzinski notes that 'though political parties in different nations may share similar names [. . .] unique historical and national experiences have made these parties distinct from one another' (1995: 144).

However, convergent tendencies are also detected at the societal, economic and political levels of nations. Wilensky (2002) argued that modernity is equivalent to nine major structural and demographic shifts leading to convergences between nations whereby parties across nations may converge to almost identical positions. Even if party families still differ in their blueprints for solving societal, economic and political problems, parties of the same party family would behave responsibly when they reacted to the increasingly similar real world cues. Following this normative perspective, we would expect policy positions of parties belonging to the same party family to become more similar subject to cultural constraints. For EU member countries, convergent tendencies should be prominent because ever more policies are regulated centrally and regional differences are being mitigated by regional and structural funds. Moreover, parties deviating from party family lines change groups or establish new ones. Convergent tendencies within EP party groups may be further intensified by intra-group cooperation facilitating policy learning/transfer, as well as by transnational European party federations contributing to cooperation across nations. Therefore, the programmatic compatibility of parties in EP party groups on left–right as well as on European integration issues can be expected to rise between the first and the sixth legislative period.

Empirical evidence from party manifestos

There are good reasons for analysing policy distances between and within EP party groups using content analyses of national parties' election programmes. National parties are the main collective actors in EP party groups. All existing studies on EP party group cohesion agree that the core role of national parties in the EP party groups is a function of formal rules and procedures (Bardi, 1994; Brzinski, 1995; Gaffney, 1996; Pedersen, 1996; Raunio, 1997, 1999, 2000a, b; Corbett *et al.*, 2000). Most importantly, national parties can control their EP representatives through candidate selection procedures. A study testing whether MEPs vote according to personal policy preferences, to national parties' positions or according to EP party group positions, concludes that national parties' positions are by far the most influential (Hix, 2002). Although election programmes are often criticized for being mere 'shopping lists' to attract voters and without relevance for the political behaviour of parties, a number of studies have shown that programmatic positions are translated into legislation (Pomper, 1968; Ginsberg, 1982; Rallings, 1987; Thomson, 2001) and into budgets (Klingemann *et al.*, 1994). In addition, distances between parties in EP party groups cannot be studied on the basis of election programmes issued for the European elections, because some parties compete EP elections with joint programmes produced by transnational European party federations, whereas national election programmes are issued for each election by every party contesting elections in all member states, so that changes over time can be analysed.

Measuring programmatic distances between and within EP party groups

Because the MRG/CMP collects and content analyses only election programmes from relevant parties in national parliaments, data is not available for some small parties in EP party groups (see Appendix 3.a.1 for details). Election programmes at the time of or prior to the EP elections of 1979, 1984, 1989, 1994, 1999 and 2004 have been used to estimate the positions of all parties listed as members in EP party groups during the six legislative terms.[1] This procedure yields 471 cases of parties in 40 EP party groups in the six legislative terms excluding seven groups that are not created along the lines of party families.[2] The method of the Manifesto Research Group is easily applicable and is described elsewhere in detail (Budge *et al.*, 1987). The MRG-CMP data set gives each position of a party as a percentage of the total program. The more space devoted to a position, the more important it is for a party. The measure thus combines position and saliency. With this combined measure, all positions are related as is the case with budgets: the more money spent on one goal, the less is left for another. A statement by a member of the EP party group secretariat also reveals that the salience of a position is important for MEPs: 'On issues on which members would not feel very strongly, they will vote with the majority' (Brzinski, 1995: 149).

Although the MRG/CMP data are combined measures, one can easily create separate measures for positions and saliencies from the percentages of given categories. The 'pure' position of a party can be derived by (1) adding up the percentages of all right pole categories, (2) adding up the percentages of all left pole categories, (3) subtracting the sums of the left pole from the sums of the right pole and (4) dividing this value by the sum of all left and right pole percentages (Laver and Garry, 2000). By separating positions from their saliencies, all policy positions are treated as being independent from one another. 'Pure' saliencies are equal to thematic concerns in media analysis and give the importance of a topic such as European integration without taking into account whether parties are opposed to or in favour of a specific issue. The 'pure' saliency measures can be created by adding up the percentages of all categories assigned to the two poles.

For the two policy dimensions under consideration (the left–right and the European integration dimension) all three measures – positions, saliencies, and the MRG/CMP combinations of positions and saliencies – were calculated. The left–right measure employed by Laver and Budge (1993), has been shown to have the greatest face validity as well as correlational validity (McDonald and Mendes, 2001a, b). This measure includes 13 categories that define the right pole such as free market economy, welfare state reduction, law and order, and military strength, and 13 categories that define the left pole such as market interventions, economic planning, welfare state expansions, peace and internationalism. For central and east European party programmes extra subcategories were added.[3]

Two standard categories – 'in favour of European integration' and 'opposed to European integration' – directly tackle positions of parties on European integration. But in the European multi-level arena, as Bell (1996: 229) notes: 'If taken at face value, however, the reinforcement of the EP is clearly at odds with state sovereignty: any reinforcement of supranational institutions can only be to the detriment of the state powers'. The same is true for decentralization. A party opting for national sovereignty or for decentralization will by definition oppose binding decisions to be taken at the European level. Therefore, the anti-European pole is derived by (1) adding up all percentages of sentences opposed to European integration, in favour of national sovereignty, and in favour of decentralization, whereas (2) the pro-European pole consists of all statements in favour of European integration. Saliencies, 'pure,' and combined measure positions of parties on this European-integration dimension, can be computed, as given above for the left–right dimension. The more negative the resulting values for the 'pure' positions and the MRG/CMP combined measure positions, the more anti-European a party is likely to be.[4]

EP party group means were computed by (1) weighting the six index values (two policy dimensions with three measures each) of each party with their relative strength in EP party groups, i.e. the number of representatives in relation to the number of all representatives in the party group for which programmes are available[5] and (2) summing the resulting values for all parties in each party group. Standard deviations were computed as a measure for distances within EP party groups.[6] Distances between all EP party groups were then estimated by standard deviations of EP party group means in which the means are derived from weighted positions of member parties.

Left–right and European integration distances between EP party groups

In Table 3.1, left–right as well as European integration measures for distances between groups show a clear-cut picture. From the first to the third legislative period, when the number of party groups grew from six to nine, distances between groups increased. In 1984, the group of European right parties was established. In 1989 Green parties which were previously represented mainly in the technical Rainbow Group created their own group and the Communists split into two groups. Growing distances in these legislative periods point to a strong relationship between the number of EP party groups and the policy distances between them. This relationship is equivalent to the relationship between the number of parties and polarization in national party systems.

In the mid-1990s, the two conservative groups, the European Democratic Group (EDG) and the European Democratic Alliance (EDA) dissolved and many of their member parties joined the European People's Party (EPP) that up to then represented Christian Democratic parties. In addition, the two communist camps recombined. This reduction from nine to six groups was accompanied by a significant drop in position and combined measure distances although saliency distances remained the same (Corbett *et al.*, 2000; Raunio, 2000b). Despite changes in group names, six different groups based on national cleavage lines can be distinguished from 1994 onwards.[7] But distances between the six groups declined further. This decrease was less than the reduction in distances due to the decline in group numbers although the pattern concurs with expectations derived from party families, namely that programmatic distances between EP party groups show a decreasing tendency.

Table 3.1 Policy distances between European Parliament party groups

	Number of groups[1]					
	1979–84	*1984–89*	*1989–94*	*1994–99*	*1999–2004*	*2004–09*
	6	7	9	6	6	62
1. Left–right:						
1.1 Saliency	2.52	7.07	5.29	5.29	5.15	3.74
1.2 Position	0.10	0.11	0.15	0.04	0.03	0.03
1.3 Combined	4.95	5.83	8.69	1.90	1.23	1.11
2. European integration:						
2.1 Saliency	0.37	1.18	1.38	0.22	0.41	0.17
2.2 Position	0.11	0.21	0.24	0.04	0.08	0.03
2.3 Combined	0.37	0.99	1.34	0.20	0.53	0.12

Notes
1 Excluding technical groups (see Appendix 3.A.1) and non-attached parties.
2 No programme data are available for the new group European Democracy and Diversities (EDD).

On the whole, position and saliency, as well as combined measures, display similar patterns. The difference between the 'pure' position and the combined measures in particular are marginal as far as distances between groups are concerned. When distances in positions grow, combined measure distances also grow and vice versa. The 'pure' saliency measure, though, differs from 'pure' position and combined measures. In contrast to the latter two, the distance in left–right saliencies peaks in the second legislative period and stayed the same in the fourth period although the number of groups dwindled. Therefore, the number of groups seems to have a bigger impact on distances in position than on distances in saliency.

However, these figures may overestimate convergent tendencies on the left–right as well as on the European integration dimension for two reasons. First, many of the extreme right-wing parties either entered technical groups that are not set up along the lines of party families (Corbett *et al.*, 2000: 66) or else they stayed completely unattached. Therefore, polarization measures between all parties represented in the European Parliament would show a higher degree of left–right dissent. Second, European integration distances grew a bit from the fourth to the fifth legislative period. But even more importantly, the group, Europe of Democracy and Diversities (EDD), was set up in the sixth legislative period. This group includes four parties, among them the United Kingdom Independence Party (UKIP) which is well known for its anti-European stances, as well as three other small parties. Unfortunately, no data are available for these parties. The inclusion of this group would probably have led to a growing distance between groups with regard to European integration because numbers of groups seem to impact on policy distances between groups. Furthermore, this new group is the first based neither upon national lines of conflict nor set up as a technical group in order to get resources that are accorded to groups, but built on anti-European stances of the member parties. Therefore, the creation of this group is itself an indication of growing tensions with regard to European integration.

Left–right stances of EP party groups

How do these changes in distances between groups relate to policy changes of party groups? Dominant theories of party competition predict parties will converge, i.e. left-wing parties should move rightward and right-wing parties should move leftwards, whereas modifications of spatial theory assumptions predict parties will change left–right positions quite frequently within their own ideological space. Tables 3.2 to 3.4 present the left–right stances of EP party groups for the three measures.

Even a quick glance at the tables reveals that none of the party groups shows a constant movement in the directions predicted by dominant

Table 3.2 Left–right saliencies of parties in EP party groups

Legisl. Period	1		2		3		4		5		6		Average	
Years	1979–84		1984–89		1989–94		1994–99		1999–04		2004–09		Average	
Party Groups[1]	x̄	std.	x̄	std.	x̄	std.	x̄	std.	x̄	std.	x̄	std.	x̄	std.
Communist	45.42	4.53	42.28	16.31	56.24[2]	11.17	48.82	7.06	49.73	9.18	51.03	10.90	48.92	9.86
PES	48.64	11.25	47.13	8.88	50.59	10.65	47.47	9.19	47.60	7.92	50.74	6.14	48.70	9.01
GRE	–	–	–	–	45.70	11.77	37.88	10.32	38.85	9.95	44.94	9.88	41.84	10.48
ELDR	48.33	14.32	45.10	9.70	51.40	7.44	50.49	8.76	51.00	11.46	48.91	9.80	49.21	10.25
EPP	45.36	14.04	49.91	13.02	44.74	5.03	53.52	11.07	53.99	10.77	50.54	10.98	49.68	10.82
EDG	50.90	5.35	46.91	0.95	59.53	0.35	–	–	–	–	–	–	52.45	2.22
EDA	51.12	4.74	64.20	8.13	51.18	12.67	–	–	–	–	–	–	55.50	8.51
European Right	–	–	48.89	21.40	57.85	8.72	48.17	4.17	47.13	2.29	41.95	8.26	48.80	8.97
Average	48.30	9.04	49.20	11.20	52.15	8.45	47.72	8.43	48.05	8.60	48.02	9.33		

Notes
1 See Appendix 3.A.1 for names of party groups and changes in memberships.
2 Average of EUL and LU.

Table 3.3 Left–right positions of parties in EP party groups

Legisl. Period	1		2		3		4		5		6		Average	
Years	1979–84		1984–89		1989–94		1994–99		1999–04		2004–09		Average	
Party Groups[1]	x̄	std.	x̄	std.	x̄	std.	x̄	std.	x̄	std.	x̄	std.	x̄	std.
Communist	−0.57	0.28	−0.31	0.43	−0.39[2]	0.37	−0.58	0.28	−0.54	0.32	−0.52	0.21	−0.49	0.32
PES	−0.49	0.27	−0.43	0.32	−0.31	0.31	−0.38	0.31	−0.10	0.23	−0.22	0.17	−0.32	0.27
GRE	–	–	–	–	−0.28	0.47	−0.36	0.29	−0.50	0.29	−0.37	0.29	−0.38	0.34
ELDR	0.11	0.39	0.05	0.36	0.32	0.31	0.12	0.40	0.07	0.31	0.02	0.23	0.12	0.33
EPP	0.03	0.29	0.23	0.34	0.12	0.29	0.23	0.35	0.34	0.32	0.21	0.29	0.19	0.31
EDG	0.49	0.18	0.54	0.24	0.52	0.06	–	–	–	–	–	–	0.52	0.16
EDA	0.06	0.63	0.02	0.48	0.19	0.44	–	–	–	–	–	–	0.09	0.52
European right	–	–	0.46	0.46	0.61	0.52	0.26	0.30	0.08	0.23	0.21	0.48	0.32	0.40
Average	−0.06	0.34	0.08	0.38	0.10	0.35	−0.12	0.32	−0.11	0.28	−0.11	0.28		

Notes
1 See Appendix 3.A.1 for names of party groups and changes in memberships.
2 Average of EUL and LU.

Table 3.4 Combined left–right positions and saliencies of parties in EP party groups

Legisl. Period	1		2		3		4		5		6		Average	
Years	1979–84		1984–89		1989–94		1994–99		1999–04		2004–09		Average	
Party Groups[1]	x̄	std.	x̄	std.	x̄	std.	x̄	std.	x̄	std.	x̄	std.	x̄	std.
Communist	−26.53	14.85	−12.98	22.40	−18.98[2]	18.85	−28.14	12.82	−26.06	15.90	−25.57	10.31	−23.04	15.86
PES	−24.90	14.61	−19.87	13.82	−15.22	14.97	−17.13	14.20	−3.31	11.30	−11.13	8.52	−15.26	12.90
GRE	–	–	–	–	−11.19	25.11	−14.02	12.73	−17.97	10.61	−16.14	12.97	−14.83	15.36
ELDR	8.77	21.51	5.51	15.59	17.63	16.71	8.04	20.67	4.03	14.53	1.44	11.59	7.57	16.77
EPP	4.73	16.02	14.84	17.22	6.27	13.37	14.42	20.20	20.32	18.63	9.97	16.21	11.76	16.94
EDG	25.19	13.34	25.29	11.10	30.79	3.91	–	–	–	–	–	–	27.09	9.45
EDA	4.15	35.43	−0.46	32.24	12.23	22.57	–	–	–	–	–	–	5.31	30.08
European Right	–	–	26.86	27.78	36.06	30.32	14.63	15.19	3.79	10.47	7.94	17.60	17.86	20.27
Average	−1.43	19.29	5.60	20.02	7.20	18.23	−3.70	15.97	−3.20	13.57	−5.58	12.87		

Notes
1 See Appendix 3.A.1 for names of party groups and changes in memberships.
2 Average of EUL and LU.

theories of party change. Left–right saliencies do not differ much at all. Almost all groups devoted half of their programmes to left–right issues with only minor variations over time. Today, the left–right dimension is as important for parties as it was 25 years ago. The only group that pays less attention – on average 42 per cent – to left–right matters are the Greens since this group is more concerned with issues beyond the scope of the dimension.

Again, the 'pure' position and the combined measure show similar patterns. Most party groups move along the left–right dimension quite frequently with changes to the left often being followed by changes to the right. When the first and last legislative periods are compared, three of the four centre-left groups – Communists, Party of European Socialists (PES), and European Liberal, Democrat and Reform Party (ELDR) – moved to the right, but the Green group moved to the left. In addition, the combined measure lists the rightward movement of the Communists to be marginal and although the ELDR jumped to the right in 1989, it could still count because of its later leftward moves.

The group that best exhibits expectations of dominant convergence theories is the PES. With growing emphasis on free market principles and less on welfare state expansion, these parties moved strongly to the right from 1979 to 1999, reflecting a 'Third Way' approach. However, even the Socialists seem to return to their traditional ideological space in 2004 with a noticeable move to the left between the fifth and sixth legislative periods. Since positions of parties were weighted by their strength within groups, this cannot be attributed wholly to the smaller Central and East European parties entering the group, but also to leftward changes by parties from larger, established member states.

Of the four right-wing party groups, only the European Right moved to the left as predicted by dominant theories of party competition. This result may be influenced by the fact that most of the extreme-right parties did not join this group. Contrary to expectations, the EPP moved to the right. Although this exploratory analysis cannot systematically control for the strength of shifts relating to changes in group membership or in positions of long-term members, some of these EPP rightward changes can be attributed to new group members. In 1994, the conservative groups disbanded and many conservative parties joined the EPP, which thus grew from 15 to 31. With the accession of ten new member countries in 2004, the EPP increased from 31 to 41 parties, although it moved decisively to the left.

Overall trends of changes in left–right distances between party groups, thus, can mainly be attributed to changing numbers of groups; some changes can also be explained by major change in group memberships, others are due to changing positions of long-term group members. However, convergences between party groups are contrary to assumptions of decreasing distances being due to leftward parties moving to the right and rightward parties moving to the left. Left–right distances decreased because of complex movements sometimes rightward, at others leftward, by almost all groups.

Tables 3.2 to 3.4 also display the left–right distances between parties within party groups. On average, the heterogeneity of parties in terms of saliencies reached a height in the second legislative period and a low in the fourth period, but grew again from this time onwards. However, a look at the single party groups shows that heterogeneity in saliency peaked at quite different points in time. Apart from these peaks, almost all groups became more similar in terms of left–right saliency, despite the number of parties within groups increasing in many legislative periods due to the accession of new member countries. As a rule, differences in left–right saliencies were much bigger in 1979 than they are today, apart from the Communist group. In 1989, the group split into the Euro-communist European United Left (EUL) and the orthodox Left Unity Group (LU) which were reunited in 1994. After enlargement in 1995, the group gained Swedish and Finnish members. At the insistence of the new members, the group added the reference 'Nordic Green Left' (NGL) to the name of the group (Corbett *et al.*, 2000). Because of all these transformations of the Communist and Allies Group, the Confederal Group of the European United Left – Nordic Green Left (GUE-NGL) of 1999 is usually considered to be a completely new group (Bardi, 1996). The same general pattern of growing programmatic compatibility is also visible in the left–right positions of parties. As was the case with saliency distances, the differences in left–right positions peaked in some, though different, periods, but decreased over time. With respect to 'pure' positions, two exceptions from this rule occur. First and foremost, the European Right group of 2004 is much more dissimilar than in 1979 although the bulk of the extreme right-wing parties were not included in 2004. Today, it is the most heterogeneous of all groups. The left–right dissent of the EPP was greatest in 1994 when Conservative parties combined with Christian Democrats. Today the group is as heterogeneous as it was in 1979, although Christian Democrats and Conservative parties became noticeably more compatible in left–right terms from 1994 onwards.

Again, the combined measure for left–right distances does not differ much from the tendencies displayed by the 'pure' position. The distances between parties generally peak at the same time points and exhibit more programmatic compatibility over time. The only obvious difference between the two measures concerns the Green group which, since 1999, comprises member parties of the European Federation of Green Parties besides parties from the European Free Alliance, a federation of regionalist parties. The regional parties seemed to fit quite well into the group and their inclusion did not lead to growing programmatic heterogeneity. After a drop in 1994, the 'pure' position measure shows the homogeneity to be constant, whereas the combined measure attests to rising heterogeneity from the fifth to the sixth period although no new members joined as a result of enlargement. Overall, though, the three measures of left–right heterogeneity of party groups do not differ much. All three display the same general pattern of growing left–right compatibility over time for most party groups.

European integration stances of EP party groups

With respect to European integration saliency, groups were predicted to converge because European issues were judged to be getting more important for all parties. Table 3.5 presents (weighted) group means and distances between parties within party groups for European integration saliencies. In all party groups, European issues became much more important from the first to the fifth legislative period as was predicted. In the sixth period, however, this trend is reversed as four of the six groups, (PES, ELDR and, in particular, EPP and European Right) paid less attention to European integration issues. The time point of this reversal certainly comes as a surprise. Despite of the accession of ten new countries and discussions about the European constitution, four of the six groups put less emphasis on European integration than they did in the preceding period.

Table 3.5 clearly shows that the programmatic heterogeneity of party groups with respect to European integration saliency did not decrease as predicted. Parties in all groups became more dissimilar in terms of emphasis on European integration from the first legislative period to the fifth. Although many parties in all groups paid more attention to Europe, some did not mention Europe much in their election programmes so that saliency distances grew. With less emphasis on Europe in the sixth legislative period, dissent between parties dropped. This is particularly true for the EPP and European Right, which mentioned Europe less.

According to expert judgements, all parties are expected to become more pro-European over time apart from far-left and far-right parties. Therefore, centre-right and centre-left party groups should be getting more homogeneous, but distances within Communist and European Right groups may increase when some of the member parties remain Euro-sceptic whereas others grow more Europe-friendly. Tables 3.6 and 3.7 present the (weighted) means of party groups and standard deviations between parties in EP party groups on European integration for the 'pure' position and the combined measure.

Contrary to both expectations and left–right positions, most groups were growing more heterogeneous over time on European integration matters. Both measures display the same pattern of increasing programmatic differences within groups with one exception. The Communist group is shown to be getting less heterogeneous by the 'pure' position measure, but more so by the combined measure. The reason for this difference is that the French and the German Communist parties changed position as well as saliency on European integration.

Table 3.5 European integration saliencies of parties in EP party groups

Legisl. period	1		2		3		4		5		6		Average	
Years	1979–84		1984–89		1989–94		1994–99		1999–2004		2004–09		Average	
Party groups[1]	x̄	std.	x̄	std.	x̄	std.	x̄	std.	x̄	std.	x̄	std.	x̄	std.
Communist	5.61	2.05	5.47	2.21	3.70[2]	1.47	4.76	3.45	7.15	4.06	7.76	5.49	5.74	3.12
PES	5.75	2.41	5.46	3.14	5.42	2.77	5.62	3.15	6.84	3.03	5.81	2.30	5.82	2.80
GRE	–	–	–	–	3.35	3.06	3.77	4.65	9.37	6.36	7.28	6.43	5.94	5.13
ELDR	4.44	1.54	3.65	4.82	8.34	3.88	7.84	4.56	9.65	7.58	9.30	6.55	7.20	4.82
EPP	4.44	1.60	3.70	4.11	7.95	7.43	6.15	4.72	9.60	6.51	6.73	2.68	6.43	4.51
EDG	2.41	0.57	3.18	1.56	3.44	3.43	–	–	–	–	–	–	3.01	1.85
EDA	2.25	–[3]	1.83	0.06	9.05	7.31	–	–	–	–	–	–	4.38	3.67
European Right	–	–	7.33	3.56	5.46	1.52	7.12	3.48	5.99	4.32	3.58	2.97	5.90	3.17
Average	4.15	1.63	4.37	2.78	5.84	3.86	5.88	4.00	8.10	5.31	6.74	4.40		

Notes
1 See Appendix 3.A.1 for names of party groups and changes in memberships.
2 Average of EUL and LU.
3 Position taken by one party, only.

Table 3.6 European integration positions of parties in EP party groups

Legisl. Period	1		2		3		4		5		6		Average	
Years	1979–84		1984–89		1989–94		1994–99		1999–2004		2004–09		Average	
Party Groups[1]	x̄	std.	x̄	std.	x̄	std.	x̄	std.	x̄	std.	x̄	std.	x̄	std.
Communist	−0.36	0.63	−0.70	0.23	−0.25[2]	0.48	−0.62	0.35	−0.56	0.45	−0.28	0.49	−0.46	0.44
PES	−0.03	0.72	−0.38	0.61	0.08	0.68	0.03	0.45	0.40	0.61	0.04	0.49	0.02	0.59
GRE	–	–	–	–	−0.85	0.44	−0.16	0.56	0.21	0.65	0.10	0.74	−0.12	0.60
ELDR	0.36	0.30	−0.58	0.65	0.25	0.55	−0.25	0.49	−0.07	0.52	0.07	0.55	−0.04	0.51
EPP	0.09	0.57	0.25	0.75	0.56	0.53	0.46	0.50	0.00	0.63	−0.04	0.58	0.22	0.59
EDG	0.59	0.28	0.30	0.55	−0.77	1.33	–	–	–	–	–	–	0.04	0.72
EDA	−0.22	–[3]	−1.00	0.00	0.79	0.23	–	–	–	–	–	–	−0.14	0.12
European Right	–	–	−0.69	0.19	−0.53	0.54	0.17	0.40	−0.78	0.37	−0.46	0.70	−0.46	0.44
Average	0.07	0.50	−0.40	0.43	−0.09	0.60	−0.06	0.46	−0.13	0.54	−0.10	0.59		

Notes
1 See Appendix 3.A.1 for names of party groups and changes in memberships.
2 Average of EUL and LU.
3 Position taken by one party, only.

Both parties became pro-European over time and today devote considerable proportions of their programmes to statements in favour of more integration whereas the Euro-sceptic Communists do not mention Europe much. Apart from this deviation, both the 'pure' position measure and the combined measure point to wider European integration distances between parties. Only one group, the PES, became more compatible on European integration issues.

An unexpected result occurred with regard to European integration, in that whilst distances between groups decreased, distances within most increased. The mean positions of groups shown in Tables 3.6 and 3.7 demonstrate a marked difference between the groups. Left-wing groups as well as the European Right, which were traditionally anti-European, grew less sceptical over time, whereas traditionally pro-European centre-right groups became more critical, so that the groups converged. As this is true for many parties in the groups, the mean position of groups changed, but the resistance of some parties to the general group trends led to considerably wider distances between parties in most party groups.

Conclusions

In normative terms, globalization processes pose particular challenges to parties as collective actors: ever more problems are beyond the reach of nation states and delegates need to further responsible parties' policy positions in ever more international settings. The European Parliament is a specific case of a multilevel system in which representatives of national parties have to cooperate across countries to produce joint policy outputs. This analysis has yielded unambiguous patterns of change over time. Both left–right and European integration distances between groups decreased when the first legislative period is compared to the sixth, suggesting that cooperation between most groups should be easier today than it was 25 years ago. But this does not mean that voters no longer have choices. In the first place, policy distances between EP party groups are heavily influenced by the number of groups, and polarization between party groups increased between the first and third legislative periods when the number of groups grew, and declined in the fourth period when groups merged.

Assumptions of dominant theories of left–right party convergence are not substantiated. Instead, patterns of policy change concur with expectations derived from modifications of spatial theories: shifts in programmatic left–right distances between groups derived from complex movements of groups, sometimes to the right, at other times to the left, without any obvious patterns for left- or right-wing parties. The PES is the only group with strong and continual changes to the right from the first to the fifth legislative term. But even the PES seems to be returning to its traditional ideological space because it moved leftwards between the fifth and sixth terms.

Table 3.7 Combined European integration positions and saliencies of parties in EP party groups

Legisl. Period	1		2		3		4		5		6		Average	
Years	1979–84		1984–89		1989–94		1994–99		1999–2004		2004–09		Average	
Party Groups[1]	$\bar{x}$	std.	$\bar{x}$	std.	$\bar{x}$	std.	$\bar{x}$	std.	$\bar{x}$	std.	$\bar{x}$	std.	$\bar{x}$	std.
Communist	-2.12	3.23	-3.31	1.21	-0.54[2]	3.00	-3.10	4.08	-4.04	5.05	-1.62	6.62	-2.46	3.87
PES	-0.18	4.22	-2.88	3.58	0.61	3.82	-0.32	2.62	2.91	4.05	0.35	3.36	0.08	3.61
GRE	–	–	–	–	-2.66	2.81	-2.02	5.24	2.98	6.37	-0.73	7.43	-0.61	5.46
ELDR	2.08	2.12	-2.33	3.28	2.50	4.97	-3.11	5.34	-1.53	6.83	0.72	5.42	-0.28	4.66
EPP	0.68	1.93	0.99	4.17	4.86	8.65	2.64	4.66	0.29	6.31	-0.09	3.24	1.56	4.83
EDG	1.46	0.14	0.69	1.26	-2.14	7.62	–	–	–	–	–	–	0.00	3.01
EDA	-0.58	–[3]	-1.83	0.06	6.33	4.35	–	–	–	–	–	–	1.31	2.21
European Right	–	–	-5.39	4.20	-3.05	2.83	0.84	4.56	-4.81	5.49	-1.70	4.37	-2.82	4.29
Average	0.22	2.33	-2.01	2.54	0.74	4.76	-0.85	4.42	-0.70	5.68	-0.51	5.07		

Notes
1 See Appendix 3.A.1 for names of party groups and changes in memberships.
2 Average of EUL and LU.
3 Position taken by one party, only.

European integration distances between party groups also decreased, but there is a marked difference between expert judgements on party position developments and programmatic statements of parties in offering explanations for this convergence. Experts judged the left-wing parties to be anti-European and centre-right parties to be pro-European in 1979 and detected convergent tendencies because almost all parties were seen as growing more pro-European. However, programmatic differences on European integration between party groups diminished as left-wing party groups grew more pro-European over time, whereas centre-right parties grew more Euro-sceptic. In addition, a new group – Europe of Democracy and Diversities (EDD) – was created in 2004, which is built on the anti-European stances of its member parties and is an indication of growing tensions with regard to integration.

As predicted, the left–right positions of member parties in EP party groups became more compatible over time, so that the groups today are better able to unite on left–right matters than 25 years ago although the number of member countries, and hence the number of parties within most groups, has grown considerably. Contrary to expectations and despite decreasing tendencies in left–right distances, European integration positions of parties within groups grew less compatible over time. The only exception to this rule is the PES which became more homogeneous and is, on the whole, the most compatible of all groups in terms of programmatic statements on left–right, as well as on European integration issues. In all other groups, European integration distances between member parties have grown. Most put increasingly more emphasis on European issues so that, on average, European integration matters became more important for all groups, although some parties do not pay much attention to Europe. These overall trends were, however, resisted by some parties with the result that programmatic dissent on EU positions within groups has increased. This pattern of growing programmatic dissent indicates that all party groups except the Socialists are increasingly faced with internal conflicts whenever basic questions arise over which of three levels (the European, the national or the regional) binding decisions are to be taken.

Throughout the analysis, 'pure' position and the combined measure results display similar patterns of change. The group means on left–right saliency do not change much over time; parties almost always devote the same amount of their national election programmes to left–right issues which indicates continuing importance of left–right cleavages. But even with growing emphasis on European issues, differences between the 'pure' position and the MRG/CMP combined measure were shown to be marginal. Up to now, the predictive capacity of the three measures has never been systematically checked and it remains to be seen whether small differences in values lead to important differences in predictions. Until then, there is good reason to suggest that a party as well as a party group will take action if it can come up with a joint position and if this position is of some importance to the party or the party group as is assumed by the saliency theory of party competition.

Appendix

Table 3.A.1 Number of parties and seats in European Parliament party groups, number of available manifestos and seats covered by manifestos

EP party groups	Legislative periods	Number of parties		Number of seats	
		Actual	Available	Actual	Available
Communist					
COM	1979–84	5	4	48	47
COM	1984–89	9	6	48	45
EUL	1989–94	4	3	28	24
LU	1989–94	4	4	14	14
GUE	1994–99	8	8	33	33
GUE-NGL	1999–2004	14	12^1	42	35^1
GUE-NGL	2004–09	16	14	39	37
PES					
	1979–84	14	12	122	120
	1984–89	15	14	165	164
	1989–94	17	16	180	179
	1994–99	20	18	214	212
	1999–2004	18	16	180	177
	2004–09	25	24	199	196
GRE					
	1989–94	12	9	30	26
	1994–99	11	10	28	27
	1999–2004	18	14	48	41
	2004–09	18	13	43	36
ELDR	1979–84	10	8^2	40	22^2
	1984–89	14	10	44	37
	1989–94	12	12	49	48
	1994–99	17	17	43	42
	1999–2004	17	16^3	51	44^3
	2004–09	31	30	93	91
EPP					
	1979–84	10	8	116	106
	1984–89	14	12	115	112
	1989–94	15	12^4	121	113^4
	1994–99	23	20	181	176
	1999–2004	31	26	233	228
	2004–09	41	37	261	257
EDG					
	1979–84	4	3	64	63
	1984–89	3	3	66	66
	1989–94	2	2	34	34

Table 3.A.1 continued

EP party groups	Legislative periods	Number of parties		Number of seats	
		Actual	Available	Actual	Available
EDA					
	1979–84	4	2[5]	22	6[5]
	1984–89	7	2	29	23
	1989–94	4	2	20	17
European Right					
ER	1984–89	4	2	17	15
ER	1989–94	3	2	17	11
EN	1994–99	5	0	18	0
EDU	1999–2004	5	0	16	0
UPE	1994–99	9	8	57	55
UEN	1999–2004	5	4[6]	30	18[6]
UEN	2004–09	6	6	27	27

Legend:
Party Groups

10	COM	Communist and Allies Group
11	EUL	European United Left
12	LU	Left Unity Group
13	GUE-NGL	European United Left-Nordic Green Left
20	PES	Party of European Socialists
30	GRE	Green Group, EG/EFA European Greens/European Free Alliance
40	ELDR	European Liberal, Democrat and Reform Party; ELDR-EDP European Democratic Party
50	EPP	European People's Party; EPP-ED European Democrats
60	EDG	European Democratic Group
70	EDA	European Democratic Alliance
80	ER	European Right
81	EN	Europe of Nations
82	EDU	Europe of Democracies and Differences
83	UPE	Union for Europe
84	UEN	Union for a Europe of Nations

Comments to Legislative Periods
1979–1984: Including Greece
1984–1989: Including Portugal and Spain
1994–1999: Including Austria, Finland, and Sweden

Sources:
Elections around the world (2004) http://www.electionworld.org/europeanuinion.htm;
Mackie,1990 Statistisches Bundesamt, 1985, 2000.

Notes
1 Major missing: France: U.F.E. Union pour la France en Europe
2 Major missing: Italy: I Democratici
3 Major missing: France: CDS Democratic Social Centre
4 Major missing: France: D.I.F.E. Centre National des independents et paysans
5 Major missing: France: RPFIE Rassemblement pour la France et l'Independance
6 Major missing: Denmark: Folksbehægelsen mod EF

Notes

1 Between 1979 and 1999, the parties covered split and joined two or even three different EP party groups 18 times. In five of these cases, parties divided up equally between two groups. In eight cases a considerable number (between one-third and one-seventh) of MEPs joined for another group than the majority of the party. In five cases, one dissident MEP defected to another group. Such splits prevailed after the 1994 EP election in French, Italian and Spanish parties. The European Liberal, Democrat and Reform Party (ELDR) was the party group from which MEPs defected most frequently. Even the five dissidents have been taken into account because many cohesive party delegations do not hold more MEPs.
2 Data for this analysis will be published on a CD-ROM appended to Klingemann *et al.* (forthcoming 2006).
3 See Volkens (2002) for precise definitions of subcategories.
4 European integration as defined in this chapter is not mentioned in 20 of the 471 programmes so that the number of available cases is reduced to 451 although the number of representatives in EP party groups is only marginally reduced.
5 The strength of parties in EP party groups can differ a lot from the strength of parties in parliaments because numbers of MEPs for each country are roughly accorded to the number of citizens.
6 Other distance measures such as the range between furthest left and furthest right party of a party system or party group or absolute distances between pairs of parties correlate strongly (about 0.85) with standard deviations used here. Although a large distance between two strong parties certainly contributes more to the conflict potential within a group than a large distance between two small parties, no weighting procedure is used for standard deviations to keep the EP party groups' distances comparable to party families. As a rule, polarization measures between parties in national party systems are not weighted according to the strength of parties.
7 Many changes have taken place during legislative terms when party groups divided or joined together and parties from new member countries entered the EP. See Appendix 3.A.1 for details.

References

Adams, J. (2001) 'A Theory of Spatial Competition with Biased Voters: Party Policies Viewed Temporally and Comparatively', *British Journal for Political Research* 31: 121–138.
Adams, J. and S. Merrill III (1999) 'Modelling Party Strategies and Party Policy Representation in Multiparty Elections: Why Are Strategies So Extreme?', *American Journal of Political Science* 43: 765–791.
Bardi, L. (1994) 'Transnational Party Federations, European Parliament Party Groups, and the Building of Europarties', in Richard S. Katz and Peter Mair (eds) *How Parties Organize. Change and Adaptation in Party Organizations in Western Democracies* (London/Thousand Oaks/New Delhi: Sage), pp. 357–372.
Bardi, L. (1996) 'Transnational Trends in European Parties and the 1994 Elections of the European Parliament', *Party Politics* 2: 99–114.
Bell, D. (1962) *The End of Ideology* (New York: Free Press).
Bell, D. (1996) 'Western Communist Parties and the European Union', in John Gaffney (ed.) *Political Parties and the European Union* (London and New York: Routledge), pp. 220–234.
Bowler, S. and D.M. Farrell (1999) 'Parties and Party Discipline within the European Parliament: A Norms-Based Approach', in Shaun Bowler, David M. Farrell

and Richard S. Katz (eds) *Party Discipline and Parliamentary Government* (Columbus: Ohio State University Press), pp. 208–222.

Brzinski, D.B. (1995) 'Political Group Cohesion in the European Parliament, 1989–1994', in Carolyn Rhodes and Sonia Mazey (eds) *The State of the European Union*, Vol. 3 (London: Longman), pp. 135–158.

Budge, I. (1987) 'The Internal Analysis of Election Programmes', in Ian Budge, David Robertson and Derek Hearl (eds) *Ideology, Strategy and Party Change. Spatial Analysis of Post-War Election Programmes in 19 Democracies* (Cambridge: Cambridge University Press), pp. 15–38.

Budge, I. (1993), Parties, Programs and Policies: A Comparative and Theoretical Perspective', *American Review of Politics*, 3: 695–716.

Budge, I. (1994) 'A New Spatial Theory of Party Competition: Uncertainty, Ideology and Policy Equilibria Viewed Comparatively and Temporally', *British Journal of Political Science* 24: 443–467.

Budge, I. (2001) 'Validating the Manifesto Research Group Approach: Theoretical Assumptions and Empirical Confirmations' in Michael Laver (ed.) *Estimating the Policy Positions of Political Actors* (London and New York: Routledge), pp. 50–65.

Budge, I. (2002) 'Mapping Policy Preferences: 21 Years of the Comparative Manifestos Project, *EPS*' (ECPR Central Services, Colchester: University of Essex).

Budge, I. and D. Farlie (1977) *Voting and Party Competition. A Theoretical Critique and Synthesis Applied to Surveys from Ten Democracies* (London/New York/Sydney/Toronto: John Wiley & Sons).

Budge, I. and D. Farlie (1983) 'Saliency Theory of Party Competition – Selective Emphasis or Direct Confrontation? An Alternative View with Data', in Hans Daalder and Peter Mair (eds) *Western European Party Systems* (London: Sage), pp. 267–306.

Budge, I., H.-D. Klingemann, A. Volkens, J. Bara and E. Tanenbaum (2001) *Mapping Policy Preferences. Estimates for Parties; Electors, and Governments, 1945–1998* (Oxford: Oxford University Press).

Budge, I., D. Robertson and D. Hearl (eds) (1987) *Ideology, Strategy and Party Change: Spatial Analysis of Post-War Election Programs in 19 Democracies* (Cambridge: Cambridge University Press).

Corbett, Richard, MEP, Francis Jacobs and Michael Shackleton (eds) (2000) *The European Parliament*, 4th edn (London: John Harper).

Downs, A. (1957) *An Economic Theory of Democracy* (New York: Harper & Row).

Enelow, J.M. and M.J. Hinich (1984) *The Spatial Theory of Voting* (Cambridge: Cambridge University Press).

Gabel, M. and C.J. Anderson (2002) 'The Structure of Citizen Attitudes and the European Political Space', *Comparative Political Studies* 35: 893–913.

Gabel, M. and C. Carrubba (2004), 'The European Parliament and Transnational Political Representation: Party Groups and Political Conflict', in *Europolity* – virtual conference, http://fes.de/europolity.

Gabel, M. and S. Hix (2002) Defining the EU Political Space. An Empirical Study of the European Election Manifestos, 1979–1999', *Comparative Political Studies* 35: 934–964.

Gaffney, J. (1996) 'Introduction. Political Parties and the European Union', in John Gaffney (ed.) *Political Parties and the European Union* (London/New York: Routledge), pp. 1–30.

Ginsberg, B. (1982) *The Consequences of Consent. Elections, Citizen Control and Popular Acquiescence* (New York: Random House).

Hix, S. (1999) 'Dimensions and Alignments in the European Union Politics: Cognitive Constraints and Partisan Responses', *European Journal of Political Research* 35: 69–106.

Hix, S. (2002) 'Parliamentary Behavior with Two Principals: Preferences, Parties, and Voting in the European Parliament', *American Journal of Political Science* 46: 688–698.

Hix, S. and C. Lord (1997) *Political Parties in the European Union* (Houndmills, Basingstoke: Macmillan).

Hooghe, L., G. Marks and C.J. Wilson (2002) 'Does Left–Right Structure Party Positions on European Integration?', *Comparative Political Studies* 35: 965–989.

Iversen, T. (1994a) 'Political Leadership and Representation in West European Democracies: A Test of Three Models of Voting', *American Journal of Political Science* 38: 45–74.

Iversen, T. (1994b) 'The Logics of Electoral Politics. Spatial, Directional, and Mobilizational Effects', *Comparative Political Studies* 27: 155–189.

Janda, Kenneth, Robert Harmel, Christine Edens and Patricia Goff (1995) 'Changes in Party Identity. Evidence from Party Manifestos', *Party Politics* 1: 171–196.

Katz, R.S. and P. Mair (1995) 'Changing Models of Party Organization and Party Democracy', *Party Politics* 1: 5–28.

Klingemann, H.-D., R.I. Hofferbert and I. Budge (1994) *Parties, Policies, and Democracy* (Boulder, CO: Westview).

Klingemann, H.-D., A. Volkens, J. Bara, I. Budge and M. McDonald (forthcoming 2006) *Mapping Policy Preference II: Estimates for Parties, Electors and Governments in Eastern Europe, the European Union and OECD, 1990–2003* (Oxford: Oxford University Press).

Kirchheimer, O. (1966) 'The Transformation of the Western European Party Systems', in Joseph LaPalombara and Myron Weiner (eds) *Political Parties and Political Development* (Princeton: Princeton University Press), pp. 117–200.

Laver, M. (2001) 'Position and Salience in the Policies of Political Actors', in Michael Laver (ed.) *Estimating the Policy Positions of Political Actors* (London and New York: Routledge), pp. 66–75.

Laver, M. and I. Budge (eds) (1993) *Party Policy and Government Coalitions* (New York: St. Martins Press).

Laver, M. and J. Garry (2000) 'Estimating Policy Positions from Political Texts', *American Journal of Political Science* 44: 619–634.

McDonald, M.D. and S.M. Mendes (2001a) 'The Policy Space of Party Manifestos', in Michael Laver (ed.) *Estimating the Policy Positions of Collective Actors* (London: Routledge), pp. 90–114.

McDonald, M.D. and S.M. Mendes (2001b) 'Checking the Party Policy Estimates: Convergent Validity', in Ian Budge, Hans-Dieter Klingemann, Andrea Volkens, Judith Bara and Eric Tanenbaum (eds) *Mapping Policy Preferences. Estimates for Parties; Electors, and Governments, 1945–1998* (Oxford: Oxford University Press), pp. 127–142.

Macdonald, S.E. and G. Rabinowitz (1998) 'Solving the Paradox of Nonconvergence: Valence, Position, and Direction in Democratic Politics', *Electoral Studies* 17: 281–300.

Mackie, T.T. (ed.) (1990) Europe Votes. *European Parliamentary Election Results 1989* (Brookfield, USA/Hong Kong/Singapore/Sydney/Dartmouth: Aldershot).

Marks, G. and M. Steenbergen (2002) 'Understanding Political Contestation in the European Union', *Comparative Political Studies* 35: 879–892.

Pedersen, M. (1996) 'Euro-parties and European Parties: New Arenas, New Challenges and New Strategies', in Svein S. Andersen and Kjell A. Eliassen (eds) *The European Union: How Democratic Is It?* (New Delhi: Sage), pp. 15–39.

Pomper, G.M. (1968) *Elections in America. Control and Influences in Democratic Politics* (New York: Dodd, Mead).

Rabinowitz, G. and A.E. Macdonald (1989) 'A Directional Theory of Issue Voting', *American Political Science Review* 83: 93–121.

Rallings, C. (1987) 'The Influence of Election Programmes. Great Britain and Canada, 1945–1979', in Ian Budge, David Robertson and Derek J. Hearl (eds) *Ideology, Strategy and Party Change: Spatial Analysis of Post-War Election Programs in 19 Democracies* (Cambridge: Cambridge University Press), pp. 1–14.

Raunio, T. (1997) *The European Perspective. Transnational Party Groups in the 1989–1994 European Parliament* (Aldershot: Ashgate).

Raunio, T. (1999) 'The Challenge of Diversity: Party Cohesion in the European Parliament', in Shaun Bowler, David M. Farrell and Richard S. Katz (eds) *Party Discipline and Parliamentary Government* (Columbus: Ohio State University Press), pp. 187–207.

Raunio, T. (2000a) 'Losing Independence or Finally Gaining Recognition? Contacts Between MEPs and National Parties', *Party Politics* 6: 211–223.

Raunio, T. (2000b) Second-Rate Parties? Towards a Better Understanding of the European Parliament's Party Groups', in Knut Heidar and Ruud Koole (eds) *Parliamentary Party Groups in European Democracies. Political Parties Behind Closed Doors* (London/New York: Routledge), pp. 231–247.

Ray, L. (1999) 'Measuring Party Orientation Towards European Integration: Results from an Expert Survey', *European Journal of Political Research* 36: 283–306.

Robertson, D. (1976) *A Theory of Party Competition* (London: John Wiley & Sons).

Statistisches Bundesamt (1985) Bevölkerung und Erwerbstätigkeit, Wahl der Abgeordneten des Europäischen Parlaments, Fachserie 1, Heft 1: Ergebnisse und Vergleichszahlen für 1979 und 1984 (Stuttgart: Metzler-Poeschel).

Statistisches Bundesamt (2000) Bevölkerung und Erwerbstätigkeit, Wahl der Abgeordneten des Europäischen Parlaments, Fachserie 1, Heft 1: Ergebnisse und Vergleichszahlen für 1994 und 1999 (Stuttgart: Metzler-Poeschel).

Stokes, D.E. (1963) 'Spatial Models of Party Competition', *American Political Science Review* 57: 368–377.

Thomson, R. (2001) 'The Programme to Policy Linkage: The Fulfilment of Election Pledges on Socio-Economic Policy in the Netherlands, 1986–1998', *European Journal of Political Research* 40: 171–197.

Volkens, A. (2002) 'Manifesto Coding Instructions (Second Revised Edition)'. Discussion Paper FS III 02–201 (Berlin: Wissenschaftszentrum Berlin für Sozialforschung (WZB)).

Volkens, A. (2004) 'Policy Changes of European Social Democrats, 1945–98', in Guiliano Bonoli and Martin Powell (eds) *Social Democratic Party Policies in Contemporary Europe* (London/New York: Routledge), pp. 21–42.

Volkens, A. and H.-D. Klingemann (2002) 'Parties, Ideologies, and Issues. Stability and Change in Fifteen European Party Systems 1945–1998', in Kurt Richard Luther and Ferdinand Müller-Rommel (eds) *Political Parties in the New Europe. Political and Analytical Challenges* (Oxford: Oxford University Press), pp. 143–167.

Wilensky, H.L. (2002) *Rich Democracies: Political Economy, Public Policy, and Performance* (Berkeley/Los Angeles/London: University of California Press).

4 Parties in democracy, democracy in parties

Lessons from Ian Budge and the CMP data

Michael D. McDonald

Introduction

The Manifesto Research Group and its offspring, the Comparative Manifesto Project (CMP), have produced important benefits. Its benefits are too many to enumerate, but its importance is easy to appreciate by considering the role of party position, taking in democratic theory and practice. An essential promise of democracy for polities operating on the scale of a nation state is to translate multifaceted popular preferences into a meaningful electoral statement that, in turn, has foreseeable policy consequences. Political parties first organize the packages of policies on offer to electors and later have the responsibility of seeing to it that they translate into policy. Each party does this by stating publicly what, in its view, are the desirable policy emphases, and, in exchange for a promise to make good on the emphases, it asks citizens for vote support.

Knowing whether, how and how well this promise of democracy is fulfilled depends fundamentally on knowing what policies parties have emphasized. This is what the CMP tells us. It has created and released a record of party policy emphasis over the post-war period for 25 nations (Budge *et al.*, 2001). And, at the time of this writing, it is preparing to release records of party policy position emphasis in Central and Eastern Europe (Klingemann *et al.*, 2006).

My purpose here is not to celebrate the CMP as such. That has been done by the Comparative Politics Section of the American Political Science Association when, in 2003, it recognized the outstanding contribution to scholarship made by the project. Instead, I intend to consider the implications of a feature of the CMP that some scholars and commentators, myself included at one time, find disorienting. The feature is the positional volatility that the CMP data tell us is a prominent feature of every party's policy position taking. Most other measurements of party policy positions – e.g. expert surveys – leave the impression that parties by and large take fixed positions, say, along the left–right dimension (McDonald and Mendes, 2001). Many analyses, too – those that use party dummy variables to estimate whether different parties advocate and pursue different policies – implicitly assume parties stand in more or less fixed policy positions (e.g. Stimson *et al.*, 1995). The CMP data tell us these stability findings and assumptions are unfounded. Party positions are volatile. One wonders, therefore, is the volatility fact or artifact; is it real or measurement error?[1]

The short version of my answer can be stated in two conclusions and one hypothesis. *Conclusion 1*: the volatility of party position taking revealed by the CMP data should not be taken as nuisance measurement error to be identified and smoothed over so as to reveal the true essence of each party's policy position. *Conclusion 2*: positional volatility may be the spice of life in party democracy that animates party competition so as to produce accurate representation in the long run. *Hypothesis*: parties do not 'develop' positions as a strategic means to their office-seeking ends nor do they 'have' policy positions formed from their principled policy desires; rather, parties take positions reflective of the faction that has gained temporary control within the party.

The long version of my answer takes the remainder of this chapter. It starts in the middle, with a re-report of just how accurate the representation in party democracies is. One plausible reaction to the accuracy finding is disbelief, thinking it must be nothing more than a consequence of merging errors in the measurement of party positions into derivative measurements of median voter and government positions. In section three, I recount where my own skepticism took my thoughts and how, in the end, I came to see that the volatility of party positions could just as well be attributable to truly erratic party behavior as to faults in the measuring instrument. Section four asks, as Ian Budge several times has asked me, what if we ignore the so-called measurement error. I show theoretically that one should expect positionally volatile parties to carry a democratic political system a long way toward producing accurate representation. This 'long way' is further than parties in fixed positions can carry accurate representation and, in absolute terms, is very close to what empirical analysis of accurate representation looks like using the CMP data. Finally, because all that I will have said begs the question of why parties would be positionally volatile in the first place, section five circles back and develops a hypothesis to suggest that we should stop theorizing about parties as either strategic or principled actors, seeking office or policy and, instead, look at them as organizational conveniences of ambitious politicians.

What are the lessons to be learned? The CMP data tell us party positions need to be characterized in terms of their two prominent features: (1) they are distinctly different, seldom leapfrogging one another, *and* (2) they are volatile. Try as one might to look through the volatility and find the essence of party position taking in distinct party differences, it turns out that an important contribution of parties in democracy could come from their positional volatility. And, try as one might to find party strategy in the volatility and to find party principles in the essential differences, it turns out that an important contribution of within-party democratic leadership selection may be to sustain the essential differences and, through time, supply the volatility. The consequences, if all this is so, are democratic parties wandering hither and yon around their ideologically home neighborhood with boundaries set by their ideologically distinct memberships, thereby creating enough distinctiveness *and* volatility in their policy positions to produce accurate representation of median voters for a nation at large, in the long run.

Accurate representation: how can it be?

Ian Budge, Silvia Mendes and I have reported that governments of Western parliamentary democracies provide accurate representation of the median voters in their respective countries, when considered over the long run (McDonald *et al.*, 2004). This is an amazing revelation, perhaps so amazing as not to be believed. For one thing, it appears to conflict with the theoretical proposition that democratically decided outcomes can end up anywhere in a policy space (McKelvey, 1976; Schofield, 1978). It also appears to be at odds with the empirical findings that representational distortions exist in all Western democracies and, relatively speaking, exist to an especially large extent in nations that elect their parliaments through single-member districts (Huber and Powell, 1994; Powell, 2000; Powell and Vanberg, 2000).

One feature of the analysis does much to resolve the seeming conflicts. The CMP data permit a long-run view. Seen from that perspective it is possible to understand that no one electoral outcome is easily predicted, just as theory tells us to expect and just as one-off empirical analysis shows us is true. Moreover, even if one were to aggregate the congruence/incongruence over a few elections in order to record average distortion, the average represents a mean level of absolute values over a series of one-off distortions. Since each single election produces distortion, the average absolute value itself has to record distortion. But, as we see immediately below, despite these short-run shortcomings, the mis-predictions and distortions balance out in the long run.

Table 4.1 reports the average distortion between median voters and governments, by nation and electoral system type, for 20 parliamentary democracies. Distortion is the absolute difference between the left–right position of the median voter and the left–right position of governments (Powell, 2000), as measured using the CMP data (see McDonald *et al.*, 2004). Every nation shows sizable distortion, and the average distortion is about twice as large under SMD systems compared to PR systems.

Fortunately, with a long enough sweep of time the analysis of representation can go two steps further. First, it can reveal whether the one-off distortions compensate one another by canceling a leftward distor-

Table 4.1 Representational distortion, bias, and responsiveness between left–right positions of governments, weighted by party size, and left–right position of median voters, 20 democracies 1950s to 1995

System	Country	Distortion[a] Mean (std dev)	Long-term Bias[b] Mean (std dev)	Intercept (s_a)	Responsiveness[c] Slope (s_b)	R^2	s_e	N
SMD	Australia	17.4 (8.8)	5.6 (19.0)	7.3 (4.4)	0.69* (.38)	0.13	19.1	24
	Canada	5.5 (7.8)	3.9 (8.7)	3.2 (2.4)	0.75* (0.41)	0.18	8.8	17
	France	18.5 (8.0)	10.9 (17.2)	9.2 (4.4)	0.68 (0.48)	0.08	17.4	25
	New Zealand	12.3 (7.2)	2.5 (14.3)	1.8 (4.4)	0.90* (0.39)	0.21	14.6	22
	United Kingdom	15.6 (12.1)	8.7 (18.0)	13.7** (5.0)	1.56** (0.33)	0.58	17.1	18
SMD Summary		14.4 (9.7)	6.5 (16.2)	6.5** (1.8)	0.98** (0.15)	0.28	16.2	106
PR	Austria	6.6 (4.3)	0.8 (8.0)	1.1 (2.1)	1.07** (0.17)	0.71	8.2	18
	Belgium	6.7 (6.0)	–0.8 (9.1)	–2.1 (2.0)	0.70** (0.25)	0.25	9.0	27
	Denmark	16.3 (11.5)	3.1 (19.9)	3.5 (4.5)	1.09* (0.48)	0.17	20.3	27
	Finland	11.7 (10.6)	4.9 (15.1)	1.2 (3.7)	0.73** (0.19)	0.33	14.8	32
	Germany	11.2 (9.8)	3.4 (14.6)	3.6 (3.2)	1.28** (0.30)	0.50	14.7	21
	Iceland	8.8 (10.5)	7.4 (11.5)	6.7* (3.0)	0.85** (0.25)	0.43	11.7	18
	Ireland	11.0 (10.5)	0.9 (15.4)	2.6 (3.5)	0.64** (0.21)	0.36	14.5	19
	Italy	2.2 (2.1)	1.3 (2.8)	2.1 (0.5)	1.14** (0.06)	0.91	2.6	43

continued

Table 4.1 continued

System	Distortion[a]	Long-term Bias[b]		Responsiveness[c]			
Country	Mean (std dev)	Mean (std dev)	Intercept (s_a)	Slope (s_b)	R^2	s_e	N
Luxembourg	5.0 (4.0)	0.7 (6.5)	3.1 (3.8)	1.15** (0.22)	0.70	6.6	14
Netherlands	7.5 (4.3)	1.4 (8.7)	–0.2 (2.6)	0.75** (0.19)	0.57	8.5	14
Norway	10.1 (6.9)	0.4 (12.4)	–12.9 (10.0)	0.45 (0.40)	0.07	12.2	21
Portugal	4.1 (2.5)	1.5 (4.8)	3.6 (2.4)	1.25** (0.22)	0.80	4.7	10
Spain	3.1 (2.3)	–0.1 (4.1)	1.8 (3.1)	1.15** (0.22)	0.84	4.3	7
Sweden	9.4 (9.0)	–3.6 (12.7)	2.4 (4.3)	1.33** (0.19)	0.73	12.0	21
Switzerland	4.5 (3.1)	0.6 (5.5)	0.6 (1.0)	1.00** (0.10)	0.68	5.6	45
PR Summary	7.9 (8.3)	1.5 (11.3)	1.4 (0.7)	0.97** (0.05)	0.56	11.3	337

Notes

*$p<0.05$; ** $p<0.01$; two-tail critical values for intercepts and one-tail critical values for slopes.

a Distortion is the absolute value of the difference between the weighted-mean left–right position of governments (with weights proportional to the number of seats held by each party in government) and the left–right position of median voters. N is the number of governments. Totally undistorted (congruent) systems have a mean equal to zero.

b Bias is the average difference between the weighted-mean left–right position of governments (with weights proportional to the number of seats held by each party in government) and the left–right position of median voters. N is the number of elections the weighted-mean left–right position of governments (with weights as above) and the left–right position of median voters. A mean of zero indicates accurate (i.e., unbiased) long-term representativeness.

c Responsiveness is evaluated by the linear relationship between the weighted-mean left–right position of government (Y) and the left–right position of the median voter (X). Left positions are negative, centre equals zero; right positions are positive

tion at one time with a rightward distortion at a later time, or vice versa. Second, it can reveal whether the positions of governments tend to respond to the positions of median voters so as to produce a one-to-one correspondence.

Consideration of compensatory distortions shows that representation is far less biased than the distortions alone might be taken to imply – compare the magnitude of numbers under 'distortion' to those under 'long-term bias.' As for responsiveness, the analysis shows that in 18 of 20 countries government positions systematically respond to median voter positions. Moreover, there is no nation for which one can reject the hypothesis that the responsiveness is one-to-one.

Arguably, such accurate representation may be too good to be true, even in the long run and maybe most especially because it can only be seen in the long run. The measurements of median voter positions are created using Kim and Fording's (1998) idea of overlaying the voter distribution party percentages on the party positions as measured by the CMP. Similarly, government positions are measured by averaging the CMP party positions of parties in government, weighted by each government party's number of seats in parliament. Imagine a situation in which the voter distribution remains exactly the same between two elections and the same parties entered government with the same number of seats. Under that set of facts, so far as one could tell, nothing changed. However, if party positions as measured by the CMP change, the recorded positions of median voters and governments would move in tandem as a mere reflection of the measured party positions. In that sense, the measurement of party positions might be the source of the long-run correspondence between voters and governments. Worse, if much of the party position movements reflects nothing more than noise in the CMP measurements, it could be mis-measurement that produces the correspondence.

Looking for the essence and thinking about the noise

That the CMP data are available for Western-democratic party systems over more than a 50-year period makes them the one and only currently available data source for analyzing party dynamics. But the claim that the CMP data are all that we have cannot justify an argumentum *ad ignorantiam* that since we cannot tell whether they are bad measurements they must be good.

Figure 4.1 provides an overview of party positions as scored, on average, by the CMP. Each party is located according to its mean position on the CMP left–right score calculated over all elections of the post-war period. This is a way of using the CMP data that assumes party left–right positions are static. The figure also provides a perspective on the distinctiveness of party positions within each party system. Shaded and boxed parties have positions that, while numerically distinguishable in their mean values, are not reliably distinguishable given their over-time variation. As a summary statement of distinctiveness within national party systems, the R^2 values in the right-most column indicate how much of a party system's total left–right variation is between-party as opposed to within-party variation across time. From top to bottom, the nations are ordered according to the

	Left	Center		Right		R^2
	−40	−20	0	+20	+40	
Denmark		SF DKP SD RV		RF VEN KrF CD KF FP		0.760
Sweden	VP SDP	FP CP			MSP	0.709
Norway		SV DNA VEN	[SP KF] H			0.642
Netherlands post-CDA		PvdA D'66 CDA		VVD		0.736
Netherlands pre-CDA		PvdA D'66	KVP	ARP CHU VVD		0.612
Canada		NDP	LIB/SC PCP			0.669
Belgium pre-split		PSB/BSP	VU PSC/CVP	PLP/PVV		0.645
Belgium post-split		SP FDF CVP	PS PSC VU PRL PVV			0.442
Luxembourg	KPL LSAP		CSV DP			0.588
United Kingdom		LAB	LIB	CON		0.462
Germany			SPD	FDP CDS		0.404
Austria			SPÖ	FPÖ ÖVP		0.301
France		PCF PS		Gaul		0.796
Switzerland		SPS		SVP FDP CVP		0.553
United States			DEM	REP		0.531
New Zealand		LAB SC	NP			0.514
Australia		LAB		LIB CP		0.478
Iceland		LAB		FF FG		0.347
Italy		PSI PCI PSDI	PRI DC PLI MSI			0.281

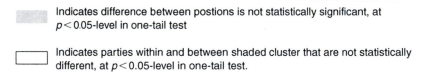

Indicates difference between postions is not statistically significant, at $p < 0.05$-level in one-tail test

Indicates parties within and between shaded cluster that are not statistically different, at $p < 0.05$-level in one-tail test.

R^2 is the proportion of between-party variance relative to total party position variance in a system, OLS estimation using k-1 party dummy variables.

Figure 4.1 Distinctiveness of choices offered by parties along the left–right dimension, by country over post-war period.

number of distinct party clusters (Denmark has five, Sweden and Norway four, . . . Italy two) and secondarily by their R^2s.

The first issue is whether such a static representation as portrayed by the mean values, in the face of the over-time variation of each party's position, is a reliable characterization. It is not. Regressing the observed positions onto the party mean values reveals a slope of 1.0, as required by definition. The R^2, however, is only 0.649. That means that slightly less than two-thirds of the systematic variance in the data is coming from differences in means across parties. The remaining one-third is either noise or real movements in party positions. If the movements are all or mostly noise, then the CMP is not an especially reliable statement of static party position taking. If it reflects all or mostly real party dynamics, then static portrayals of party positions – e.g. as would result from classifying parties by their families or scoring them by expert surveys – are not valid statements of where parties stand across time on the left–right dimension.

To investigate the extent to which party movements around the party means reflect systematic change versus noise I employ Hausman's approach to measurement error. Hausman reasons that predicted values (Y-hats) from regression analysis provide a statement of an outcome without measurement noise, because the noise of the measurements is relegated to the error term of the equation (Hausman, 1978; see also Pindyck and Rubinfeld, 1991: 160–162; Johnston and DiNardo, 1997: 153–156). In the context of the CMP data, I have first estimated the dynamics of party positions by estimating a separate autoregressive equation for each of 81 parties. I then use the predicted positions, Hausman Y-hats, as my set of smoothed estimates and relate them to the actual CMP party left–right positions.

Considered over all 81 parties throughout the post-war period, the association between the predicted values generated by applying the estimated dynamics and the observed CMP data has an R^2 of 0.806. This is a reliability estimate for the data. A total of 80 to 81 percent of the observed variance is reliable; the balance, 19 to 20 percent, is error variance. We can go one step further. Over all 81 parties, there is an estimated R^2 of 0.649 for association between the mean and the observed data. Therefore 64.9 percent of the variance in the CMP data records stable differences across party positions, 15.7 percent records change and 19.4 percent records error. By implication, 19.5 percent of the reliable variation throughout the post-war period is reliable dynamic variation (i.e. $[0.157/0.806] \times 100$). This might seem a convenient place to stop thinking about measurement error and move back to the substantive consideration of accurate representation, but it is not. There remains an important question as to the sources of the estimated measurement error. The label 'measurement error' tends to make one think first of a faulty instrument, but that is not necessarily the inference one should draw. When Philip Converse originally estimated and later elaborated his thesis of non-attitudes among the American mass public, he did so by estimating the degrees of measurement error in mass attitudes (Converse, 1964, 1970; Converse and Markus, 1979). Having found a good deal of error, Converse indicted the public's unstable attitudes as its source. It was not until a decade later that Chris Achen pointed a finger at the survey instruments as a source of the error (Achen 1975; see also Pierce and Rose, 1974; for a discussion of this issue and a third interpretation see Erikson, 1979: especially 90–91 and 110).

An inferential difficulty arises when trying to decide between noise attributable to a faulty instrument versus noise attributable to erratic behavior, because measurement models are constructed on the back of behavioral models. A model used to uncover measurement error requires one to have in mind a model of 'true behavioral change.' That is what permits one to separate noise in the measurements from change in the behavior (Heise, 1969). In effect, the assumption says that when behavior truly changes it does so systematically (i.e. in predictable ways, usually via a Markovian process). It then adds by implication that to the extent behavior is not predictable the remaining portion of the measured signal is noise.

Taking account of these dual possibilities, it is interesting to ask which is a more plausible interpretation of the CMP record of party left–right positions. Few party scholars doubt that noise comes into the CMP scores from the loose way in which words are used, misinterpretations by a coder of a manifesto, the exclusive reliance on 26 left–right CMP categories and exclusion of the 30 others, coding transcription errors, and input errors (see Volkens, 2001). But, also, few party scholars doubt that party positions sometimes change in erratic ways. Seldom does one find characterizations of parties as totally solid, dependable and (if one will) reliable political actors. More typical are characterizations such as these. A party 'cannot be defined in terms of its principles' (Schumpeter, 1942: 283). Parties are 'ever hungry for new members' (Michels, 1949: 374). Parties are motivated by a specific goal of maximizing votes (Downs, 1957: 30). Parties engage in a political strategy that 'appears to center on finding out what the public wants to hear and marketing the product accordingly' (Farrell and Webb, 2000: 122).

Given that there is as much, perhaps more, reason to credit the observations of party scholars who see erratic party positions as erratic behavior than to credit my own, one-time suspicions of noise in the CMP data, it proves to be an interesting exercise to allow the erratic behavior into serious theoretical consideration.

Representational consequences of positional volatility

Let us move away from purely methodological concerns by going directly to theoretical considerations in a way that provides full control over measurements and behavior. This is accomplished by simulating the representational process. Simulations allow one to specify the dynamics of party position taking with complete knowledge (no error) and to assign voters a simple deterministic policy voting decision rule – i.e. each voter supports the closest party along the left–right dimension. The results, perhaps as surprising as the empirically based results using the CMP data, show that in the context of volatile parties the crucial mechanism in the representational process is voter choice. By offering varied choices, at least one party will usually be positioned in the vicinity of the median voter. That leaves it to electors to make the choice on the basis of policy packages on offer. When they choose the closest party, the theoretically expected electoral consequences are responsive, unbiased and, mostly, congruent representation. In much the same way that models of under-informed parties indicate party policy offerings are drawn toward the median voter as a by-product of random searches for a winning position (McKelvey and Ordeshook, 1985: 492–495), positionally volatile parties can create accurate representation with electors as the centripetal force.

For the sake of brevity I report simulations of 1,000 elections for only two-party systems[2] – the most difficult circumstance to find accurate representation – and evaluate the accuracy of collective representation for positionally fixed versus volatile parties. The highest quality representation exists when (1) the left–right positions of policies are directly responsive to the left–right position of median voters – i.e. a slope of 1.0 (2) there is no bias – a zero intercept – and (3) congruence is exact – the average distance between policy and median voter positions is zero.

The simulations place a Left Party at –13 and a Right Party at +13. Parties are assumed to take (1) fixed positions marked by their own central tendency and (2) to move around that central tendency with standard deviations of 13. As for electorates, they are assumed in the long run to have a mean and median position of zero. The median voter movements involve both a more volatile electorate, with a standard deviation of five, and a less volatile electorate, with a standard deviation of two.

The representational consequences for parties at fixed positions and a more volatile electorate are shown in Figure 4.2. A median voter to the left of zero elects the Left Party at policy position –13. Likewise, anytime the median voter is to the right of zero, the electorate elects the Right Party at +13. Considered in detail the consequences for representation have a totally unresponsive outcome to any elector movement except that which goes from negative to positive or vice versa. At the transition point of zero, the movement is an overly responsive 26 points. Generalizing about the details across all elections by summarizing the movements, the

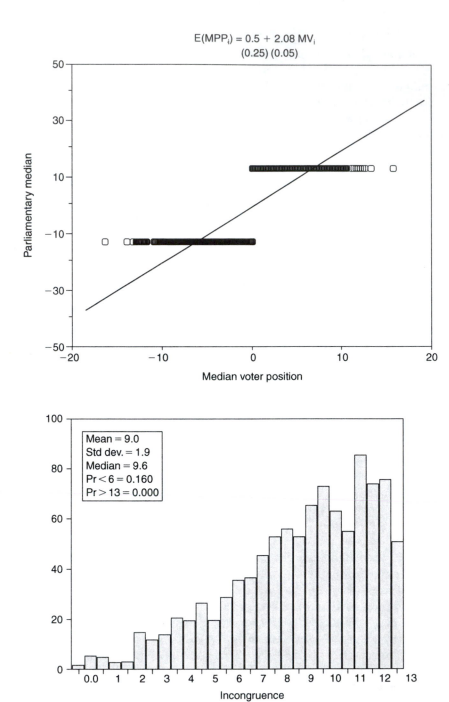

Figure 4.2 Responsiveness, bias and congruence in two-party systems, given parties presenting fixed positions.

linear equation at the top of the scatterplot indicates that a one-unit movement by the median voter, on average, translates into more than a two-unit movement in the policy position of the elected party (b = 2.08).[3] In other words, responsiveness is 2.08 to 1.0 and, given the small and statistically insignificant intercept, there is no bias.

Congruence results are shown in the histogram. They average 9.0, meaning that for any given election the policy position of a median party in parliament and electorate's median voter have an expected difference of nine units. Median incongruence is 9.6; half the outcomes are above 9.6 and half are below. Furthermore the probability that the two actors are within six units of one another is only 0.160. Briefly stated, one sees an overly responsive relationship, no bias, a typical mismatch between nine and ten units, and a low probability that the match is within six units.

Figure 4.3 shows the relationship and congruence results for a situation when party positions vary. The relationship is certainly less orderly than when parties stand at fixed positions. Disorder, notwithstanding, the quality of representations is mostly enhanced when party positions vary. The associated equation shows responsiveness is now close to one-to-one, b = 1.07, and there is no statistically significant bias.

Average incongruence is nearly the same as when parties are at fixed positions, but median incongruence is 7.6. One of two important differences in the congruence results is that the probability of close congruence is considerably higher when parties vary. The probability that the policy and median voters are within six units of one another is 0.401 (compared to 0.160 for fixed parties). The downside is that varying party positions hold an almost one-in-four chance that incongruence will exceed 13, which never happens in our simulations using fixed party positions.[4] Therefore, while there is a risk of high incongruence when party positions vary, varying versus fixed party positions create more direct responsiveness, leave bias at essentially zero and increase the probability of good congruence.

Does the accuracy of representation change in a less volatile electorate? Some details are different, but relative comparisons stay much the same. For parties at fixed positions competing in a less volatile electorate, the relationship is

$$MPP_i = 0.05 + 5.20 \, MV_i + e_i$$
$$(0.25) \quad (0.12)$$

Bias is unaffected compared to the more volatile electorate; it has the same numerical value, 0.05, which is statistically insignificant. Responsiveness more than doubles, however, which makes more than doubly responsive something that was overly responsive to begin with.[5] Congruence is worse; average incongruence grows to 11.4, and its median value is 11.6. The probability of being less than six units apart falls to one in 1,000.

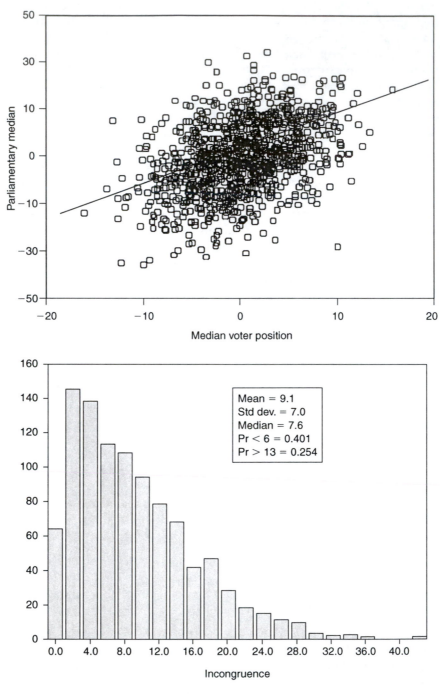

Figure 4.3 Responsiveness, bias and congruence in two-party systems, given parties presenting varied positions.

In short, with fixed party locations, decreasing electoral volatility increases responsiveness, leaves bias unaffected, and reduces congruence.

In the case of varying party positions, low electorate volatility also makes responsiveness overly responsive, but the increase is only to a value of 1.32. The relationship involving varying parties is

$$MPP_i = -0.54 + 1.32 \, MV_i + e_i$$
$$\quad\;\; (0.37) \quad (0.18)$$

Relatively speaking, parties with varying positions are still more directly responsive than were parties at fixed positions. Furthermore, average congruence is better with varying as compared to fixed parties. Mean incongruence for varying parties is 9.2 versus an average of 11.4 for fixed parties, and median incongruence is 8.0 compared to 11.6. Also, the probability of the median party in parliament being within six units of the MV is 0.395 for varying parties, compared to only 0.001 for fixed parties.

To summarize, the quality of representation in two-party systems is expected to be reasonably close to directly responsive and unbiased when parties have distinct central tendencies around which their left–right offerings to voters vary. At any given election, however, one can expect a mismatch between the policy position offered by the winning party and the location of the median voter. And, under the circumstances specified, one has to expect that in one of four elections the mismatch will be especially large.

Is it plausible to characterize electors as purely deterministic policy voters? Probably not: for one thing that would require them to know the left–right location of parties while the parties are moving around; for another, it means that electors are not from time to time attracted to one party or another on the basis of the leader's appeal. We can ask (1) what are the consequences when electors have no information about party positions other than their central tendencies and (2) what happens when electors base their decisions on leadership appeals rather than pure policy considerations?

The effect of low information on responsiveness recreates the situation seen for fixed party positions (see the slope value in Figures 4.2). Any movement of the median voter to the left leads to selection of the Left Party and likewise for selecting the Right Party after any movement of the median voter to the right. Voters therefore forego selecting a party closer to the median about half the time in favor of one that is typically on their side of the zero-divide, regardless of how extreme a party is. From that half-of-the-time extreme selection, the voter choice tends towards extremism, creating an overly responsive selection that is less congruent than it needs to be. Responsiveness almost doubles for the more volatile electorate, and it nearly quadruples for the less volatile electorate. In addition, average incongruence is 13 or higher for both more and less volatile electorates, and the probabilities of selecting a party more than 13 units away are greater than 0.4. The short version of the outcome is that a little information harms accurate representation. If the only information voters have is about the central tendency of party positions, more accurate representation would come from the parties offering fixed positions. Responsiveness and bias would be the same, but standing still would improve congruence.

What are the effects on accurate representation when an electorate selects solely on the basis of personal appeals of party leaders? To find an approximate answer, assume such appeals have no policy bent. Attractive leaders are as likely to come from the Left Party as the Right Party. Further, assume leadership appeals are the sole basis of electoral decisions up to half the time. As a result, electors will make a policy mistake a quarter of the time – i.e. half of their mistaken choices, in terms of the non-policy basis of their choice, will reach the correct policy choice by inadvertence.

Not surprisingly, the consequence of focusing on leadership qualities and not policy is to make the choice less responsive to policy. For both more and less volatile electorates, leadership-only choices half the time reduce responsiveness to just about half of direct responsiveness. In order for the choices to be in the vicinity of direct responsiveness, electors would have to base their decision on non-policy leadership appeals no more than one in four or five elections. With reduced responsiveness in this situation comes less congruence as well. Average and median incongruence are two to three points higher when electors base their choice on non-policy leadership appeals half the time. As with having too little information, using non-policy information as the basis of choice is harmful to accurate representation.

Of course, as one's intuition would suggest, were one to combine having too little information all the time and using non-policy information half the time, the result would be something close to direct responsiveness and congruence close to that for the baseline case with deterministic policy voters.

In a world with no measurement error and positionally volatile parties, the type of accurate representation can be expected to be quite similar to that found by using the CMP data. Furthermore, the results stand robust in the face of a combination of low information and sometime-leadership appeals. This is no proof-positive that the analysis using the CMP-based measures of voter, parliament and government positions are leading us to the truth. It is proof-positive, however, that throwing away the measured volatility of party positions due to suspicions that they might contain error is theoretically wrongheaded. Positional volatility could be the missing theoretical link that allows voters the opportunity, over the long run, to keep their governments on track with the expressed preferences of electorates.

Speculation on sources of positional distinctiveness and volatility

I suppose many would find the idea of gaining accurate representation through positionally volatile parties interesting but unconvincing unless there is a plausible reason to think party positions move around their individual mean value as if by some sort of random process. One possibility comes from a model developed by James Snyder and Michael Ting, based on an informational rationale for parties (Snyder and Ting, 2002). In their model the value of a party to a candidate depends on where the party's policy program is located along something like a left–right dimension. For voters, the value of a party comes from the policy information conveyed by its label – a brand name. At the time of entry, candidates sort themselves according to parties' general policy tendencies, thereby helping to establish and maintain each party's policy-related reputation as a central tendency. Diverse candidate positions around a party's central tendency hold the potential to be the source of within party faction. As candidates-turned-elected-representatives vie for party leadership positions, as long as platforms are selected democratically rather than dictatorially, the policy character of a party is likely to shift to reflect the views of the current winning faction (Snyder and Ting, 2002: 102–103).

How plausible is this way of thinking about parties? I submit that among the three pre-eminent frameworks used to analyze party activities – an electoral competition model, a responsible party model and a diverse coalition model (see Aldrich, 1995: 7–14) – the diverse coalition model, of which Snyder and Ting's thesis is one version, is the most plausible. To substantiate this claim let us examine the three in detail.

An idea that sets the first two frameworks apart from one another and from the diverse coalition framework is the different assumption each makes about party goals. According to the electoral competition model, in order to understand how parties operate one assumes they want to win elections. With that in mind, theory develops by reasoning through to how a party can most effectively compete for votes. Figuring out a party's most effective strategy leads to hypotheses about how a party behaves before an electorate, in parliament and in government. A party offers policies to electors (e.g. Downs, 1957) and promotes policies for adoption (Austen-Smith and Banks, 1990) that best secure its chances of winning votes and holding office. Anthony Downs puts the point succinctly: 'The major force shaping a party's policies is competition with other parties for votes' (Downs, 1957: 102).

The responsible party model is organized around the issue of how parties should operate (Schattschneider, 1942; APSA, 1950). The model's useful analytical function comes from taking its prescriptive requirements and using them as standards to help figure out what makes the 'ideal type' more or less realizable. It assumes the goal of parties should be to create policy offerings in accordance with their different images of what is needed to bring about an improved human condition. One type of empirical analysis that follows concerns itself with the choices parties offer (Ginsberg, 1972, 1976; Robertson, 1976; Budge *et al.*, 1987; Budge *et al.*, 2001; Laver *et al.*, 2004). Others ask what the choices mean for accurate representation (Huber and Powell, 1994; Powell, 2000; Powell and Vanberg, 2000), for government formation (e.g. Laver and Shepsle, 1996; Müller and Strøm, 2000), and for actual policies (Budge and Hofferbert, 1990; Erikson *et al.*, 2002). At some times and in some places, parties appear to live up to the model's requirements; at other times and in other places they do not. The evaluations are, at best, conditional.

As I have said, the diverse coalition model, too, is set apart from the preceding models by the assumption it makes about party goals. It looks at parties as organizations and finds it dubious to assume they have goals. Rather, parties exist because they serve the interests of ambitious politicians, who presumably want to win their own elections and promote policies in line with their own preferences (Katz, 1980; Aldrich, 1995).

Born as legislative factions or organizations sympathetic to the policy aspirations of newly enfranchised segments of society, parties locate themselves on different sides of the dominant cleavage lines in a society (Lipset and Rokkan, 1967). This makes make it possible for close observers to look across a variety of issues and see policy distinctions between and among the parties (Laver and Hunt, 1992). On most issues party leaders and party adherents among the public line up in much the same way (Dalton, 1985; Table 3, 282; Iversen, 1994: Figures 2 and 3, 168–169). Probably for these reasons it is easy for 'expert' observers and the general citizenry to characterize party positions along a left–right continuum (Castles and Mair, 1984; Huber and Inglehart 1995; Inglehart and Klingemann ,1976). There, too, leaders and adherents align similarly (Dalton, 1985: Table 3, 282).

Why do parties line up on different sides? The answer, I propose, follows from how ambitious politicians sort themselves into parties in the first place. It seems entirely plausible to think that ambitious politicians want to affiliate with a party that serves their interests. If one assumes, as is usual, that a politician wants first and foremost to hold elective office, she or he will join a party that best serves that particular goal. In some circumstances, such as American South from 1880 through 1970, only one party provides a realistic opportunity for electoral victory. However, most developed democracies have competitive party systems; in them two or more parties offer reasonable electoral prospects for an aspiring politician. Under competitive circumstances an ambitious politician is expected to join a local party organization providing the best opportunity.

Which party that is depends on which side of a line of cleavage predominates in a locale. Assuming politicians have policy ideas that, other things equal, they prefer not to sacrifice to their ambition for office, the choice they face is not a mere either/or proposition. They can move or be assigned to a constituency that offers a good opportunity for election given their policy views, or they can have district lines drawn that match their views to a constituency. Also, where two or more parties offer reasonable opportunities, a simple tie-breaking rule is for a politician to join the party with a program he or she most agrees. By sorting along policy lines at the time of entry, the particular politicians affiliated with a party help to maintain its policy-related reputation and thereby create divergent central tendencies.

Difficult as it is to distance oneself from the notion that parties have goals, theoretically there is not much to commend the idea. The main theoretical problem is the collective nature of a party, meaning goal-based theory requires a unitary actor assumption to keep it afloat. What individuals within a group may want is as difficult to read as is what the group as a unit wants. A composite of elements needed by each individual to achieve his or her goal does not amalgamate to some fixed value for each composite element as it might apply to each person in a group. Thus, when the issue is to find an ideal policy position, the diverse coalition model implies that the ideal position is a candidate characteristic not a party characteristic. Each candidate has an ideal policy position to offer his or her constituency; a party does not.

We expect two competing candidates facing a policy-interested constituency with partisan predispositions to take positions close to their particular constituency median though separated slightly, perhaps as a reflection of their uncertainty (Downs, 1957: 100–102) or to accommodate electors' partisanships (Erikson and Romero, 1990). The most thorough evidence on candidate locations across multiple constituencies comes in relation to House elections in the United States. It corroborates the expectation for candidates. Within a single constituency, Democratic and Republican candidates for the House almost always stand apart (Sullivan and O'Connor, 1972). And, in accordance with the ideological leanings of one's constituency, each set of partisan candidates takes positions different from their co-partisans who have to face different constituencies.

As good as the correspondence between theory and evidence of candidate position taking is, attempts to extend its logic to party position taking have led to predictions not much supported by evidence. Comparative investigations report little tendency for party policy programs to respond to problems of the day, such as unemployment and inflation (McDonald *et al.*, 2004), or to public opinion and recent election results (Adams *et al.*, 2004). In US presidential elections, it is difficult to explain party liberal–conservative positions with other variables, showing a 'hint' of an effect from macropartisanship and little evidence of platform response to public mood (Erikson *et al.*, 2002: 261, note 17).

By refusing to assume parties have vote and office goals, because they do not have any goals as such, is it not also necessary to refuse to assume parties have ideologies as such? Yes, but that is not to say that parties do not espouse policy programs. They do. Announcing a policy program is among the initial steps taken by virtually all parties preceding virtually all elections. Why are their announced positions volatile, when set along a left–right dimension? This answer, too, has to do with the sorting process. Because politicians with diverse views sort themselves according to party policy central tendencies, a party is expected to host politicians with a range of views. Within-party differences over policy become a source of party faction. As individuals in each faction vie for party leadership positions, sometimes winning and other times losing, the policy character of a party is likely to shift to reflect the views of the current winning faction. Through such individually based rational choices, a party tends to offer policy programs with identifiable mean tendencies and substantial positional volatility over time.

Conclusion

Party theorists search for predictable party positions because they assume they exist. Empiricists assume stable positions exist and implicitly rely on that assumption to draw inferences about the representational role of parties. One has to suspect the assumption has important consequences for what one sees and infers. For instance, when it comes to reasoning about the representational consequences of stable positions, one can be led to the following type of conjecture about how parties affect policy in the Westminster Model. 'Alternation of parties in office may ... make policy trajectories shift dramatically back and forth' (Aldrich, 1995: 11). Analyses of representation relying on a stability assumption appear to corroborate that conjecture. Relying on expert survey data of what are effectively measured as stable party positions, G. Bingham Powell reaches this conclusion: '[T]he persistent superiority of the proportional influence designs in linking the citizen median and the policymakers should give pause to those attracted by the idea of the decisive election as a direct tool for citizen control' (Powell, 2000: 252).

All of these hypotheses and findings amount to very little, however, if the party position taking is what the CMP data tell us it is – volatile. On what basis, theory or fact, should one choose to ignore that the most thorough record of party positions, the Comparative Manifesto Project, indicates substantial party movements? Should the stability results of expert surveys trump the CMP record? Why not suppose that the stability reported in the results of expert surveys is the consequence of experts reporting what they see as the central tendencies of party positions? When asked about party movements other, and perhaps sometimes the same, highly informed case-specific experts report volatility (see, e.g. country-specific commentaries in Müller and Strøm, 2000).

An important lesson I have learned from working with Ian Budge and the CMP data, which I have attempted to pass on here, is that evidence of unpredictable party position volatility does not have to be assigned to the rubbish bin labeled 'noisy error.' Letting go of the unfounded stability assumption draws back the curtains to see how party systems, as observed in fact, can contribute to policy representation that democratic theory so dearly values.

Notes

1 The ideas put forth here owe large debts to collaborative efforts with Ian Budge, most especially, and Robin Best, Rachel Cremona, Richard I. Hofferbert, Hans Keman, Silvia M. Mendes, Aida Paskeviciute and Paul Pennings. I am also pleased to acknowledge my heretofore unacknowledged debts to Michael Laver and Olga Shvetsova, for prodding me into reconsidering what I thought, until they wrote, were good ideas.
2 Elsewhere, with others, I report simulated results for three-party systems (see McDonald *et al.*, 2004).
3 Intuitively one might be inclined to think that the slope would be 3.25. The mean MPP policy values (Y) are −13 and +13, and these are obtained for a mean MV position (X) of −4 when MV is less than zero and +4 when MV is greater than zero. Drawing a line through the mean Ys and Xs would produce a slope of (26/8) or 3.25. However, the general linear tendency takes account of the non-responsiveness from $0 \to \pm 18$ by treating the within-segment MV variation as if it were measurement error. Since 36 per cent of the MV variation is in the ranges 0 to −18 or 0 to +18, the proportion of as-if error is 0.36. Therefore the estimated slope is [3.25 * (1 − 0.36)] or [3.25 *0.64] or 2.08.
4 It could happen, but that would require the electorate to move more than five standard deviations. Such an outcome has about a three in five million chance.
5 The more than doubling of responsiveness follows from the facts that the mean values of MPP are ± 13 while the mean values of MV are now ± 1.6 instead of ± 4.0 when MV is above or below zero. Therefore, the relationship runs generally from (−1.6, −13) to (+1.6, +13), which has a slope of 8.125. But, as before (see note 2), the as-if error in MV amounts to 0.36 of the total variance, and 0.64 * 8.125 = 5.20.

Bibliography

Achen, C. (1975) 'Mass Political Attitudes and the Survey Response' *American Political Science Review* 69: 1218–1231.

Adams, J., M. Clark, L. Ezrow and G. Glasgow (2004) 'Understanding Change and Stability in Party Ideologies: Do Parties Respond to Public Opinion or to Past Election Results?' *British Journal of Political Science* 34, 589–610.

Aldrich, J. (1995) *Why Parties? The Origin and Transformation of Party Politics in America* (Chicago: University of Chicago Press).

American Political Science Association (APSA) Committee on Political Parties (1950) 'Toward a More Responsible Two-Party System', *American Political Science Review* 44:3 (supplement), pp. 1–99.

Austen-Smith, D. and J. Banks (1990) 'Stable Governments and the Allocation of Portfolios', *American Political Science Review* 84:3, 891–906.

Budge, I. (1994) 'A New Theory of Party Competition: Uncertainty, Ideology, and

Policy Equilibria Viewed Comparatively and Temporally', *British Journal of Political Science* 24:. 443–467.

Budge, I. and R.I. Hofferbert (1990) 'Mandates and Policy Outputs: U.S. Party Platforms and Federal Expenditures', *American Political Science Review* 84:1, 111–131.

Budge, I. and H.-D. Klingemann (2001) 'Finally! Comparative Over-time Mapping of Party Policy Movement' in I. Budge, H.-D. Klingemann, A. Volkens, E. Tanenbaum and J. Bara *Mapping Policy Preferences: Estimates for Parties, Electors, and Governments 1945–1998* (Oxford: Oxford University Press).

Budge, I. and M.J. Laver (1992) 'The Relationship between Party and Coalition Policy in Europe: An Empirical Synthesis', In M.J. Laver and I. Budge (eds) *Party Policy and Government Coalitions* (London: St. Martin's).

Budge, I., D. Robertson and D.J. Hearl (1987) *Ideology, Strategy and Party Change: Spatial Analyses of Post-War Election Programmes in 19 Democracies* (Cambridge: Cambridge University Press).

Budge, I., H.-D. Klingemann, A. Volkens, E. Tanenbaum and J. Bara (2001) *Mapping Policy Preferences: Estimates for Parties, Electors, and Governments 1945–1998* (Oxford: Oxford University Press).

Castles, F. and P. Mair (1984) 'Left-Right Political Scales: Some "Expert" Judgements', *European Journal of Political Science* 12:1, 73–88.

Converse, P.E. (1964) 'The Nature of Mass Belief Systems in Mass Publics' in David Apter (ed.) *Ideology and Discontent* (Glencoe, IL: Free Press).

Converse, P.E (1970) 'Attitudes and Non-Attitudes: Continuation of a Dialogue' in Edward R. Tufte *The Quantitative Analysis of Social Problems* (Reading, MA: Addison-Wesley).

Converse, P.E. and G.B. Markus (1979) 'Plus ça change . . .: The New CPS Election Study Panel', *American Political Science Review* 73: 32–49.

Dalton, R.J. (1985) 'Political Parties and Political Representation: Party Supporters and Party Elites in Nine Nations', *Comparative Political Studies* 18:3, 267–299.

Downs, Anthony (1957) *An Economic Theory of Democracy* (New York: Harper & Row).

Erikson, Robert S. (1979) 'The SRC Panel Data and Mass Political Attitudes', *British Journal of Political Science* 9: 16–49.

Erikson, R.S. and D.W. Romero (1990) 'Candidate Equilibrium and the Behavioral Model of the Vote', *American Political Science Review* 84:4, 1103–1126.

Erikson, R.S., M.B. MacKuen and J.A. Stimson (2002) *The Macro Polity* (New York Cambridge University Press).

Farrell, D.M. and P. Webb (2000) 'Political Parties as Campaign Organizations' in Russell J. Dalton and Martin P. Wattenberg (eds) *Parties without Partisans: Political Change in Advanced Industrial Democracies* (Oxford: Oxford University Press).

Ginsberg, B. (1972) 'Critical Elections and the Substance of Party Conflict: 1844 to 1968', *Midwest Journal of Political Science* 16:4, 603–625.

Ginsberg, B. (1976) 'Elections and Public Policy', *American Political Science Review* 70:1, 41–49.

Hausman, J.A. (1978) 'Specification Tests in Econometrics', *Econometrica* 46, pp. 1251–1271.

Heise, D.R. (1969) 'Separating Reliability and Stability in Test—Retest Correlation', *American Sociological Review* 34: 93–101.

Huber, J.D. and G. Bingham Powell (1994) 'Congruence between Citizens and Policymakers in Two Visions of Liberal democracy' *World Politics* 46:1, 291–326.

Huber, J.D. and R. Inglehart (1995) 'Expert Interpretations of Party Space and Party Locations in 42 Societies', *Party Politics* 1:1, 73–111.

Iversen T. (1994) 'The Logics of Electoral Politics: Spatial, Directional, and Mobilization Effects', *Comparative Political Studies* 27:1, 155–189.

Inglehart, R. and H.-D. Klingemann (1976) 'Party Identification, Ideological Preference and the Left–right Dimension among Western Mass Publics' in Ian Budge, Ivor Crewe and Denis Farlie (eds) *Party Identification and Beyond* (London: Wiley).

Johnston, J. and J. DiNardo (1997) *Econometric Methods*, 4th edn (New York: McGraw-Hill).

Katz, R. (1980) *A Theory of Parties and Electoral Systems* (Baltimore: Johns Hopkins University Press).

Kim, H.M. and R. Fording (1998) 'Voter Ideology in Western Democracies', *European Journal of Political Research* 33:1, 73–97.

Klingemann, H.-D., A. Volkens, J. Bara, M. McDonald and I. Budge (2006) *Mapping Policy Preferences II. Estimates for Parties, Electors and Governments: Eastern Europe, EU and OECD, 1990–2003.* (Oxford: Oxford University Press).

Knutsen, O. (1998) 'Expert Judgements of the Left-Right Location of Political Parties: A Comparative Longitudinal Study', *West European Politics* 21:2, 63–94.

Laver, M.J. and I. Budge (1992) *Party Policy and Government Coalitions* (London: St. Martin's).

Laver, M. and W.B. Hunt (1992) *Policy and Party Competition* (New York: Routledge).

Laver, Michael and Kenneth Shepsle (1996) *Making and Breaking Governments* (Cambridge: Cambridge University Press).

Laver, M., K. Benoit and J. Garry (2004) 'Extracting Policy Positions from Political Texts Using Words as Data', *American Political Science Review* 98:2, 311–331.

Lipset, S.M. and S. Rokkan (eds) (1967) 'Cleavages Structures, Party Systems and Voter Alignments: An Introduction', in S.M. Lipset and S. Rokkan (eds) *Party Systems and Voter Alignments* (New York: Free Press).

McDonald, M.D. and I. Budge (n.d.) 'From Preferences to Policy: The Median Mandate Theory of Elections', unpublished manuscript Binghamton University and University of Essex.

McDonald, M.D. and S.M. Mendes (2001) 'The Policy Space of Party Manifestos', in Michael Laver (ed.) *Estimating the Policy Position of Political Actors* (London: Routledge).

McDonald, M.D., I. Budge and P. Pennings (2004) 'Choice versus Sensitivity: Party Reactions to Public Concerns', *European Journal of Political Research* 43: 845–868.

McDonald, M.D., S.M. Mendes and I. Budge (2004) 'What Are Elections For? Conferring the Median Mandate', *British Journal of Political Science* 34:1, 1–26.

McDonald, M.D., A. Paskiviciute, R. Best and R. Cremona (2004) 'Out of Equilibrium: A Positive Theory of Parties and Representation' Paper presented at the 2004 meeting of the Public Choice Society, Baltimore, MD.

McKelvey R.D. (1976) 'Intransitivities in Multidimensional Voting Models and Some Implications for Agenda Control', *Journal of Economic Theory* 12: 472–482.

McKelvey R.D. and P.C. Ordeshook (1985) 'Sequential Elections with Limited Information', *American Journal of Political Science* 29:3, 480–512.

Michels, Roberto (1949) *Political Parties,* Glencoe (Free Press).

Müller, W.C. and K. Strøm (eds) (2000) *Coalition Governments in Western Europe* (Oxford: Oxford University Press).

Pierce, J.C and D.P. Rose (1974) 'Nonattitudes and American Public Opinion', *American Political Science Review* 68: 626–49.

Pindyck, R.S. and D.L. Rubinfeld (1991) *Econometric Models and Econometric Forecasts,* 3rd edn (New York: McGraw-Hill).

Powell, G. Bingham (2000) *Elections as Instruments for Democracy: Majoritarian and Proportional Visions* (New Haven, CT: Yale University Press).

Powell, G.B. and G. Vanberg (2000) 'Election Laws, Disproportionality and Median Correspondence: Implications for Two Visions of Democracy', *British Journal of Political Science* 30:3, 383–411.

Robertson, D. (1976) *A Theory of Party Competition* (London and New York: Wiley).

Schatteschneider, E.E. (1942) *Party Government* (New York: Holt, Rinehart, Winston).

Schofield, N. (1978) 'The Instability of Simple Dynamic Games', *Review of Economic Studies* 45: 575–594.

Schumpeter, J.A. (1942) *Capitalism, Socialism and Democracy* (New York: Harper & Row).

Snyder, J.M. Jr. and M.M. Ting (2002) 'An Informational Rationale for Political Parties', *American Journal of Political Science* 46:1, 90–110.

Stimson, J.A., M.B. MacKuen and R.S. Erikson. (1995) 'Dynamic Representation', *American Political Science Review* 89: 543–565.

Sullivan, J.L. and R.E. O'Connor (1972) 'Electoral Choice and Popular Control of Public Policy', *American Political Science Review* 66:4, 1256–1268.

Volkens, A. (2001) 'Manifesto Research Since 1979: From Reliability to Validity', in Michael Laver (ed.) *Estimating the Policy Positions of Political Actors* (London: Routledge).

5 Do parties reflect public concerns?

Judith Bara

Introduction

The Manifesto Research Group (MRG) project is regarded as a landmark in empirical political science, not only in its own right, nor simply because of its rich, publicly available data set, but also because it provides a well-validated standard for parallel types of study. The project has shown that it is possible to create reliable time series estimates of party preferences across a broad range of strategic policy areas by content analysing election manifestos. This has allowed us, *inter alia*, to map changes and trends in what parties see as important over time. (Budge *et al.*, 2001) In recent years, computerisation of content analysis has also been employed not only to speed up the actual process of coding but also to enhance reliability. Examples of different approaches attesting to greater or lesser degrees of success now abound. (See; *inter alia*, Bara, 2001a; Bara 2001b; Laver, 2001; Laver and Garry, 2000; Laver *et al.*, 2003). Much of this is related to developing accurate measures, not only of issue salience, but also of direction/ideological positioning, using 'leftist' or 'rightist' language and discourse.

It is long been argued that such research into party 'preferences' is at the heart of rational choice theories of democracy (Downs, 1957). This taps into the core of what parties are really all about, not only in terms of their ideological 'space' but also in relation to their representative nature. Who or what do parties represent in a democratic polity? Is it a series of philosophically informed ideas about how society 'ought to be'? Is it a group (or groups) of people who are bound together by cultural ties? Or is it to try to solve problems that the public believe to be important and bring about truly popular government? This discussion will suggest how we might investigate part of this last suggestion by offering some thoughts on a revised analysis of the content of political party manifestos in relation to public opinion data.

Of course this is not the first time such an approach has been embarked upon. It is a contested area of study both within and outside the political science community, and is also grounded in a much more fundamental debate at the root of liberal democratic theory. V.O. Key Jr (1961) indeed hypothesised that a successful democracy has to engage the public in the policy process. Downs (1957) had already created the possibility for the median voter theorem in the sense that the electorate's preferences coalesce with those of the winning party – thus inferring shared outlook, beliefs, concerns between a majority of the voting public and the agenda of the winning party. Dahl (1989) suggested that a 'reasonable justification' for democracy might be reflected by the fact that governments can be persuaded to do what the majority of the public really want them to do in policy terms. Riker (1993) edited a series of essays on the specification, origin and manipulation of issues, although much of this was speculative since data was lacking for a systematic comparison of party and public concerns.

Although much of the research associated with late twentieth century efforts to link public, party and government concerns has related to 'median voter' studies, there is another focus which deals with the link between public opinion and party policy preferences, using manifestos as a major data source. Among the more notable examples of this approach are Budge and Farlie (1983), Budge *et al.* (1996a), Huber and Powell (1994), Monroe (1998), McCombs and Zhu (1995), McDonald *et al.* (1998) and Budge *et al.* (1999). These focus on a variety of concerns and tend to concentrate on 'left–right' comparisons. Most prioritise the interface between public policy preferences and *government* policy outcome, rather than public and *party* preferences. Budge *et al.* (1996a, b) are exceptions in that they do use a *party* focus, but they also use standard Manifesto Research Group (MRG) estimates to effect comparisons. The majority of these studies have used responses to the most important problem (MIP) question: 'What is the most important problem facing the country today?' as a source for public opinion data.

In order to examine how far parties reflect concerns nominated by the public as 'important', Bara (2001a) focused on a different content analysis of party manifestos and platforms based on the public's perception of issue or policy importance as expressed in responses to the MIP question. This was done partly for methodological purposes to test the 'goodness of fit' between computerised coding and manual coding by validating a data set based on fully computerised estimates. The results of this analysis not only demonstrated good face validity, but also produced interesting and substantive information about trends in policy priorities favoured by the major political parties in Great Britain and the United States from 1945 to 1997. The current study builds on the more successful elements of this analysis in order to engage in a preliminary assessment of how far parties actually do reflect public concerns.

Using party election programmes as a vehicle for analysing the party – public opinion interface

It is not the intention here to reiterate the development of content analysis of party manifestos, which can be found in succinct form elsewhere (Budge and Bara, 2001). What is necessary, however, is to show whether or not party programmes reflect patterns of issue/policy/problem/concerns reported by the public. In other words, we need to code party programmes into categories constructed in the terms indicated by the electorate's responses to the MIP question. Such an undertaking is, needless to say, not without its problems.

The MIP question itself has come under significant scrutiny in recent years, mainly in relation to work on American data. Contributions by McCombs (1999), Burstein (2003), Wlezien and Franklin (1997) and Wlezien (2004) to this debate are good illustrations. Indeed, these authors question what precisely the MIP question seeks to measure – saliency or importance? issues or problems? – to say nothing of the possibility that responses to the question might be both 'a function of importance *and* the degree to which it is a problem' (Wlezien, 2004: 23). There are also problems relating to the fact that the wording of 'MIP' questions has altered over time.

Whilst noting such concerns, this discussion will not engage with questions such as these. It reports what is primarily an exploratory venture and will take the view that the issue areas cited by respondents to the MIP question signify that these are things that 'matter' to them and might reflect a variety of different concerns which the issue encapsulates for such respondents. It also recognises that sometimes answers to MIP questions may have little to do with considered and informed responses or rational judgement. Rather, many answers might well reflect short-term, often non-political, frustrations or general patterns of attitudes and values. For example, giving 'transport' as the MIP because the respondent had missed a bus and was late for work, or 'immigration' because s/he had seen an inflated figure relating to the volume of 'bogus' asylum seekers entering the country in the newspapers.

Riker (1993) took a robustly straightforward approach to such matters. He conceptualised issues as being 'whatever some people think are issues'. In other words, there does not necessarily need to be a tight, universally accepted definition. What is important is that such matters or concerns are able to be politicised and, as such, are worthy of investigation. Problems of definition and measurement notwithstanding, answers to such a direct and simple question as the MIP can tap into popular concerns and facilitate the construction of a relatively straightforward computerised coding scheme – such as that constructed for this exercise.

The purpose of this study is therefore to investigate how far major British political parties reflect public concerns by creating a new manifesto data set derived from a coding scheme (dictionary) based on MIP responses. This will then be compared with MIP responses themselves. The proposition under investigation is that manifestos for each party *will* reflect these concerns *but* that this relationship will be *less reflective of the public's concerns than of the concerns of the other parties.* After all, parties which are serious contenders for office *all* monitor MIP responses quite closely and indeed may well also try to 'guide' public opinion to their own way of thinking in this respect often with the help of the media.

Data

The particular data used for such a purpose in this study are derived from the responses of Gallup MIP questions carried out regularly intervals in Great Britain between 1964 and 2000 and published in a single volume. (King, 2001) For 2001, this is supplemented with data derived from the British Election Study (2001) and compared with the data published in the Gallup Political and Economic Index.[1] However, as we are aware, even over time data derived from a single source is not always without its problems and the case here is no exception. Indeed there are at least four problems relevant to this exercise, besides the well-known difficulties associated with coding!

First, the 'MIP' question may not always be as it seems, since the wording varies among the separate surveys. Up to 1964, the question was 'which of these [areas or issues] is the most important problem facing the country today?' From 1966 this was changed to 'What would you say is the most urgent problem facing the country at the present time?' (King, 2001). Despite this – and bearing in mind that most discussion will relate to the post-1970 period – the term 'MIP' will be retained for purposes of this exercise as a convenient shorthand. In any case, we are examining estimates and inferences rather than precise measures of causality. That said, we should nonetheless be aware that there *is* a difference in terms of what we understand by 'urgency' as compared with 'important', discussion of which forms part of the debate presented by Wlezien (2004) *inter alia.*

Second, the question itself may not have been asked in every politically oriented survey carried out by Gallup. Hence, there are uneven numbers of results able to be tracked throughout the period. For example, for the 1966 and 1970 elections, only one set of figures was easily available in standardised form.

Additionally, there are instances where respondents might insist that there is more than one concern of urgency or importance and refuse to be drawn on making a choice between these. Some surveys do contain supplementary questions of 'and what is the next most important/ urgent?' type. Finally, prior to 1968, respondents were shown lists of issues to choose from, rather than be allowed to present their own choice in answering a completely open-ended question, which for our purposes would certainly have been preferable and more directly comparative over time.

These problems notwithstanding, this material is still a good source to draw on. The actual data compiled for this exercise represents (apart from 1966 and 1970) mean percentage mentions of problems/concerns in surveys reported during the 12 months prior to the election, excluding the month of the election itself. Percentages are calculated on the basis of the total number of responses to the MIP question. The choice of 12 months is in many ways arbitrary. The logic behind it is that in previous studies, averages or annualised figures for the election year have been used (see for example, Budge *et al.*, 1996a, b; Bara, 2001a). However, these are less than satisfactory for a number of reasons. The task of producing a manifesto is not something that is done immediately prior to the election. It takes place over several months and has become a much more institutionalised process. Indeed, one might be tempted to suggest that this starts the day following the previous election! Using the data for election years is also problematic as the election may take place early in the year and much of the material contained in poll responses after this will be of dubious relevance. By using an estimate of public concerns covering a period of several months leading up to the election, it is possible to tap more relevant material.[2] We should also bear in mind that the public are much more fickle, volatile, and reactive and focused on shorter time spans than parties. Parties tend to think further ahead in terms of what they can do in the future to progress policy – and of course to win electoral support – rather than wishing to dwell on mistakes of the past.

With regard to the MIP responses, all reported Gallup categories were taken as the basis for the coding scheme for the party manifestos as well as for reporting public concerns. Some of these are very minor and are either discounted or collapsed into a relevant, larger category, for example 'Petrol Prices' became part of the 'Other/General economic' category. In the event, 19 categories were taken as indicative of both public and policy concerns over the period. Seventeen of these were then collapsed to form four substantive domains which focused on the areas of Economic, Social, Foreign and Environmental policy. The precise configuration of these categories is shown in Table 5.1.

The party programmatic data were derived from computerised content analysis of the full manifestos of the British Conservative, Labour and Liberal/Liberal Democrat parties[3] for eight general elections 1964–70 and 1979–97. These were generated from electronic sources and prepared in appropriate format for computer analysis. As far as possible, the original MRG units of analysis (quasi-sentences) were replicated.

Producing reliable and valid estimates

One of the greatest strengths of computerised coding is indeed its potential for providing reliable estimates derived from content analysis. We can be certain that when we apply the same coding procedure to the same

Table 5.1 Coding categories and domains

Category number	Category name	Domain
1	Cost of living	Economy
2	Unemployment	Economy
3	Other/General economic	Economy
4	Education	Social
5	Health	Social
6	Housing	Social
7	Immigration	Social
8	Strikes	Economic
9	Pensions	Social
10	Law and order	Social
11	Poll tax/rates	–
12	Fuel shortages	Economic
13	Benefits	Social
14	Defence	Foreign
15	International	Foreign
16	Europe	Foreign
17	Ireland	–
18	Environment	Environment
19	Farming	Environment

document by means of a computer this will always be applied in exactly the same manner so, assuming the dictionary is appropriate, there are virtually no reliability problems. Application of the computerised dictionary based on MIP responses to the manifesto texts thus gives us a general indication of how far manifestos reflect public concerns.

There are however problems relating to validity which become especially relevant when assessing the results of computerised coding. Validity issues are not a new problem for textual analysis of political material (Budge, 2001) but are especially relevant to computerised analysis. Once we go beyond the simple procedure of building frequencies based on word-counts we need to infer context, specific meaning and possibly direction of ideological tendency, for example in terms of policy reflecting ideological positions on the 'left' or 'right' (Bara, 2001b). Earlier attempts to create a computerised dictionary which used MIP responses as a guide were thus validated against a parallel set of manual codings, as well as assessing face validity using mapping techniques and statistical testing. Given the high correlation across more than three-quarters of the results (Bara, 2001a), the present study is based entirely on computerised coding using the 19 category dictionary. Each category comprises a series of words, word strings (e.g. Common Agricultural Policy), word stems (e.g. 'migra', 'milit') and relevant abbreviations (e.g. BSE). Categories may tap both direct mention and associations, surrogates or euphemisms used in the manifesto.

The dictionary was applied using *TEXTPACK 7* software[4] as this provides for the creation of dedicated dictionaries, a 'keyword in context' facility to check instances where words might have two meanings (e.g. 'drugs' in terms of health and/or law and order issues) and interfaces fairly easily with other software packages. It was also possible to apply the dictionary to analytic units which replicated those of the manual scheme as far as possible.

Reporting the results

Results of the analysis are reported in terms of three sets of indicators, each of which will assess whether there is evidence of party policy estimates reflecting public concerns, and will address the proposition suggested earlier – that manifestos for each party will reflect these concerns but that the distribution will be less reflective of the public's concerns than of those of the other parties.

- Rankings of 'Top Ten' concerns for the two 'critical' elections of 1979 and 1997 (as examples) will be reported for the public opinion data and the party manifestos.
- Maps for public opinion and party manifesto concerns along the policy domains.
- Basic statistical analysis: means and correlations.

The second and third of these will encompass comparisons between the computerised estimates and original MRG data – a well-accepted 'standard' for validation purposes. In order to provide for a 'level playing field' it is necessary to recompute the original economic, social and foreign domains, and to create a new environmental domain. This is created by grouping together variables as set out in Table 5.2.

Rankings of 'Top Ten' concerns

It is inevitable that economic matters are of considerable importance for all parties and for the public. In the case of public opinion, the margin between concern for economic matters and all others is very great. Likewise, although of lesser magnitude, economic matters predominate for the parties across a large section of the post-war period. When considering rank ordering we thus have to be clear that there are considerable differences of emphasis with regard to the positions. Some of the lower ranks are indeed often occupied by concerns that certainly represent less than 5 per cent of total estimates. 'Other' or 'general' economic matters are consistently ranked first for all parties across the eight elections considered here, whereas for the public, this category averaged fourth – although other categories reflecting economic concerns, unemployment and, often, cost of living, ranked first and second.

Table 5.2 Manifesto categories and domains

Category number	Category name	Domain
401	Free enterprise	Economic
402	Incentives	Economic
403	Market regulation	Economic
404	Economic planning	Economic
405	Corporatism	Economic
406	Protectionism positive	Economic
407	Protectionism negative	Economic
408	Economic goals	Economic
409	Keynesian demand management	Economic
410	Productivity	Economic
411	Technology and infrastructure	Economic
412	Controlled economy	Economic
413	Nationalisation	Economic
414	Economic orthodoxy	Economic
701	Labour groups positive	Economic
702	Labour groups negative	Economic
504	Welfare state expansion	Social
505	Welfare state limitation	Social
506	Education expansion	Social
507	Education limitation	Social
601	National way of Life positive	Social
602	National way of Life negative	Social
603	Traditional morality positive	Social
604	Traditional morality negative	Social
605	Law and order	Social
607	Multiculturalism positive	Social
608	Multiculturalism positive	Social
101	Foreign special relations positive	Foreign
102	Foreign special relations negative	Foreign
103	Anti-imperialism	Foreign
104	Military positive	Foreign
105	Military negative	Foreign
106	Peace	Foreign
107	Internationalism positive	Foreign
108	European community positive	Foreign
109	Internationalism negative	Foreign
110	European community negative	Foreign
416	Anti-growth	Environment
501`	Environmental protection	Environment
703	Agriculture and farmers	Environment

Rankings for 1979 and 1997 are examined as these are the two most 'critical' elections since 1945 in terms of bringing about not only change of government but also significant changes in policy emphasis. This notwithstanding we can see that despite a few idiosyncrasies there is still a generally high level of 'agreement' among parties about what are seen as significant issues than there is between any of the parties and the public. If

Table 5.3a Ranking of 'top ten' issues, 1979

Issue	POP	Conservative	Labour	Lib Democrat
Unemployment	1		8	
Cost of living	1		9	
Strikes	3	6		
Economy	4	1	1	1
Law and order	5	2	3	2
Immigration	6			
Housing	7	9	7	7
Health	8	5	4	9
Benefits	9	8	9	10
Education	10			5
International		3	2	3
Environment				4
Defence		4	5	5
Europe				7
Farming		6	6	9
Pensions		9		
% within two places of POP position		20%	30%	30%

Table 5.3b Ranking of 'top ten' issues, 1997

Issue	POP	Conservative	Labour	Lib Democrat
Unemployment	1			
Health	2	5	5	2
Education	3	4	3	5
Law and order	4	2	2	3
Europe	5	6	9	8
Cost of Living	6			
Farming	7			
Economy	8	1	1	1
Housing	9			
Pensions	10	10	10	
Environment		9	7	4
International		3	4	7
Benefits		8	8	9
% within two places of POP position		40%	30%	30%

we take a fairly arbitrary indication based on how many concerns voiced by the public fall within two ranks for the parties, we can see that this is fairly low for both elections. Nor is there any discernible relationship between winning parties being closer to public concerns in terms of rankings. What emerge as interesting, however, are changing trends in terms of the political agenda, with social matters overtaking the economy as subjects of concern. This is seen even more clearly in the party maps.

Mapping trends in domain importance

We can appreciate the ebbs and flows in the importance of different policy domains if we look at maps of their contribution to party manifesto content and proportion of overall MIP responses in the case of public opinion. The prevailing wisdom of recent years is that 'it is the economy, stupid'. But is this borne out by the evidence available here?

With regard to the public opinion picture (Figure 5.1), economic concerns clearly predominate through the sixties to 1992. However, we can also see that these reached a high in the mid-eighties and subsequently began to diminish, gradually being overtaken by social concerns. Notable here are concerns over law and order and health. Indeed, from the mid-seventies, an inverse relationship between economic and social matters seems to be developing. By 2001 social concerns overtake economic concerns for the public – as indeed an MRG-based analysis also shows in the case of the parties (Bara and Budge, 2001).

As expected, foreign policy concerns are clearly of much less interest to the public than to the parties from the mid-sixties. The slight surge in 1983 undoubtedly reflects worries related to the Falklands crisis, just as a similar move in 1997 is probably due to slightly greater concern over European matters. Environmental matters show a remarkable steadiness in terms of lack of interest until 1997, where the rise is surely related to the BSE crisis. How do these patterns compare with party policy estimates?

The Conservative picture is reflective of public opinion patterns despite differences in degree of importance afforded to the domains. The

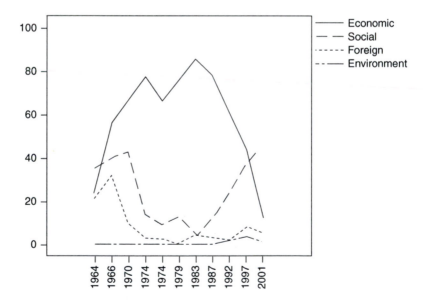

Figure 5.1 Public opinion by domain.

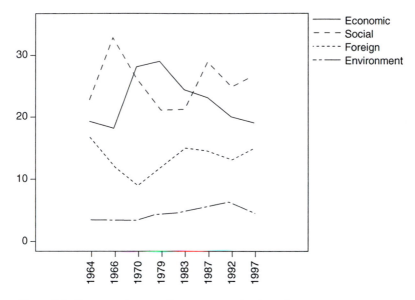

Figure 5.2 Conservative manifesto content by domain.

domestic agenda is clearly dominant with between 25 and 50 per cent of manifesto content taken up by economic and social matters. Whilst these have an essentially inverse relationship, this is less marked than that perceived in the public opinion data. The foreign policy domain, however, is almost the opposite of the public opinion result, while environmental concerns show a similar pattern for both party and public.

For Labour like the Conservatives, the relationship between economic and social concerns is much closer than is the case for the public, and both occupy similar proportions of space across the manifestos. Unlike the public opinion and Conservative patterns, Labour does not show a significant rise in concern for social matters – indeed there is a decrease after 1992. Foreign policy also shows declining importance and the environment is slightly more important (and volatile) than in the public or Conservative maps – but less erratic than in the case of the Liberal Democrats.

The Liberal Democrats show a much more volatile picture across all four domains than either of the other parties or public opinion. Indeed, it is striking that concern over social matters emerges much earlier in their case, although until the nineties, its movement is parallel to that of the economic domain. Foreign policy also appears somewhat higher on the agenda – no doubt reflective of the party's longstanding concerns with internationalism and Europe. The environment is also more prominent.

But of course public opinion estimates are not the only material with which this new data can be compared. The original MRG data also had a

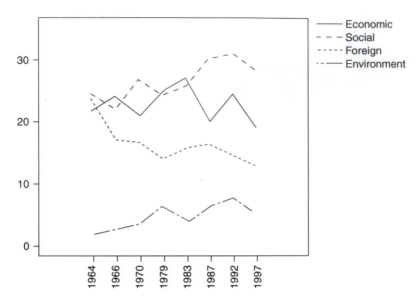

Figure 5.3 Labour manifesto content by domain.

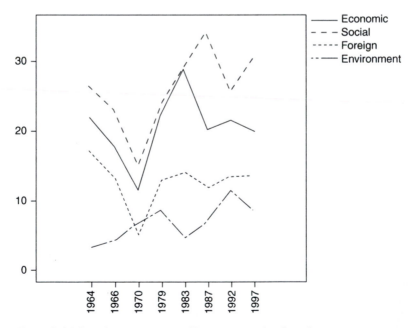

Figure 5.4 Liberal Democrat manifesto content by domain.

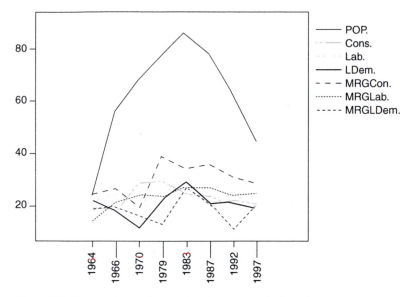

Figure 5.5 Comparing estimates for the economic domain.

great deal to say about much of this and can act as a benchmark for validating this new computerised analysis of the documents. This will be shown by reference to the economic domain.

In the case of the economic domain we can see immediately that the new computerised estimates are closer in terms of degree of emphasis shown by the MRG estimates than to public opinion patterns, despite broad similarities in patterns of movement. Overall, the party positions are closer to each other than to the public opinion estimates. However, even though this is clear at face value, correlations between the different positions are not significant – possibly in part a function of low numbers of cases (see Table 5.5).

The results concerning the social domain present a similar picture, although here the Conservatives also manifest a much greater degree of closeness than was the case with economic matters. It is also interesting that there is a closer relationship with the public opinion trend than in the case of the economic domain. The positions of the parties are also quite close as are differences between the computerised estimates and the MRG ones. Indeed in the case of the environment domain, correspondence in terms of closeness of fit between the MRG and computerised estimates is more decisive. However patterns relating to foreign policy are less clear. The Conservatives show the greatest degree of similarity between MRG and the computerised coding. From 1979, the public opinion estimates also show a similar pattern. Labour and the Liberal Democrats fail to provide such a clear pattern.

Means and correlations

If we compare means, there is little difference between the computerised and MRG estimates for Labour and Liberal Democrat in the case of the economic domain and for the social domain; differences in means are quite low for all parties – between 1.9 and 2.2.

In relation to foreign policy the mean difference for the two sets of Conservative estimates is quite high at 6 per cent. Labour and the Liberal Democrats show lower average differences – especially in the case of the Liberal Democrats at 0.9. The environment domain, however, suggest a good fit with mean differences of between only 0.1 and 1.0 across all three parties.

We now come to the overall correlations across the domains for all party and public opinion estimates. These are encouraging in that all the relationships are shown as significant and there are some interesting trends within these results (see Table 5.5).

The lowest sets of figures that emerge are for the relationship between the public opinion estimates and the party policy estimates. There is no material difference between the magnitude of the coefficients for the MRG and computerised estimates in relation to public opinion. Indeed, the only discernible difference is in the case of the Conservatives, and even here it is only 0.121. The correlation results for computerised party estimates set against the MRG standard are somewhat higher, especially for Conservative and Labour, which is a convincing endorsement of the estimates based on computerised coding.

Finally, when the correlations for different pairs of party estimates are examined, the results suggest that the proposition that parties will tend to reflect each other's concerns to a greater degree than those of the public is clearly corroborated. The set of inter-party correlations with the highest coefficients is that based on computerised coding.

These results suggest that the parties are not simply responding to public considerations in terms of setting their policy agendas. Rather, whilst all parties clearly pay some attention to public concerns, they con-

Table 5.4 Means

Party	Economic domain		Social domain		Foreign domain		Environment domain	
	Comp	*MRG*	*Comp*	*MRG*	*Comp*	*MRG*	*Comp*	*MRG*
Conservative	22.5	29.3	25.5	22.8	13.2	8.1	4.3	5.1
Labour	22.7	22.8	26.4	28.3	16.3	10.3	4.4	4.5
Lib. Democrat	20.4	18.1	25.9	23.7	12.6	11.7	6.7	7.7

Table 5.5 Correlations for domains, parties and public opinion estimates

		POP	Cons	Lab	LDem	MRGCon	MRGLab	MRGLDem
POP	Pearson Correlation	1	0.698(**)	0.613(**)	0.491(**)	0.829(**)	0.619(**)	0.464(**)
	Sig. (2-tailed)	.	0.000	0.000	0.004	0.000	0.000	0.007
	N	32	32	32	32	32	32	32
Cons	Pearson Correlation	0.698(**)	1	0.905(**)	0.830(**)	0.811(**)	0.873(**)	0.668(**)
	Sig. (2-tailed)	.000	0	0.000	0.000	0.000	0.000	0.000
	N	32	32	32	32	32	32	32
Lab	Pearson Correlation	0.613(**)	0.905(**)	1	0.876(**)	0.794(**)	0.890(**)	0.781(**)
	Sig. (2-tailed)	0.000	0.000	0	0.000	0.000	0.000	0.000
	N	32	32	32	32	32	32	32
LDem	Pearson Correlation	0.491(**)	0.830(**)	0.876(**)	1	0.795(**)	0.850(**)	0.739(**)
	Sig. (2-tailed)	0.004	0.000	0.000	0	0.000	0.000	0.000
	N	32	32	32	32	32	32	32
MRGCon	Pearson Correlation	0.829(**)	0.811(**)	0.794(**)	0.795(**)	1	0.821(**)	0.674(**)
	Sig. (2-tailed)	0.000	0.000	0.000	0.000	0	0.000	0.000
	N	32	32	32	32	32	32	32
MRGLab	Pearson Correlation	0.619(**)	0.873(**)	0.890(**)	0.850(**)	0.821(**)	1	0.778(**)
	Sig. (2-tailed)	0.000	0.000	0.000	0.000	0.000	0	0.000
	N	32	32	32	32	32	32	32
MRGLDem	Pearson Correlation	0.464(**)	0.668(**)	0.781(**)	0.739(**)	0.674(**)	0.778(**)	1
	Sig. (2-tailed)	0.007	0.000	0.000	0.000	0.000	0.000	0
	N	32	32	32	32	32	32	32

Note
** Correlation is significant at the 0.01 level (2-tailed).

tinue to set their own agenda in terms of their own priorities and ideological base. However, there is a suggestion that parties also pay attention to what their rivals are saying. Manifestos are no longer conceived in secret and their general content is discussed publicly for some time prior to an election. The major parties in Britain are concerned neither to be outflanked on policy initiatives by their rivals, nor to ignore the priorities of their own membership. Manifestos are not yet simply the products of focus group research.

Conclusion

The results of this investigation of correspondence between public and party priorities in terms of policy areas suggest that indeed there are differences in terms of both ranking of specific concerns and degree to which these – and indeed broader policy domains – are viewed as important. In general, the parties and the public are interested in matters concerning economic well-being and social stability, but these concerns do not always manifest themselves in the same manner, or to the same degree of concern.

It is also the case that most of the time the public are not very interested in foreign and defence matters – especially since the end of the Cold War. Certainly specific events, such as the Falklands or Iraq crises, or even a development concerning the European Union may trigger an interest. Most of the time, however, the domestic agenda, and especially day-to-day concerns over the economy, crime, education, health etc. are seen as considerably more important or urgent. Parties likewise manifest a declining prioritisation for foreign and defence matters, but by no means to such a low level as the public. There is also evidence that economic concerns have declined in importance in favour of social matters.

The environmental domain shows a similar pattern, with particular crises such as BSE triggering greater degree of concern, and the parties overall showing somewhat more interest. Whilst prioritising economic and social matters over the past 40 or so years, the parties nevertheless manifest a more balanced approach. The public tend to throw their weight behind a single area and sometimes a single element within it, such as unemployment in the case of the economy.

With regard to the parties themselves, the results also back up the initial proposition that they are more likely to show affinity with each other in terms of policy areas or discrete aspects of these, than with the public.

However, we must always bear in mind the pitfalls of investigations such as this. Not only are the public notoriously subjective, fickle and prone to volatile behaviour in terms of what they regard as politically important – often as a function of media coverage – but the data reflecting public opinion is itself less than completely reliable. This does not preclude us from using it as a guide but we should be aware of its shortcomings.

Parties are more concerned with medium-term issues, relating to the span of one, or sometimes two parliament(s). They take a more measured view of what should be prioritised in terms of policy. They not only need to have policies for the whole gamut of government activity, as opposed to the 'concern of the moment', but they also have to produce the basis for feasible policy outcomes. In order to be able to achieve all this they need to get themselves elected, so they will need to keep a weather eye on what their opponents are planning and try to find something which will give them an edge. This is where paying some attention to what the public is concerned about may well produce results. Hence, party policy preferences are bound to differ, at least in degree, when compared to those of the public, and this is reflected in the results discussed above.

There are also a further series of investigations which could indeed provide additional insight into how far parties are leading or responding to public concerns, and whether the time lags involved produce effects which are indeed 'delayed' reactions. This might be identified more clearly by focusing on a monthly MIP cycle rather than simply looking at annual estimates based on means or other calculations. Additional content analysis might also locate when instances of concerns being satisfied by government, or at least dispelled, could be triggers for new issues of concern to emerge between elections.

One thing clearly demonstrated by this study is that the computerised coding shows a close degree of correspondence with the MRG estimates. This could indeed be related to the fact that the dictionary used in the study is simple, relatively unambiguous and based on plain language and easy to apply. However this may be a doubled-edged situation as these benefits might also signify limitations. Before we decide to go along a fully-fledged computerised route in the future, let us be clear that problems still remain, despite improvements in coding techniques in recent years. We may indeed not be tapping into sufficient variables and thus might not be exposing a full picture or set of relationships between parties, public and government. So, as far as the computerised coding is concerned, we should remain cautious about applying the dictionary used here as a fully-fledged investigative aid. The fact that not all policy domains yielded significant comparisons between manual and computer coding suggests that more work remains to be done.

On the other hand, this investigation does demonstrate that, at least for a range of the election programmes of the major parties in Great Britain, computerised content analysis can produce estimates that appear to be as valid as those produced by manual coding. The present results, provide further evidence to suggest that there is cause for optimism that computerised coding can become a valid alternative, certainly in order to engage in future investigation into the degree of correspondence between perceptions of policy areas held by the public and by political parties.

Notes

1   I am very grateful to Anthony King for providing relevant 2001 Gallup Poll material. I also appreciate comment on an earlier presentation of the material discussed in this chapter from Hugh Ward, John Bartle, Ian McLean and Paul Whiteley.
2   The number of surveys concerned varied as follows. 1964 and 2001 = 10; 1966 and 1970 = 1; 1979, 1983 and 1987 = 12; 1992 and 1997 = 14.
3   The term Liberal Democrat will be used throughout the discussion to denote 'Liberal' prior to 1983 and Liberal-Social Democrat Alliance, 1983–87.
4   Investigation into the suitability of *TEXTPACK 7* and initial training in its application was conducted at the ZA-EUROLAB, Zentralarchiv für Empirische Sozialforschung at the Universität zu Köln. I should like to thank especially Ekkehart Mochmann, Ingvill C. Mochmann and Bruno Hopp for their advice and support during my time spent there on study visits, 1997–99 and afterwards. I am also grateful to the European Union's TMR-LSF initiative for funding these visits.

References

Bara, J. (2001a) 'Tracking Estimates of Public Opinion and Party Policy Intentions in Britain and the USA' in Michael Laver (ed.) *Estimating the Policy Positions of Political Actors* (London: Routledge).

Bara, J. (2001b) 'Using Manifesto Estimates To Validate Computerized Analyses' in Ian Budge, Hans-Dieter Klingemann, Andrea Volkens, Judith Bara and Eric Tanenbaum *Mapping Policy Preferences: Parties, Electors and Governments, 1945–1998* (Oxford: Oxford University Press).

Bara, J. and I. Budge (2001) 'Party Policy and Ideology: Still New Labour?' in Pippa Norris (ed.) *Britain Votes 2001* (Oxford: Oxford University Press).

British Election Study (2001) Accessed via http://www.essex.ac.uk/bes/data.html on 27 April 2004.

Budge, Ian (2001) 'Validating Party Policy Placements', *British Journal of Political Science* 34:1, 210–223.

Budge, I. and J. Bara (2001) 'Content Analysis And Political Texts' in Ian Budge, Hans-Dieter Klingemann, Andrea Volkens, Judith Bara and Eric Tanenbaum *Mapping Policy Preferences: Parties, Electors and Governments, 1945–1998* (Oxford: Oxford University Press).

Budge, I. and D.J. Farlie (1983) *Explaining and Predicting Elections: Issue Effects and Party Strategies in Twenty-Three Democracies* (London: George Allen and Unwin).

Budge, I., R.I. Hofferbert and P. Pennings (1996a) 'Public Opinion and Party Programs in Modern Democracies', ECPR Joint Sessions, Oslo.

Budge, I., H.E. Keman and P. Pennings (1996b) 'Organising Democratic Choice: Public Opinion Data', unpublished paper based on results of analysis carried out at NIAS.

Budge, I., H.-D. Klingemann, A. Volkens, J. Bara and E. Tanenbaum (2001) *Mapping Policy Preferences: Parties, Electors and Governments, 1945–1998* (Oxford: Oxford University Press).

Budge, I., E. Tanenbaum and J. Bara (1999)   'Monitoring Democratic Five-Year Plans: Multiple Coding of British Manifestos and US Platforms' (Swindon: ESRC Report R00022289).

Burstein, P. (2003) 'The Impact of Public Opinion on Public Policy: A Review and Agenda', *Political Research Quarterly* 56:1, 29–40

Dahl, R.A. (1989) *Democracy and its Critics* (New Haven, CT:Yale University Press).

Downs, A. (1957) *An Economic Theory of Democracy* (New York: Harper).

Huber, J. and G.B. Powell Jnr (1994) 'Congruence Between Citizens and Policy-makers in Two Visions of Liberal Democracy' *World Politics* 46: 291–326.

Key, V.O. Jnr (1961) *Public Opinion and American Democracy* (New York: Knopf).

King, A. (ed.) (2001) *British Political Opinion, 1937–2000* (London: Politicos).

Laver, M. (ed.) (2001) *Estimating the Policy Positions of Political Actors* (London: Routledge).

Laver, M. and J. Garry (2000) 'Estimating Policy Positions from Political Texts', *American Journal of Political Science* 44:3, 619–634.

Laver, M., K. Benoit and John Garry (2003) 'Extracting Policy Positions From Political Texts Using Words as Data', *American Political Science Review* 97:2, 311–331.

McCombs, M. (1999) 'Personal Involvement with Issues on the Public Agenda', *International Journal of Public Opinion Research* 11:2, 152–168

McCombs, M. and J.-H. Zhu (1995) 'Capacity, Diversity and Volatility of the Public Agenda', *Public Opinion Quarterly* 59: 495–525.

McDonald, M.D., I. Budge and R.I. Hofferbert (1998) 'American Party Platforms and Dynamic Representation: Responsiveness, Choice and rationality', APSA Annual Meeting, Boston.

Monroe, A (1998) 'Public Opinion and Public Policy, 1980–1993', *Public Opinion Quarterly* 62: 6–28.

Riker, W.H. (ed.) (1993) *Agenda Formation* (Ann Arbor: University of Michigan Press).

Wlezien, C. (2004) 'On the Salience of Political Issues: The problem with the "Most Important Problem"', accessed via http://www.nuff.ox.ac.uk/Politics/ papers on 2 May 2004.

Wlezien, C. and M. Franklin (1997) 'The Responsive Public: Issue Salience, Policy Change and Preferences for European Unification', *Journal of Theoretical Politics* 9: 247–263.

Part II

Methodological directions and challenges

6   The dimensionality of party ideologies

Iain McLean

Introduction: garbage in, gold out?

The Manifesto Group data series has only one equivalent of equal weight in the whole of political science, namely the time-series of national election surveys in most democracies. The world needs both series if it is to test even the most commonplace generalisations about the interaction between voters and politicians. However, many observers are sceptical of the value of Manifesto Group data, unlike that of the national election studies. This section considers the criticism that content analysis, however sophisticated, offers only *garbage in, garbage out*. It defends the method by reference not only to the MRG/CMP project but also to the other most important content analysis in political science, namely W.H. Riker's analysis of arguments for and against ratifying the Constitution of the United States. The second section compares the Budgean analysts of the CMP with other work in neighbouring fields of political science. The final section considers how many political dimensions there truly are in a large democracy.

Budge and Bara (2001: 4–5) show that measuring media coverage by the column inch predates the Second World War. Harold Lasswell found out that in the summer of 1939 negative references to the Soviet Union in German papers tailed off ahead of the Nazi–Soviet Pact, which nevertheless came as a total surprise to the governments of the UK and the USA (not to mention Poland). Meanwhile, in a different sector of political science, the then-ignored Lewis Richardson was engaged on his huge categorisation of dyads and moods in international relations. Richardson's idea was both to collect data and to derive equations for the mathematical physics of war (Sutherland, 1993; Nicholson, 1999). The Richardson categorisation of dyads and moods is formally similar to the MRG/CMP's procedure of classifying all sentences in party manifestos. Perhaps a group of international relations scholars with money and devotion might bring the two together. They could compare CMP statements in the party manifestos of dyads of countries about one another – as part of the Democratic Peace research project (e.g. Russett 1994), of which Richardson would have thoroughly approved?

Nevertheless, content analysis has always aroused some suspicion. Is it not *garbage in, garbage out?* Most of what politicians say and the papers write is garbage: so how can one justify analysing it, by howsoever sophisticated a method? The MRG are not the only group to have been exposed to this criticism. So was Richardson, whose recognition was limited to the USA and whose reception by UK international relations scholars was frosty until as late as Nicholson (1999). The pioneer study of Commons Early Day Motions by Berrington *et al.* (Finer *et al.*, 1961; Berrington, 1973; McLean, 1995) met with similar scorn in some circles. The tough question is this. Are party manifestos (and political speeches about foreign relations, and Early Day Motions) such cheap talk that they are not even worth analysing?

I think that the MRG/CMP team are entitled to give a weak and a strong answer. The weak answer runs: *The data are what they are. Content analysis of them is better than anecdotal discussion, unsystematic sampling, or ignoring them altogether, which are the only three alternatives.* The strong answer runs: *The data yield real, reliable and valid results, which are consistent with results from other methods and which combine to form the counterpart to data on electoral opinion.*

Even the weak answer says something to historians and to those who typically use historians' methods of archival study. Anybody who has worked in political history has to get gold from dross: must process a great deal of ore, some of much higher quality than other, in order to derive a few ounces of precious metal. Historians do not spend long enough thinking about sampling and representativeness. For some documents, it is appropriate to take a 100 per cent sample. The records of the central policy departments of a government may be a case in point. But even there, the serious historian will become weighted down in departmental archives before she has gone very far. How can she assure her readers that what she quotes is representative of what was said and done? For other documents, such as newspapers, social scientists are primarily interested in the generalisable; historians primarily in the unique. But even historians cannot always operate on a 100 per cent sample. Life is too short, and research grants are even shorter. The problems of appropriate sampling from historical records are real, serious and far too little discussed.

The MRG/CMP begins with an unassimilable amount of primary data – all party manifestos since 1945 in its set of countries (with the exceptions candidly listed in Budge *et al.*, 2001, Appendix IV). This unassimilable can be assimilated in three ways: by unsystematic sampling, by systematic sampling, or by reduction of the 100 per cent sample to an interpretable body of data. All historians and many political scientists follow the first route. The second route would be better than the first, but the third – the MRG/CMP route – is better than the second.

The Manifesto group report their reliability and validity testing in Volkens (2001). Reliability includes inter-coding reliability and inter-language reliability. Garry (1999, 2001) reports that, without knowing any Norwegian, he computer-coded Norwegian party manifestos at a number of elections and the resulting policy positions replicated those derived from the MRG/CMP coding of the same manifestos. This establishes the MRG/CMP hand-coding as the bedrock on which future electronic coding could be built.

The MRG method assumes that party manifestos do not argue with one another. They talk past one another. The Conservatory Party says "We will preserve Ruritania's military greatness". The Laboratory Party says "We will free the wretched people of Ruritania's oppressed colonies". Using this insight, the MRG/CMP has generated 56 coding categories for manifesto sentences, such as "Foreign Special Relationships: Positive" and "Keynesian Demand Management". It has also, perhaps more controversially, generated a unidimensional left–right positioning for the parties in its set. A party gains "left" points for sentences classed into the left-hand column of Table 6.1, and "right" points for sentences classed into the right-hand column.

Budge *et al.* (2001: 22–23) make two points about Table 6.1. First, that factor analysis confirms that these sentences are associated. A manifesto which contains one of the left-column sentences tends to contain others, and the same for the right-column sentences. Second, that the MRG scoring scheme scores the "leftness" of a manifesto not by the simple ratio of left to right sentences, but by the net leftness of its left–right sentences *as a proportion of all sentences in the manifesto*. The following explanation is thoroughly Richardsonian:

[A] party that makes 200 statements with 100 (or 50%) of them about Left items and 40 (or 20%) about Right items receives a score of −30

Table 6.1 Sentences that give rise to "left" and "right" scores in the MRG coding scheme

Left-wing sentences	*Right-wing sentences*
Decolonisation	Military: positive
Military: negative	Freedom, human rights
Peace	Constitutionalism: positive
Internationalism: positive	Effective authority
Democracy	Free enterprise
Regulate capitalism	Economic incentives
Economic planning	Protectionism: negative
Protectionism: positive	Economic orthodoxy
Controlled economy	Social services limitation
Nationalisation	National way of life: positive
Social Services: expansion	Traditional morality: positive
Education: expansion	Law and order
Labour groups: positive	Social harmony

Source: Budge *et al.*, 2001, Table 1.1.

(i.e., 20–50)..... Imagine that at the next election this party says exactly the same things it had said last time but adds 200 new statements about an issue that is not of concern to the Left-Right scale (e.g., favourable statements about protecting the environment). Now the party is making 400 total statements, and relative to that total they are making only half as many Left statements (25%) and half as many Right statements (10%) as they did for the first election. The party's Left-Right position is recorded as moving from -30 to -15.

(Budge *et al.*, 2001: 23)

Thus the MRG scaling procedure is not quite a unidimensional scheme. Other dimensions enter it in a shadowy way (see also McDonald and Mendes, 2001). This becomes important when we compare it with other schemes, and attempt to comment on the true dimensionality of politics in an industrial democracy, below.

In his last completed book, *The Strategy of Rhetoric*, W.H. Riker independently used the same technique as the Manifesto Group (Riker, 1996). This book concludes Riker's lifelong study of the 1787 Philadelphia Convention, which drafted the US Constitution. Riker analysed the motives and tactics of the Federalist Framers and their Anti-Federalist opponents, before, during and after the convention. The records of the Federal Convention, and the newspaper controversies over whether or not to ratify it, are very high-grade ore. They are also in part ready-smelted. A peerless record of the secret discussions of the Convention itself was kept by its most assiduous and cleverest delegate, James Madison, and published after his death. And American historians have proudly and reverently published all the surviving paper they can find, on both the Federalist and the Anti-Federalist sides, in multi-volume sets.

In *The Strategy of Rhetoric* Riker asks: how on earth was a Constitution ratified? It required nine out of 13 states to ratify. Anti-Federalists were strong in most states and dominant in at least four, including two of the biggest (Massachusetts and Virginia). A further two (North Carolina and New Hampshire) probably had Anti-Federalist majorities in the state, even though they sent Federalist delegates to Philadelphia.

Americans revere their Constitution, but rarely notice how simply *improbable* it is. The Americans wrote a constitution, and had it popularly ratified, in 1787–88. The French, in the heartland of the Enlightenment, failed to produce a popularly ratified constitution in 1789, again in 1791, again in 1793 and again in 1830. The Constitution of 1848 lasted only until 1851. The Canadians never submitted their founding 1867 constitution for popular ratification. On electoral evidence, it would have lost if they had. Their struggles through the 1980s to amend the constitution suggest that nothing has changed. The UK has never had a written constitutional text, and therefore has never had a ratification debate. The British–Irish Treaty of 1921 was debated in the Irish Parliament, but ratified only as a result of the pro-treaty party winning the ensuing civil war. At this writing, the Giscard constitution of the European Union seems likely to fail ratification. Only the Australians followed the US pattern, with their ratification process of 1892–1901 – over a century after the pioneer of popular ratification.

Riker asks why the rhetoric of the Federalists was more effective than that of their opponents. By content analysis of the huge volume of texts on both sides he derives what he calls the Dominance Principle and the Dispersion Principle. The former states that "when one side dominates in the volume of rhetorical appeals on a particular theme, the other side abandons appeals on that theme" and the latter that "when neither side dominates in volume, both sides abandon it" (Riker, 1996:6).

If both of these principles applied fully, then in equilibrium the two sides would totally talk past one another. They would reach this equilibrium – where no actor has a rational incentive to change strategy – once they had found out on which issues they could dominate in the volume of electoral appeals. After that, every possible issue would be raised either by precisely one side or by precisely zero sides. Riker's data (especially Riker, 1996: Table 8.4) show that the Dominance and Dispersion Principles, although suggestive, do not totally explain the rhetorical strategies of the two sides. One hostile reviewer of this "in some respects unfortunate book" concluded that "those interested in the substance of the debate . . . would do better to examine the primary sources for themselves". That would be the four volumes of Max Farrand's *Records* and the 18 of Jensen, Kaminski and Saladino's *Documentary History of the Ratification of the Constitution*, then? (Wall, 1998; Jensen *et al.*, 1976; Farrand *et al.*, 1966). This review so magnificently misunderstood Riker's whole point that it makes mine. A historian cannot possibly make a fair précis of 22 huge volumes of priceless primary records without either unsystematic or systematic sampling. Systematic sampling is better than unsystematic sampling. Riker's central insight is the same as the MRG's: that politicians largely talk past one another rather than debate with one another.

Budgeans and other sects

The Holy Grail is a reliable and valid measurement of party ideology. The Budgeans (as I shall call the MRG/CMP) are one of the leading groups of questers for it. As with any other object of religious reverence, though, many sects are engaged in the quest. There are Budgeans, Macdonaldites, Downsians, Laverites, Aydelottians, Pooleans, Rikerians, and doubtless more. Also as with any other religion, the sects sometimes fight among themselves with a passion that outsiders cannot always understand. To this outsider the sects appear much closer than they sometimes say to each other that they are.

The Budgean approach is that parties try to "own" issues. It is rational for a party to speak much on an issue where public opinion is on its side and little where it is not. It is very predictable that the UK Conservative manifesto for the 2005 General Election will contain more sentences on asylum, and fewer sentences on the NHS, than the Labour manifesto. In its stress on direction and saliency the MRG/CMP is closer to the directional theory of Macdonald and Rabinowitz (e.g. Macdonald and Rabinowitz, 1998) than to classic Downsian stress on parties' position in Euclidean space. Nevertheless, probably because of the sheer dominance of the Downsian model in empirical political science, most of the intellectual engagement of the MRG/CMP has been with Downsian political science. Indeed the attempt, reported above, to produce a summary statistic of the "leftness" of all parties in all countries in the MRG/CMP set seems driven by the wish to provide empirical data for Downsian analysis. That is certainly how other political scientists tend to approach MRG/CMP data.

Here, the main rivals to the MRG/CMP are the Laverites and the Aydelottians. The Laver expert survey approach is in one sense an offshoot from the MRG/CMP. Laver and associates contact academic specialists in the politics of a country and ask them to position the country's political parties in issue space (see e.g. Laver and Hunt, 1992; Laver, 2001). The spatial measures of parties' position produced by each method act as a reliability and validity check on the other method. As far as I am aware, there has been no case in which the Laver and MRG/CMP estimates of a party's location have been seriously at odds. Several chapters of Laver (2001) report impressive intercorrelations between different methods of coding the spatial location of parties across many democracies. As mentioned above, Garry (1999, 2001) compared expert survey generated policy positions to word frequency based computer coding generated positions and to MRG/CMP generated positions, with reassuring results.

The Budge method locates parties by the statements in their manifestos; the Laver method by whatever signals the country specialists hear when they respond to one of Laver's expert surveys. A third method, which I label the *Aydelotte method* in honour of its originator, estimates party positions in a legislature by examining roll-call votes there. The method has become an industry standard in the USA, but is only now spreading to other jurisdictions. In particular, nobody attempted to replicate Aydelotte's own work on the UK Parliament for 40 years after he started.

With co-authors I have analysed the Aydelotte programme elsewhere (especially McLean and Bustani 1999; McGillivray *et al.*, 2001). Beginning in the 1950s when computers barely existed, Aydelotte collected data on a heroic Richardsonian scale on the UK Parliament of 1841–47. A total of 815 MPs sat in that Parliament. Aydelotte collected up to 300 pieces of information about each member, including his vote on each of 114 (later expanded to 186) divisions. It was an ideal case for examining the dimensionality of legislative voting, because in 1846 the Tory Prime Minister, Sir

Robert Peel, proposed the Repeal of the Corn Laws, an action that flew in the face of the vested interest and ideology of his own party. Repeal was enacted on the votes of most of the opposition and a minority of the governing party, with two-thirds of Peel's own MPs opposing him.

Like the MRG/CMP, Aydelotte constructed a unidimensional measure of opinion, which he called the Big Scale. All of Aydelotte's 24 scales were derived by Guttman scaling. The Big Scale linked votes on the Corn Laws, Ireland, the relief of working-class distress and income tax, among other things. If Tory MPs are regarded as the "right" and their Whig and Liberal opponents as "left", then the right-wing cluster is opposition to working-class relief combined with support for the Corn Laws; for coercion in Ireland, and for the reintroduction of income tax in 1842. (The last of these might surprise Gordon Brown). The left-wing cluster is the opposite position on each of these. The formal similarity with the MRG/CMP method of left–right scaling is evident.

American political scientists in the 1960s, unlike those in Britain, were not scared of numbers. Therefore, the Iowa school founded by Aydelotte rapidly spread its wings into the US Congress. Because of weak party discipline, Congress was in any case a more suitable forum for roll-call analysis than the House of Commons (no subsequent Parliament having been as fluid as that of 1841). The culmination of the Iowa programme is therefore the work of Poole and Rosenthal (1997). Poole and Rosenthal's programme NOMINATE and its derivatives enable them to estimate the dimensionality of House voting in every Congress since the First (1789–91). NOMINATE is in turn a descendant of Aydelotte's Guttman scales.

According to Poole and Rosenthal, the dimensionality of voting in the House of Representatives is low. Except in the 1820s and the 1850s, most votes in the House scaled into a single dimension, from whatever might be labelled "left" in the context of the time to whatever might be labelled "right". The biggest exception was a chaotic period in the 1850s, in which the old party alignment was destroyed by the irruption of slavery – an issue which politicians had consciously tried to suppress in the interest of national harmony since the writing of the Constitution in 1787.

How many dimensions?

But how many issue dimensions are there really in the national politics of a typical democracy? The question is vital because if politics is unidimensional, a powerful existence theorem predicts that it will be stable. If politics is pluridimensional, an equally powerful impossibility theorem predicts chaos. The existence theorem is Duncan Black's Median Voter Theorem (MVT); the impossibility theorem is Kenneth Arrow's.

According to the MVT, the ideal platform of the median voter is a strongly stable, Condorcet-winning position: that is, it would defeat any other in a straight binary vote. Therefore, Downsian (which should really be called Blackian) political science predicts powerful convergence on the median voter. As the MVT is a valid piece of reasoning, any observed failure to converge must be due to some pathology. This may be:

- A defective electoral system. Example: plurality rule in the UK suppressed the median when Conservative and Labour ideology diverged symmetrically to right and to left in the 1980s.
- Imperfect information. Example: politicians who falsely believe that their issue position coincides with the electoral median, such as Joseph Chamberlain (1903); Barry Goldwater (1964); George McGovern (1972); Tony Benn (1982); Howard Dean (2004).
- Future-oriented campaigns. Perhaps some of the politicians just mentioned were trying to bring the electorate round to their position, rather than adapting their position to the electorate's. Tony Benn hailed the eight million Labour votes cast in the UK 1983 General Election as votes for socialism.
- Multidimensionality. Here we are in contested terrain. Most Downsians deny it exists. Rikerians insist that it does.

The MVT fails to generalise to more than one issue dimension. When Duncan Black discovered the failure of the MVT in two dimensions, he reports that it made him feel sick (Black *et al.*, 1991). Arrow (1951) proved that no ranking system could simultaneously satisfy transitivity, universal domain, the weak Pareto principle, independence of irrelevant alternatives and non-dictatorship. Black's condition of single-peakedness imposes a domain restriction. If single-peakedness holds, then so does the MVT (the converse is not necessarily true).

Arrow's theorem is powerful in itself, but it generates a set of striking corollaries known as the chaos theorems most associated with McKelvey (1976) and Schofield (1978). There are many technical discussions of the domain and range of these theorems and subsequent refinements, and this is not the place for them (cf. McLean, 2002 and references cited there). The theorems state that chaos is always possible. *Chaos* here means the property that majority-rule outcomes could wander anywhere in issue space – that there may be a global cycle among all possible outcomes.

Riker was the high priest of chaos. Having felt that political science lacked a deductive basis, he leapt on the work of McKelvey and Schofield, which he first saw in preprint in the mid-1970s, because he felt that it supplied that basis. If economics was the study of general equilibrium, then let political science be the study of general disequilibrium. Accordingly, Riker developed the new art, or science, of heresthetic(s) (McLean, 2002). Heresthetics is the art of political manipulation. In a series of stories that rapidly spread around the discipline, Riker celebrated the wiles of those who could manipulate the dimensionality of US politics to bring about unexpected outcomes such as the ratification of the Constitution in 1787 or Abraham Lincoln's victory (on less than 40 per cent of the vote) in the 1860 presidential election.

Riker therefore celebrates disequilibrium. All other schools, whether Downsian, Budgean or Aydelottian, prefer to examine low-dimensional equilibria. What do the schools have to teach one another?

Riker's more extreme claims of universal chaos are not sustainable. Chaos is always possible – the chaos theorems are valid pieces of reasoning – but rarely observed. This may be because institutions suppress chaos, so that voting in any one institution (say a Congressional committee) is one-dimensional, and the rules of aggregation prevent an issue settled in committee from being raised again on the floor of the whole House. Or it may be because opinion in mass democracies really can be validly fitted into a single issue dimension. Or, most controversially, it may be that opinion is truly multidimensional, but that the measuring instruments available to us give a false reading, showing it to be of lower dimensionality than it truly is. The rest of this chapter explores the last two alternatives.

As Converse (1964) canonically argued, nothing logically constrains mass opinions on one subject, given opinions on another. Budge *et al.*'s (2001) list of constituents of left-wing and right-wing issue space (Table 6.1) would disappoint both Robert Nozick and Gordon Brown. Nozick (1974) argued that economic liberalism implied social liberalism. He would have been disappointed to see "Free enterprise" and "Economic incentives" in the same column as "Traditional morality: positive" and "Social harmony". Brown (2003) makes "Protectionism: negative" definitive of his version of social democracy, while abandoning "Economic planning" and "Controlled economy". He argues that:

> A progressive government seeking a strong economy and fair society should not only support but positively enhance markets in the public interest....[I]t is not only unwise but impossible to shelter our goods and services markets by subsidies or by other forms of protectionism without incurring long-term damage.
>
> (Brown 2003: pp. 270–1)

As to "Peace", Benjamin Disraeli boasted at the end of the Congress of Berlin in 1878 that "Lord Salisbury and myself have brought you back peace – but a peace I hope with honour". Neville Chamberlain echoed Disraeli when he brought home the Munich Agreement of 1938: "I believe it is peace for our time . . . peace with honour". Do these examples mean that while "Peace" is left-wing, "Peace with honour" is right-wing: or that Salisbury, Disraeli and Chamberlain were closet leftists? Would Labour under Brown become a more right-wing party? Is *Anarchy, State and Utopia* a left-wing manifesto?

These are all rhetorical questions, not to be taken very seriously. Even as ruthlessly logical figures as Nozick and Brown do not insist that only one combination of attitudes to market and to state is logically consistent. Converse was right. Factor analysis of both popular opinion and party manifestos shows that there is usually a single principal dimension, and that attitudes (of people or parties) on one subject predict their attitudes on another. Politicians want low dimensionality to sell their package. Voters want low dimensionality for information saving. Similarly, Guttman's analysis of roll-calls, as in the Aydelotte and Poole–Rosenthal schools, also shows parliamentary voting to be of low dimensionality. The 1846 Repeal votes shattered the UK party system for a generation and hover like some distant echo of the Big Bang over every successive Conservative leader who "will not be another Peel" as numbers of them from Balfour to Howard have proclaimed. However, McLean and Bustani (1999), and Schonhardt-Bailey (1994) have found that they were not orthogonal to votes on other matters in the 1841–47 parliament.

And yet, and yet. Some methods suppress dimensionality. The pioneer expert survey by Mair and Castles (see Mair and Castles, 1997) invited respondents to classify parties on a left–right scale, even parties that did not define themselves by their leftness or rightness but by something else entirely. Laver and associates do not do this, but summarise their responses so as to give left–right spatial locations to all the UK parties including the nationalists in Wales, Scotland and Northern Ireland. A critic might argue that to evaluate Plaid Cymru, the SNP and Sinn Fein by their degree of leftness is to miss the essential point about each of them (Budge, 1999). As to roll-call analysis, McLean and Spirling (2003) found an interesting quirk when we applied Optimal Classification (OC), a cousin of Poole and Rosenthal's NOMINATE suite, to voting in the House of Commons.

> The rank ordering for the parliamentary session between the general elections of 1997 and 2001 did not accord to common understandings and anecdotal knowledge of which MPs should be properly considered of the left and those that should be properly considered of the right. Particularly, several left-wing Labour MPs are given scores placing them to the right (i.e. more conservative than) the bulk of the Labour party . . .

> [T]he Labour party MPs count in from the 'left' to position 428. The last 30 scaled positions include MPs such as Tam Dalyell (position 404), Robert Marshall-Andrews (405), Dennis Skinner (411), Jeremy Corbyn (416), Diane Abbott (420), Tony Benn (421), Ken Livingstone (422) and Bernie Grant (427). To be clear, OC classifies these MPs as some of the most right-wing of the Labour party. Ideologically then, they are the closest to the Conservatives. This seems odd. Commentators have not been slow to cite some or all of these individuals as Labour rebels, but not for the reason suggested by the attendant analysis. Rather, these

members are widely accepted as ideologically left-wing – disagreeing with the government on foundation-hospital NHS reform, the Iraq war and social-security/disability benefits to name but three policy areas. Yet here we observe them being placed right of their Prime Minister and, in fact, the entire Cabinet.

Who then were the most left wing members of the Commons (1997–2001) if it is not these individuals? Apparently, MPs Galbraith and Radice, with members Morris, Stevenson, Maxton and Ashton not far to their right.

(McLean and Spirling, 2003: 2, 4; data from Firth and Spirling, 2003)

McLean and Spirling go on to argue that OC (and therefore any Guttmanoid technique, because the whole family descends from Guttman scaling, as used by Aydelotte) gives misleading signals and spurious validity statistics. Almost every division in the Commons of 1997–2001 is perfectly consistent with the ranking of MPs listed above. The reliability of the scale is tremendous. Its validity is zero. The anomaly arises because sophisticated voting exists. In a party-controlled legislature, the governing party sets the agenda. Those who dislike its proposals can only vote against them or abstain. Typically, rebels on the Government side and members of the Opposition dislike the government's proposals for opposite reasons, but they vote in the same lobby. At least one of the groups casts a sophisticated vote. *Even if the underlying dimensionality is low,* the observed dimensionality, if correctly measured, would be higher. It is the measuring instrument that has failed, not reality. Where sophisticated voting exists, so does the scope for cycles. Therefore the Riker approach is not invalidated for legislatures. When Poole and Rosenthal report that the dimensionality of Congressional voting is low throughout the entire history of the USA, their measure may be under-recording the true dimensionality of voting. It certainly cannot pick up, and correctly assign, instance of sophisticated voting. And yet these instances are the mainspring of Riker's stories.

Analogously, it may be that the MRG/CMP is closer to capturing true underlying multidimensionality than is conventional Downsian spatial analysis, and yet that the willingness of the MRG/CMP to generate and discuss a left–right scale for their parties may have obscured this. I take as a starting point the Mannheim Manifesto, as I shall label Budge's (2001) typically feisty defence of the MRG/CMP coding procedure. Here Budge counter-attacks those who had expressed "doubts about the extent to which the one-position saliency codes typically used by the MRG/CMP really measure the kind of policy spaces assumed by classical theories of party competition and coalition formation" (Budge, 2001: 53). He quotes Stokes, (1966) on the primacy of "valence" over "position" issues, an approach which informed the US and UK election studies in the waves with which Stokes was concerned (e.g. Butler and Stokes, 1974), but has progressively given way to the now standard Downsian spatial view. Stokes was a pungent critic of the Downsian approach. Budge further quotes Robertson's (1976) analysis as showing that "parties do not directly oppose each other on an issue by issue basis" (p. 57). This discovery of Robertson's determined the MRG/CMP coding scheme, described above, to which it has stuck ever since.

Nevertheless, the Budgeans compromise with the Downsians to the extent of deriving a left–right scale from an underlying dataset that has Stokes' characteristics of saliency and valency. Parties make statements about things that are salient to them, and/or to the voters to whom they hope to appeal. Most of those statements are univalent. Few party manifestos promise lawlessness and disorder, social disharmony, war or the contraction of social services. Actually, this finding is perfectly consistent with Downsianism. The median voter in all democracies is almost certainly at the univalent position: in favour of law, order, social harmony, peace and the expansion of social services (well, some of them).

The left–right scale derived from the univalent sentences of Table 6.1 is displayed country by country by Budge and Klingemann (2001). They argue that it shows some real facts, consistent with results from other traditions. As an observer would expect, the US Republican position moves sharply to the right in 1964 and from 1980 to 1988; the Democratic position moves sharply left in 1972 and sharply right in 1992. (The US manifestos analysed are those for the presidential, not the congressional, campaign.) But the results for the two most interesting Westminster regimes are more mixed. For the UK, Budge and Klingemann show Labour as moving to the right of the Liberal Democrats for 1997. For New Zealand their graph actually has Labour moving *left* in 1984 and 1987, the two elections which hailed a rightward transformation of New Zealand politics more extreme than anything that has happened in any other Westminster regime since the Repeal of the Corn Laws (Nagel, 1998). In the British case their graph captures a partial truth but in a perhaps misleading way. In the New Zealand case it obscures more than it clarifies.

Undoubtedly, the British Labour Party stopped talking in 1997 about many of the things in the left-hand column of Table 6.1, and talked for the first time in its history about some of the things in the right-hand column. Meanwhile, I assume that the British Liberals' *relative* use of those sentences did not change (and recall that it is relative use that matters most). Furthermore the two intellectual leaders of "New" Labour, Tony Blair and Gordon Brown, were consciously developing a more market-friendly, less producer-group oriented, ideology. But it is hard to say that Gordon Brown (in particular) is more right-wing than Hugh Gaitskell or Jim Callaghan. In Brown (2003) and other writings, he is developing a new ideology of state and market: essentially that the two roles of the state are to redistribute to the poor and to intervene in market failure, such as collusion among capitalists or patients' ignorance of their medical condition. In contrast to vacuities about the Third Way that have emanated from some Blairite advisors, this is gritty and novel policy making. Yet much of it is too subtle to be caught in manifesto coding. For instance, the Brownite redistribution to the poor has been a remarkable achievement of the 1997 and 2001 Labour administrations, yet it is one about which they have been almost totally silent. The reason is probably that the lowest two deciles of the income distribution include people who are socially excluded; liable to be stigmatised (Welfare Scroungers!! Bogus Asylum Seekers!!!! Slovakian Gipsies!!!! Vandals!!!!! Teenage Mothers!!!!!!), and not particularly likely to vote, for Labour or any other party. They are not median voters. Budgean principles explain why Labour makes no mention of its generosity to the bottom deciles in its manifestos. But therefore they fail to capture how left-wing the party is, in this dimension.

And then there is free trade. To be mischievous, one might say that the most left-wing Labour Chancellor before Brown was Philip Snowden (Chancellor in 1924 and from 1929 until his break with Labour in 1931). Brown and Snowden shared the view, which too many of the Labour Chancellors in between have failed to share, that free trade is better for the British working class than protectionism. The overwhelming weight of economic theory and evidence since Ricardo is with them. Brown adds, what is certainly correct, that free trade is the best thing for the poor of the Third World. The best thing, in at least the following sense: that the best thing that governments of the rich world can do for them is to remove the outrageous protection of farm produce, steel and other commodities where the comparative advantage lies with the South but the political clout with the North. Brown may not be the most left-wing Chancellor since Lloyd George, but he is the most effective left-wing Chancellor since Lloyd George.

The New Zealand case maybe shows up a more direct problem with the MRG/CMP method. Nagel (1998) explains the transformation there by arguing that the Labour leaders David Lange and Roger Douglas opened up a new issue dimension. In the dimension of social liberalism, they took a distinctively "left" or "liberal" position on nuclear weapons, the environment and Maori land rights. This package appealed to post-materialist Labour activists, horrified by the diagonally opposite policy platform (economically welfarist and socially conservative) of the National Party's dominant incumbent Robert Muldoon. Hence they did not notice, or even (ahead of Labour's coming to power) did not care about Labour's New Right economic policies. The MRG methodology obscures this heresthetical shift. It reports New Zealand Labour as having shifted in a minor way in one dimension, where it actually shifted tectonically in two.

Although there are thus good reasons for caution about the dimensionality of politics in a democracy, I end this chapter as I started by honouring the achievements of the Comparative Manifesto Project. Political science would be much the poorer without it.

References

Arrow, K. (1951) *Social Choice and Individual Values* (New York: Wiley).

Berrington, H.B. (1973) *Backbench Opinion in the House of Commons 1945–55* (Oxford: Pergamon).

Black, D., I. McLean and D. Squires, (1991) "Arrow's work and the normative theory of committees", *Journal of Theoretical Politics* 3: 259–275.

Brown, G. (2003) "State and Market: Towards a Public Interest Test", *Political Quarterly* 74:3, 266–284.

Budge, I. (1999) "Expert Judgements of Party Policy Positions: Uses and Limitations in Political Research", University of Essex, Department of Government, Working Paper 140.

Budge, I. (2001) "Validating the Manifesto Group Approach: Theoretical Assumptions and Empirical Confirmations", in M. Laver (ed.) *Estimating the Policy Positions of Political Actors* (London: Routledge), pp. 50–65.

Budge, I. and J. Bara, (2001) "Content analysis and political texts", in I. Budge, H.-D. Klingemann, A. Volkens, J. Bara and E. Tanenbaum (eds) *Mapping Policy Preferences: Estimates for Parties, Electors, and Governments 1945–1998* (Oxford: Oxford University Press), pp. 1–16.

Budge, I. and H.-D. Klingemann, (2001) "Finally! Comparative Over-time Mapping of Party Policy Movement", in I. Budge, H.-D. Klingemann, A. Volkens, J. Bara and E. Tanenbaum (eds) *Mapping Policy Preferences: Estimates for Parties, Electors, and Governments 1945–1998* (Oxford: Oxford University Press), pp. 21–50.

Budge, I., H.-D. Klingemann, A. Volkens, J. Bara and E. Tanenbaum (eds) (2001) *Mapping Policy Preferences: estimates for parties, electors, and governments 1945–1998* (Oxford: Oxford University Press).

Butler, D.E. and D. Stokes, (1974) *Political change in Britain* 2nd edn. (London: Macmillan).

Converse, P. (1964) "The Nature of Belief Systems in Mass Publics", in D. Apter (ed.) *Ideology and Discontent* (New York: Free Press), pp. 206–261.

Farrand, M. (1966) *The Records of the Federal Convention of 1787*, revised edn, 4 vols (New Haven: Yale University Press).

Finer, S.E., H.B. Berrington and D. Bartholomew (1961) *Backbench Opinion in the House of Commons 1955–59* (Oxford: Pergamon).

Firth, D. and A. Spirling, (2003) *Parliamentary Division Data*, MS, Nuffield College, Oxford.

Garry, J. (1999) "Using Computer-Coded Content Analysis of German and Norwegian Election Manifestos to Estimate Party Policy Positions", Paper for Mannheim ECPR 1999 Panel – Estimating the Policy Positions of Political Actors.

Garry J. (2001) "The Computer Coding of Political Texts: Results from Britain, Germany, Ireland and Norway", in M. Laver (ed.) *Estimating the Policy Positions of Political Actors* (London: Routledge), pp. 183–192.

Jensen, M., J. Kaminski and G. Saladino (1976) *The Documentary History of the Ratification of the Constitution*, 18 vols (Madison, WI: State Historical Society of Wisconsin).

Laver, M. (ed.) (2001) *Estimating the Policy Positions of Political Actors* (London: Routlege).

Laver, M. and B. Hunt, (1992) *Policy and Party Competition* (London: Routledge).

McDonald, M.D. and S.M. Mendes (2001) "The policy space of party manifestos", in M. Laver (ed.) *Estimating the Policy Positions of Political Actors* (London: Routledge), pp. 90–114.

Macdonald, S.E and G. Rabinowitz (1998) "Solving the Paradox of Nonconvergence: Valence, Position, and Direction in Democratic Politics", *Electoral Studies* 17:3, 281–300.

McGillivray, F., I. McLean, R. Pahre and C. Schonhardt-Bailey (2001) *International Trade and Political Institutions: Instituting Trade in the Long Nineteenth Century* (Cheltenham: Edward Elgar).

McKelvey, R.D. (1976) "Intransitivities in Multidimensional Voting Models and Some Implications for Agenda Control", *Journal of Economic Theory* 12: 472–482.

McLean, I. (1995) "Backbench opinion revisited", in P. Jones (ed.) *Party, Parliament, and Personality: Essays Presented to Hugh Berrington* (London: Routledge), pp. 121–140.

McLean, I. (2002) "William H. Riker and the Invention of Heresthetic(s)", *British Journal of Poltiical Science* 32:3, 535–558.

McLean, I. and C. Bustani (1999) "Irish Potatoes and British Politics: Interests, Ideology, Heresthetic, and the Repeal of the Corn Laws ", *Political Studies* 47: 817–836.

McLean, I. and A. Spirling (2003) "UK OC OK? A Note on Interpreting Optimal Classification Scoring for the United Kingdom", Nuffield College, Working Papers in Politics, 2003 W-9.

Mair, P. and F. Castles (1997) "Revisiting Expert Judgements", *European Journal of Political Research* 31, pp. 150–157.

Nagel, Jack H. (1998) "Social Choice in a Pluralitarian Democracy: The Politics of Market Liberalization in New Zealand", *British Journal of Political Science* 28: 223–265.

Nicholson, M (1999) "Lewis Fry Richardson and the Study of the Causes of War", *British Journal of Political Science* 29: 541–563.

Nozick, R. (1974) *Anarchy, State and Utopia* (Oxford: Basil Blackwell).

Poole, K.T. and H. Rosenthal (1997) *Congress: a Political-Economic History of Roll Call Voting* (New York: Oxford University Press).

Riker, William H. (edited by R.L. Calvert, J. Mueller and R.K. Wilson) (1996) *The Strategy of Rhetoric: Campaigning for the American Constitution* (New Haven, CT: Yale University Press).

Robertson, D.B. (1976) *A Theory of Party Competition* (London: Wiley).

Schofield, N. (1978) "Instability of Simple Dynamic Games", *Review of Economic Studies* 45: 575–594.

Russett, Bruce (1994) *Grasping the Democratic Peace: Principles for a Post-Cold War World* (Princeton, NJ: Princeton University Press).

Schonhardt-Bailey, C. (1994) "Linking Constituency Interests to Legislative Voting Behaviour: The Role of District Economic and Electoral Composition in the Repeal of the Corn Laws", *Parliamentary History* 13: 86–118.

Stokes, D. (1966) "Spatial models of party competition", in A. Campbell, P. Converse, W. Miller and D. Stokes (eds), *Elections and the Political Order* (New York: Wiley), pp. 161–179.

Sutherland, I. (ed.) (1993) *Collected Papers of Lewis Fry Richardson vol. 2: Quantitative Psychology and Studies of Conflict* (Cambridge: Cambridge University Press).

Volkens, A. (2001) "Manifesto Research since 1979: From Reliability to Validity", in M. Laver (ed.) *Estimating the Policy Positions of Political Actors* (London: Routledge), pp. 33–49.

Wall, F. (1998) "Review of Riker (1996)", *Canadian Journal of Political Science* 31: 389–390.

7   Occam no, Archimedes yes

Jack H. Nagel

Introduction

In the debate over the dimensionality of political issue spaces, two great motives impel most scholars toward a unidimensional conception. One is Occamite; the other, Archimedean.

The Occamite motive is empirical. As political scientists, we have absorbed – practically along with our mothers' milk – the conviction that parsimony ranks high among virtues. If one can explain most of the variance in terms of just one dimension – the conventional left–right spectrum – why complicate one's model with lesser issues?

The Archimedean motive is normative. As would-be constitutional engineers, we need an evaluative standpoint that enables us to judge the performance of institutions – and perhaps even to move the world by designing new constitutions or recommending reforms in old ones. Unidimensional models furnish that criterion. When preferences are arrayed along one dimension, the outcome most preferred by the median voter is the Condorcet winner – the option that can defeat all others in pairwise voting. The median-voter standard therefore provides a widely accepted test of whether majority rule has been achieved.

Among its many advantages as a method for locating political parties ideologically, the content analysis of manifestos developed by Ian Budge and his collaborators imposes no built-in bias toward the detection of just one issue dimension. In that respect, as in several others, it compares favourably with the two main alternatives, surveys eliciting experts' judgements and analyses of roll-call votes.[1] Nevertheless, the trajectory of Budge's thought follows the familiar Occamite and Archimedean pulls toward a one-dimensional destination.

In *Mapping Policy Preferences*, the invaluable definitive book on the MRG/CMP programme, Budge and Bara (2001: 58–62) note that early factor analyses of manifesto data produced solutions with two, three, five and even 20 dimensions (e.g. Budge *et al.*, 1987). However, when spaces of higher and lower dimensionality were systematically compared (Laver and Budge, 1992), the only ones generalizable across ten countries were the unidimensional left–right representation and an exceedingly complex 20-dimensional space. In tests of 'a whole range of theories', the single dimension performed equally as well as the 20-dimensional version.[2] Following the lead of Budge and Bara (2001: 59), who 'on grounds of parsimony prefer the simpler representation', over the past decade CMP research and publications have increasingly focused on the left–right scale, which Budge and Klingemann (2001: 19) hail as the 'crowning achievement of the Manifesto Research Project'.

Whether or not parsimony was the only empirical reason for adopting a unidimensional vision (it would be unparsimonious to claim otherwise), Budge has recently exploited the normative value of a one-dimensional conception (McDonald *et al.*, 2004). By positing conformity to the wishes of the median voter as the test for majority rule, he and his co-authors redefine mandate theory so that it can be extended from the Westminster systems that Arend Lijphart (1984, 1999) (mis)names 'majoritarian' to all parliamentary democracies. If the left–right position of the pivotal median party in parliament corresponds to the left–right position of the median voter in the electorate, then elections have presumably empowered the median voter, and the legislature can be said to satisfy the median mandate. Using manifesto data to apply that test to the performance of democracies in 1949–95, McDonald *et al.* find that legislatures elected by proportional representation satisfy the median mandate more consistently than do those elected by plurality from single-member districts (first-past-the-post).[3] This is a devastating result, because, along with similar findings by Powell (2000), it hoists single-member plurality with its own petard, the majoritarian justification.

For many scholars, the Occamite and Archimedean motives became fused and intensfied because of a challenge that the late William Riker (1982) hurled at democratic theory more than two decades ago. He built on the 'chaos theorems' of the 1970s, which showed that when political competition occurs in a space of two or more dimensions, there usually is no majority-rule equilibrium – in pairwise voting, any outcome can be defeated by some other combination of positions across the multiple dimensions. Extrapolating provocatively from those mathematical results, Riker made two claims, one empirical and the other normative: empirically, he contended that politics typically *is* multi-dimensional, because losing politicians have an incentive to activate and exploit cross-cutting issues in order to break up previously winning majorities. Combined with the chaos theorems, Riker argued, that generalization fatally undermines the version of democratic theory that he labelled 'populism' – the belief that major policies in a democracy should, and under the right institutions, *can* reflect the will of the majority of the people. If all majorities are fundamentally arbitrary and temporary, there can be no substantive content or moral force to notions of majority rule and popular will. 'Populism fails, not because it is morally wrong, but merely because it is empty' (Riker, 1982: 239).

Obviously, Budge's theory of the median mandate is an example of populism in Riker's sense. Because they are well aware of the Rikerian argument, Budge and his collaborators take pains to justify their assumption that politicians and voters are oriented to a shared, unidimensional policy space. Unlike Riker's, Budge's texts are never dogmatic, but they vary in the strength of their claims. While denying any 'need to debate the "true" dimensionality of the space', Budge and Bara (2001: 59, 62) nevertheless conclude, 'The compelling reasons for representing policy space as a unidimensional Left-Right continuum should be accepted until the latter can be conclusively shown to be untenable.' McDonald *et al.* (2004: 13), on the other hand, adopt a more 'relaxed tone on unidimensionality', requiring only that 'the basic ordering of preferences ... be characterized reasonably well as spread along the well-known left–right continuum'.

As the last part of this chapter will show, I am close to agreement with the McDonald *et al.* statement. Believing, however, that readers always take away the most extreme lines, I intend to take up the cudgels against the mindset reflected in the quotation from Budge and Bara. I shall begin with a stark statement of my own thesis: elsewhere (Nagel 2001a), I have contended that Riker was empirically right, but normatively wrong. If so, then *Budge is empirically wrong, but normatively right.*

The remainder of the chapter will consist of two sections, one devoted to each part of that thesis. The argument is preliminary and far from systematic. It will take the form of a series of claims, together with enough support to establish, so I hope, their plausibility – but that is for others to judge.

Why one dimension is insufficient to explain politics

As the title of this section signals, I don't actually want to insist on the stark version of my indictment. 'Insufficient' is not the same thing as 'wrong' *tout court*. Budge and his colleagues show persuasively that scholars, as well as popular pundits, can interpret most party competition in most democracies most of the time using the left–right spectrum. I also concede with admiration that their left–right scale postdicts historical judgements about party movements remarkably well (though not perfectly). These data are better than anything else we have, and they provide an invaluable resource for anyone who wants to see how far one get with a one-dimensional explanation.[4] There's a lot of mileage in them, but not enough! I differ from Budge and his associates in believing that explanations that stop with the left–right scale are often, perhaps even usually, insufficient.

This disagreement may result from the criteria we apply. Budge's tests are statistical, whether to develop cross-national comparisons or generalizations about single countries (Laver and Budge, 1992). My goal is to achieve insightful understanding of party strategies, election outcomes and public policies within individual countries for single elections or, even better, for a series of elections in a country's political history. Although such insight may require thick idiographic research and detailed narratives, it should not be atheoretical. I shall argue that the theory provided by multidimensional issue analysis is especially helpful and needed for five reasons, beginning with those that are most nearly compatible with the unidimensional view, and then moving to more fundamental challenges.

Even if voters are predisposed to choose within a unidimensional space, they may find it necessary to resort to other dimensions

Assume that voters wish to choose between two parties according to the basic Downsian model – preferring the party that takes a position closest to their ideal points on a unidimensional line, and assume also that the MRG/CMP left–right scale represents that space.

1   If the parties converge fully, their left–right ideologies are indistinguishable, so *all* voters must resort to some other test in order to make a choice. That criterion may be a valence attribute not directly tied to policy positions, such as the candidates' competence, personal morality or likability. It may, however, be some other issue, independent of the Left–Right spectrum, that can be characterized in positional terms as a 'dimension'.

2   Similarly, if the parties do not converge completely, but take positions some distance apart, then *some* voters – those half-way between the two parties – must decide according to some other test, which again may be an orthogonal issue. In both cases, the new dimension influences voters' choices lexicographically, coming into play only when they are unable to decide using left–right positions.

Cross-cutting issues that are small statistically may be crucial politically

Suppose that in an electorate of 101 voters, 100 decide according to parties' left–right positions, 50 opting for each party, while just one person votes on the basis of some other issue. To explain the outcome, it is essential to include the second issue, because it determined a crucial vote. *We must not equate political importance with statistical significance.*

In the 1996 US presidential election, Bill Clinton and his consigliere Dick Morris (Morris, 1999) developed into an art form the identification and espousal of such small issues – framed in a non-ideological way, appealing across party lines and to independents, each influencing relatively few voters but with the potential in the aggregate to swing a close election. One of those issues that helped Clinton – the question of research using human embryonic stem cells – also played a prominent role in the 2004 election. Reversing Clinton's policy, President George W. Bush imposed restrictions on the use of federal funds for stem-cell research. His stance was risky for Republicans because the diseases that such research might help cure – including diabetes, Parkinson's and Alzheimer's – strike families without regard to ideology or partisanship. In May 2004, Nancy Reagan spoke out publicly in opposition to the President's position. She pleaded for lifting the ban so that others might be spared the Alzheimer's disease that had taken her husband 'to a distant place where I can no longer reach him'.[5] Subsequently, at the Democratic National Convention, the former President's son, Ron Reagan, gave a featured address emphasizing the stem-cell issue. Nevertheless, the stem-cell debate did not swing the 2004 election to Democrat John Kerry. Instead, the outcome hinged on 'values' positions identified with the political right, such as a ban on gay marriage. Despite the conventional assimilation of such issues into the left–right spectrum, I contend that it is too simplistic to understand them in purely undimensional terms, for the reason to be developed next.

Unidimensional explanations of voters' choices do not take saliency theory seriously enough

Saliency theory was the key that enabled the Manifesto Research Group to convert simple counts into scalar positions. Thanks to the work of Budge and his co-authors, it is now widely recognized that parties compete mostly by 'talking past each other', selectively emphasizing issues on which they think they have the advantage. But if parties present themselves in that way, how do voters choose between (or among) them? Voters do not actually decide in the way that literal-minded application of the MRG/CMP scale to their choices might seem to imply – by summing across dozens of 'left' and 'right' statements, distilling them into a single score, and then comparing that score to one's 'own' position on the same left–right scale. Perhaps there are voters who do something like that – but I am sure they are a minority even within the chattering classes.

Instead, saliency is a two-way street, depending not only on the strategies of the parties but also on the prominence of issues in voters' minds. Consistent with Budge and Farlie (1983), I suggest that voters typically attend to only a few issues, the saliency of which can vary over time, and then choose the candidate or party that more successfully emphasizes the issue(s) most salient in the voter's own mind – whether because of the party's propaganda, exogenous events or the voter's personal predilections. Often, such issues will be components of the left–right scale. If so, it might be said that the party has moved toward the voter along that scale, or vice versa; but such an interpretation explains too little and hides too much. To take a commonplace example, suppose that many voters favour the party of the right when their country is menaced by foreign enemies. Should we infer that those voters have moved to the right (as opposed to choosing the party of the right)? Their preferred position on other components of the scale, such as economic policy, may not have changed at all – a possibility that is important to remember, both to avoid inferring too much (empirically and normatively) from shifts in votes and to understand how opposite flows might occur as a result of fluctuations in salience, without any mass ideological conversion.

In the preceding example, politicians are not the prime movers. Instead, their fortunes depend on salience in the minds of voters, who in turn respond to external events. However, seeing the Budge left–right spectrum as fundamentally multidimensional also enables us to appreciate opportunities for heresthetic manoeuvre of the kind that Riker emphasized. For decades now, many analysts of US politics have distinguished two dimensions of liberalism-conservatism – economic and cultural (or social).[6] The two are collapsed in the MRG left–right scale, and they do indeed correlate, but the constraint is far from absolute, especially at the mass level. Bill Clinton exploited the resulting room for manoeuvre by extolling 'people who work hard and play by the rules' and accepting welfare reform (thus embracing traditional social values), while also dramatically expanding the Earned Income Tax Credit (a repackaged version of the negative income tax, a policy that helped place George McGovern far to the left in 1972). The two stands would neutralize each other in the MRG method, putting Clinton in the centre, which agrees with a widespread perception; but we get more insight by recognizing that conservatism of one sort made possible liberalism of another. Moreover, along with his more widely-remarked personal rapport with blacks, policies like the Earned Income Tax Credit help explain – in a way that a simple 'centrist' characterization cannot – why Clinton enjoyed such enthusiastic and near-unanimous support from African-Americans despite ending 'welfare as we know it'.

Both of Clinton's moves probably accorded with majority values, but of two different majorities that only partly overlap. In other situations, exploiting variations in the salience of different policies across groups can result in rule by a combination of minorities. I have argued elsewhere (Nagel, 1998) that a good example of this phenomenon is provided by New Zealand during its period of radical economic liberalization in the 1980s. Besides leftist policies on non-economic social and foreign-policy issues (noted by Iain McLean elsewhere in this volume), the Labour government of 1984–90 enacted an economic programme combining wide-ranging radical free-market reforms, policies favoured by trade unions (restoration of compulsory unionism, continuation of the national wage-setting system, substantial wage hikes), and maintenance of generous welfare-state benefits for the poor. The free-market reforms enabled the party to attract a pivotal bloc of business and professional people who were rebelling against the interventionist economic policies of the otherwise rightist National Party. Meanwhile, the two 'left' economic policies enabled the party to cling to support from its traditional base among trade unions and the poor. Those two old Labour groups were deeply unhappy about most of the free-market reforms, while the party's trade union and welfare-state policies were on the hit list of the liberalizers if they could have had their way entirely (as they soon did). Over the electorate as a whole, a majority would surely have rejected key policies enacted for each part of the triad if given a chance to vote on them one at a time.

Unidimensionality hides too much about the dynamics of party support

In the New Zealand example, the MRG characterization of the Labour Party's programme as moderately centre-left and the convergence toward it of the National Party in 1990 (Budge and Klingemann, 2001: 27) would suggest a period of basic political tranquillity and moderate policy change.[7] In contrast, multidimensional social-choice theory better explains the instability that actually characterized this period, including open warfare within the Labour cabinet during its second term, desertion of the party by many voters from all three economic groups (as well as from the non-economic left) and victory in 1990 for the National Party, which – having recaptured its free-market defectors – proceeded to complete their right-wing economic revolution with harsh cutbacks in benefits and a draconian anti-union policy.

On the larger stage of the United States, the watershed election of 1964 similarly shows how a unidimensional conception obscures political dynamics. Promising to offer 'a choice, not an echo', Barry Goldwater, the Republican candidate, moved his party sharply to the right, as the MRG scaling duly records (Budge and Klingemann, 2001: 25). Goldwater's landslide loss to Lyndon Johnson is usually taken as a classic confirmation of Downsian theory. As a first approximation, that is correct, but stopping the analysis there gives no clue about subsequent developments. Goldwater's bundle of conservative policies included one element, his policy on racial integration, that reversed his party's historic position. Ever since its founding, the party of Lincoln had been positioned as more sympathetic to African-Americans than the Democrats (which, admittedly, wasn't saying much from 1876 until the mid-twentieth century). Goldwater leapfrogged over the Democrats on race by endorsing states' rights at a time when Southern states were engaged in all-out resistance to integrationist policies imposed by Federal courts and Congress. As a result, besides his own Arizona, Goldwater carried only the Deep South states of Alabama, Georgia, Louisiana, Mississippi and South Carolina. Their defection from the Democrats encouraged the Republicans' subsequent Southern Strategy. As racial politics lost the moral clarity of the mid-1960s, the Republicans staked out popular positions consistently to the right of the Democrats on race-linked issues such as law and order, school bussing, affirmative action and welfare dependence. Aided by the shift of population to the Sunbelt (including the migration of the Bush clan from Connecticut to Texas and Florida), the strategy paid off handsomely over the next 40 years, with victories in seven of ten presidential elections and House majorities from 1994 onwards. As a result, the electoral map of the US became nearly the reverse of what it had once been. Comparing the two close elections of 1916 and 2004, 41 of 48 states voted for different parties; and the previously Democratic Solid South is now nearly as solid for the Republicans. These changes cannot be understood solely in terms of movements on an aggregate left–right dimension. The distinguishable role of race must be part of the story.

Unidimensionality misses most of the really big stories

Both of the preceding cases exemplify major political changes. In general, dramatic shifts in power and policy are likely to involve multiple issue dimensions for either or both of two reasons: first, as in the New Zealand example, the recombination of policies across relatively independent dimensions can enable a minority that espouses radical policies to dominate an issue even though it has not done (and might never be able to do) the hard, patient work of persuasion needed to shift the political centre to its own position. Second, the most severe political convulsions often result from emergence onto the agenda of previously suppressed dimensions of conflict. Race has played that role twice in American history, during the 1960s and a century earlier, when the struggle over extension of slavery precipitated the Civil War and ushered in a 72-year era of Republican dominance, ending a 60-year period when Democrats had been similarly ascendant.

In arguing for a multidimensional conception of politics, Riker developed as his primary example Abraham Lincoln's use of the free-soil issue to destroy the antebellum Democratic majority. In a recent, exhaustively researched book, Gerry Mackie (2003) challenges two elements of the Riker thesis – that Lincoln and the Republicans heresthetically manipulated the slavery issue, and that Lincoln won because of a voting cycle in the election of 1860. Rather than a cycle in two dimensions, Mackie contends, politics had become organized by a new unidimensional alignment along sectional lines. On that dimension, Lincoln's Democratic opponent, Stephen Douglas, was the Condorcet winner (median choice), but the four-candidate contest gave the Electoral College victory to Lincoln, who won only 39.8 per cent of the popular vote. However, Mackie's account does not challenge the central point of the Riker thesis – that the Republican victory followed emergence to the fore of a distinct dimension of conflict, one that previously had been secondary because political leaders, helped by institutions designed for the purpose, succeeded in keeping it off the agenda most of the time before 1860.

In one-dimensional competition, a party that changes its programme radically is likely to lose unless a corresponding shift in the median has already occurred or occurs simultaneously. The two most likely causes of such a large movement in preferences are (a) dramatic changes in the demographic composition of the electorate or (b) exogenous shocks that strongly affect public opinion. Historical developments that would seem to fit those patterns are, respectively, the enfranchisement of the working class, accounting for the rise of socialist and labour parties, and the Great Depression, explaining the adoption of welfare-state policies. On closer examination, however, cross-cutting issues played a crucial role in celebrated instances of each.

1 In a well-known passage, Downs (1957: 128–129) explains how the Labour Party supplanted the Liberals in Britain:

> Before 1900, there were two major British parties, the Liberals ... and the Tories. ... They were under the usual two-party pressure to converge. However, the enfranchisement of the working class in the late nineteenth century had shifted the center of the voter distribution far to the left of its old position. And the Liberal Party, even after it moved to the left, was to the right of the new center of gravity, although it was the more left of the two parties. The founders of the Labour Party correctly guessed that they could out-flank the Liberals by forming a new party ... to the left of the latter, which they did. This trapped the Liberals between the two modes of the electorate, and their support rapidly diminished to insignificant size.

Downs' stylized account ignores that fact that the Liberals had adapted very well to the expanded electorate, controlling government through three elections in 1906 and 1910, and keeping Labour in a subordinate position. The proximate cause of their downfall was the First World War, which divided the party over orthogonal issues such as conscription, provided the occasion for a fatal power struggle between Asquith and Lloyd George, and made the latter a prime minister dependent on Tory support (Searle, 1992; Sykes, 1997). If the First World War and the Asquith–Lloyd George split had never occurred, would the Liberals have remained a major party, as did their Canadian and Australian namesakes? No one knows, but Downs' simplified history is clearly much too one-dimensional.

2 In Sweden, the Depression brought to power the Social Democratic Party, which built the world's model welfare state. The Social Democrats led in the 1932 election, but did not win a majority of seats. They formed a minority government, but required help from members of the non-socialist majority to pass their 'crisis policy', which would implement the party's new economic theories. They won the necessary votes not by

moving back to the centre, but instead by striking a deal on another dimension with the Agrarian Party, who were 'persuaded to support Social Democratic unemployment policy, and in exchange the Social Democrats abandoned their traditional free-trade stance and adopted a protectionist position on the farm issue' (Lewin, 1988: 140).[8] That classic logroll opened the way to an economic programme that proved to be both successful and popular, securing for the Social Democrats a hegemonic position that has lasted more than 70 years.[9]

Why the median test is nevertheless a good standard for political evaluation

If there are so many reasons for rejecting the Occamite motive for adopting a unidimensional conception of politics, how can one defend its normative use in providing an Archimedean standpoint for judgement, the median test? Doesn't that run afoul of Riker's objection that multidimensionality entails cycles, the absence of a Condorcet winner and the meaninglessness of majority rule? I don't agree, for reasons that I'll now propose and briefly discuss.

The left–right median remains a valid test if other dimensions enter lexicographically

If voters resort to other issues only because parties' positions leave them unable to decide on left–right grounds – either because parties have converged or because they are equidistant from centrist voters – then majority rule unequivocally demands an outcome at the left–right median. (Outcomes on any other issue considered separately may or may not be majoritarian.) Because the left–right dimension enters voters' decision processes before all others, any party position that differs from the median can be defeated by it. Thus outcomes that depart from the left–right median must be due to defects in the electoral or party system, which the median mandate test will properly detect and condemn. For example, the frequent failure of Westminster systems to satisfy the median test (Powell, 2000; McDonald *et al.*, 2004) can be explained by the combination of plurality rule and multiparty electoral politics.

The median remains a valid test in some instances where the main use of multidimensionality is to develop dynamic insights

In the example of the 1964 US election, I do not doubt that Goldwater's position generally was far from the left–right median (and also that his specific stand on civil rights did not accord with majority preferences at that time). Thus I see no problem in applying the median mandate test to judge that the system worked properly in electing Lyndon Johnson (setting aside the fact that he soon betrayed the foreign policy component of his programme by going to war in Vietnam). The value of pointing to the race dimension is to highlight Goldwater's departure from the historic position of his party and the process of voter alignment his stand set in motion, as well as to foreshadow the subsequent success of the Southern strategy, as the race issue evolved and Republicans developed subtler ways to exploit it. In the same vein, it may be that the two-dimensional Swedish logroll of 1933 enabled the government to enact an economic programme that did not yet accord with median preferences. However, experience with that policy in practice soon shifted preferences, as is indicated by the Social Democrats' later successes. In 1936, unlike 1932, they occupied the median position by winning, in combination with parties to their left, an absolute majority of votes and seats; and in 1940, they won an absolute majority unaided (Mackie and Rose, 1991).

A median test (albeit it on a different scale) remains valid when another dimension supplants the conventional left–right spectrum

If, like Lincoln's Republicans, a party succeeds in the ultimate heresthetic manoeuvre – replacing a dominant dimension on which it loses with a new dominant dimension on which it wins – then a median test can be applied, provided that one uses the the new unidimensional spectrum, rather than the old one. That is essentially Mackie's argument about 1860 (although, if he is right, Lincoln's plurality victory in that year failed to satisfy the median mandate). Such rotations of the policy space will be rare events, but analysts using the MRG left–right scale should be alert to the possibility. A polity that departs from the conventional left–right median may have decided to march to a different drummer.

When politics is fully multidimensional, the median on each dimension remains a plausible, if not irrefutable, standard

Finally, suppose that a large proportion of voters make their choices within a multidimensional space, in either of two senses – most people evaluate more than one dimension before deciding how to vote, or most people consider only one dimension but collectively divide into groups that respond to distinctly different issues. In some of these cases, MRG analysis of party programmes will conceal the existence of multiple dimensions, because issues that I contend are, or can be, independent are forced into the left–right scale – for example, economic versus cultural liberalism/conservatism, or the three distinct elements of economic policy in 1980s New Zealand. In other cases, when a second dimension involves policies not coded into the left–right dimension, manifesto analysis will readily identify it – for example, the language dimension in Belgium or Canada.

If there are multiple dimensions (whether or not manifesto analysis recognizes them), the possibility arises that minorities rule on one or more, perhaps all, dimensions in a pattern of implicit or explicit vote trades. From the viewpoint of democratic theory, are such outcomes always undesirable, because they are non-majoritarian (taking one issue at a time); or might they be desirable, because they solve the intensity problem and produce more efficient outcomes? Riker and Brams (1973) tackled this question with respect to legislative decisions in an essay published more than three decades ago, before Riker became enamoured of chaos. Applying cardinal and ordinal analyses, they showed that both judgements are possible – vote trades sometimes increase overall welfare, but can also decrease it. When decisions are by majority rule, trades always impose external costs on those who are not involved in the logroll. The question is whether the accumulation of such external costs outweighs the benefit each group gets when it is part of a winning exchange. Riker and Brams conclude that the more pervasive the pattern of minorities rule, the greater the aggregate losses, whereas a single vote trade necessarily produces more gainers than losers.[10] Therefore, except for such isolated exchanges, vote trades ought to be discouraged.

The alternative to vote trading is one-issue-at-a-time decision making, which produces majority rule on every issue, a median on all dimensions (Feld and Grofman, 1988). After his conversion, Riker (1982: 189, 192) contended that such an outcome has no normative significance, because it can be defeated by a new majority comprised of frustrated minorities. However, as I have pointed out elsewhere (Nagel, 1993: 170–171), there is a strong majority-rule argument for one-issue-at-a-time decisions. Riker's potential 'majorities' whom that pattern frustrates are mere coalitions of minorities. If victorious, they are likely to impose extreme positions with substantial external costs. In contrast, one-issue-at-a-time decisions do not frustrate but instead satisfy the majority *on each issue.* Indeed, we cannot define majority rule with respect to a particular dimension except by examining the distribution of preferences on that dimension alone – the test intended by the median mandate as applied to the left–right scale.

Conclusion

Is it possible to have it both ways? Can we appreciate the rich complexity of politics while also enjoying the bracing simplicity of a clear standard for evaluating political performance? As the preceding arguments indicate, I believe we can and should – most of the time. Nevertheless, I conclude with cautions about two situations in which applying the median mandate can lead one astray. One occurs when the test yields a false positive, the other when it produces a false negative.

False positives

Normally, a finding that the legislative and electoral medians correspond on the left–right scale will be prima facie satisfactory, because any of several acceptable situations can bring about such correspondence – political competition may in fact be essentially one-dimensional; other dimensions may be active, but only in a secondary, lexicographic fashion; or decisions across multiple dimensions may be made one at a time, satisfying the median voter on each. There is, however, one possibility where the methods of Budge and his colleagues lead us astray. Because their left–right scale incorporates logically distinct issues that may in fact attract relatively independent groups of voters, it may show a median outcome when closer examination suggests a pattern of minorities rule, as in the case of New Zealand's economic liberalization.

False negatives

Findings that legislative and electoral medians do *not* correspond should also be probed to protect against accepting false negatives. Many of the cases of incongruence detected by McDonald, Mendes, and Budge can be readily explained in one-dimensional terms. In single-member-district electoral systems, intra-party politics may pull the two major competitors towards the extremes, while the bias of the system against third parties leaves voters no option at the median position. Alternatively, if a centrist third party survives in defiance of Duverger's Law, its occupation of the electoral centre may help keep the major parties apart, while the lack of proportional representation keeps it from playing a pivotal role in the legislature (Nagel, 2001b). Nevertheless, two other possibilities should be considered. Rarely, outcomes may depart from the left–right median because a new dimension of conflict has superseded the conventional one, as in Mackie's account of the US in 1860. Less infrequently, departure from the median may occur because minorities rule in a truly multi-dimensional pattern. If those minorities are sufficiently few, encompassing, and intense, then we might judge the non-median outcome welfare-enhancing for that polity.

It is a tribute to the remarkable methods developed by Budge and his collaborators that they offer tools to detect failures of Budge's own median mandate test. If a false positive is suspected, the elements that comprise the MRG left–right scale are numerous and explicit, so researchers can unpack them to check whether some are influencing voters independently, producing a functional (or perhaps dysfunctional) equivalent of multidimensionality beneath the left–right umbrella. If it is thought that a departure from the median is 'false' because another dimension is at work, then by expansion of policy categories and relaxation of statistical screens, the method is flexible enough to reveal its presence. By keeping in mind these caveats about possible indigestion, we can usually eat our cake and have it too.

Notes

1 In the earliest expert survey, Castles and Mair (1984) *required* respondents to locate parties only on a left–right scale. In a modest improvement, Huber and Inglehart (1995) asked respondents if there are 'some other policy dimensions' that are also very important, but only after beginning with the expectation that 'the most important differences' between parties can be distilled into locations on a unidimensional left–right scale and then inviting respondents to assimilate other 'key issues' to that division. Their questionnaire is thus analogous to stepwise regression. The first explanatory variable (the left–right dimension) is allowed to explain all the variance it can; then subsequent variables are entered to see if anything is left for them to do. As Koford (1989) points out, the dimensional analysis of roll-votes pioneered by Poole and Rosenthal (1997) operates the same way.

2 However, in four of the ten countries – Belgium, the Netherlands, France and Israel – multidimensional models performed better (Laver and Budge, 1992: 413).

3 As do many other analysts, McDonald, Mendes and Budge lump single-member-district systems together, whether they use plurality rule, as in Britain, Canada, and pre-reform New Zealand, or majority rule, as in Australia (the alternative vote) and France (a two-round system). It is not clear from their article how they estimate electoral preferences in the two majoritarian countries. If it is only by first preferences in Australia and first-round votes in France, the results are misleading, because voters also influence outcomes by second-preference votes in Australia and second-round votes in France.

4 As I have learned in research that uses the left–right scale to investigate the vote for centre parties in Britain (Nagel, 2001b)

5 Juvenile Diabetes Research Foundation, press release, 12 May 2004 (http://www.jdrf.org/index.cfm?fuseaction=home.viewPage&page_id=79C7022 1-2A5E-7B6E-1976DDFA1B71E539).

6 For example Scammon and Wattenberg (1970), Shafer and Claggett (1995), Miller and Schofield (2003), Barone *et al.* (2003).

7 As Budge and Klingemann (p. 29) correctly suggest, plans for market liberalization were not adequately presented in manifestos. In fact, due to internal conflicts, Labour did not issue its 1987 manifesto until two weeks *after* the election (Nagel, 1998: 251).

8 Note that the MRG coding would score the adoption of a pro-protection policy as a move to the left. Coding protectionism on the left–right scale seems to me highly dubious. Who supports free trade – labour or capitalists, agriculture or industry – varies from country to country and time to time, depending on the vagaries of comparative advantage, as well as the influence of ideas.

9 A similar alliance between workers and farmers (though intra-party and not involving agricultural protection) formed the basis of the model welfare state of a generation earlier, built in New Zealand by the Liberal government of 1890–1912 (Hamer, 1988; Nagel, 1993)

10 Olson (1982) reached a similar conclusion, showing that 'encompassing' interest groups impose less economic harm than narrow 'distributional coalitions'.

References

Barone, M. with R.E. Cohen and G. Ujifusa (2003) *The Almanac of American Politics 2004* (Washington: National Journal).

Budge, I. and J. Bara (2001) 'Manifesto-Based Research: A Critical Review', in I. Budge, H.-D. Klingemann, A. Volkens, J. Bara and E. Tanenbaum (eds) *Mapping Policy Preferences: Estimates for Parties, Electors, and Governments 1945–1998* (Oxford: Oxford University Press), pp. 51–74.

Budge, I. and D.J. Farlie (1983) *Explaining and Predicting Elections: Issue Effects and Party Strategies in Twenty-three Democracies* (London: George Allen and Unwin).

Budge, I. and H.-D. Klingemann (2001) 'Finally! Comparative Over-Time Mapping of Party Policy Movement', in I. Budge, H.-D. Klingemann, A. Volkens, J. Bara and E. Tanenbaum (eds) *Mapping Policy Preferences: Estimates for Parties, Electors, and Governments 1945–1998* (Oxford: Oxford University Press), pp. 19–50.

Budge, I. H.-D. Klingemann, A. Volkens, J. Bara, and E. Tanenbaum (2001) *Mapping Policy Preferences: Estimates for Parties, Electors, and Governments 1945–1998* (Oxford: Oxford University Press).

Budge, I.D. Robertson and D.J. Hearl (eds) (1987) *Ideology, Strategy and Party Change: Spatial Analyses of Post-War Election Programmes in 19 Democracies* (Cambridge: Cambridge University Press).

Castles, F.G. and P. Mair (1984) 'Left–Right Political Scales: Some "Expert" Judgments', *European Journal of Political Research* 12: 73–88.

Downs, A. (1957) *An Economic Theory of Democracy* (New York: Harper).

Feld, S.L. and B. Grofman (1988) 'Majority Rule Outcomes and the Structure of Debate in One-Issue-at-a-Time Decision-Making', *Public Choice* 59: 239–252.

Hamer, D. (1988) *The New Zealand Liberals: The Years of Power, 1891–1912* (Auckland: Auckland University Press).

Huber, J. and R. Inglehart (1995) 'Expert Interpretations of Party Space and Party Locations in 42 Societies', *Party Politics* 1: 73–111.

Koford, K. (1989) 'Dimensions in Congressional Voting', *American Political Science Review* 83: 949–962.

Laver, M.J. and I. Budge (eds) (1992) *Party Policy and Government Coalitions* (New York: St. Martin's Press).

Lewin, L. (1988) *Ideology and Strategy: A Century of Swedish Politics* (Cambridge: Cambridge University Press).

Lijphart, A. (1984) *Democracies: Patterns of Majoritarian and Consensus Government in Twenty-One Countries* (New Haven: Yale University Press).

Lijphart, A. (1999) *Patterns of Democracy: Government Forms and Performance in Thirty-Six Countries* (New Haven: Yale University Press).

McDonald, M.D., S.M. Mendes and I. Budge (2004) 'What Are Elections For? Conferring the Median Mandate', *British Journal of Political Science* 34: 1–26.

Mackie, G. (2003) *Democracy Defended* (Cambridge: Cambridge University Press).

Mackie, T.T. and R. Rose (1991) *The International Almanac of Electoral History*, 3rd edn (Washington: Congressional Quarterly Press).

Miller, G. and N. Schofield (2003) 'Activists and Partisan Realignment in the United State.,' *American Political Science Review* 97: 245–260.

Morris, D. (1999) *Behind the Oval Office: Getting Reelected Against All Odds* (Los Angeles: Renaissance Books).

Nagel, J.H. (1993) 'Populism, Heresthetics, and Political Stability: Richard Seddon and the Art of Majority Rule', *British Journal of Political Science* 23: 139–174.

Nagel, J.H. (1998) 'Social Choice in a Pluralitarian Democracy: The Politics of Market Liberalization in New Zealand', *British Journal of Political Science* 28: 223–267.

Nagel, J.H. (2001a) 'Salvaging Heresthetic: Six Theses on the Riker Program', Paper presented as the Public Choice Society Annual Meeting, San Antonio, 9–11 March 2001.

Nagel, J.H. (2001b) 'Center-Party Strength and Major-Party Polarization in Britain', Paper presented at the Annual Meeting of the American Political Science Association, San Francisco.

Olson, M. (1982) *The Rise and Decline of Nations: Economic Growth, Stagflation, and Social Rigidities* (New Haven: Yale University Press).

Poole, K.T. and H. Rosenthal (1997) *Congress: A Political-Economic History of Roll-Call Voting* (Oxford: Oxford University Press).

Powell, G.B. (2000) *Elections as Instruments of Democracy: Majoritarian and Proportional Visions* (New Haven: Yale University Press).

Riker, W.H. (1982) *Liberalism Against Populism: A Confrontation Between the Theory of Democracy and the Theory of Social Choice* (San Francisco: W. H. Freeman).

Riker, W.H. and S.J. Brams (1973) 'The Paradox of Vote Trading', *American Political Science Review* 67: 1235–1247.

Scammon, R.M. and B.J. Wattenberg (1970) *The Real Majority* (New York: Coward-McCann).

Searle, G.R. (1992) *The Liberal Party: Triumph and Disintegration, 1886–1929* (London: Macmillan).

Shafer, B.E. and W.J.M. Claggett (1995) *The Two Majorities: The Issue Context of Modern American Politics* (Baltimore: Johns Hopkins University Press).

Sykes, A. (1997) *The Rise and Fall of British Liberalism, 1776–1988* (London: Longman).

8   On the dimensionality of political space and on its inhabitants

David Robertson

Introduction

The idea that political life can usefully be described in terms of spatial dimensions seems to stem from an improbable juxtaposition of French Revolutionary legislature seating plans and the geography of American small towns. The terms 'left' and 'right' are usually thought to have come from the relative seating of the commoners and the aristocrats during the meetings of the Estates General in France in 1789, though had this directly led to a spatial model it would be unlike the ones we are used to. For one thing, the seating was in a semicircle, and for another the clergy, forming one of the three estates, were in the centre. Yet the idea that the clerical position was in any useful sense half way between the commoners and the aristos is unclear. In fact 1789 would have lead directly to a multi-dimensional model – something not to trouble political science until much later. Left and right, useful or otherwise, is a simple dichotomy which does not necessarily entail any dimensional model at all. Dimensionality probably made its real impact on political science when Anthony Downs adapted Harold Hotelling's model of spatial competition between retailers in linear American urban environments. There were many other influences on social science thinking in the early and mid-1950s which helped spread the idea of dimensional analysis. Hans Eysenck produced a study of political psychology which made extensive use of multidimensional depictions, following his general dimensional approach which had been first published in 1947 and much read by those seeking a new, more 'scientific' way of studying politics.[1] The original Michigan school of electoral studies was deeply influenced by social psychology, and whilst this did not predispose them to the rational choice approach, it did lead to them seeing spatial descriptions of politics as natural. And, of course, there was factor analysis. Again, using factor analysis does not require one to think dimensionally. At its most innocent it is just a technique for extracting a measure of an assumed underlying variable from repeated measures. But because the mathematical model which underlies it, principal components (also, revealingly, known as principal axes), is inherently spatial it was a short leap to taking this 'behind the scenes' spatial model seriously in giving intuitive accounts of politics. For these and other reasons it rapidly became normal to describe differences between political actors as at least akin to distances in a space, and to conjure with the dimensionality of this space. Little thought was – or is now – given to whether such approaches are metaphors or analogies, and whether, either way, they are useful. Perhaps there was no particular need to worry, but it would be wrong to dismiss discussion about the number of dimensions underlying political space as useless 'Angels on Pin Heads' discourse. (Not that the medieval debates thus referenced were in fact useless.) Some, at least, wish to claim a reality to their preferred dimensional models which profoundly affects how we go about theorising about politics. Some caution does seem to be required, some thought needs to be undertaken before we describe politics, anywhere, as dimensional, or before we assert the primacy of one, or the necessity of N, dimensions. As in any academic discourse, it is dangerous to play fast and loose with terminology.

Consider the following example. Since about the time I am talking about it has been automatic to claim that the politics of the Fourth Republic in France required two dimensions if it was fully to be understood. This became even more fully accepted after the publication of one of the earlier works actually to use dimensional models in empirical political science, MacRae's classic *Parliament, Parties, and Society in France.*[2] One was, of course, a left–right dimension. The second dimension posited as necessary to grasp the realities of French politics was an anti-clerical dimension, a claim similarly made for much of Europe at the time and even later for Italy. I have no doubt at all that anti-clericalism was crucial – the whole history of the French Radicals shows this. I do not doubt that coalitions between the MRP and other parties able to find a socio-economic consensus programme were inherently unstable because of the clerical/anti-clerical tension. But in what useful sense does the fact that there existed an issue on which views could be held by people of varying socio-economic beliefs, that is, the legitimacy of Catholicism in public life, require us to believe that it constituted a *dimension* in any way similar to the left/right socio-economic policy dimension? A more famous interpreter of French politics of the period, Philip Williams, nowhere characterises anti-clericalism as a dimension, though he fully uses the left–right idea.[3] How could it be a dimension? What, for example, would constitute a position half way between the MRP and the Radicals? There is no metric, not even a theoretical but unmeasurable one. Would a Huguenot party, had one sprung up, have fitted somewhere on that 'dimension'? What would have constituted the MRP 'moderating' or 'moving to the centre' on an anti-clerical/clerical dimension? Some minimal conditions must apply before we can intelligibly talk about a political 'difference' being a dimension. (And rather more criteria have to be satisfied before we can 'intelligently' so do.) Let us look at an example of a dimensional analysis from a quite different area of political science to demonstrate this.

Almost as long as people have been subjecting parties to dimensional analysis, they have been doing the same thing to constitutional courts, an approach fully developed by the judicial behaviour school around Glendon Schubert.[4] Nearly always a simple liberal/conservative axis has been used in such work, where the axis is just the result of trying to extract a scale from data about judicial voting. Very few pieces of jurimetric research have gone beyond this, in large part because they have not been based on actually reading and thinking about the cases and judicial opinions. Yet nothing as intellectually complex as constitutional review is very likely to be summarised in such naive terms. Figure 8.1 gives a very basic dimensional model of judicial differentiation from the Constitutional Court of South Africa.

The spatial portrayal is based on agreement/disagreement scores in terms of judicial voting, treated as similarity scores in a multidimensional analysis. So far, so much like Schubert *et al.* My addition is to interpret those dimensions by extensive reading of the opinions. As a consequence I can offer an understanding which would almost certainly make sense to the judges themselves, and will not surprise any court watcher in South Africa. (I am not claiming very much by this – I use the example only for illustrative purposes here, and not to announce some wonderful insight of mine.) There are two dimensions in this modelling of the South African court because the very nature of the judicial decision making requires it.

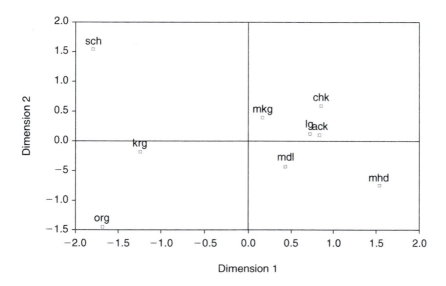

Figure 8.1 Derived stimulus configuration Euclidean distance model.

When presented with the question of whether some legislative or administrative act is outwith the constitution the court first has to answer that precise question – has a protected right been trampled on, has a central (or local) government body exceeded its authority? Answering such a question throws up differences in the readiness of judges to give an expansive or narrow interpretation of the constitution, to reign in the state or to hold it to tight boundaries. Chaskalson (Chk) has been the chief justice since inception, and has been committed to winning legitimacy for his court against often hostile politicians. He has tended towards a restricted interpretation. Ackner (Ack) has most of his experience as a senior lawyer in the UK, and lacks, as do most English judges, great enthusiasm for judicial review. Sachs (Sch), O'Regan (Org) and Kriegel (Krg) are clear enthusiasts for a court-led remaking of South African social values, and it is natural that they would be at the opposite end of such a narrow/ extensive reading dimension. However judicial interpretation in South Africa (as in Canada, but not the USA) is, by the actual terms of the constitution, two-dimensional. If the court finds that there has been a breach of a right, it has to go on and decide separately whether such a breach is, nonetheless, justified, that the aims of the legislation are sufficiently important that, in a modern democracy, this breach should be ignored. So judges are differentiated by this second, orthogonal dimension. As it happens, Sachs very frequently does find the breach he acknowledges to have been made, nonetheless justified. O'Regan, in contrast, seldom applies this test of proportionality in a way that gives the state victory. Mohamed (Mhd), though restrictive as an interpreter and not likely to see the state as acting unconstitutionally in the first place, is nonetheless hard to satisfy when it comes to assessing the proportionality of breeches he does recognise. And so on. Fully to prove my interpretation would take too long for my heuristic purposes here, though I believe it correct[5]. My point here is to show at least one way in which one might need, and benefit from, a dimensional, and in this case a multidimensional, model. The South African court can usefully be characterised by these dimensions because:

1   They are derived from objective data relating to public acts. Thus it is possible in outline to answer questions like, 'what would X have to do to move closer to Y'.
2   They generate a metric – albeit in any particular analysis one determined in detail by the choice of data analytic technique. This allows for statements about X being 'nearer to' Y and so forth.
3   Either the dimensionality is directly perceived by the actors described or – generally more likely – it arises from 'facts' about the action context the actors would recognise.

More generally, the dimensionality in my example arises because the action-world described has a structure which enforces it, and is, at least indirectly, consciously grasped by the actors. This leads to the first general point I wish to insist on, which is that questions about how many dimensions exist, or are needed for analysis, are secondary to two other, potentially but not necessarily related, questions. First, where do these dimensions exist – in the minds of which set of actors? Second, what is it that structures the world to produce these dimensions? To revert to Eysenck for a moment – he thought that the dimensionality of his political space was in the minds of voters, and was shaped by the more fundamental personality factors in all of us. Political dimensions were projections into the political world of basic truths about human personality – conservatives were superstitious, for example. In my South African example the preferences which give rise to spatial positioning are consciously in the minds of the judges, and are shaped by the external constraints imposed by the constitution. To develop that example slightly further, the Canadian constitution is less directive about how the courts must with constitutional challenges, and the US Constitution hardly directive at all. Thus Canadian judges have themselves set the shape of the tests they apply – judges could refuse to deal with issues by the thought processes that yield this model, and sometimes do. American Supreme Court justices almost never use a similar analysis. Were the two dimensions nonetheless to appear in a jurimetric analysis of either of these jurisdictions, one would probably end up talking about some more deeply rooted structuring inherent in constitutional argument of any type. More probably the essentially 'voluntary' nature of the two stage test in America, and its less binding nature in Canada would lead us to doubt the reality of the dimensions.

There is, of course, another tack one might take. This is to be highly positivist, to say that the dimensionality of political space exists only in the mind of the analyst and takes all the justification it needs from its utility in generating predictions. My reason for ignoring this orientation is twofold. First, I prefer a Weberian approach – explanation ought to be cast in terms that could in principle make sense to the actors involved. Second, unless dimensions do exist in the minds of the actors, it is in fact extremely unlikely that the researcher will achieve even positivist success. Certainly rational choice frameworks require the possibility of translation into something which makes sense to actors.

The minds of the actors

We need to explore this idea of where exactly the dimensions exist more fully, and in so doing it will turn out that the question usually involves the question of what structures the dimensionality as well. In fact the question of where a political space exists, although always important, is particularly pertinent to theories of party competition. I shall use an example drawn for purely expository purposes from the 1987 British General Election

survey. One battery of questions was specifically designed to allow measurements both of where a respondent stood on an issue and where he
thought each of the three main parties stood. Conveniently for my purposes this battery of six questions, if treated as an attempt to uncover an
underlying ideology space, produces two factors from a standard factor
analytic approach. One factor is a typical 'left–right' factor in as much as it
is primarily about socio-economic distributive politics. The second is
about security – it is characterised by two questions, one on defence
policy, one on law and order. (Brief details of the factor analysis and so
forth are given in footnote 6 to this chapter.) Figure 8.2 plots the average
position of the voters for the three parties in this two-dimensional space. It
looks perfectly predicable.

But how do we get the parties onto this map, in order to consider the
dynamics of party competition, either from a Downsian or any other
perspective? If political space inheres in voters' minds, the position of
each party must be a question of the voters' perceptions. But which
voters? An 'average perception' of all the voters? A separate space for each
voter? The next three figures, Figures 8.3–8.5, show the party positions as
perceived differently by each of the three blocs of voters.[6]

Not surprisingly the patterns vary considerably. The differences in perception can even be shown to matter. Table 8.1a/b gives the results of a

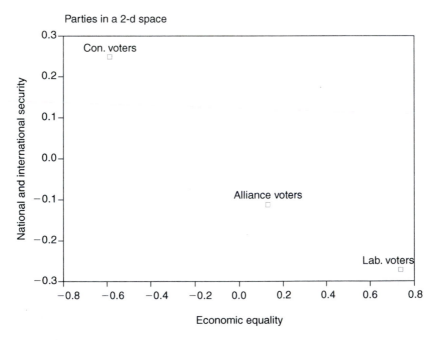

Figure 8.2 Parties in a 2-d space.

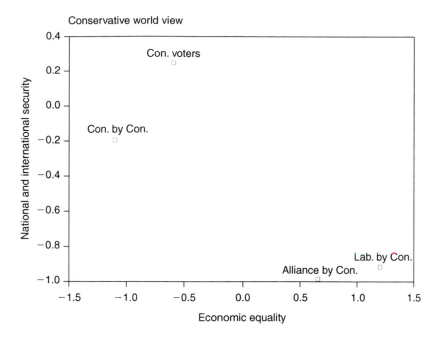

Figure 8.3 Conservative world view.

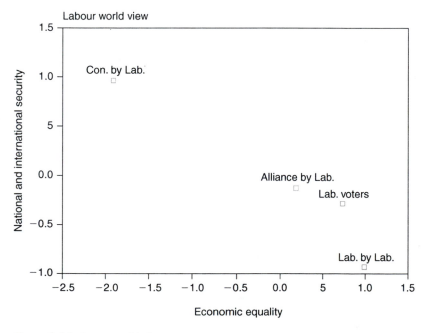

Figure 8.4 Labour world view.

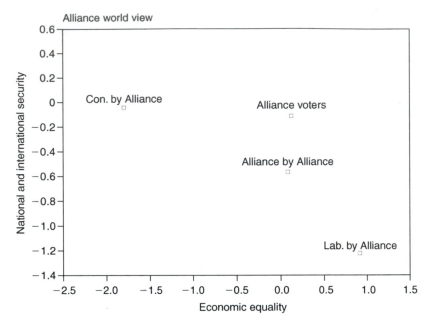

Figure 8.5 Alliance world view.

Table 8.1   Predicting vote in 1987 by distance between party and voter

a) using distances to overall sample estimate of party positions.

Nearest Party	Party predicted Cons	Lab	Alliance	Total
Cons	78.1	13.3	8.5	100%
Labour	16.1	69.2	14.7	100%
Alliance	44.9	36.3	18.8	100%

Percentage of grouped cases correctly classified: 61.0%

b) Using distances to estimate of party positions, separately for each voting block

Nearest Party	Party predicted Cons	Lab	Alliance	Total
Cons	81.7	3.2	15.1	100%
Labour	3.2	72.8	24.2	100%
Alliance	13.4	34.6	52.0	100%

Percentage of grouped cases correctly classified: 71.7%

multiple discriminant analysis predicting vote by perceived distance from each party. If one calculates for each respondent his 'nearest party', more than 40 per cent would be predicted to vote other than the way they did. If, instead, party positions attributed to each party are derived from the different spaces for each parties supporters, the per cent correctly predicted rises to 71.7 per cent. Perhaps more important is the differential effect. The correct prediction rate only varies for the Conservative voters by about 3 per cent. But where Alliance voters are allowed their own estimates of relative party positions they move from being correctly predicted less than 20 per cent of the time to be over 50 per cent.

Everything we have known for years about cognitive dissonance would predict this, and one might argue it does not matter, because it has always been recognised that voter ignorance was high, or that imperfect information reduces the detailed accuracy of a party competition model. This argument will not quite work, because it is predicted on voters having an inaccurate (but probably roughly adequate) perception of the parties' 'true' positions. If there is a true position, however, it must mean that the dimensions do not exist primarily in the voters' minds, but somewhere else. Where? There would seem to be two possible sorts of answers. One answer would be that the dimensions inhere in the minds of the parties, which must mean some combination of leaders and activists. The alternative would be that the dimensionality exists independently of its perceivers, voters or politicians. Which is why the 'where are the dimensions?' and the 'how do they come about?' questions led into each other, and are together prior to the 'how many are there?' question.

Why are there (any) dimensions?

This is, in fact, a curiously difficult question to answer, especially if one hopes to avoid a deeply metaphysical, Locke style reference to political essences, to an underlying 'something I know not what'. It is easiest to approach it via examples. A simple version of the answer is the reason the 1987 BES study produces two factors from that battery of questions. (And, being generous, why very similar solutions arise from many batteries of policy preference questions in many surveys.)[7] It is just that the pattern of correlations between the survey questions treated as variables can be 'decomposed' into a smaller number of factors, are axes which represent the commonality in the answers. Back at the dawn of time, Phil Converse indeed used the absence of such correlations to claim that the mass electorate had no ideologies. But the fact that we take party positions in space seriously must mean we have rejected this claim. The variables correlate, we are forced to believe because people do have something amounting to an ideology, even if this is little more than an organising principle to help us make rational utility decisions faced with political complexity. The correlations represent, therefore, an ordered patterning of our preferences, views and desires. Where these ideologies (I will call them that for convenience) are multidimensional, something else must be true. It must be true that a voter's preferences on some issues cannot be predicted from knowledge of his position on some others. In fact, as a dimension to be meaningful must relate to more than one issue, one could make a minimum definition of two-dimensional political space as follows: the voter must have preferences on at least two pairs of issues such that each item in a pair is predictable by the other, and neither is predictable from either issue in the other pair. Lest this seem unduly formulaic, it is merely an effort to spell out the minimal content of the idea of a space of two orthogonal dimensions. (Non-orthogonal, intercorrelated dimensions make little sense for our purposes.)

What sociological or psychological factors lead to this structuring is beyond discussion here, except for one thing – it is unlikely that the multidimensionality, or indeed the correlation pattern that leads to even one dimension, has a quality I want to call being 'compulsory'. People really can want incompatible things and can bundle together issues an analyst would think unconnected in such a way as to lead to high correlations. Converse's mistake, amongst others, was to dismiss correlations he did not think made sense, and to treat as ideological and cognitive failure the absence of correlations he thought ought to be present. Put like this it would seem very unlikely that politics anywhere at any time would be one-dimensional to *the extent that the dimensions inhere in mass consciousness.* What is much more likely is that multidimensional mass ideologies are reduced to effective unidimensionality for one of two reasons. It may be that a strong lexicographic ordering arises because of the intense salience of issues making up one of the dimensions. It used to be argued, for example, that an explanation for Macarthyism in the USA in the early 1950s went along these lines. The orthogonal dimension of patriotism/ American identity anxiety which cross-cut the socio-economic dimension was thought to be smothered by the salience of the latter in normal times. When the post-war economic boom reduced the pressure on 'bread and butter issues' the second dimension could come to influence some voters. They were not thought to have changed positions from earlier ones, but to be free to express political preferences marked on that dimension.[8] Perhaps the more recent 'post-materialism' thesis might be cast in these terms, rather than as a replacement of one 'old' dimension by a newer one. That certainly seems to be the implication of the common assumption that post-materialism, if it exists at all, is subject to the vagaries of the Western economies.[9] These examples link to the second reason that an actual multidimensional world might appear unidimensional.

It may also be that the dimensionality of the space in the minds of the parties only maps partially onto mass space, essentially making one or more of the mass dimensions redundant. One needs here to make a careful distinction between two similar seeming situations. One is where the mass culture already contains a second dimension along which the parties normally refuse to compete, or at least neglect. The second situation is where political actors invent and educate the mass into a cross-cutting dimension. This latter is the sort of case much discussed by writers like McLean and Nagel, following Riker's lead, on which more later.[10] In either case the crucial role played by political parties in creating or intensifying dimensions, originally pointed out most forcefully by Dunleavy and Ward must be taken very seriously, and rather suggests that the answer to the question 'How many dimensions?' must vary with the other quite separate aspects of party competition.[11]

When we turn to thinking about political parties, the range of answers to the general question 'why are there any dimensions?', as opposed just to bundles of issues, becomes more theoretically interesting. I have already mentioned the idea that some dimensions may be 'compulsory'. This is actually a double duty concept. The political context may make it unavoidable for all parties, or at least all serious players, to have a position on each of a series of issues. Not to speak out on issues X, Y and Z would make a party electorally highly vulnerable. The actual position taken on any one or more of these issues may be highly restricted by preferred positions on other issues. These constraints may be logical/technical – it is just not possible both to end conscription, remain a leader in NATO and refuse to develop nuclear weapons, perhaps. They may be electoral – if one does not advocate taking away professional monopolies at the same time one advocates the end of the union's closed shop, the accusations of class bias will be too dangerous. They may be ideological – the vision of the good society requires both nationalisation of industry and worker participation in it. (Or the priority for economic efficiency in the nationalised economy requires state planning and precludes worker participation ...) For these and other sorts of reasons, positions on issues are interlinked; they form a dimension because movement on any policy requires changes in others. In practice dimensions come into existence for a mixture of all of these reasons, so that some policies have to change for technical reasons and others change with them because of political vulnerability, and still others because of the incremental shift the first set of changes produce in the articulation of the vision of the good society and so on. The policies are involuntarily bundled into a dimension in a way that I shall call, for convenience, a logical compulsion.

How many such dimensions there are depends on whether or not there are two or more such bundles which have the additional character of not wielding any logical compulsion on each other. The example I gave from South African constitutional jurisprudence is apt here. The judge does not have a choice about developing a position on each of the dimensions, but neither exerts any compulsion on the other. Inside each dimension though there are distinct logical compulsions on sub-issues, on precise questions of legal doctrine.[12] The great temptation here is to take something like the 'domestic and international security' dimension I sketched earlier and treat it as not having any compulsory link to the socio-economic dimension and thereby constituting a genuine second dimension of politics. Though it is true that the internal connections between issues in a domain like this are rather weak – they would stem from the overall idea of the good society rather more than from technical incompatibilities between, let us say, a preference both to reduce police arrest powers and to have a nuclear based defence policy.

This is where the second sense of compulsion comes in. The judges do have to operate in a two-dimensional space. But do the parties? There would seem to be two conditions that both have to be satisfied before the fact that issues bundled into two dimensions will produce two-dimensional party politics. And it has to be stressed that it is this sense of multidimensionality that concerns us – the actuality of two-dimensional party competition, rather than the sociological possibility of such. The dimensions would have to have roughly equal salience. If this is not the case, then party positions on the 'second' dimension would be important only as tiebreakers for voters unable to discriminate on the main dimension. An alternative scenario, harder to think through, is where one dimension has salience to one section of the electorate and the other to another section. In other words one finds two, opposed, lexicographic orderings. If one leaves aside the cultural identity politics of religion or language, it is actually rather hard to come up with a plausible example of such a polity, but it is certainly a possibility. The number of effective dimensions would be dependent to a very great degree on the relative sizes of the groups. But it would equally depend on the second factor that determines the compulsory nature of a second dimension. This is the question of whether one or more parties of sufficient weight themselves have this dimension as primary in their ordering and will capitalise on their position. Again, leaving aside identity politics, examples do not spring to mind. If the two dimensions are genuinely orthogonal in policy-making terms as well as in ideological or psychological terms, there is no reason for parties not to compete on both of two equally salient dimensions, except, perhaps, because of campaigning resource limitations. The most important resource constraint might well be the need to simplify the battlefield both to aid voter decision making, and to maximise control of the image the party projects. However the fact that there seem to be very few known examples of genuinely two-dimensional competition may speak then to the primacy, for the as yet unstated reason, of single dimensional politics.

Somehow or other it does not seem quite right to talk about a dimension, of political importance, where either voters or parties can have preferences quite unconnected to their preferences on another important dimension. It is important to remind ourselves here about the stipulative definition I gave of a dimension, because there are plenty of examples of what at first glance might seem important cross-cutting dimensions. A prime example would be the opposition to Britain's EEC membership (as it then was) in the 1970s. Notoriously this united the right of the Conservative party with the left of the Labour party – surely then, it was possible for people of whatever position on the left–right dimension to take up any position on the European dimension? But this would be to conflate policy and dimension. For very different reasons it was possible for the right and left to agree that Britain should leave the EEC – the one because it regarded Europe as a capitalist plot, the other because it feared loss of sovereignty. But in no way did this mean that the two extremist supporting groups agreed on a position on an underlying long-term political dimension. Indeed the positions on the two dimensions were not genuinely uncorrelated, given that the moderates in both parties agreed on Europe. What we had was a rather strong, but non-linear correlation between a dimension and a specific issue.

Why there might (effectively) be only one dimension?

The main reason we have few true examples of multidimensional politics is probably this: in a fundamental sense it is impossible to conceive of governments going about their business in a world they conceive of as having two or more independent spaces for policy development. For one thing, a second dimension cannot really be independent of the first if it relates to public expenditure, or more broadly to the nature of the state. For all but the most highly symbolic of policies the question of resource constraint arises. This need not merely be a financial constraint which makes even apparently disconnected policies have mutually retraining consequences, though that is the most obvious commonality. States run on other resources, both technical, like administrative capacity, and less measurable but crucial resources like legitimacy and authority.

The point about financial constraint is too obvious to need much spelling. Put simply, a cost cutting low tax Conservative party may operate primarily on a dimension of economic laissez-faire and minimal welfarism which appear to have no ideological connection to defence and criminal law policies which, following my data example earlier, constitute a second dimension. It does not follow that the party is free to advocate any policies it likes or might find electorally advantageous there. Defence equipment and prisons are both very expensive; the mere fact that governments are forced to optimise returns, including electoral returns over a huge range of policy ares for rare financial reasons; resources suggests that they must all be considered in some single metric, and what is a dimension but a metric common to a series? Depending on a party's overall vision, its political 'tone' almost, other factors may constitute a resource restriction with a similar effect. One good candidate for this is the idea of authority, particularly the authority of central government. Highly liberal policies in terms of the private sphere have, amongst other consequences, the tendency to diminish the public's sense of the state's right to control. Can a party simultaneously support authority dependent policies like mass nationalisation and highly privatised individual lifestyle policies? In a more general sense, there are what one might best call 'governing methodologies' which constrain across otherwise arguably separate dimensions. If anything at all is meant by 'New Labour', we know by now that it involves detailed management by target setting towards the aim of reducing any form of social or economic exclusion. No policies based on government entirely abandoning some field to the market or to free and perhaps selfish individual choice is likely to recommend itself. There is something, an idea, a methodology, a prime value, which tends towards organising a party's policy offerings across all of what it does. Consider again the 'fact' I started with about the French Fourth Republic's putative clerical/anti-clerical second dimension. Had this really been a dimension orthogonal to a socio-economic left/right dimension it would be suggesting something rather odd. The precise question, the legitimacy of church involvement in the state or society via, usually, education, might just about be seen as genuinely one on which one's position was unconnected to what one thought about welfare and economic planning. But from the viewpoint of the MRP itself this would amount to saying that, though Catholicism was so important they would risk losing office rather than abandoning a pro-clerical stance, this same religious credo had no effect on what they thought was just or acceptable in terms of welfare or the rights of private property.

What all this amounts to is saying that there is only one image of a political party which is capable of making sense of multidimensional policy space. This is the pure Downsian party committed, in its inner councils, to nothing but winning an election. Such a party, especially if it had little long-term ambition, might be able to adopt policies as though they were living in a space of orthogonal dimensionality. At most, financial constraint issues could operate as a restriction – as long as there was no pressing desire to repeated re-election, such matters as maintaining state authority or not overburdening administrative capacity, would not restrict policy choice. For any other type of party there has to be some source of policy selection, some *fons et origo* of the party's positioning which makes the idea of multidimensionality exceptionally improbable. I am hardly insisting here on a full-blooded idea of ideology in some quasi-Marxian sense. Yes it is surely part of any definition of ideology that it contains an image of the good society, as well as something like a sociology which explains to its adherents how the world works. How easily can such an ideology produce an image of politics in which there is any great degree of freedom in choice of policy preferences in one set of issues not contained by policy choice in any other set of issues? It will always be a mistake to see similarity of party positions on one suggested dimension between parties vastly apart on another as evidence of true multi dimensionality. To take another French example – throughout both the Fourth and much of the Fifth Republic the PCF and the Gaullistes were united on at least three issues – distrust of NATO, distrust of the EEC and opposition to devolution. This could be presented, perhaps has been somewhere, as a second dimension to French politics characterised by attitudes to the sovereignty of the central state versus challenges from either below or above. There may have been French voters who could, lexicographically, have made their choice based on that 'dimension'. But the idea that either the PCF or the UDR could choose its position on this dimension because it was unconnected to the positions they had to espouse on a central left/right dimension is absurd. The opposition to the two external alliances are derived from completely different sources of political inspiration. The agreement that devolution was dangerous did, indeed, stem from a common desire for strong central authority – but one party wished to have that authority to abolish, and the other to protect, private property. The example may seem to raise the possibility that voters and parties might inhabit space of different dimensionality, but this would be true in an very uninformative sense, given that the voter only gets to choose what parties offer. Lexicographically a voter might hate NATO/EEC and local government so much that he would prefer any party at one end of that dimension to any at the other. But the voter would have to be indifferent to the nationalisation issue actually to have a free choice on this second dimension.

Historically there has been a very basic understanding about the nature of the primary opposition in politics, one that operates not merely on one dimension, but on a dichotomous basis. Political science certainly requires more than a dichotomy, and a multiparty system would enforce more sophistication anyway. But does it require much more? Politics in France particularly has often been characterised, in all its Republics, as quite simple – there are forces of Progress (or movement) and forces of Reaction. Stated like that, we are invited to think of motion, and therefore of space, in basically simple terms. There is a road to travel on. Some want to go back, others to press on. Interestingly exactly this metaphor was used by Tony Blair addressing the Spring Conference of the Labour Party in 2005, a few months before the election. He consciously reduced politics to one dimension, saying that whether one chose the Conservatives or the Liberals, the effect would be the same – progress could be found only with the Labour party. We might get much further with our problem by reflecting on this sense of movement in politics. Voters may very well see parties as nearer or further from them, and they may see them as likely to travel further forward or backwards along a road. But they will neither see this, nor express it, in the city block metric of multidimensionality – it will be a direct measurement of distance in Euclidian space. Oxford is 120 miles from Colchester – it is not to its inhabitants 50 miles south and 109 miles east. One can always reduce a two-dimensional space by plotting the projections of the positions of its inhabitants onto a single principal component line drawn through the origin. As long as one does not give content to the meanings of the end points, this is fine. And the best way to *label* the end points is going to be left and right. One can also alter the metric so that the range of scores on the two dimensions is equivalent. This is one crude way of dealing with a question that cannot be avoided by exponents of multidimensional space – how big is each dimension? A 'short' dimension equates to a low salience dimension, and one cannot dodge the question of weighting. Lexicographic orderings are equivalent to spaces where the second and further dimensions have very low weightings except in cases of ties on the prime dimension. The analogy to modern speculative physics is hard to avoid – string theory, championed as the hope for the General Unified Theory requires, in some models, seven dimensions. My own first foray into party competition also, improbably, required seven dimensions.[13] The difference is that I (surely wrongly) weighted them equally. String theory regards three or four of the 'extra' dimensions to be very short, so short, indeed, that we are unaware of them in ordinary life. So even if a full description of political space is multidimensional, it may be that we should expect the occasions when more than one is effective to be almost pathological.

This brings me to one of my earlier arguments I need to address slightly further. This is my dismissal of the common idea that multidimensionality does exist where one has cross-cutting social cleavages like religion or language. Although I do doubt that religion in the Fourth Republic was a 'dimension' of politics, as opposed to an unfortunate fact about coalition difficulties, it is probably wrong to dismiss the idea of such 'political identity' dimensions altogether. But brief reflection on the politics of systems with serious identity issues suggests that fitting a common space with an identity 'dimension' may not work at all well, and may do violence both to the idea of political space and to our ability to understand the politics in question. A more interesting example than France in the 1950s may be the Netherlands at the same time. Given that there were three religiously based parties actually fitting extra dimensions would be conceptually complex – the Calvinist parties were, surely, not at one end of a dimension opposing the Catholic party with the lay parties between, while at the same end as the Catholics on a dimension contrasting religion with secularism, both dimensions orthogonal to each other and to a (at least) socio-economic dimension. What would an appropriate dimensionality be? One needs to think a little about how a voter might orient himself. At least one plausible model is that for the devout Calvinist or Catholic; some parties just fall off the space altogether. It would be as unthinkable for a Roman Catholic to vote Calvinist as for a Communist to vote Roman Catholic. What this means is that rather than having a single space with complex dimensionality one is faced with more than one space, none of which has all the parties present. This in fact is going to be a highly empirical matter. If we consider Italy, a good case could be made out for it changing over time from having two spaces, one for devout Catholics and one for the determinedly lay, which merged into one space with a highly pragmatically flavoured minor religious dimension.

Identity politics can, in principle, lead to an extra dimension, but only if the actual policies in question are capable of compromise. Take the issue of state aid to religious schools. Because the Canadian constitution specifically requires this, Canada could have a 'dimension' of religion in its politics, where parties could offer varying degrees of state support, and state support in return for various educational commitments to multiculturalism, etc. But in France state aid to Catholic schools was a dichotomous and hotly contested definition of the nature of the Republic itself, and quite incapable of the sort of compromise that leads to dimensionality and party manoeuvring. By the latter days of the Italian first Republic the PCI had managed to find ways of making it possible for at least some Catholics to vote for it, and had indeed turned the dichotomy clerical/anti-clerical into a dimension on which it could position itself. It will always be a matter of serious doubt however whether the politics of identity, ongoing inside a system of pragmatic utility politics, is best regarded as an extra dimension. We must always be careful of promoting a political 'fact about some voters and parties' to the status of a dimension open to manoeuvre.

It is possible that this distinction between a second dimension and a 'fact about' may help with some other problems. No one can deny the logical correctness of the famous 'cyclical majorities' argument, whereby, faced with three alternatives, A, B and C a majority prefers A to B, and B to C, but, unfortunately for democratic theory, C to A. Part of the problem of cyclical majorities is that they appear to crop up very rarely. It may be that this has something to do with the way in which the preferences are formed and can be expressed. It has never been true, something careless readings have sometimes led people to believe, that the theory posited that voters would prefer A over B, and B over A, but C over A, for *the same reasons*. Such a theory would deny ordinary language meaning to the verb prefer. The cycles arise because the motivation for the AB and BC choices are different from the CA choices. This has often been thought of as a problem underlying a multidimensional space, making impossible, amongst other things, the theory of the median mandate. If my suggestion above, that voter preference is made by minimising direct Euclidian distance in a space or its equivalent, that voters are arrayed along projected a single dimensional summary, the cyclical majority issue vanishes, because, except in the case of a tie, there just is one party to whom more people are nearer than any other. The cyclical majority problem arises because voters are seen as switching from one judgement method to another when they consider the rival attractions of A and C. As an illustration, suppose an economic left–right dimension such that party A is socialist, Party B moderate and Party C conservative. Six of ten voters are socialist and prefer A to B. An overlapping group of liberals also produce a majority when faced with a choice between B and C. But six out of ten voters, regardless of their economic ideology, are also vegetarians, for whom animal welfare is a paramount value, and Party C is, as well as conservative, strongly in favour of animal rights. There is a voting paradox here if one allows this form of 'criterion switching' into a model. If one takes as the criterion just the minimisation of Euclidian distance in two-dimensional space there is no reason not to have a simple winner. If, on the other hand, there is one economic left–right dimension, but there is also the question of animal rights, which for some reason or other takes on a virtually dichotomous nature in the minds both of voters and party leaders, we have cycle problem.

Why then do cycles occur, at least in theory and possibly in history? Another way of looking at much the same set of concerns is to suggest that the sort of analysis popularised under the name of 'heresthetics', a leading practitioner of which is Iain McLean, maybe depends on the 'dimension' versus 'fact about' distinction. McLean's account of Peele's reform of the Corn Laws gives a convincing account of how Peele manoeuvred politicians on both sides of the house into having to support tariff reform because of their prior and more pressing commitment to governmental stability. It is not entirely clear whether McLean prefers to think of the politics in multidimensional terms or not. Certainly he is dismissive of one research project which suggests from roll-call data a large number of political dimensions in the minds of the parliamentarians of the period. Nothing in his account requires him to see the political word he describes as multidimensional – it is just as satisfactory to say that Peele introduced, arranged for, a new and awkward 'fact', which is that if the MPs voted as might be predicted from their position on some economic interest dimension, all hell would break loose. I am running together these actually disparate parts of Riker's lessons for political science because they both depend on the distinction I have drawn. The existence, or creation, of awkward political facts about which parties cannot compete but towards which they must bow is both a potential characterisation of some politics at some times, and something one can imagine a 'great politician' using. I do not believe that Peele could create a real dimension, a set of interlinked and long-lasting issues on which positions were uncorrelated with policies in the space people were used to. I do believe he could take advantage of a special situation where a one-off unrefusable choice was presented. In much the same way I can go along with the idea that Republicans in nineteenth-century America could capitalise on the slavery issue by forcing voters to think about a fact which made it impossible for politics as normal to go on along its usual, Democrat dominated, dimension.[14] Indeed slavery/abolition is the nearest one can imagine to an awkward dichotomy. Attempts to 'dimensionalise' it by compromises signally failed. The Dredd Scott case came out the way it did precisely because there was no halfway house between treating a slave as property or not.[15] (A little remembered fact about the case which suggests how hard it was to handle in constitutional argument is that it was the first case after *Marbury* v. *Madison* in 1803 that the Supreme Court overruled a federal act.)

An easier way to say much of what I have discussed in the last section may be a slogan – Single Issues Are Not Dimensions. They are not, usually anyway, dimensions when they relate to political identities, when they concern the very fragility of cabinet government, when they touch on the most appalling moral issue in American history. If they cannot be bundled up into an existing dimension, they are best analysed as exogenous shocks to, or restraints on, party competition in a much simpler space. Is politics unidimensional? Yes. Is the single dimension aptly called left/right? Why not. Does it have a constant transnational and transtemporal identity? That is for the historians of ideas.

Notes

1 Eysenck and Himmelweit (1947) was followed a few years later by Eysenck (1954).
2 MacRae (1967).
3 Williams (1964).
4 The first major statement was Schubert (1965). An early effort at making this more comparative can be found in Schubert and Danelski (1969). The seldom noticed extent to which Schubert sought to develop a fully-fledged theory of political ideology along dimensional lines, as well as the social–psychological basis for this can be seen in Schubert (1974).
5 This analysis is derived from more thorough work on the South African court in Robertson (2006). It is based on data published annually in *the South African Journal on Human Rights*. The most recent version is Klaaren and Stein (2004).
6 I calculated these party positions by creating three new 'cases' in the data set, one for each party. They were accredited with answers to the battery of questions according to the mean score attributed to them on each question, and their factor scores calculated accordingly. This was repeated for each of the three voting blocs, to generate three separate sets of spatial coordinates for each party.
7 For example the robust two-dimensional model of voter ideology first shown in my own book on elections in the seventies, Robertson (1982) and discovered independently later by Evans (1993).
8 Kornhauser (1968) or Bell (2000).
9 Ingleheart (1997).
10 Nagel (1993). McLean and Bustani (1999). Both are heavily influenced by Riker's work, as best exemplified in Riker (1980).
11 Dunleavy and Ward (1981).
12 Iles (2004).
13 Robertson (1976).
14 I am thinking of Riker's use of this example, well discussed in McLean (2002).
15 Fehrenbacher (1978).

References

Bell, D. (2000) *The End of Ideology: On the Exhaustion of Political Ideas in the Fifties* (Cambridge, MA: Harvard University Press).

Dunleavy, P. and H. Ward (1981) 'Exogenous Voter Preferences and Parties with State Power – Some Internal Problems of Economic Theories of Party Competition', *British Journal of Political Science*, 11: 351–380.

Evans, G. (1993) 'The Decline of Class Divisions in Britain – Class and Ideological Preferences in the 1960s and the 1980', *British Journal of Sociology*, 44:3, 449–471.

Eysenck, H.J. (1954) *Psychology of Politics* (London: Routledge & Kegan Paul).

Eysenck, H.J. and H.T. Himmelweit (1947) *Dimensions of Personality* (London: Routledge & Kegan Paul).

Fehrenbacher, Don E. (1978) *The Dredd Scott Case: Its Significance in American Law and Politics* (New York: Oxford University Press).

Iles, K. (2004) 'Limiting Socio-Economic Rights: Beyond the Internal Limitations Clause', *South African Journal on Human Rights* 20:3.

Ingleheart, R. (1997) *Modernization and Postmodernization: Cultural, Economic, and Political Change in 43 Societies* (Princeton, NJ: Princeton University Press).

Klaaren, J. and N. Stein (2004) 'Constitutional Court Statistics for the 2003 Term', *South African Journal on Human Rights* 20:3.

Kornhauser, W. (1968) *The Politics of Mass Society* (London: Routledge).

MacRae, D. Jr (1967) *Parliament, Parties, and Society in France, 1946–1958* (London: Macmillan).

McLean, I. (2002) 'William H. Riker and the Invention of Heresthetics', *British Journal of Political Science* 32:2, 535–558.

McLean, I. and C. Bustani (1999) 'Irish Potatoes and British Politics: Interests, Ideology, Heresthetics and the Repeal of the Corn Laws', *Political Studies* 47: 817–836.

Nagel, Jack H.(1993) 'Populism, Heresthetics, and Political Stability: Richard Seddon and the Art of Majority Rule', *British Journal of Political Science* 23: 139–174.

Riker, W. (1980) 'Implications from the Disequilibrium of Majority Rule for the Study of Institutions'. *American Political Science Review* 74: 432–446.

Robertson, D. (1976) *A Theory of Party Competition* (London: Wiley & Co).

Robertson, D. (1982) *Class and the British Electorate.* (Oxford: Blackwell).

Robertson, D. (2007) *Constitutional Review: A Comparative Study of the Nature and Role of Constitutional Courts in Liberal Democracies* (forthcoming).

Schubert, Glendon A. (1965) *The Judicial Mind: The Attitudes and Ideologies of Supreme Court Justices, 1946–1963* (Evanston, IL: Northwestern University Press).

Schubert, Glendon A. (1974) *The Judicial Mind Revisited: Psychometric Analysis of Supreme Court Ideology* (New York: Oxford University Press)

Schubert, G.A., and D.J. Danelsk,(eds). (1969) *Comparative Judicial Behavior: Cross-Cultural Studies of Political Decision-Making in the East and West* (New York: Oxford University Press).

Williams, Philip M. (1964) *Crisis and Compromise: Politics in the Fourth Republic*, 3rd edn (London: Longman).

9 "Party-defined" spaces revisited

Michael Laver

Introduction

Spatial models of politics are characterised by the postulation of some kind of underlying political space that can be used to describe the preferences and choices of key actors. Such spaces are intellectual constructs, bordering on the metaphysical, that provide theorists with a common conceptual language with which to describe specific models of political choice. This common language relies upon an explicit analogy with physical space when it uses terms such as "distance", "movement", "dimensions" and "direction" to describe the preferences and choices of political decision makers.

The psychological micro-foundations of the spatial analogy in political science have not been a source of overwhelming concern to the majority of spatial modellers. Rather, theorists building spatial models of politics have developed a common understanding or folk wisdom about the underlying choice processes involved – a folk wisdom largely imported from micro-economics. Spatial models of politics have been more interested in unfolding the logical implications of a set of axioms deriving from this folk wisdom than with agonising about whether these axioms are themselves well grounded in any consistent psychological theory about how real human beings make real choices.

This is an intellectual can of worms I do not propose to open here. I do propose to leave it on the kitchen table in plain sight, however, in the certain knowledge that it is indeed full of worms. The reason for drawing attention at all to the psychological micro-foundations of the spatial analogy is that I want to revisit a "spatial" approach proposed nearly three decades ago by Ian Budge and Denis Farlie. This involves a "party defined", "likelihood ratio space" (LiRaS), which in one sense is a straightforward spatial description of voting propensities, however derived, but in its practical application tends to rely upon psychological micro-foundations that differ from those underlying the more conventional spatial model (Budge *et al.*, 1976a, b; Budge and Farlie, 1976, 1977; Farlie and Budge, 1976).

The stimulus for doing this has been the publication of a unique new data set of real votes cast by real voters in a real election, arising from trials of electronic voting in the 2002 general elections in Ireland. Ireland's STV electoral system requires voters to rank order candidates on the ballot. A total of 138,011 Irish voters, voting in one of three Dáil constituencies, registered these rankings electronically in 2002. All of these rankings were subsequently published, generating a data matrix of 138,011 voters' expressed preferences that is amenable to dimensional, and hence spatial, analysis. (See Laver, 2004, for a description and preliminary analysis of these data.) As we shall see, the resulting "party defined" spaces bear effectively no resemblance to the "policy" spaces that have conventionally used to describe Irish party competition. We should not discount the possibility that Irish politics is peculiar, in that Irish voters are more concerned with party, and less concerned with policy, than voters in other modern democracies. Nevertheless, these results provide a prima facie case for revisiting the notion of a "party defined" space.

In what follows I briefly review the conceptual language of both "policy" and "party defined" spaces. I then report the results of various spatial analyses of Irish party competition, derived from expert surveys, the Irish National Election Study and the dimensional analysis of electronic voting data. I attempt to reconcile these quite different spatial representations of Irish party competition and ruminate briefly on the implications of these differences.

On policy spaces and "ideal points"

The essential idea underlying any spatial representation of politics is that of a perceived psychological "distance" between sets of political stimuli. Thus, without reading any psychology, many people do find it intuitively reasonable, when thinking for example of two politicians X and Y, to take the view that "X is closer to me politically than Y". Thinking of two potential outcomes, P and Q, the intuitively meaningful statement "I prefer P to Q" can be translated, apparently without loss of meaning, into the statement "P is closer than Q to the potential outcome I most prefer".

Once we accept the concept of political distance, in this sense, we have a political space. This is because distance implies the potential for movement. Movement has direction. Direction is defined in terms of a set of basis vectors, or dimensions. A set of basis vectors spans a space. Political distance is the key concept in the spatial analogy. All else follows from this.

Thus "policy spaces" depend on a concept of the "policy distance" between two stimuli. The folk wisdom of spatial modellers typically regards policy distances as expressing how an actor feels about different political stimuli. Typically these stimuli are actual or potential political outcomes, and distances are expressed in terms of how "close" each stimulus is to the actor's most preferred potential political outcome, or "ideal point".

The concept of an ideal point is itself deeply metaphysical. It is another matter on which spatial modellers typically form a pact with each other on a set of definitions and spare themselves the angst of delving too deeply into the micro-foundations of these. Personally, I would ideally like to live in a world with zero taxes, infinite public services, zero poverty, infinite tolerance, perfect equality and unlimited opportunity. Anyone who would not like to do this is not my friend. When I make political choices in the real world, however, I am painfully aware of my belief that my unconstrained ideal point can currently be realised only in science fiction novels. My practical political thinking is radically conditioned by my technological and social *weltanschauung*. Given this *weltanschauung*, which is in effect taken by spatial modellers as an exogenous constraint on my feelings about political stimuli, I have an ideal point i in the sense that there is no other potential policy outcome that I both perceive to be technologically and socially feasible and prefer to i. Changes in my *weltanschauung* change my ideal point.

If we accept that I have constrained preferences about potential political outcomes in this sense, we have a policy space that will allow us to locate my ideal point in relation to any set of potential political outcomes. This remains a long way from the policy spaces of conventional spatial models, which locate the ideal points of many different actors, relative to many potential political outcomes, all in the same space. Even if we assume that all actors in the system share the same *weltanschauung*, it remains possible that they do not all see the same policy space when they look at the political world. In politics as in life, I may love you more than you love me so that we disagree on the distance between us, which is of course utterly subjective.

The bottom line is that there are many, many assumptions underlying the conventional representation of a common policy space within which a diverse set of ideal points and potential political outcomes can be located. As intrepid and fearless theorists, let's make all of the necessary assumptions and further assume that political choices, including the choice of which party and/or candidate to support in a real election, are made in terms of the matrix of policy distances encapsulated in the resulting space. This leaves us in a position to specify a model of voting behaviour. A model of "sincere" Downsian voting, for example, would have each voter supporting the party proposing the policy position closest to his/her own ideal point. A model of instrumental voting, on the other hand, would have each voter casting a vote in such a way, taking into account the consequences and probabilities of potential election results, as to increase the probability of an outcome close to his/her ideal point. Decisions made by party activists and funders may be added to the model; the credibility of party policy promises may be brought into the equation; new entrants to the party system may be envisaged; and so on. In effect the notion of a policy space provides a conceptual tool kit with which a wide variety of different models, sharing similar micro-foundations, can be constructed. The common feature of all of these actual and potential models is that the relative locations of voter ideal points and party policy positions lie at the heart of some explanation or another of voting behaviour in real elections.

On party-defined spaces and "likelihood ratios"

All political "spaces" depend upon some underlying notion of political distance but the type of "party defined", "likelihood ratio" (LiRaS) space proposed by Budge and Farlie (1976, 1977) depends upon a notion a distance quite different from that underlying the conventional spatial modelling literature. The stimuli generating distances in a policy space are potential policy outcomes. The stimuli in a LiRaS space are actual political parties. (*Potential* political parties might also be considered, but I am not aware that this possibility has actually been developed.)

To take a simple example, imagine only two political parties, A and B. Ignoring non-voting for the moment, one underlying psychological assumption in an LiRaS space is that every voter can be thought of as having a relative probability, however generated, of voting for Party A, and the inverse probability of voting for Party B. This allows us to conceive of an underlying dimension running from A to B, on which every voter can be located in terms of his/her relative probability of voting for the two parties (Budge and Farlie, 1976: 106–107). A voter 100 per cent certain to vote for A would be "at" A. A voter equally likely to vote for either A or B would be at the midpoint on this dimension. A voter twice as likely to vote for B as to vote for A would be two-thirds of the way down this dimension, towards B, and so on.

If there are three parties in contention, A, B and C, then these can be placed at the corners of an equilateral triangle. Each voter can be located somewhere inside this triangle in terms of his/her relative likelihood of voting for each party. Thus a voter equally likely to vote for each party would be at the centroid of the triangle; a voter 80 per cent likely to vote for A and 10 per cent likely to vote for each of B and C would be on the perpendicular running from A to the line BC, at a point eight times closer to A than to B or C. Four parties would form a regular pyramid, while five parties would form a regular four-dimensional hyper-pyramid; and so on. Any n-party system can be described as a LiRaS space of dimension n-1, with the parties located by definition at the apices of the n-1 dimensional hyper-pyramid and voters located inside it, at a position reflecting their relative likelihoods of voting for each party in the system (Farlie and Budge, 1976: 390). Assuming that these relative likelihoods have some psychological meaning for each voter, the LiRaS space simply describes them in spatial terms. The underlying psychological assumption is that two voters who have similar relative likelihoods of voting for each of the set of parties on offer are close to each other politically, in some sense. This would arise even if the two different voters arrived at their relative voting likelihoods for utterly different reasons.

An LiRaS space, no more than a policy space in itself, is thus not a model of voting behaviour, but a graphical representation of voting likelihoods. A striking difference between an LiRaS space and a policy space is that, as political competition unfolds and voters change the relative likelihoods with which they will support different parties, the parties remain fixed and it is the voters that move around the space.

Thus, as with policy spaces, we may use the LiRaS framework as a tool kit from which to build a model of voting behaviour. The model of voting behaviour discussed by Budge and Farlie when they advocate the use of LiRaS spaces is in effect the "party identification" model of the Michigan School. "[M]any of the original assumptions associated with party identification can also be used to build a descriptive model of voting and party competition based in LiRaS" (Farlie and Budge, 1976: 390; see also Budge and Farlie, 1977). The party identification approach has very explicit psychological micro-foundations. It posits the "party identification" of a given voter as an underlying psychological attachment to a political party, developed as a result of long-term political socialisation (Miller *et al.*, 1954; Miller *et al.*, 1966). Party identification creates an underlying tendency to vote for the party in question, a tendency also influenced by "short-term political forces". In a two party system, absence of short-term political forces, a voter's likelihood ratio of voting for each party will be a function of the strength and direction of his/her party identification. Election campaigns generate the short-term forces that modify this likelihood ratio, although these forces are rarely modelled explicitly. As we have seen, short-term forces thus cause voters to move around the LiRaS space, and Farlie and Budge (1976) suggest that this short-term voter movement may arise from party competition in the policy space.

The concept of party identification is much more problematic in a multiparty context, both theoretically and empirically. This is because in a two party context, as we have seen, the resulting LiRaS space is one-dimensional. Weakening party identification for, or short-term forces damaging to, one of the parties implies only one direction of "movement" – towards the other party. In a multidimensional LiRaS environment, however, weakening support for one of the parties may imply "movement" in many different directions. Indeed the LiRaS approach helps us to see that, in order to specify a coherent model of party choice in a multiparty environment, the party identification approach must provide an account of how multidimensional likelihood ratio vectors would emerge and change. If such an account could be provided, then we would have a "spatial" model that explained voter movements around a multidimensional LiRaS space.

I am not sure what this model might look like but, in the best traditions of political theory, let us leap into the unknown and imagine that such a model already exists or could conceivably be constructed.

Prima facie evidence for party defined spaces

The reason we might want to resume the hunt for an explicit model of voter movement in an LiRaS space has to do with prima facie evidence that party defined spaces, at least in Ireland, appear to capture something of what real voters actually do. In order to illustrate this I first estimate policy spaces for parties and voters in the 2002 Irish election. I then compare this with a space derived from electronic voting data on party rankings. I then estimate a LiRaS space from survey data. The LiRaS space and the electronic voting space are remarkably similar.

The dimensionality and dimensions of the Irish policy space, 2002

Table 9.1 shows estimates of the relative salience of nine a priori policy dimensions during the 2002 general election in Ireland, derived from an expert survey (Benoit and Laver, 2006). Country specialists were asked for judgements of the salience of each policy dimension for each party, and Table 9.1 reports the mean salience of each policy dimension, weighting each party's contribution to the mean by its vote share in the 2002 election. By far the two most important policy dimensions relate to the classical left–right dimensional of economic policy and to Northern Ireland policy. One plausible representation of Irish *country specialists'* views of the Irish policy space in 2002 is thus two-dimensional.

Table 9.1 Expert judgements of policy dimension salience: Ireland 2002

Dimension	Weighted mean dimension salience*
Northern Ireland	13.9
Economic policy	13.8
EU neutrality	12.4
EU strengthen	12.3
EU enlarge	12.0
Immigration	11.8
Social policy	11.1
Environment	10.8
Decentralisation	10.2

Source: Benoit and Laver, 2005.

Note
* This is the mean of each of the dimension saliences for each party, weighted by party vote share in 2002.

The results of an attempt to estimate the dimensions and dimensionality of the Irish policy space, *as perceived by voters,* can be seen in Table 9.2. This reports a principal components analysis of a set of attitude scales derived from the Irish National Election Study (INES).[1] Sets of survey questions were combined into five additive scales with high scale reliability. These scales captured respondents' attitudes on: economic policy (left–right); "social" issues such as divorce, abortion and gay rights (liberal-conservative); immigration (liberal-conservative); European Union (pro-conservative); and Northern Ireland (republican-unionist). The top panel of these results show that the eigenvalues suggest either a one- or a two-dimensional policy space. The bottom panel, giving scale loadings on the varimax-rotated principal components, shows that first dimension is characterised by Northern Ireland policy and the second by economic policy. It is quite striking that the completely independent expert survey and INES survey of electors both suggest effectively the same policy space.

Table 9.2 Principal components analysis of INES survey respondents' positions on various attitude scales

Total variance explained						
	Initial eigenvalues			*Rotation sums of squared loadings*		
Component	*Total*	*% of variance*	*Cumulative %*	*Total*	*% of variance*	*Cumulative %*
1	1.404	28.084	28.084	1.289	25.784	25.784
2	1.058	21.163	49.247	1.173	23.464	49.247
3	0.914	18.286	67.533			
4	0.857	17.136	84.669			
5	0.767	15.331	100.000			

Note
Extraction method: Principal Component Analysis.

Rotated Component Matrix	*Component*	
	1	*2*
Economic policy: L/R	0.306	0.751
Social policy: lib/con	0.495	−0.442
Immigration: lib/con	0.663	−0.054
EU: pro/con	−0.264	0.640
N. Ireland: rep/un.	0.664	0.045

Source: Author's calculations from the Irish National Election Study, 2002.

Notes
Extraction method: Principal Component Analysis.
Rotation method: Varimax with Kaiser Normalization.

Table 9.3 shows expert survey estimates, taken from Benoit and Laver (2005) of party policy positions on the Northern Ireland and economic policy dimensions, as well as estimates of the mean policy positions of party supporters on the same policy dimensions, calculated from the INES. (The latter are the mean respondent positions on standardised versions of the Northern Ireland and economic policy INES attitude scales, broken down by the party to which the respondent gave his/her first preference vote.) The parties in Table 9.3 are ordered from left to right according to the country specialists' judgements of their economic policy positions.

The patterns in Table 9.3 are most easily seen by looking at Figure 9.1, which superimposes plots of the standardised estimates of party (expert survey) and voter (INES) positions and shows a fairly conventional two-dimensional spatial representation of Irish party politics, albeit one with some interesting divergences between the estimated policy positions of parties and party supporters. Country specialists rate Sinn Féin as having an economic policy position on the left, whereas Sinn Féin voters do not present themselves as being especially left-wing when reporting their attitudes on matters relating to economic policy. A similar situation can be seen on the economic right, with the Progressive Democrats (PDs) being rated by country specialists as having the most right-wing policies, while it is Fine Gael party supporters who have the most right-wing views on the economy. On Northern Ireland policy, the judgements of country special-

Table 9.3 Party policy positions in the 2002 Dáil election: expert judgements party supporter issue positions

	SF	Green	Labour	FG	FF	PD
Economic policy						
Expert judgements						
Mean	4.8	5.7	6.5	12.4	13.7	17.4
SE	0.31	0.28	0.35	0.38	0.38	0.24
INES respondents						
Mean	0.00	−0.20	−0.14	0.18	0.00	0.10
N	114	116	231	395	919	68
SD	1.02	0.84	0.90	1.05	1.02	0.89
Northern Ireland						
Expert judgements						
Mean	1.5	8.7	9.1	10.9	6.3	11.0
SE	0.19	0.40	0.35	0.47	0.37	0.44
INES respondents						
Mean	−0.47	0.24	0.09	0.07	−0.06	0.43
N	128	117	249	460	1,037	73
SD	1.03	1.07	0.99	1.04	0.97	0.98

Source: Benoit and Laver, 2005; author's calculations from the INES, 2002.

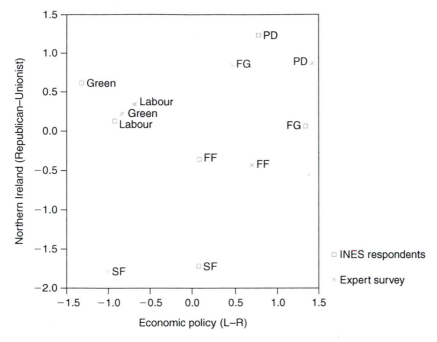

Figure 9.1 Two-dimensional representation superimposing standardised INES respondent positions, by party of first preference, and standardised expert survey judgement of party policy positions: Ireland 2002.

ists on party policy positions and the attitudes of party supporters are generally in line, with the main divergence being that Fine Gael supporters are on average more republican than the country specialists judge FG policy to be.

Thus it is easy to generate plausible policy spaces for Irish politics in 2002 and the policies we generate for parties and voters are encouragingly similar. The fly in the ointment is that the positions of INES respondents on the relevant policy dimensions add very little to our ability to predict how they voted. This can be seen from Table 9.4, which reports the likelihood ratios generated by binary logistic regressions setting out to predict party voting from the spatial policy positions of INES survey respondents.

For each of the three main parties, it is almost impossible to predict any party voting from policy positions alone, as the tiny Cox and Snell (pseudo) r-squared values show. Only for Fine Gael was there a strong association between party voting and policy position, with a one standard deviation unit move rightwards on economic policy increasing the likelihood of voting Fine Gael by 24 per cent. Labour voters did tend to be more left-wing on the economy and FF voters more republican on Northern Ireland. The reasons for the failure of policy positions to say much

Table 9.4 Policy positions, political socialisation and voting behaviour in the 2002
        Dáil election (likelihood ratios)

Dependent variable	FF voter?		FG voter?		Labour voter?	
N. Ireland policy	1.10*	1.06	0.92	0.98	0.91	0.91
Economic policy	1.01	1.01	1.24***	1.21**	0.86*	0.87
Party father		2.57***		3.13***		2.04**
Party mother		1.57***		2.58***		2.35**
Cox and Snell r²	0.002	0.089	0.007	0.097	0.003	0.017

*$p<0.05$, **$p<0.01$, ***$p<0.001$

about voting behaviour can be seen from Figure 9.2. While the mean
policy positions of party supporters reported in Table 9.3 did generate
reasonable looking party positions, the variation around those means was
enormous as Figure 9.2 shows, with box plots of INES respondents' policy
positions, broken down by party. There is massive overlap between parties
in the distributions of party supporters' policy positions, which is why it is
so hard to predict voting from voters' policy positions.

Table 9.4 also estimates an alternative logistic regression model for
each of the three main parties, adding two variables that we can assume to
capture a substantial element of political socialisation. For each group of
party supporters, this is whether or not the respondent's father and/or
mother were supporters of the party in question. Thus in explaining FF
voting we supplement respondents' policy positions on the two most
salient dimensions with variables reflecting whether the respondents'
fathers and mothers were FF supporters. Equivalent parental vote variables are used to predict FG and Labour support. The effects of these
"political socialisation" variables both dramatically improve predictive
power and typically reduce the effect of policy positions to insignificance.
Thus a voter whose father supported FF was 2.57 times more likely to vote
FF, controlling for policy position; a voter whose father supported FG was
3.13 times more likely to vote FG. Only in the case of FG did the voter's
(economic) policy position retain some independent effect on voting
after parental party support was added to the equation.

Table 9.4 and Figure 9.2 thus tell us that the Irish policy spaces described
in Figure 9.1 do not add hugely to our ability to predict Irish voting behaviour in 2002, and that parental voting, which might plausibly be taken to
capture some of the "political socialisation" micro-foundations of the party
ID approach, tends to swamp any policy effects that we can discern.

Dimensional Analysis of Irish Electronic Voting Data, 2002

If we want to characterise the actual voting behaviour of Irish citizens in
spatial terms, then the published electronic votes from the 2002 election,

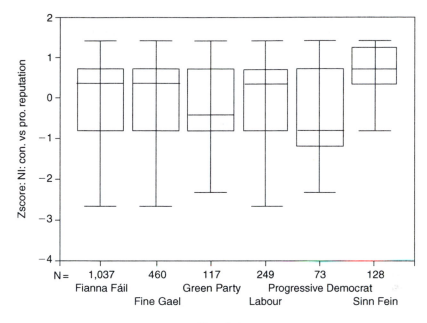

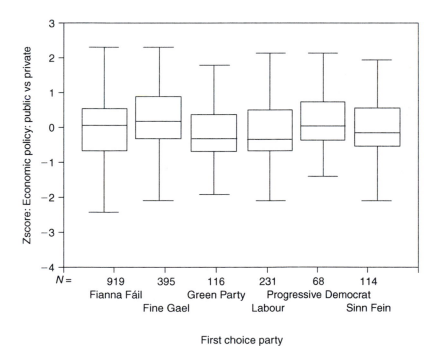

Figure 9.2 Box plots of INES respondents' positions on two most salient policy dimensions, by party.

ranking all candidates contesting each of the three pilot constituencies in which electronic voting machines were deployed, offer us a unique opportunity to do this. Unfortunately, in only one of these three constituencies, Dublin West, did all main Irish parties field at least one candidate. In the other two constituencies, Dublin North and Meath, the Progressive Democrats (who were government coalition partners both before and after the election) did not run a candidate. In what follows, therefore, I base the analysis on the 29,988 electronic ballots ranking the nine candidates running in Dublin West. Fianna Fáil ran two candidates and all other parties contesting the race ran one candidate.[2] Unusually for an Irish election these days, but fortunately for us in the present context, no independent candidate contested Dublin West in 2002.

One result of publishing full STV ballots for the first time was to confirm anecdotal evidence that most voters register very incomplete rankings. Despite the fact that there were nine candidates on the ballot, the mean number of rankings registered by voters in this constituency was 4.4, the median number was four and the modal number three. Only 12.7 per cent of Dublin West voters ranked all candidates (Laver, 2004). An unranked candidate on a ballot is not missing data in the traditional meaning of the term (in the sense that the dog ate the ranking), but rather it can reasonably be inferred that unranked candidates are ranked lower than ranked candidates. Therefore, rather than treating unranked candidates as missing data and confining ourselves to a highly biased subset of the 12.7 per cent of fully-completed ballots, preferences can be imputed for unranked candidates on each ballot. Of various possible ways of doing this, the method selected was to give all unranked candidates on a ballot the median of the unfilled rankings on the ballot. In effect, and for want of any other information, this treats all unranked candidates as being ranked "last equal", and destroys less information than treating them as missing data (see Laver (2004) for a discussion of imputing rankings in this context). This imputation also reflects how votes are counted in an STV election.

These rankings, including the imputed rankings discussed above, can be used to calculate a matrix of inter-party distances, which can then be scaled. For an individual voter, the distance between any pair of parties was estimated as the absolute difference in the voter's ranking of those two parties. For any given voter, the distance between explicitly ranked parties could thus range between one (when two parties were given adjacent rankings) to eight (when one party was ranked one and the other nine). Unranked parties have an inter-party distance of zero, since the voter has registered indifference between them. The distance between a pair of parties in Dublin West is thus taken as the sum of the individual voter inter-party distances for that pair.

If this inter-party distance matrix is scaled using MDS,[3] the result can be seen in Figure 9.3. This dimensional analysis of voter rankings of the various parties looks nothing at all like the policy spaces in Figure 9.1. Indeed it is effectively impossible to interpret this figure in policy terms, no matter how we might rotate it, flip it or stand on our heads. The parties are arranged in a triangle with Fianna Fáil (FF), Fine Gael (FG) and Sinn Féin (SF) at its apices. Indeed it is hard to escape the interpretation of this picture of Irish voting behaviour as one of "Fianna Fáil versus the rest" – an interpretation that has pervaded popular accounts of Irish politics since the Civil War. On one side of the horizontal dimension is FF, on the other are the serried ranks of FF's opponents. FF's coalition partner, the PDs, occupy an intermediate zone between the two. The vertical dimension does distinguish between FF's opponents, placing FG and SF as farthest apart, a divergence that could be interpreted in terms of Northern Ireland policy.

The overwhelming impression from Figure 9.3, however, is that this is a party defined space rather than a policy space – in other words that Irish voters did not rank the parties on their ballots in a manner consistent with these parties' locations in the Irish policy space. At the very least, Figure 9.3 suggests that the primary decision for Irish voters concerned whether or not to vote for Fianna Fáil, with this decision being very little structured by party and voter policy positions. It seems to have been much more of a "party defined" decision deriving, if we are to take seriously the evidence from Table 9.4, from much longer-term political socialisation. The vertical

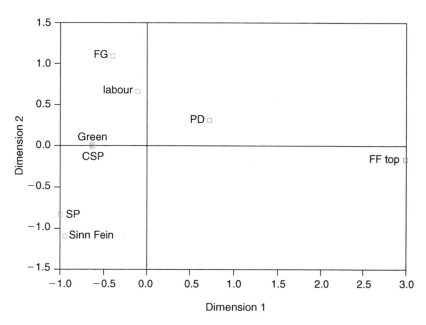

Figure 9.3 Two-dimensional Euclidean MDS of party distance matrix based on electronic preference votes cast in Dublin West, 2002.

dimension in Figure 9.3, with SF at one end and FG at the other also representing opposite ends of the "republican" policy dimension, does however suggest that those voters who chose *not* to support FF did perhaps distinguish the other parties on a basis that could be systematically related to party and voter policy positions.

Dimensional analysis of "probability of party support" data in the INES

If Figure 9.3 puts the notion of party-defined spaces back on the agenda, then the INES provides data with which to estimate something like a party defined LiRaS space for the 2002 Irish election. The INES asked a battery of questions designed to estimate the probability that respondents would ever vote for each party.[4] These "probability of a party vote" questions can be used to generate an inter-party distance matrix in a manner similar to that used on the electronic voting data. For an individual INES respondent, the distance between any pair of parties can be estimated as the absolute difference in the voter's probability of ever voting for each those two parties. For any given voter, the distance between explicitly ranked parties could thus range between zero (when the respondent reported that s/he was equally probable to vote for either party) to nine (when the respondent reported that s/he was maximally probable to vote for one party and minimally probable to vote for the other). Indeed, although these distances are self-evidently not likelihood *ratios*, they do capture relative likelihoods of party voting in a systematic way. The inter-party "relative likelihood" distances for the entire INES are the aggregate of the inter-party distances of each respondent. Scaling this in the same way as the electronic voting distances in Figure 9.3, we get the result in Figure 9.4.[5] The similarity between Figures 9.3 and 9.4 is uncanny, despite the fact that they were estimated using utterly independent data, the former using real electronic votes in one constituency, the latter using INES survey responses for the country as a whole. In other words, survey data on respondents' relative voting probabilities generates what looks like precisely the same party space as that generated by electronic voting data on actual voter rank orderings of the parties.

Mapping policy into a likelihood ratio space

The supreme act of heroism (or folly) in this paper is displayed in Figure 9.5. This takes the party-defined space that appears so clearly in both the electronic voting data and the INES party voting probabilities and sets out to map actual voting behaviour and voter policy positions into this. Figure 9.5 in effect shows a LiRaS space *á la* Budge and Farlie, with added information about actual voting behaviour and attitudes on key policy dimensions mapped into this.

The equilateral triangle defining this space was taken, given the strong

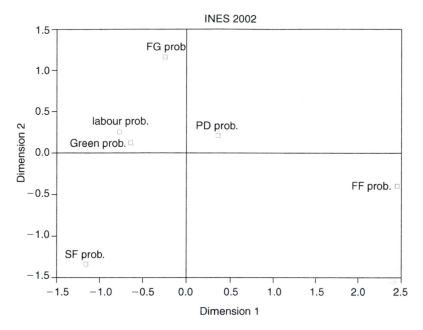

Figure 9.4 Two-dimensional Euclidean MDS of distances between "probability to give first preference vote to party" scores, INES 2002.

empirical patterns in Figures 9.3 and 9.4, to have FF, FG and SF at its apices. The bisectors of this triangle partition the space into six segments. Thus the horizontal line in Figure 9.5 divides INES respondents into those (above the line) who had a higher likelihood of voting FG at some time in the future than they had of voting SF, and those (below the line) for whom the converse was true.[6] The other bisectors sort respondents in terms of their relative likelihoods of supporting FF and FG, and relative likelihoods of supporting FF and SF. For each segment of INES respondents, the small tables inside the figure report mean levels of actual first preference party support, and mean positions on the two main policy dimensions.

These tables confirm the prima facie impression that the "north–south" dimension in the party defined spaces is indeed related to Northern Ireland policy. Northern Ireland policy scores become more republican as we move south in the space. The policy basis of the "east–west", or "FF versus the rest", dimension is harder to interpret in policy terms, however.

Conclusions

The most striking finding reported in this paper is that the party space generated by dimensional analysis of party distances calculated from actual electronic votes cast, closely resembles the party-defined LiRaS(ish)

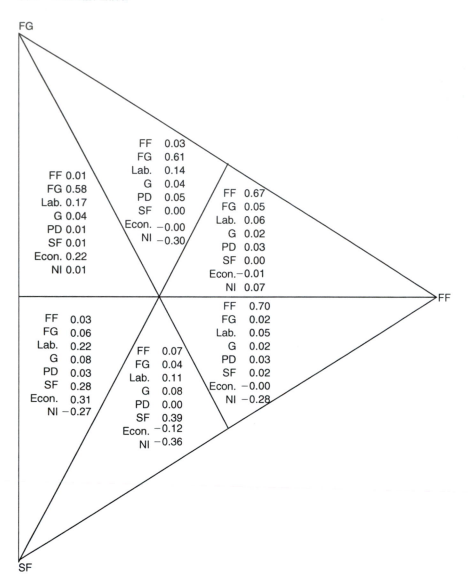

FG

FF 0.03
FG 0.61
Lab. 0.14
G 0.04
PD 0.05
SF 0.00
Econ. −0.00
NI −0.30

FF 0.01
FG 0.58
Lab. 0.17
G 0.04
PD 0.01
SF 0.01
Econ. 0.22
NI 0.01

FF 0.67
FG 0.05
Lab. 0.06
G 0.02
PD 0.03
SF 0.00
Econ.−0.01
NI 0.07

FF   0.70
FG   0.02
Lab.   0.05
G   0.02
PD   0.03
SF   0.02
Econ. −0.00
NI −0.28

FF

FF   0.03
FG   0.06
Lab.   0.22
G   0.08
PD   0.03
SF   0.28
Econ.   0.31
NI −0.27

FF 0.07
FG 0.04
Lab. 0.11
G 0.08
PD 0.00
SF 0.39
Econ. −0.12
NI −0.36

SF

Figure 9.5 "Likelihood ratio space" of INES survey respondents, with voting behavi-
    our and policy positions of various categories of respondent.

space calculated from the party voting probabilities in the Irish National
Election Study. At the same time, this looks quite unlike the conventional
Irish policy spaces generated using expert surveys or INES attitude scales.
If one was strongly wedded to the view that voters' locations in the Irish
policy space determine their rank orderings of political parties when they
vote at elections – and this is indeed what is implied by conventional

spatial voting models – then the differences between 9.1, on the one hand, and Figures 9.3 and 9.4, on the other, might be grounds for considering a divorce.

Despite all talk of the demise of Civil War politics in Ireland, the old characterisation of Irish party politics as "Fianna Fáil versus the rest" appears from an analysis of both the electronic voting data and the INES party voting probabilities to have lost none of its potency by the time of the 2002 election. There was even a strong hint of a civil war policy dimension, essentially "republican" in substance, distinguishing FF's opponents – to a large extent the product of deep policy divisions on Northern Ireland between FG and SF.

Of course, Ireland might indeed be peculiar and it is not at all clear how far we can generalise these results. We have been fortunate when analysing Irish voting behaviour in having access to a wide variety of independent data sources, of which the most unique and intriguing is the full set of published electronic votes from 2002.[7] This is supplemented by INES estimates of relative probabilities of party support, INES estimates of voter policy positions and by expert survey estimates of party policy positions. Of all of these data sources, the most challenging for any spatial model of policy-based party voting are the electronic voting data. If Ireland is not peculiar, then the fact that real voters clearly do not rank order political parties according to their positions in conventional policy space does indeed imply a serious re-evaluation of conventional spatial models of mass voting behaviour.

Appendix

Table 9.A.1 "Likelihood ratios" for different sets of party supporters: INES, 2002

First choice party		Prob (FF)/ Prob(FF+FG+SF)	Prob (FG)/ Prob(FF+FG+SF)	Prob (SF)/ Prob(FF+FG+SF)
Fianna Fáil	Mean	0.57	0.24	0.18
	n	1,019	1,019	1,019
	Std Dev.	0.15	0.13	0.12
Fine Gael	Mean	0.28	0.55	0.17
	n	454	454	454
	Std Dev.	0.16	0.18	0.12
Sinn Fein	Mean	0.28	0.16	0.56
	n	125	125	125
	Std Dev.	0.16	0.12	0.16
Green Party	Mean	0.35	0.36	0.29
	n	119	119	119
	Std Dev.	0.17	0.17	0.19
Labour	Mean	0.36	0.37	0.27
	n	246	246	246
	Std Dev.	0.18	0.17	0.17
Prog. Dems	Mean	0.43	0.38	0.19
	n	72	72	72
	Std Dev.	0.17	0.18	0.12
Total	Mean	0.44	0.33	0.23
	n	2,281	2,281	2,281
	Std Dev.	0.20	0.20	0.17

Table 9.A.2 Numbers of INES survey respondents in various likelihood ratio categories

SF vs FG relative likelihood	FF vs FG relative likelihood	FF vs SF relative likelihood			Total
		More SF than FF	Equally FF and SF	More FF than SF	
More FG than SF	More FG than FF	81	192	237	510
	Equally FG and FF			238	238
	More FF than FG			611	611
Total		81	192	1,086	1,359
Equally FG and SF	More FG than FF	28			28
	Equally FG and FF		201		201
	More FF than FG			358	358
Total		28	201	358	587
More SF than FG	More FG than FF	70			70
	Equally FG and FF	79			79
	More FF than FG	119	89	273	481
Total		268	89	273	630

Table 9.A.3 First preference votes and policy positions of INES survey respondents in various likelihood ratio categories

FF vs FG relative likelihood	SF vs FG relative likelihood		FF vs SF relative likelihood		
			More FG than FF	Equal FG and FF	More FF than FG
More FG than SF					
	More SF than FF	FF voter?	0.01	.	.
		FG voter?	0.58	.	.
		Labour voter?	0.17	.	.
		Green voter?	0.04	.	.
		PD voter?	0.01	.	.
		SF voter?	0.01	.	.
		Economic policy	0.22	.	.
		Northern Ireland	−0.01	.	.
	Equal FF and SF	FF voter?	0.02	.	.
		FG voter?	0.61	.	.
		Labour voter?	0.09	.	.
		Green voter?	0.11	.	.
		PD voter?	0.04	.	.
		SF voter?	0.00	.	.
		Economic policy	0.15	.	.
		Northern Ireland	−0.26	.	.
	More FF than SF	FF voter?	0.03	0.32	0.67
		FG voter?	0.61	0.26	0.05
		Labour voter?	0.14	0.10	0.06
		Green voter?	0.04	0.05	0.02
		PD voter?	0.05	0.05	0.03
		SF voter?	0.00	0.00	0.00
		Economic policy	−0.00	0.19	−0.01
		Northern Ireland	−0.30	−0.21	−0.07
Equal FG and SF					
	More SF than FF	FF voter?	0.02	.	.
		FG voter?	0.38	.	.
		Labour voter?	0.19	.	.
		Green voter?	0.07	.	.
		PD voter?	0.00	.	.
		SF voter?	0.09	.	.
		Economic policy	0.09	.	.
		Northern Ireland	0.17	.	.
	Equal FF and SF	FF voter?	.	0.19	.
		FG voter?	.	0.10	.
		Labour voter?	.	0.15	.
		Green voter?	.	0.10	.
		PD voter?	.	0.02	.
		SF voter?	.	0.01	.
		Economic policy	.	−0.07	.
		Northern Ireland	.	−0.10	.

Table 9.A.3 continued

FF vs FG relative likelihood	SF vs FG relative likelihood		FF vs SF relative likelihood		
			More FG than FF	Equal FG and FF	More FF than FG
	More FF than SF	FF voter?	.	.	0.68
		FG voter?	.	.	0.02
		Labour voter?	.	.	0.05
		Green voter?	.	.	0.03
		PD voter?	.	.	0.01
		SF voter?	.	.	0.01
		Economic policy	.	.	–.18
		Northern Ireland	.	.	0.17
More SF than FG					
	More SF than FF	FF voter?	0.03	0.06	0.07
		FG voter?	0.06	0.01	0.04
		Labour voter?	0.22	0.21	0.11
		Green voter?	0.08	0.06	0.08
		PD voter?	0.03	0.02	0.00
		SF voter?	0.28	0.33	0.39
		Economic policy	0.31	–0.00	–0.12
		Northern Ireland	0.27	0.34	0.36
	Equal FF and SF	FF voter?	.	.	0.35
		FG voter?	.	.	0.00
		Labour voter?	.	.	0.05
		Green voter?	.	.	0.03
		PD voter?	.	.	0.03
		SF voter?	.	.	0.19
		Economic policy	.	.	–0.21
		Northern Ireland	.	.	0.26
	More FF than SF	FF voter?	.	.	0.70
		FG voter?	.	.	0.02
		Labour voter?	.	.	0.05
		Green voter?	.	.	0.02
		PD voter?	.	.	0.03
		SF voter?	.	.	0.02
		Economic policy	.	.	–0.00
		Northern Ireland	.	.	0.28

Notes

1 Full details of, and data from, the Irish National Election Study of 2002 can be found at www.ucd.ie/issda/dataset-info/ines.htm.
2 In the analysis that follows each voter's ranking of Fianna Fáil is taken as his/her highest ranking for a Fianna Fáil candidate.
3 The results were created using a Euclidean distance model and the Alscal routines in SPSS.
4 These questions took the following form: "We have a number of political parties in Ireland each of which would like to get your vote. How probable is it that you will ever give your first preference vote to the following parties? Please use the numbers on this scale to indicate your views, where '1' means 'not at all probable' and '10' means 'very probable'."
5 The Socialist Party and the Christian Solidarity Party have been omitted because there is insufficient data on these very small parties in the INES.
6 There are actually many INES respondents "on" these lines, having reported that they were equally likely in the future to vote for either of a given pair of parties. These respondents are not considered here, for the sake of clarity of exposition, but their characteristics would not change our conclusions.
7 In May 2004, the Irish government postponed the full introduction of electronic voting, pending further tests of the proposed system, and it is not clear when new electronic voting data will be generated and published.

References

Benoit, K. and M. Laver (2006) *Party Policy in Modern Democracies* (London: Routledge) (forthcoming).

Budge, I. and D. Farlie (1976) 'A comparative Analysis of Factors Correlated with Turnout and Voting Choice', in Budge, Crewe and Farlie *Party Identification and Beyond* (London: Wiley), pp. 103–126.

Budge, I. and D. Farlie (1977) *Voting and Party Competitio* (London: Wiley).

Budge, I., I. Crewe and D. Farlie (eds) (1976a) *Party Identification and Beyond* (London: Wiley).

Budge, I., I. Crewe and D. Farlie (eds) (1976b) 'Introduction: Rational Choice, Policy Spaces and Party Identification'. in I. Budge, I. Crewe and D. Farlie *Party Identification and Beyond* (London: Wiley), pp. 277–283.

Farlie, D. and I. Budge (1976) 'Placing Party Identification within a Typology of Representations of Voting and Party Competition and Proposing a Synthesis', in I. Budge, I. Crewe and D. Farlie *Party Identification and Beyond* (London: Wiley), pp. 383–393.

Laver, M. (2004) 'Analysing structures of party preference in electronic voting data', *Party Politics* 10: 521–541.

Miller, Warren E., Angus Campbell and Gerald Gurin (1954) *The Voter Decides* (Evanston, IL: Paterson and Co.).

Miller, W.E., A. Campbell, Philip E. Converse and Donald E. Stokes (1966) *The American Voter* (New York: Wiley).

Part III

Democratic processes and values

10 Ideological considerations and voting behaviour

A comparison of individual and aggregate level approaches

John Bartle

Introduction

Many of those who write about democracy often suppose that individual vote decisions and aggregate election outcomes owe something to ideological considerations. Elections are, therefore, regularly scrutinised for what they tell us about the appeal of 'ideas', whether in the form of ideational wholes ('isms') or general solutions to social problems. In the mid-1980s, for example, the Conservative Party's three successive victories were often supposed to owe something to the appeal of 'Thatcherism' or policies that 'rolled back the frontiers of the state'. At the same time, Ronald Reagan's landslide victories were widely interpreted as signalling a demand for more 'conservative' policies or marking a 'shift the right' (Shanks and Miller, 1990). Indeed, elections at all times and in all places are interpreted in 'ideological' terms (Stokes, 1963).

The tendency to invoke ideological explanations doubtless owes something to the need among the political elite to make sense of elections. After all, commentators need to explain and politicians need to respond (or, at least, to be seen to do so). Both must, therefore, distil a message if they are to perform their roles. This need to explain, of course, may lead them to produce unduly complex interpretations of elections (Stokes, 1963). Yet the tendency to appeal to 'ideology' also undoubtedly reflects the normative belief that elections *should* link voters to outcomes. Ideological accounts are important, therefore, simply because they suggest that that the democratic promise of self-government can be fulfilled.

Although it is widely supposed that ideological considerations play an important role in democratic elections, political scientists have tended to play down their role. This is particularly true of individual level models of vote decisions. It is a little less true of aggregate level models, where parties are assumed to compete on the basis of their 'ideological reputations' (Webb, 2000). Yet, even here, there has been surprisingly little effort to empirically demonstrate that ideological considerations do influence the vote. This is an omission that is only slowly being addressed.

Political science has, therefore, produced two (apparently contradictory) conclusions. Most individual level research suggests that ideological considerations are irrelevant, while aggregate level research suggests that they are of great importance. In this chapter I propose to explore the reasons for this curious – but also curiously ignored – disjuncture (Scarbrough, 1984: 4). I begin by exploring the approach of individual level modellers: their prior beliefs, their model of voting behaviour and measurement assumptions. I will then explore the beliefs of aggregate level modellers in order to understand this state of affairs, before examining the impact of ideological considerations in British elections.

Individual level models and ideological considerations

Most laypersons – and doubtless some analysts too – maintain that scientific research is objective and free from bias. They believe that the scientist merely gathers the relevant facts and produces conclusions based on well-rehearsed rules of statistical or logical inference. Most reflective analysts of social behaviour, of course, are all too well aware that their prior beliefs can (consciously or subconsciously) influence their working practices, shape their expectations and influence their interpretations of ambiguous evidence. They are, furthermore, acutely aware that the validity of such priors are rarely examined and that their successful application depends on the strength of the theory and the appropriateness of the underlying analogy. It is, accordingly, worth making a few general observations about the 'priors' associated with those who adopt an individual level approach.

Prior beliefs

At the risk of being trite, it is important to realise that most analysts assume that they need to explain the behaviour of individual voters. By and large most analysts have simply sought to establish what factors distinguish supporters of party A from those for party B or, alternatively, to reveal the causal processes by which variables influence the vote. In principle, analysts can then combine evidence about the estimated impact of each variable with information about its distribution, in order to provide an estimate of its impact on the aggregate election outcome (Miller and Shanks, 1996). In practice, however, this additional step is rarely undertaken. It is as if analysts have been so aware of the difficulties that confront any attempt to produce a general model for the 'typical voter', that they have despaired of producing truly general characterisations of election outcomes.

This reluctance to produce an explanation of the aggregate outcome in part owes something to the realisation that individual voters are subject to complex and almost unfathomable motivations. Most analysts accept, for example, that voters are not simply guided by their preferences. Rather they wish to understand the world about them, to connect themselves to others and that they value those like themselves (Smith and Mackie, 2000). In order to facilitate this understanding, they naturally attach labels both to themselves and others. These 'identities', once acquired, shape political attitudes and political preferences because individuals wish to gain the love, approval or acceptance of fellow group members. Political attitudes and preferences are continually adjusted to fit in with family, workmates and neighbours. While identities do change, they do so only as a result of glacial social change; a marriage, religious conversion or social and regional mobility and this results in considerable continuity of electoral preferences. The vote is, therefore, a complex expression of identities, rather than as a purposive choice (Campbell *et al.*, 1960).

Most analysts of voting behaviour have also been struck by the remarkable range of factors that appear to have some visible influence on political preferences (Miller and Shanks, 1996). When faced with such a bewildering array of possible causes, a few have been prepared to set aside consideration of some variables, relying either on 'strong theory' or the principle of parsimony to focus on 'relevant' variables. Invariably, if not inevitably, the 'strong theory' is some version of the utility choice model (Alvarez and Nagler, 1995).[1] Most analysts of voting behaviour, however, do not believe that the principle of parsimony can be used to justify oversimplified representations of 'patently complex' phenomena (Campbell *et al.*, 1960: 19). Consequently, they have tried to arrange variables into an order that best approximates the process by which voters acquire their attitudes, opinions and evaluations. This attempt to unravel cause and effect has added to the complexity of their models and shifted attention away from the aggregate outcome.

Models of the vote

Most analysts of individual level voting behaviour have accepted that their models should be as inclusive as possible and not exclude consideration of variables by theoretical fiat (Miller and Shanks, 1996). In this context it is important to note that analysts did not simply declare that ideological considerations were unimportant on a priori grounds alone. Having defined ideology in very precise terms and having produced well-specified indicators they felt compelled to conclude that voters were largely 'innocent' of ideology. Only in retrospect has it become apparent that the definition was too restrictive and the measures inadequate (Scarbrough, 1984).

Before exploring why early research concluded that voters did not possess ideologies, it is important to understand exactly how individual level analysts tried to assess the influence of variables on votes. The three keys to simplifying the task were to recognise (1) the crucial implications of voter ignorance, (2) the special role played by parties in organising choice and (3) the utility of the 'funnel of causality' heuristic.

The most striking, and in many ways, the most theoretically significant

Social characteristics

Social identities

Party identification and ideological positions

Policy preferences and evaluation of conditions

Retrospective evaluations of governmental performance

Prospective evaluations of party performance and assessments of leaders

VOTE

Figure 10.1 The funnel of causality.

observation of the early surveys on voting behaviour was that most voters know surprisingly little about politics (Butler and Stokes, 1974). Although most participate in general elections, few pay much attention to politics. Most voters, therefore, know little about their programmes for office and even less about specific policies. Apart from the leaders of the major political parties, they recognise few politicians. In order to perform even their minimal roles, therefore, voters have to simplify the political world. The chief way that voters simplified things was by forming an identity with a party. Voters simply came to think of themselves 'being' 'Democrat', 'Republican' or 'Conservative'.

Once established, this party identification is held to be largely resistant to change, thus ensuring considerable electoral stability. This identification is the core element in the voter's belief system and shapes their basic beliefs and preferences. Partisans are held to interpret information through the rose tinted spectacles of their partisanship, discounting information critical of their party and reducing 'dissonance' (Campbell *et al.*, 1960: 141). This is illustrated in Figure 10.1, which displays the 'funnel of causality' heuristic, showing how voters are assumed to acquire their configuration of attitudes, opinions and evaluations. Social characteristics shape identities and these in turn determine partisan self-identifications. These long-term predispositions in turn shape short-term factors, such as policy preferences, evaluations of conditions and assessments of leaders.

If this model approximates the process by which voters acquire their attitudes, preferences and evaluations then, in order to assess the unique impact of any given variable, one must control for those variables that are both a cause of the current variable under consideration and the vote decision (Miller and Shanks, 1996). 'Explanation', therefore, consists in providing a finely grained explanation linking remote (or long-term) predispositions to more proximate (or short-term) factors. This can be sharply distinguished from mere 'prediction', which can be achieved by focusing on the proximate causes of the vote.

Defining and measuring ideology

The earliest studies of ideology and voting behaviour equated ideology with sophistication. Indeed, one of the most influential studies defined it as 'a particularly elaborate, close-woven, and far ranging structure of attitudes' (Campbell *et al.*, 1960: 192). In order to establish whether voters held anything approaching an ideology they sought to establish whether voters used and understood abstract terms (such as 'conservative', 'liberal', 'left' or 'right') or whether they associated the parties with such terms. Faced with overwhelming evidence that they did not, the early researchers felt compelled to conclude that voters were not familiar with the language of ideology (Campbell *et al.*, 1960; Butler and Stokes, 1974). They further reasoned that if voters had ideologies then their opinions on issues of current controversy would be 'constrained', so that to know their opinion on issue X_1 would enable them to predict their opinions on related issues X_2 and X_3. Further, if enduring ideas underpinned their opinions, they should find that opinions on X_1 in time t_1 should predict the same opinions in t_2 and t_3. Faced with evidence of considerable temporal instability, they again felt compelled to conclude that voters' opinions were not structured by ideology and that voters were largely incapable of responding to ideological appeals (Campbell *et al.*, 1960; Converse, 1964; Butler and Stokes, 1974).

Later studies have demonstrated that the early studies were marred by both conceptual and methodological flaws. The use and recognition of abstract terms is not, for example, an indicator of 'ideological thinking', but of sophistication (Luskin, 1987). It is, therefore, perfectly possible to believe in a good society in which individuals are left alone and the state is as small as possible and yet mistakenly think of oneself as 'left-wing'. Moreover, parties do not, on the whole, stand before the electorate and say 'vote for me I'm right wing' (Scarbrough, 1984). They appeal to the electorate in general terms by advocating 'a smaller state and larger citizens' or by advocating policies such as tax cuts, deregulation and privatisation. An individual who mistakenly believes himself to be 'left-wing' would, therefore, be still able to cast his vote on the basis of belief.

There was a further problem with the early studies, which is simply stated. Real ideologies are not coherent wholes. Indeed, many apparently contradictory ideas can be made to 'stand together' via elaboration. Ideologies can, therefore, be more straightforwardly and more usefully defined as a 'set of beliefs characteristic of a group' and analysts can try to uncover evidence that voters hold those fundamental beliefs rather than 'constrained opinions' on current controversies (Scarbrough, 1984).

Those who take the study of ideology seriously have increasingly sought to identify political enduring conflicts that underpin partisan debate (Scarbrough, 1984). Since partisans tend to rationalise, however, analysts have employed questions that avoid all direct reference to the parties themselves. They have also shifted attention away from the specific and contemporary to the general and the enduring. This has revolutionised our understanding of the role of ideological considerations and revealed that many voters do, indeed, have quite stable opinions after all (Heath *et al.*, 1994). Once responses to individual items are adjusted for measurement error, respondents' opinions are overwhelmingly stable (Achen, 1975). Aggregating individual responses, reduces the effects of random error and further suggests that voters do have stable general positions (Heath *et al.*, 1994). Even those who were responsible for the early research on ideology have accepted that 'policy-related predispositions' (or ideological considerations) merit a prominent place in the 'funnel of causality' (see Figure 10.1). The major, unresolved, issue is the precise relationship between ideological considerations and partisanship (see below).

Despite this revolution in thinking, many survey analysts have continued to downplay the role of ideological considerations in the vote. In part, of course, this reflects the enduring influence of the early studies and lingering suspicions about voters' capacities for self-government. The tendency to ignore ideology has increased in recent years with some noting the rise of the 'catch-all' party that downplays any attempt to characterise it in 'ideological' terms (Kirchheimer, 1990). More mundanely, however, the absence of ideological considerations from vote models often simply reflects the fact that the appropriate indicators are not available because they are so very expensive to measure. This is particularly true where ideological considerations are viewed in terms of 'ideational wholes'. The most comprehensive study of voting behaviour and political ideology ever published, for example, required a questionnaire that was several pages long and permitted open-ended responses, which are notoriously difficult to code (Scarbrough, 1984). Even if ideology is defined more narrowly in terms of 'ideological positions' on underlying dimensions of conflict, large batteries of questions are still required (Heath *et al.*, 1994). While incorporation of ideological considerations may thus clarify assumptions about causal order, most principal investigators are reluctant to include such items because they reduce the coverage of 'topical' ('sexier') issues.

The response to this tension between causation and topicality has been predictable. Time and time again researchers have relied either on voters' self-locations on abstract 'left versus right' dimensions or their opinions on current issues as indicators of general beliefs. The former, of course, represent a measure of sophistication rather than ideology (Luskin, 1987), while the latter reflect measurement error as well as the influence of ideological considerations (Zaller, 1992). It is hardly surprising, therefore, that both these indicators have modest correlations with behaviour (Bartle, 2003).

While there has been a fundamental reappraisal of ideology, many principal investigators fail to take ideological considerations seriously. The recent resurgence of interest in 'valence', moreover, has further served to obscure the extent to which 'position' issues underpin the latter (Stokes, 1963). Voters cannot *evaluate* an outcome until they know what is to be 'valued'. 'Position issues' and ideological considerations are logically prior to 'valence' issues. Most individual level models must, therefore, understate the extent to which vote decisions are based on disagreements about fundamental issues. Just as Converse has wryly noted, the study of ideology seems proof that 'what is important to study cannot be measured and .... what can be measured is not important to study' (Converse, 1964: 206).

Aggregate level models

The majority of research into voting behaviour has focused on the micro-level behaviour of individuals and used survey data to produce comprehensive explanations of individual vote decisions. By contrast, however, an increasing number of analysts have sought to bypass direct consideration of the individual voter and focus instead on aggregate outcomes (Erickson *et al.*, 2002). Most such studies naturally assume that 'ideological reputations' are *the* fundamental basis of party appeals and that parties can increase their appeal via a process of programmatic adaptation (Webb, 2000).

Before examining these models, it is again useful to examine the prior beliefs of analysts: particularly those relating to explanation, modelling and purposive behaviour. As I shall argue, yet again, these assumptions account, in large part, for the 'curious disjuncture' noted above.

Prior beliefs

Again at the risk of stating the obvious, it is important to realise that aggregate (or macro) models focus on aggregate electoral outcomes: the total votes received by the major parties. Macro-level analysts believe that the purpose of political science is to produce truly general inferences about the fundamental forces influencing behaviour and happily endorse the principle of parsimony (Budge, 2004). Explanations of elections, therefore, need not be based on a detailed understanding of individual vote decisions, which are – by definition – subject to a range of trivial or idiosyncratic influences. That is a task that should be left to contemporary historians (Budge, 2004). Truly scientific (or general) 'explanations' of the vote should strip away 'inessential detail' to reveal the fundamental forces that drive voting behaviour (Erickson *et al.*, 2002). In contrast with their micro-level counterparts, macro-level analysts also tend to believe that there is a fairly close relationship between explanation and prediction and are willing to 'shave off' 'unnecessary' assumptions. Abstraction and simplification is viewed as an essential requirement for all good explanation. The aggregate level analyst accordingly revels in simplicity just as much as his individual level counterpart revels in complexity.

A further illustration of this tendency to simplify in order to explain is the way in which most aggregate models tend to assume that the vote is an instrument used to achieve desired ends. Since voters are instrumental, their decisions can be analysed in the same way as the decision about which brand of toothpaste or car to purchase (Brennan and Lomasky, 1993). The vote decision is held to represent a choice based on a (more or less) rational calculation of benefit to the voter, their household or groups to which they belong. Thus, the simplest 'rational choice' models suggest that voters would calculate an 'expected party differential' by acquiring information about the parties' policies, estimating the impact of those policies on their welfare and then supporting the party that offers them the highest utility income (Downs, 1957: 39–40).

Whatever their theoretical elegance and intuitive plausibility, all purposive theories of voting behaviour run into sand on the 'paradox of voting'. Put quite simply, instrumental voters are unlikely to vote, since the probability that their single vote will be decisive is infinitesimal and the resulting expected net benefits from voting are always less than the associated costs. For some, the fact that the basic motivational assumption is unable to account for turnout represents an insuperable objection to all instrumental models and illustrates the superiority of expressive models of mass behaviour (Brennan and Lomasky, 1993). For others, including most aggregate analysts, the identification of the paradox illustrates the power of instrumental theories to account for what must be the most consistent finding of survey research over the last 40 years. Voters are ignorant simply because they have no incentive to pay attention to politics. They can, however, reduce the cost of acquiring and processing information and still arrive at a reasonable decision that is guided by calculations of personal benefit (Popkin, 1994).

One way that voters might simplify their decision is by judging parties according to their 'ideology', defined as beliefs about: the way the world is, the way the world should be and the chief means of getting from one to the other (Downs, 1957: 96). Voters can, therefore, compare the basic socioeconomic stances of the parties and support the one most like their own. While use of this 'ideology differential' drastically simplifies decision making, it does not reflect the triumph of (irrational) hope over (rational) experience. Parties wish to establish a reputation for trustworthiness and thus keep their promises and do not repudiate past positions (Downs, 1957: 103–109). The ideology differential, therefore, enables voters to predict what parties would do in the uncertain future. The adoption of an ideology also serves the interests of parties, since it enables them to distinguish themselves from their competitors and avoid the need to relate 'each policy decision to voter reaction', allowing them to formulate policy according to a few principles (Downs, 1957: 101). While these may ultimately restrict the

parties' room for manoeuvre, they enable them to adopt a range of positions and accommodate voters by incremental adjustments.

Having informed themselves about the parties' basic stances, therefore,
voters can arrive at 'synoptic' judgements, without having to inform themselves about the details of policy, or to work through the consequences of
policy for their welfare. Since voters have little incentive to pay attention to
politics, they focus on a few fundamental issues: the scope of state inter-
vention, the freedom of the individual and the general direction of foreign
policy. If political debate can be reduced to just a few fundamental issues,
this idea can be reduced to a single spatial representation on a left–right
dimension, whereby voters support the party that they feel they are closest
to (Downs, 1957). Yet voters need not think in spatial terms or share the
language of 'left' and 'right'. All they need to do is form a synoptic evaluation of the parties on various important dimensions of conflict.

The calculation of an ideology differential, of course, is only one of the
ways in which voters can reduce the cost of acquiring and processing
information. Voters can also follow the cues of social groups that they
share an interest with (religious leaders, trade union leadership and so
on) (Popkin, 1994). They may even be able to make use of information
drawn from the statements of those with whom they do not share an interest (Lupia and McCubbins, 1998). Some have even suggested that voters
may form a rational attachment to a party, akin to party identification
(Downs, 1957: 85). Thus, although the social–psychological and rational
choice approaches start from very different assumptions they quickly
agree on a list of 'usual suspects'. This is hardly surprising; good data
makes for considerable agreement (Achen, 1992).

There are, however, at least two major sources of disagreement. The
first relates to the relationship between party identification and ideological considerations. The social–psychological approach, so dominant in
individual level studies, suggests that voters acquire beliefs from parties.
Most rational choice accounts, on the other hand, suggest that voters form
loyalties with a party as a result of the correspondence between their
beliefs and those of the parties (Robertson, 1976; Adams, 1998). This contention is supported by evidence that partisans who find themselves at
odds with their party on key issues either defect or become weaker identifiers (Crewe *et al.*, 1977). Yet, as the process of realignment in the southern United States illustrates, the process can take a long time indeed
(Miller and Shanks, 1996). The speed with which party loyalties adjust is,
ultimately, an empirical issue. The second issue relates to the measurement of party identification. Considerable doubt has been expressed as to
whether responses to the traditional battery of party identification items
does reveal genuine psychological attachments, since responses are sensitive to question wording effects and unstable (Bartle, 2003). Individual
level modellers have maintained that this reflects measurement error and
that, once the necessary adjustments are made, identification is

overwhelmingly stable (Green *et al.*, 2002). Others have expressed scepticism about such claims (Clarke *et al.*, 2004) Yet again, it appears that interpretation is a matter of prior beliefs rather than 'proof' (Fiorina, 1981: 89).

The measurement of ideological positions in aggregate level analyses

Models of electoral competition suggest that ideological considerations link the worlds of the voter and parties. Parties appeal to voters by formulating ideological packages. Voters respond by supporting the parties. In order to examine this proposition, however, it is necessary to measure the positions of the parties. It is here that the work of the Manifesto Research Group (MRG), has proven so important (Budge, 1994; Budge *et al.*, 2001). By taking each authoritative statement of the party's proposals and subjecting it to systematic content analysis, they have established the parties' positions on dimensions of conflict. Somewhat more controversially, MRG also provide data on the parties' overall positions on a left–right scale (Budge *et al.*, 2001). Whatever one's reservations about this measure, however, it cannot be doubted that the MRG produces indicators of the parties' appeals that are uniquely authoritative.

Since manifestos are published around six weeks before each election they represent relatively unambiguous causes of vote or changes in vote. Unlike their micro-equivalents, macro-models do not, therefore, depend upon dubious reports of respondents' psychological states or perceptions of party position. Party positions are 'objective' since they are estimated according to clear rules rather than subjective opinions. It is, therefore, a simple task to observe how positions are related to support. As I shall demonstrate, even naive analyses of the MRG data can pay dividends.

The role of ideological considerations in the vote

In this section I will demonstrate that both individual and aggregate level models provide evidence of a link between ideology and the vote. In both cases, however, the crucial (and unresolved) issue is about the relationship between ideology and partisanship. Do ideological considerations promote partisanship or vice versa?

Individual level

The earliest British election studies gathered little direct evidence that voters were influenced by ideological considerations. Later studies made some efforts to reassess 'issue voting' but were constrained by the methods available and the need to maintain continuity. By the early 1990s, however, two new batteries of relatively non-partisan questions were introduced to measure voters' positions on two dimensions of enduring conflict: the scope of state activity (socialist versus laissez-faire) and the freedom of the individual (liberal versus authoritarian) (Heath *et al.*, 1994). In this section I use data drawn from the 2001 BES to assess whether voters are influenced by ideological considerations. Moreover, I am also able to add further information about voters' attitudes towards immigration and law and order, as well as their self-reported left–right positions.

Table 10.1, which displays the results from a multinomial logistic regression, underlines the crucial importance assumptions about causal order. The base (or reference) category in each case is Conservative. Moreover, the explanatory variables are coded so that the coefficients should be positive. Model 1 displays the effect of ideological positions without further controls. All the coefficients are correctly signed and statistically significant. Those with leftist, liberal, pro-immigration ideas and so on, are all less likely to vote Conservative than Labour or Liberal Democrat. Indeed, even self-reported position on the left–right scale is significant and correctly signed. Ideological positions appear collectively to 'explain' 20 per cent of the variation in the dependent variable.

Table 10.1 Ideological positions, party identification and vote, 2001 (multinomial logistic regression)

	Model 1	*Model 2*	*Model 3*
Conservative v. Labour			
Socialist-laissez-faire	5.67***	—	2.14***
Liberal authoritarian	1.59**	—	1.72*
Law and order	2.15***	—	0.43
Left–right self-location	1.61**	—	0.57
Immigration	1.51***	—	1.63***
Labour party ID	—	2.63***	3.25***
Conservative party ID	—	−3.30***	−2.26***
Liberal Democrat party ID	—	0.05	0.13
Intercept	−5.84***	0.41**	−3.02***
Conservative v. Liberal Democrat			
Socialist-laissez-faire	4.64***	—	2.56***
Liberal authoritarian	2.69***	—	2.36**
Law and order	2.65***	—	1.47*
Immigration	1.84***	—	2.03***
Left–right self-location	1.66*	—	0.10
Labour party ID	—	1.95***	1.82***
Conservative party ID	—	−1.82***	−1.47***
Liberal Democrat party ID	—	2.04***	1.96***
Intercept	−6.83***	0.07	−4.30***

Source: British Election Study, 2001.

Notes
Cox and Snell Pseudo R^2 = 0.194 0.551 0.562.
*** $p < 0.01$.
** $p < 0.05$.
* $p < 0.1$.

The estimates in Model 1 can be regarded as maximal estimates of the impact of ideological positions on vote, since they make no allowance for the prior influence of social characteristics or the contribution of partisanship to ideological positions. Model 2, therefore, similarly sets out the effect of party identification without controls for ideological positions. Most of the coefficients are again correctly signed and statistically significant and can be regarded as maximal estimates of the impact of party identification. Collectively partisanship 'explains' 55 per cent of the vote.

Model 3 finally displays the coefficients from a regression that simultaneously controls for both types of predisposition. This model explains more of the variation than either the two previous models (56 per cent).[2] Although self-reported ideological positions are no longer statistically significant in the Conservative versus Labour model, socialist laissez-faire and liberal-authoritarian positions are still significant, as are attitudes to immigration. There are similar – albeit somewhat stronger – findings in the Conservative versus Liberal Democrat model. As well as illustrating that self-reported positions are inappropriate indicators of the impact of ideological conditions, these findings together suggest that beliefs have an impact on vote that is not simply mediated by partisanship.[3] Moreover, if some accounts of the origins of partisanship are correct, ideology should be given additional credit for its effect on that variable (Robertson, 1976). While it is also undoubtedly true that party identification also has an effect on vote, it is clear that political scientists need to resolve the relationship between partisanship and beliefs if they are to understand the role of long-term factors on the vote.

Aggregate level studies

Most aggregate level analyses of the vote have, to date, relied on relatively informal – indeed, almost casual – observations about the relationship between party positions and vote share. In part this is because the evidence drawn from such studies is compelling and ties in so well with common understandings of electoral history. Figure 10.2, for example, shows that Labour shifted sharply to the left in 1974 and 1983; years when they lost six points and nine points of the popular vote respectively. It further shows how the party moved toward the centre over the course of the next 14 years, resulting in its landslide victories in 1997 and 2001. The same evidence suggests that support for the Liberals and their successors appears to be related to major party polarisation. As the 'distance' between the Conservative and Labour parties increases Liberal support appears to increase, providing support for a simple 'vacated centre' theory of the rise in support for the Liberals.

Of course neither these analyses are entirely convincing. According the to the MRG data Labour moved left between 1987 and 1992, yet the party gained around four points. Similarly, according the MRG data, the major

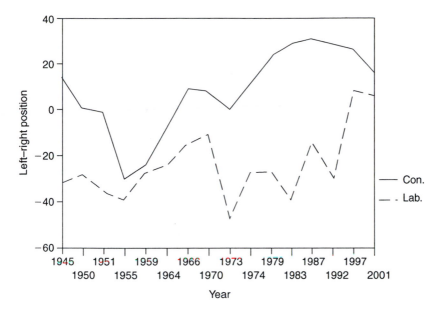

Figure 10.2 Major party positions, 1945–2001.

parties converged more in 2001 than 1997 and yet the Liberal Democrat vote increased slightly. It is also far from clear, moreover, why the Conservatives were able to win so many elections as they moved to the right in the 1980s. Thus, as suggestive as such analyses are, ideological accounts provide only part of the story.[4] Ideological explanations of the aggregate vote, therefore, may need supplementing with additional information about voters' assessments of the parties' competence, unity or appeal of the leaders.

One part of the story that is missing, of course, are the ideological positions (or 'policy mood') of the public in any particular election. If public opinion had moved to the left in 1992, for example, Labour's shift to the left would not necessarily have cost them votes, because they would be no further away – and possibly nearer – to the average voter. Another part of the story that is missing is party identification. If party identifiers do follow their leaders, then the impact of programmatic shifts in position may be reduced. It may be that only dramatic shifts in position, such as those between 1970 and February 1974, 1979 and 1983 or between 1992 and 1997 might shake voters free of their prior loyalties (Crewe *et al.*, 1977). What is really missing from all this, of course, is any attempt to estimate the precise impact of these factors on the vote; something that I now attempt to do.

In order to establish the apparent relationship between ideological considerations and the vote I follow the approach adopted by Erickson *et al.*, (2002). Their work is striking because they conclude that it is 'the fit of voter policy preferences to party issue positions [that] is fundamental to understanding election outcomes' in the United States (Erickson *et al.*, 2002: 242). Even in the 'non-ideological' climate of the United States, therefore, it appears that the parties' general left–right positions do influence voters. Intriguingly, however, this conclusion only becomes apparent once one makes allowance for party identification. Indeed, it seems that ideological and partisan explanations are complementary, rather than competing, explanations of aggregate outcomes (Shanks and Miller, 1990).

The first step in the analysis is to recognise that current party platforms are unlikely to determine voters' perceptions of party positions. Instead, voters are assumed to estimate party position by weighting past and current party platforms. To capture this dynamic process I assume that positions can be estimated as follows:

$$\text{Party position} = 1 - \alpha \, (\text{Platform})_{t-1} + \alpha \, (\text{Platform})_t$$

For a variety of reasons explored in their book (Erickson *et al.*, 2002) set α to 0.20; a practice that, with some hesitation, I follow here.[5] The second step in the analysis is to introduce a measure of the policy mood of the electorate (the equivalent of left–right positions). Here Erickson *et al.* (2002) are able to draw upon the extensive work of Stimson (1999) who has created a measure of policy mood stretching back to the early 1950s onwards. These details relating to the production of this measure need not detain us here. Suffice it to say that it would take a great deal of effort to replicate even if the data were readily available. In the British case there are few indicators of policy mood available. Indeed, there is surprisingly little consistency in the most authoritative and comprehensive source of information about public opinion; the British Election Study. I therefore, hesitantly and reluctantly, take the net balance of people favouring further nationalisation over further privatisation as my indicator of policy mood over the period 1964 to 2001. Although this effectively limits the N to just 11 cases, the time series on this issue at least has the advantage of relative consistency and of being clearly related to the left–right battle throughout the period under study. The process of aggregating responses will reduce measurement error. This indicator, nevertheless, only dimly reflects the major battles about public expenditure and taxation that dominate elections. The principal justification, as ever, is sheer necessity: there is simply no other data to hand.

The third step in the analysis is to try to examine the proposition that spatial distance causes party support. I therefore assume that those to the left of Labour vote Labour. Those to the right of the Tories vote Tory. The voter half-way between the two is indifferent. This indifference point is, therefore, the mean of the two parties' positions. I include this variable in my models.

Table 10.2 displays results for a series of regressions in which the depend-

Table 10.2 Labour share of two party vote, party positions, policy mood and Labour party identification

	Model 1	Model 2	Model 3	Model 4
Party platform (midpoint)	0.00	–0.03	–0.15*	—
Policy mood (Election Year)	—	0.28	0.19*	—
Labour Party Identification	—	—	1.02***	0.97***
Constant	49.26	47.21	12.74	11.33
R^2	–0.11	–0.08	0.84	0.73

Source: British Election Studies, 1964–2001 and Manifesto Research Group.

Notes
*** $p < 0.01$,
** $p < 0.05$,
* $p < 0.1$.

ent variable is Labour's share of major party support from 1964 to 2001. The first model displayed in column 1 explores the relationship between party position and vote. There is none. The second model displayed in column 2 adds further evidence about policy mood. Yet again there are no significant relationships. Indeed, the negative R^2 indicates that both models predict the vote worse than would be expected by chance. The third adds controls for Labour identification and immediately the R^2 rises to 0.84. Only when this variable is added does there appear to be a relationship between policy mood and vote or party position and vote (at $p < 0.06$ and $p < 0.09$ respectively). The negative coefficient for the midpoint variable is significant and negative, indicating that if both parties locate to the right, Labour's share of the two party vote increases: just as might be expected. The positive coefficient for the policy mood variable suggests that the more 'left-wing' voters are, on average, the higher the Labour share. As column 4 makes clear omitting the party position and policy mood variables reduces the overall fit of the model from 0.84 to 0.73. It is clear, therefore, that party identification explains a great deal. It is equally clear, however, that the electorate is sensitive to the positions adopted by the parties; just as they are in the United States. There is, however, little evidence that the ideological positions of the parties and voters have an impact on aggregate vote shares independently of partisanship. Nor do they appear to have an impact on levels of partisanship.[6] Although the evidence can hardly be conclusive, it appears to lend some support for more 'traditional' accounts of partisanship. Only time will tell whether this finding is repeated after more suitable indicators of policy mood are devised.

Erickson and his colleagues go even further by bringing evidence about party positions and the median voter together in a single model, to estimate the impact that distance has on vote share, net of party identification. This step in their analysis is difficult to replicate in the British case because the indicator of policy mood is – as yet – so unsatisfactory. The steady growth in support for the Liberals makes for a further complication in the analyses. Perhaps the most problematic step, however, is that in order to locate the parties and electorate on the same scale it is necessary to assume that the two parties are equally adept at matching the policy views of the median voter. This assumption does not seem appropriate in the British context given that the Conservatives have traditionally afforded its leaders much more policy freedom than Labour (Webb, 2000). Doubtless analysts of the macro-polity would contend that, even if this assumption is unrealistic, its usefulness should be assessed by its empirical predictions. Until a more convincing indicator of policy mood has been produced, however, this is an assertion that cannot be put to the test. For the moment, the results set out in Table 10.2 should be regarded as suggestive. It does, however, appear that ideological considerations matter at both the individual and aggregate level and this alone should prompt further research.

Ideology and voting behaviour

In this final section I return to my initial question: why do ideological considerations feature so little in individual level models, when they loom so large in aggregate models of party competition? The answer in large part appears to lie in the prior beliefs of the analysts, rather than the data itself (though, to be sure, the priors of the principal investigators also shape what evidence is gathered). Differences about what is to be explained (individual decisions or aggregate outcomes), what constitutes 'explanation' (or 'prediction'), the role of parsimony, together with fundamental assumptions about voters' motivations, appear to draw analysts inevitably to their conclusions. Ultimately, the choice between the various interpretations depends on matters of 'taste' and whether one 'feels comfortable' with rational actor assumptions rather than empirical tests alone (Stokes, 1963: 377; Fiorina, 1981: 190). Prior beliefs do not yield to direct empirical inquiry.

There is some hope of progress. The old definitions of ideology have been demonstrated to be too demanding and largely incompatible with models of party competition. There is, furthermore, increasing awareness that that mere recognition and use of ideological concepts is no indicator of ideological thinking. Improvements in the measurement of ideological positions and party identification, at least, hold out the hope that the relationship between these two variables can be resolved by the use of appropriate panel data (Bartle, 2003).

The best hope for genuine progress, however, appears to lie in attempts to marry together aggregate level evidence about party positions and survey evidence about policy mood. Speaking as one who has 'slummed it' in the detail of individual detail for far too long, it is hard to disagree with those who claim that most voting behaviour research has come to resemble mere contemporary history (Budge, 2004) or an essentially journalistic enterprise (Achen, 1992). To be sure, a great many individual votes appear to be uninformed, to express identities and signify (or communicate) little. The political scientist who denies that many individuals are motivated by habit, expressive considerations or tribalism is surely missing an important aspect of individual behaviour. Such observations should not, however, distract us from the possibility that the aggregation process, which lies at the very heart of democracy, may well translate 'noise' into a relatively clear 'signal' about the preferred direction for society to take (Converse, 1990 cf. Bartels, 1996). It is, therefore, the task of the political scientist, just as much as it is the task of the commentator and politician, to work out just what that message is.

Notes

1 The utility choice family of models is, of course, rather less useful in focusing attention than many theorists think, since most variables – even apparently irrational identifications – can be interpreted as serving the basis for a rational choice.
2 The fact that some variables are still significant is all the more remarkable since the regression is on a small subsample who completed the self-completion supplement and answered the agree/disagree items.
3 The impact of ideological considerations may also be mediated by more proximate issue positions and evaluations.
4 It is worth placing on record just how surprising the MRG data is on this point. To be sure, it could be argued that Labour did make a lot of spending commitments in 1992 and, in retrospect, it could be argued that it had failed to shed its image as a 'tax and spend' party. It was widely thought at the time, however, that, under Neil Kinnock's leadership, Labour had moved to the right. I therefore leave it to the reader to judge whether the MRG evidence on this point should be discounted.
5 My hesitation is based in part on doubts about their reasoning as set out in their book and my own explorations which suggest that voters may be more responsive to party positions.
6 Both the policy mood and party midpoint variables are insignificant in a model of Labour Party identification over time.

References

Achen, C.H. (1975) 'Mass Political Attitudes and Survey Response', *American Political Science Review* 69:4, 1218–1231.
Achen, C.H. (1992) 'Social Psychology, Demographic Variables and Linear Regression: Breaking the Iron Triangle in Voting Research', *Political Behaviour* 14:2, 195–211.

Adams, J. (1998) 'Partisanship Voting and Multiparty Spatial Competition', *Journal of Theoretical Politics* 10:1, 5–31.

Alvarez, R.M. and J. Nagler (1995) 'Economics, Issues and the Perot Candidacy: Voter Choice in the 1992 Presidential Elections', *American Journal of Political Science*, 39:4, 714–744.

Bartels, L.M. (1996) 'Uninformed Votes: Information Effects in Presidential Elections', *American Journal of Political Science* 40:2, 194–230.

Bartle, J. (2003) 'Partisanship, Performance and Personality: Competing and Complementary Characterisations of the 2001 British General Election', *Party Politics* 9:3, pp. 317–345.

Brennan, G. and L. Lomasky (1993) *Democracy and Decision: The Pure Theory of Electoral Choice* (Cambridge: Cambridge University Press).

Budge, I. (1994) 'A New Spatial Theory of Party Competition: Uncertainty, Ideology and Policy Equilibria Viewed Comparatively and Spatially', *British Journal of Political Science* 24:3, 443–467.

Budge, I. (2004) 'Review of The Macro Polity', *Public Administration* 82:1, 218–220.

Budge, I., H.D. Klingemann, A. Volkens, J. Bara, and E. Tanenbaum (2001) *Mapping Policy Preferences: Estimates for Parties, Electors, and Governments 1945–1998* (Oxford: Oxford University Press).

Butler, D. and D. Stokes, (1974) *Political Change in Britain: The Evolution of Electoral Choice* (London: Macmillan).

Campbell, A., P.E. Converse, W.E. Miller, and D. Stokes (1960) *The American Voter* (New York: John Wiley).

Clarke, H., D. Sanders, M. Stewart and P. Whiteley (2004) *Political Choice in Britain* (Oxford: Oxford University Press).

Converse, P.E. (1964) 'The Nature of Belief Systems in Mass Publics' in D. Apter (ed.) *Ideology and Discontent* (New York: Free Press), pp. 206–261.

Converse, P.E. (1990) 'Popular Representation and the Distribution of Information' in J. Kuklinski and J. Ferejohn (eds) *Information and Democratic Processes* (Illinois: University Of Illinois Press), pp. 369–390.

Crewe, I., B. Sarlvik and J. Alt (1977) 'Partisan Dealignment in Britain, 1964–74', *British Journal of Political Science* 7:2, 129–190.

Downs, A. (1957) *An Economic Theory of Democracy* (New York: Harper & Row).

Erickson, R.S., M.B. Mackuen and J.A. Stimson (2002) *The Macro Polity* (Cambridge: Cambridge University Press).

Fiorina, M.P. (1981) *Retrospective Voting in American National Elections* (New Haven: Yale University Press).

Green, D.P., B. Palmquist and E. Schickler (2002) *Partisan Hearts & Minds: Political Parties and the Social Identities of Voters* (New Haven: Yale University Press).

Heath, A., G. Evans and J. Martin (1994) 'The Measurement of Core Beliefs and Values: The Development of Balanced Socialist/Laissez Faire and Libertarian/Authoritarian Scales', *British Journal of Political Science* 24:1, 115–131.

Kirchheimer, O. (1990) 'The Catch-all Party', in P. Mair (ed.) *The West European Party System* (Oxford: Oxford University Press), pp. 50–69.

Lupia, A. and M.D. McCubbins (1998) *The Democratic Dilemma: Can Citizens Learn What they Need to Know?* (Cambridge: Cambridge University Press).

Luskin, R. (1987) 'Measuring Political Sophistication', *American Journal of Political Science* 31:4, 856–899.

Miller, W.E. and J.M. Shanks (1996) *The New American Voter* (Harvard: Harvard University Press).

Popkin, S. (1994) *The Reasoning Voter: Communication and Persuasion in Presidential Campaigns* (Chicago: Chicago University Press).

Robertson, D. (1976) 'Surrogates for party identification within a rational choice framework', in I. Budge, I. Crewe and D. Farlie (eds) *Party Identification and Beyond: Representations of Voting and Party Competition* (London: Wiley), pp. 365–382.

Scarbrough, E. (1984) *Ideology and Voting Behaviour: An Exploratory Study* (Oxford: Clarendon Press).

Shanks, J.M. and W.E. Miller (1990) 'Policy Direction and Performance Evaluation: Complementary Explanations of the Reagan Election', *British Journal of Political Science* 20:2, 143–235.

Smith, E.R. and D.M. Mackie (2000) *Social Psychology* (Philadelphia: Psychology Press).

Stimson, J.A. (1999) *Public Opinion in America: Moods, Cycles and Swings* (Boulder, CO: Westview Press).

Stokes, D. (1963) 'Spatial Models of Party Competition', *American Political Science Review* 57:2, 368–377.

Webb, P (2000) *The Modern British Party System* (London: Sage).

Zaller, J.R. (1992) *The Nature and Origins of Mass Opinion* (Cambridge: Cambridge University Press).

11 Does the median voter theorem wipe out political participation?

Paul Whiteley

Introduction

The median voter theorem is one of the oldest and best known results in formal political theory. As is well known, it suggests that political parties will tend to adopt policy positions preferred by the voter who occupies the median position on the left–right ideological scale. The theorem requires a number of assumptions, but it implies that electoral politics will tend to be rather homogeneous and centrist.[1] The idea that politics should be centrist and that parties should seek to capture the middle ground is widely used in popular discourse and it originates from the median voter theorem. It derives originally from Harold Hotelling's (1929) analysis of competition in spatial markets, and was popularised and further developed in political science by Duncan Black (1948, 1958), but the best known statement of the theorem is in Anthony Downs (1957).

It has generated a great deal of theoretical and empirical research. The theoretical work has focused on elaborating models of two-party competition and extending the model from the deterministic voting to the probabilistic voting case (Calvert, 1985; Banks *et al.*, 2002). In addition it has been extended from the two-party to the multiparty competition case (Hinich, 1977; Enelow and Hinich, 1984; Lin *et al.*, 1999). On the empirical side, in addition to testing models of spatial competition (McKelvey and Ordeshook, 1990), the theorem has been used to explain government spending patterns, on the assumption that they reflect the preferences of the median voter (Pommerehne and Frey, 1976; Denzau and Grier, 1984).

Thanks to the work of Ian Budge and his associates in mapping party policy preferences along the left–right dimension, we now have a fairly clear picture of the extent to which electoral politics is actually homogeneous and centrist in reality (Budge and Farlie, 1977; Budge *et al.*, 1984; Budge and Roberston, 1987; Laver and Budge, 1992; Budge *et al.*, 2001). Put simply, their evidence suggests that parties do not converge to the centre of the left–right spectrum, and that in many instances they diverge from this position for long periods of time (Budge and Klingemann, 2001).

The evidence is more consistent with Duverger's observation that there is no political centre in a two-party system, than with the median voter theorem. Duverger explains this in the following passage:

> Every policy implies a choice between two kinds of solution: the so-called compromise solutions lead one way or the other. This is equivalent to saying the centre does not exist in politics: there may well be a Centre party but there is no centre tendency, no centre doctrine.

> (Duverger, 1954: 215)

Other work confirms this view. Estimates of party positions in Germany, the Netherlands and Norway all suggest that policy convergence does not take place (Schofield *et al.*, 1998; Adams and Merrill, 1999). A similar point can be made about the United States, a classic two-party system, which can be easily modelled by the median voter theorem (Poole and Rosenthal, 1984; Alesina and Rosenthal, 1995; Schofield *et al.*, 2003). The same point can be made about Britain (Alvarez *et al.*, 2000). Again, contrary to the median voter theorem, there is a fairly consistent finding that parties often adopt policy positions which are more extreme than those taken by their supporters in the electorate (Dalton, 1985, Holmberg, 1989; Iversen 1994). Clearly, all this work is fundamentally at odds with the median voter theorem.

The purpose of this paper is to explain why we do not observe the convergence predicted by the median voter theorem in practice. A fair amount of research exists to explain why convergence does not take place, but this research invariably makes additional assumptions in order to modify the basic spatial model and avoid convergence. In our case we explain non-convergence in a pure spatial model with a two-party system without additional assumptions. The argument is that the median voter theorem has always contained a problem when it comes to explaining electoral participation. It is just that this problem has been disguised by the assumption that all electors vote. Evidence for the model is provided by the Party Manifesto Project, and it is more comprehensively tested with data from the 2001 British Election Study (see Clarke *et al.*, 2004). We begin by setting out the median voter theorem and examining the conditions under which it does and does not apply. This leads into a discussion of a model which explains non-convergence, and this is tested subsequently.

The median voter theorem

The simplest version of the median voter theorem applies to two-party systems with a one-dimensional policy space, that is, the left–right ideological scale. To repeat an earlier point, the theorem requires that voters have single-peaked utility functions for the alternative policy positions and that they vote for the party closest to them in the ideological scale (see Enelow and Hinich, 1984). The theorem is proved in the appendix.

In his analysis of the economic model of democracy, Downs imagines that the voters are normally distributed along a 100 point left–right scale. He writes:

> (I)f we place parties A and B initially at 25 and 75, they will converge rapidly upon the center. The possible loss of extremists will not deter their movement toward each other, because there are so few voters to be lost at the margins compared with the number to be gained in the middle.
>
> (1957: 118)

Thus the gain in votes at the centre of the distribution from party convergence outweighs the loss of votes in the tails of the distribution from individuals alienated by the convergence. This mechanism explains the theorem. Downs also considers a stronger version of the theorem which assumes that everyone votes, and consequently rules out abstention by alienated voters. He writes:

> As long as there is even the most infinitesimal difference between A and B, extremist voters would be forced to vote for the one closest to them, no matter how distasteful its policies seemed in comparison with those of their ideal government. It is always rational *ex definitione* to select a greater good before a lesser, or a lesser evil before a greater; consequently abstention would be irrational because it increases the chances of the worse party for victory.
>
> (1957: 118–119)

In this strong version the incentives for parties to move to the median are overwhelming, since there is no cost imposed by the abstention of alienated voters. Thus the assumption that everyone votes guarantees convergence.

Downs was well aware that convergence would not take place under some circumstances. These relate to the distribution of the voters on the left–right ideological scale. For example, if the distribution is bimodal, then parties would locate at the two modes and not at the median. Similarly, if the distribution is rectangular and there is a multiparty system, this would prevent convergence as each party sought to protect its 'territory' in the space. If, for example, one of the parties shifted rightwards in order to capture votes from an adjacent party, it would lose an equal number of voters to a rival party on the left. For this reason it will not move.

Davis *et al.* (1970) were the first to point out that abstention will not deter convergence providing that the distribution of voters is symmetric around the median. In this case the loss of support from convergence will be symmetrical for both parties, leaving their relative share of the vote unchanged. For this reason, parties will continue to pursue convergence. Given the evidence that convergence does not generally take place, there is the need for an explanation of why this happens even when the electorate are normally distributed along the left–right scale.

One such explanation derives from the directional model of party competition introduced by Rabinowitz and Macdonald (1989; see also Macdonald and Rabinowitz, 1993, 1998). They argue that spatial models are incompatible with the way voters actually make decisions when they are thinking about which party to support. They suggest that voters respond symbolically to electoral politics rather than with cognitive calculations of the utility income streams which parties are likely to deliver. A symbolic reaction to a party issue position involves the voters focusing on two different questions. First, they must ask themselves if they favour or oppose that issue position, and this constitutes the directional component of the model. Second, voters must examine if they feel strongly about the issue, or are relatively indifferent to it, which is the intensity component. In these circumstances voters judge issues such as race relations, health care or taxation using these two criteria, rather than in terms of the detailed policy positions taken by the parties. In this situation voters will support a party which is in the same direction as themselves on a salient issue, even if that party it is further away from them on the left–right scale than a party which opposes the issue. One consequences of this type of voter decision making is that parties have no incentive to converge to the median voter. As Rabinowitz and Macdonald put it:

> A key theme in directional theory is that candidates can compete sucessfully by taking extreme stands on issues. Indeed, in districts with a clear directional preference, candidates are advantaged by taking a position close to the boundary of the region of acceptability.
>
> (1989: 111)

Thus providing parties stay within a 'region of acceptability' they may diverge from rather than converge to the centre. Building on this argument Iversen (1994) developed a model which has both proximity and directional components, and it predicts that both centrist and extreme parties will exist in such a world. Adams and Merrill (1999) have further extended the model to include non-policy variables such as partisanship, social class and religious affiliation. Again, by incorporating these into the picture, parties lose their incentive to converge. Finally, Merrill and Grofman (1999) incorporate different versions of the directional model into a spatial proximity model and this produces similar results.

A second approach to explaining non-convergence is to take into account the organisational structure of political parties as an important influence on their electoral strategies. Following May's (1973) 'law of curvilinear disparity' thesis it is argued that party activists are more extreme than both party leaders on the one hand, and party supporters in the electorate on the other. For this reason party activists will resist convergence, since they will see it as an attempt to abandon key principles which are important to them. Since activists provide a useful resource for the party in the form of campaigning and fund-raising, the leadership will not converge to the centre specifically in order to avoid alienating them (Budge and Keman, 1990; Aldrich, 1995; Whiteley and Seyd, 2002).

A third approach to non-convergence, which is quite a recent one in the literature, is to incorporate valence measures into spatial models of party competition. Following Stokes' (1963) famous critique of spatial theory, valence politics has been largely ignored in spatial models. But recent work has started to integrate valence measures into models of party competition (Ansolabehere and Synder, 2000; Groseclose, 2001). Schofield (2003) proves a theorem which shows that parties can occupy non-centrist equilibrium positions in a spatial model when valence issues are taken into account (see also Schofield and Sened, 2004). Thus valence politics can undermine convergence because questions of competence and performance are taken into account by voters when they evaluate policy proposals.

A fourth approach is to explain the lack of convergence as arising from party leader preferences for other things apart from winning votes. If party leaders wish to pursue ideological goals and at the same time they are uncertain as to where the median voter can be found then they will not necessarily pursue convergence. Calvert (1985) suggests that uncertainty will undermine convergence and Wittman (1983) shows that when candidates have policy goals in addition to the desire to win the election, then they will generally not converge. In this situation party leaders may trade off policy goal-seeking against vote maximising and arrive at an equilibrium which does not generally coincide with that of the median voter (see also Wittman, 1977).

The argument here is that while these ideas may all be relevant for explaining non-convergence, they are not required for an explanation of non-convergence in spatial models of party competition. *Convergence will not take place in a pure spatial model, if we drop the assumption that all electors vote.* We develop this idea in the next section.

Why parties will not converge in a pure spatial model

The basic argument of this section is that parties will not converge in a pure spatial model because indifferent citizens will not vote. Voter indifference occurs when the parties are so close together in the space, that the electors cannot distinguish between them. In the two-party case, if voters perceive that they will receive the same utility incomes from the election of either party, then they are faced with a dilemma; they should either vote for both parties, which is impossible, or for neither of them (see Clarke *et al.*, 2004: 248). Thus indifference produces abstention. Davis *et al.* (1970: 238) first pointed out that if citizens abstain because of indifference, then in general no equilibrium strategy for the parties will exist.

Indifference affects individual voters differently. It may be, for example, that fringe voters are more likely to be indifferent than centrist voters. This would happen in Britain if an 'extreme' voter sees no difference between Labour and the Conservatives, whilst a more centrist voter does perceive a difference. If so, fringe voters will 'peel off' into abstention while centrist voters continue to participate. Given an electorate symmetrically distributed around the median voter this will not affect the party electoral shares. So parties will continue to pursue convergence for the reasons discussed earlier.

However, this pattern breaks down at the position of the median voter because at this point all voters become indifferent. In spatial models of party competition voters must perceive a difference between the parties in terms of the utility incomes they provide. In the absence of any difference, or a difference which is so small that it cannot be perceived by anyone, then individuals have no basis for choosing between the alternatives. If the parties are located at the median none of the voters, including the median voter herself, will be able to distinguish between them and accordingly will abstain. This means that in the absence of compulsory voting the median voter theorem predicts that no one will vote.[2] This conclusion suggests that there is an electoral 'black hole' at the location of the median voter in spatial models of party competition. This 'black hole' theorem is proved in the appendix.

This has not been recognised before, since incentives to participate are routinely ignored in these models. The prevailing assumptions are either that everyone will vote, or that only fringe voters are alienated by convergence to the median. But neither of these assumptions apply in a model which relies on voters having to calculate utility incomes differentials between the parties in order to make a choice. If there is no difference between the parties in the utility incomes they provide, then voters cannot make this choice, except on grounds other than proximity. This takes the whole exercise outside the theoretical framework of spatial proximity voting models.

Downs himself was aware of the problems for any rational choice theory of party competition if abstention is allowed. He notes that if everyone but one person abstains, then that individual will be pivotal or decisive, which gives them a strong incentive to turn out and vote. By this reasoning, if everyone thinks they are going to be pivotal, this will encourage them all to vote. However, if everyone does actually vote, then they will immediately lose their pivotality along with their incentive to vote. As he puts it, the rational individual is 'trapped in a maze of conjectural variation' (Downs, 1957: 267). It should be noted, however, that this reasoning is not valid if the parties have converged at the median. In this case even if an individual knows with certainty that they are pivotal, they still have no incentive to vote because they have no basis for choosing between the parties.[3]

Does proximity reduce turnout?

This argument explains why parties do not generally converge to the position of the median voter in practice and operates alongside the other reasons for non-convergence discussed earlier. This suggests that in so far as electoral participation is motivated by proximity considerations in actual elections, then convergence will reduce turnout. In this situation parties will only pursue convergence to the median if they can be absolutely sure that the loss of support to abstention does not adversely affect them in comparison with their rivals. If they lose just a handful of voters more than their rivals, they will lose the election. If they pursue convergence to its logical conclusion electors will only vote for reasons which have nothing to do with convergence, thus making the convergence unnecessary in the first place.

The fact that a number of other variables influence turnout which are unrelated to proximity considerations, prevents the 'black-hole' appearing if convergence strategies are actually pursued in practice. But we should nonetheless expect to see a decline in turnout by electors motivated by proximity considerations, when parties converge towards the median voter in actual elections.

There is preliminary evidence to support this conclusion in Figure 11.1 which uses the party manifesto data aggregated by country for all the elections between 1945 and 1998 (see Budge *et al.*, 2001). If convergence inhibits participation then there should be a positive relationship between the standard deviation of party ideological scores on the left–right scale and turnout. The vertical axis is the average turnout in all 25 countries in the party manifesto data over this period, and the horizontal axis is the weighted standard deviation of party scores on the left–right ideological scale. The party manifesto scores are weighted by the size of the party vote share in national elections. This is done in order to ensure that larger parties 'count' more than smaller parties, when it comes to voter evaluations of their ideological position. The standard deviation measures how dispersed parties are on the left–right ideological scale – in effect how far away they are from the median voter. It can be seen in Figure 11.1 that turnout is positively related to the dispersion of parties along the left–right scale. While the correlation is not particularly strong it shows clearly that convergence – a smaller standard deviation of party ideological scores – is associated with lower turnouts.[4]

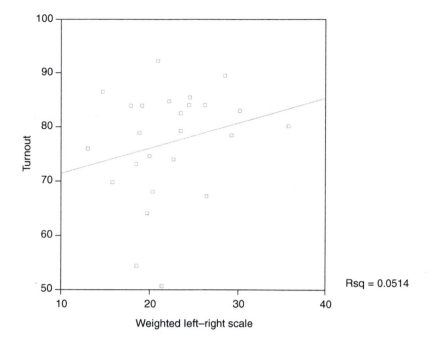

Correlation = 0.23

Figure 11.1 The relationship between turnout and the standard deviation of the left–right ideological scale in 25 OECD countries in national elections 1945–1998.

It is useful to examine the same relationships for different countries over time. This is done for Britain, Germany, the United States and Japan in Figures 11.2 through 11.5 for all the elections which took place in these countries in the post-war period up to 1998. It can be seen that with the exception of the United States, there are positive relationships between turnout and the ideological dispersion of the parties in these countries.[5] Thus in Britain, Germany and Japan convergence to the median reduced turnout during this period while in the United States it appeared to have no discernible effects.

This evidence is interesting and suggestive, but the effect of proximity on turnout needs to be tested in a properly specified model with adequate numbers of cases. In the British Election Study of 2001 an aggregate time series model of turnout in the 16 general elections between 1945 and 2001 was estimated, using the left–right proximity scale scores referred to in Figure 11.2. The results are tentative because of the small number of cases, but they showed that party competition stimulates turnout. As the ideological distance among the parties increased, so did turnout. One of the reasons why turnout was at a historically low level in 2001 was because

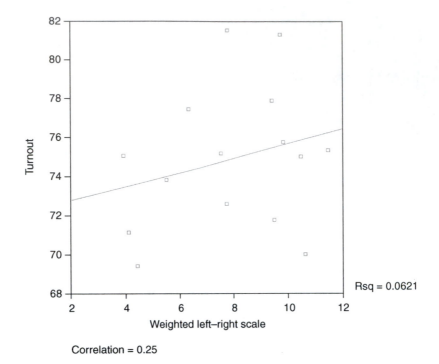

Correlation = 0.25

Figure 11.2 The relationship between turnout and the standard deviation of the left–right ideological scale in British general elections 1945–1997.

the three major parties were closest to each other on the left–right scale than at any time since the Second World War. Given this aggregate effect then there should be a relationship between proximity and turnout at the individual level. We examine this issue next.

Modelling the effects of proximity

To test the effects of proximity on turnout we can use individual level data from the British Election Study surveys of 2001. In our book, *Political Choice in Britain* (Clarke *et al.*, 2004) we analyse electoral turnout in the 2001 general election using six alternative theoretical models. These are the civic voluntarism, social capital, rational choice, general incentives, cognitive mobilisation and equity-fairness models. It is possible to include an additional determinant of turnout, that is proximity, in the equations which test these theoretical alternatives to see if it has additional explanatory power.

To describe the models briefly, the central idea of the civic voluntarism model is that resources such as the individual's educational attainment

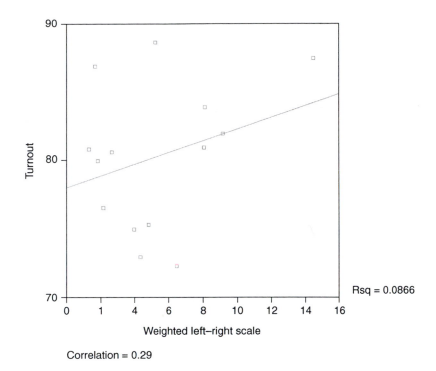

Correlation = 0.29

Figure 11.3 The relationship between turnout and the standard deviation of the left–right ideological scale in German general elections 1949–1998.

and their social class, facilitate their electoral participation. This works directly to influence participation, but also indirectly via its effects on personal efficacy and interest in politics. This theoretical approach to modelling participation was pioneered in the United States by Sidney Verba and his collaborators (see Verba *et al.*, 1995).

The social capital model has been popularised by the work of Robert Putnam (1993, 2000) and suggests that participation is promoted by interpersonal trust which arises from voluntary activity in a community. If an individual lives in a neighbourhood which contains high levels of interpersonal trust, this engenders a willingness to cooperate with others to solve collective action problems. One of the effects of this is to stimulate turnout in elections. So in this view participation is rooted in networks of civic engagement and high levels of interpersonal trust.

The rational choice model is based on the idea that individuals undertake actions only if the expected benefits of doing so outweigh the costs. This model was introduced into the analysis of turnout by Riker and Ordeshook (1968). In the model, perceptions of the individual's role in influencing the outcome of the election, or their personal efficacy, is a key

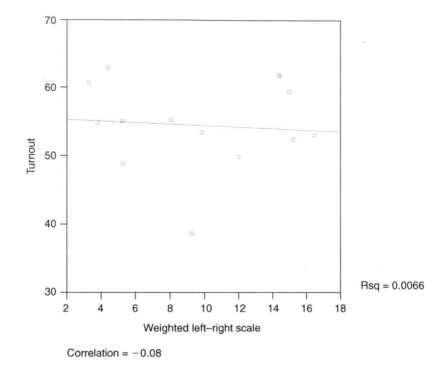

Correlation = -0.08

Figure 11.4 The relationship between turnout and the standard deviation of the left–right ideological scale in US congressional elections 1948–1996.

factor in explaining why some people participate when others do not. In the original version of the model efficacy was conceptualised in terms of the individual's 'pivotality', or the likelihood that their vote would decide the outcome. However, since this is zero in all practical cases, it cannot provide an explanation of the levels of personal efficacy actually observed among voters. Accordingly, we interpret efficacy in more collective terms to mean the individual's perceptions that people *like themselves* can influence the election outcome (Clarke *et al.*, 2004: 248).

The general incentive theory is a generalisation of the rational actor theory which incorporates variables derived from a social–psychological account of participation. Originally the theory was developed to explain high intensity participation of the type which takes place in political parties (Seyd and Whiteley, 1992, 2002; Whiteley and Seyd, 2002). It includes measures such as the influence of social norms on participation, the influence of system benefits or the perception that participation benefits the whole of society, and various other indicators.

Cognitive mobilisation theory stresses the importance of the individual's exposure to political information and their ability and willingness

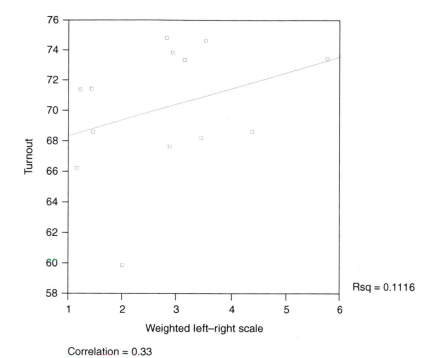

Correlation = 0.33

Figure11.5 The relationship between turnout and the standard deviation of
   the left–right ideological scale in Japanese national elections
   1948–1998.

to respond to that information as a factor in explaining why they participate. In this view the more educated, media conscious and politically interested people are more likely to vote in comparison with less educated and
politically indifferent people (see Dalton, 2002). So participation in this
model is really a matter of information processing and the individual's
ability to absorb, interpret and act on the information received.

   Finally, the equity-fairness model is developed around the core idea of
relative deprivation, or the gap between what the individual expects out of
life and what they actually experience (Runciman, 1966; Walker and
Smith, 2002). This has been shown to be associated with protest behaviour
in politics (Mueller, 1979), but arguably it will motivate individuals to vote
as they seek to oppose parties which they perceive to be responsible for
their deprivation.

   These alternative theories of participation were tested using a wide
variety of different measures in the 2001 election study (Clarke *et al.*, 2004:
237–278). A statistical tournament was set up in which the models were
pitted against each other to determine which one had the strongest
explanatory power. A variety of tests revealed that no one model explained

turnout to the exclusion of all others. Each of the models had something to contribute to the explanation of why individuals voted. However, it was also apparent that the general incentives and cognitive engagement models dominated their rivals. In general terms these can be described as choice or knowledge based models of participation, and so as a result the election study team argued that: 'The conclusion is that choice- and knowledge-based models do the best job at explaining turnout in contemporary British general elections' (Clarke *et al.*, 2004: 273).

The modelling exercise developed in *Political Choice in Britain* ended up with a composite model of turnout which provided the best account of electoral participation in the 2001 general election. Though it was dominated by the general incentives and cognitive mobilisation models, it contained variables from the other theoretical approaches as well. This composite model can provide the necessary controls in a model incorporating proximity as a predictor of turnout in the 2001 election.

Turning to measurement issues, there are two different scales which can be used to measure proximity in the British Election Study. The first is a left–right ideological scale and the second is a taxation versus spending scale.[6] The distribution of individual respondents along these scales can be seen in Figure 11.6. In the case of the left–right scale, the mean and median scores are practically the same, and the most popular response is the median position. The popularity of the median position may in part be a reflection of the fact that most people place themselves in the centre of the political spectrum. On the other hand, it may reflect the fact that some respondents are really not clear what the left–right scale means, and therefore opt for the median as the default. Credence to the latter interpretation is given by the fact that some 16 per cent of respondents opted for the 'don't know' category on the left–right scale, but only 4 per cent did so on the tax–spend scale. With regard to the latter, there is a distinct skew in the responses with the median voter being located at point seven on the scale. This indicates a distinct preference for increased taxation and spending as against cuts in spending and taxation.

Respondents were asked to locate the political parties on the same scales, making it possible to calculate the distance between them and each of the three major parties. Figure 11.7 shows the absolute distance between voters and parties on the two scales. It can be seen that with respect to the left–right scale the voters were on average closest to the Liberal Democrats (1.3 points) with Labour coming next (1.6 points) and the Conservatives (2.4 points) in third place. On the tax–spend scale again voters were closest to the Liberal Democrats (1.8 points), and then to Labour (2.1 points) and finally to the Conservatives (2.7 points). Clearly, if the election was based entirely on proximity considerations as measured by these scales, then the Liberal Democrats would have won it and Labour would have come second.

To develop a proximity measure for each voter we use a quadratic loss function, rather than the absolute difference between the respondent and

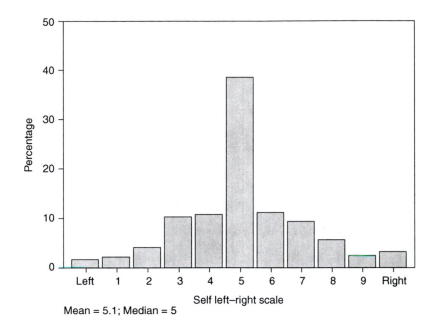

Mean = 5.1; Median = 5

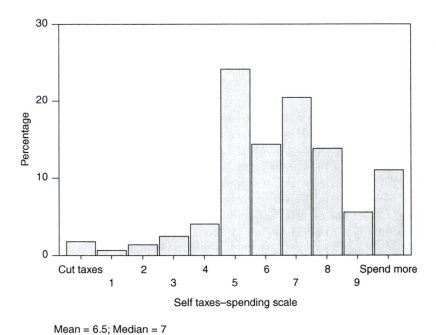

Mean = 6.5; Median = 7

Figure 11.6 The distribution of respondents on the left–right and the tax-spend scales.

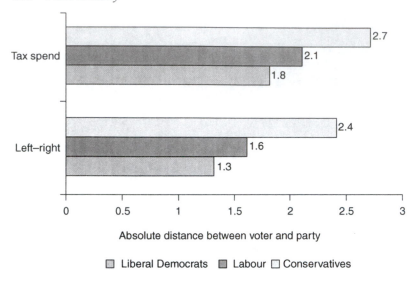

Figure 11.7 Average distances between voters and parties on the left–right and tax–spend dimensions.

the party. Thus the proximity measure for the left–right scale is the sum of the squared distances between the individual respondent and the respondent's perceptions of the position of Labour, the Conservatives and the Liberal Democrats.[7] If all three parties were perceived to be in the same position as the respondent, then this measure would be zero; if, on the other hand, the respondents perceived one or more of the parties to be in a different position on the scale then the proximity measure would be positive. It reaches a maximum when all three parties are perceived to be as far away from the respondent as possible.

In *Political Choice in Britain* we were interested in the effects of proximity on vote choice. But in this chapter the key issue is the effects of proximity on turnout. Following the earlier discussion, if a given voter believes herself to be in the same position as all three parties on the scale, then the election is uncompetitive from her point of view and she has little incentive to vote. In effect she is in the 'black hole' referred to earlier. On the other hand, if she is close to one of the parties but a long way from the others, she has a clear incentive to vote. But, if she perceives herself to be distant from all three parties then her incentive to vote is once again reduced, since none of them appears to be representing her interests. This reasoning suggests that the relationship between turnout and proximity should be curvilinear and is best approximated by a quadratic function of the type:

$$\text{Turnout} = \beta_0 + \beta_1 \text{ Proximity} + \beta_2 \text{ Proximity}^2 + ,i$$

where β_0 and $\beta_1 > 0$ and $\beta_2 < 0$.

Table 11.1 The effect of proximity on the left–right and tax-spend scales on turnout in the 2001 general election in Britain

Predictor	Model A	Model B	Model C	Prob+
Left–right proximity	0.002	–0.006	–	
Left–right proximity squared	–0.000			
	0.000	–		
Tax–spend proximity	0.0162***	0.009**	0.003**	0.15
Tax–spend proximity squared	–0.001***	–0.000	–	
Election interest	–	0.280***	0.323**	0.28
Trust in others	–	0.035	0.046**	0.09
Efficacy X benefits scale	–	0.004***	0.004***	0.28
Perceived costs	–	–0.145***	–0.144***	–0.22
Individual benefits	–	0.146***	0.112***	0.18
System benefits	–	0.202***	0.222***	0.39
Social norms	–	0.145***	0.133***	0.27
Policy dissatisfaction	–	–0.032*	–0.030*	–0.18
Political knowledge	–	0.184***	0.188***	0.24
Personal economic expectations	–	0.052***	0.037***	0.15
Social class	–	0.094*	0.088**	0.09
Party mobiliszation	–	0.174**	0.125**	0.14
Attention to the campaign on TV	–	0.090	–	–
Perceived relative deprivation	–	0.068	–	–
Sex	–	–0.344***	–0.314***	–0.06
Age	–	0.018***	0.020***	0.28
Ethnicity	–	0.748***	0.376**	0.08
McFadden R squared	0.01	0.19	0.19	
Per cent correctly classified	73	78	77	

Notes

$p < 0.01$***; $p < 0.05$**; $p < 0.20$*.

+ This is the change in the probability of voting caused by varying the predictor from its minimum to its maximum value while holding other predictors at their means.

The estimates of various logistic regression models of the turnout appear in Table 11.1. The dependent variable in these models is the respondent's verified turnout, which is a behavioural rather than an attitudinal variable and compensates for the well-known tendency of individuals to exaggerate their electoral participation.

Model A contains the estimates for the left–right and the tax–spend proximity scales using the quadratic specifications for both variables. It is apparent from this table that the left–right scale has no statistically significant impact on turnout. On the other hand the tax–spend scale is a significant predictor of turnout and the quadratic form for the specification works in exactly the way predicted. Thus turnout rises as the distance between the parties and the respondent increases, reaches a maximum and then subsequently starts to decline. It is clear that the tax–spend scale is not a strong predictor of turnout and has a rather small pseudo-R squared statistic. But it nonetheless predicts 73 per cent of the cases correctly.

Model B includes all of the variables in the best model of turnout derived in the election study analysis of the six models (see Clarke *et al.*, 2004: 259). It can be seen that the tax–spend scale remains a positive predictor of turnout, with the same signs as in model A, but the power term is no longer statistically significant, making the relationship linear rather than quadratic. Model C deletes all non-significant variables from model B, and the final column of Table 11.1 translates the coefficients in model C into probabilities for ease of comparison.[8]

It can be seen in Table 11.1 that distance on the tax–spend proximity scale has a modest positive effect in stimulating turnout, taking into account the effects of the other six models of participation. The effect is not as large as some of the variables in the general incentives model, such as efficacy time benefits and costs, or some of the variables in the cognitive engagement model such as political knowledge and interest in the campaign. But distance has an independent effect on turnout, controlling for the effects of all six other models.[9] This suggests that if an election is uncompetitive and voters perceive little difference between the parties on the taxation and spending issue, this will inhibit their willingness to participate. This is not an electoral 'black hole' because many other things influence turnout other than issue proximity. But the evidence does show that a lack of perceived party competition inherent in the median voter theorem inhibits electoral participation.

Conclusions and discussion

The main conclusion of this chapter is that convergence to the median voter in a spatial model of party competition wipes out electoral participation, if one assumes that citizens can abstain from voting. This is a purely theoretical argument, but the empirical evidence suggests that convergence inhibits electoral participation in practice and therefore is consistent with this 'black hole' theorem.

The black hole theorem has some curious implications for spatial models. In the version which assumes that voters cannot distinguish between the parties if the policy distance falls below a certain threshold, the black hole is wider than in the pure case. By implication, if parties run bland campaigns which avoid specific promises and talk in generalities and focus on personalities then the black hole will be wider as a consequence, since it is motivated by policy considerations. Electors will find it difficult to distinguish between the parties on policy grounds.

Another implication is that parties have an incentive to get as close to the edge of the black hole as possible in order to maximise votes. A party which succeeds in getting closer to the political Schwarzschild radius,[10] or the edge of the black hole, than its rival will win the election. But if they both get too close they will fall in. Party strategy in this situation is like a 'chicken game' with leaders wanting to face down rivals without losing their electoral support. So another unexpected implication of the theorem is that parties will have to collude to maintain a 'safe' distance between themselves in spatial models of party competition.

A third equally counter-intuitive conclusion is that if parties agree on policy goals, which is commonly the case in valence models of electoral behaviour, then they may want to fabricate differences between themselves in order to avoid the black hole. This is only necessary if the electorate does not share their agreement about goals or is unsure of what the goals should be. Such 'shadow' competition will preserve the impression that the parties are different, even though they may not be so in reality. Overall, it appears that spatial models of party competition are more interesting and less straightforward than they appear at first sight, once issues of voter indifference are taken into account.

Technical appendix

Let voter i's preferences be represented by a utility function $U_i(x)$ defined over a single dimensional vector x. Let x_i^* be voter i's most preferred point along the x vector. Thus x_i^* is voter i's ideal point iff $U_i(x_i^*) > U_i(x_i)$ for all x_i not equal to x_i^*.

Let $\{x_1^* \ x_2^* \ x_3^* \cdots x_n^*\}$ be the n ideal points for an electorate of n individuals. Let N_R be the number of $x_i^* >$ or $= x_m$, the ideal point of the median voter, and N_L be the number of $x_i^* <$ or $= x_m$. Then x_m is the median position iff $N_R >$ or $= n/2$ and $N_L >$ or $= n/2$.

Median voter theorem

If x is a single-dimensional issue, and all voters have single-peaked preferences defined over x then x_m, the median position cannot lose under majority rule.

Proof

Consider any z not equal to x_m, say $z < x_m$. Let R_m be the number of ideal points to the right of x_m. By definition of single-peaked preferences, all R_m voters with ideal points to the right of x_m prefer x_m to z. By definition of the median position, $R_m > n/2$. Thus, the number of voters preferring x_m to z is at least $R_m > n/2$. Thus x_m cannot lose to z under majority rule. The same reasoning applies to $z > x_m$, so that x_m cannot lose to z under majority rule.

Let $U_i(P_1)$ be the utility received by voter i from party 1's platform where P_1 is a location on the single dimensional vector x. Similarly $U_i(P_2)$

is the utility received by voter i from party 2's platform on vector x. $U_i(P^*)$ is the utility received by voter i from her ideal party platform.

Black hole theorem

If party 1 and party 2 converge to the position of the median voter x_m, then no-one will vote.

Proof

In the spatial model i votes for party 1 iff $|Ui(P^*) - Ui(P_1)| < |Ui(P^*) - Ui(P_2)|$ and for party 2 iff $|Ui(P^*) - Ui(P_1)| > |Ui(P^*) - Ui(P_2)|$. Rearranging terms and simplifying;

i votes for party 1 iff $|Ui(P_1) - Ui(P_2)| > 0$, and for party 2 iff $|Ui(P_1) - Ui(P_2)| < 0$, abstain otherwise. As the Median Voter Theorem shows, parties will adopt x_m, the platform of the median voter to avoid losing. Thus $x_m = P_1 = P_2$.

In this case $|Ui(P_1) - Ui(P_2)| = |Ui(x_m) - Ui(x_m)| = 0$. Therefore i is indifferent and will not vote.

Note that individuals will vote if parties are located infinitesimally to the left or right of the median position. But if we make the plausible assumption that voters have to perceive a minimum distance between the parties before they are willing to participate, this is no longer true. Thus assume that i votes iff $|Ui(P1) - Ui(P2)| > \epsilon_i$ for some $\epsilon_i > 0$. This term may vary across the electorate, but it has a minimum value ϵ_i. If the parties get within ϵ_i of each other, no one will vote. Note that this result applies anywhere on the left–right spectrum and not just at the median position. However, since the median is an attractor this is where the problem is likely to occur.

Notes

1 The assumptions are that there is no voter abstention, voters have single-peaked preferences, party competition is over a one-dimensional issue space, two parties are competing for office, and politicians are office-seeking (see Riker and Ordeshook, 1973).

2 The case of compulsory voting does not in fact improve the situation, from the point of view of democratic accountability. In the case of compulsory voting, electors will be forced to choose randomly between the parties since they have no basis for choosing otherwise. If the electorate is an even number of individuals, this will produce a tie, since in a two-party system each party will take exactly 50 per cent of the vote. The outcome will be settled by tossing a coin. If the electorate is an odd number of individuals the outcome will be decided by the median voter, but she will have to toss a coin to do it. Thus the median voter theorem with compulsory voting means that the election result is decided by chance.

3 This is because if the parties converge at the median, voters have no basis for choosing between them, even when that choice decides the outcome of the election.

4 The voter turnout data is taken from the website of the Institute for Democracy and Electoral Assistance and measures the turnout relative to the voting age population (see www.idea.int.).

5 Note that in the case of the United States there is a moderately strong positive correlation between turnout and the standard deviation of the parties on the planned economy scale in the party manifesto data. This is labelled PLANECO in the manifesto data set (see Budge *et al.*, 2001: 183).

6 For the left–right ideological scale respondents were given the following question: 'In politics, people sometimes talk of the left and right. Using a scale from 0 to 10, where would you place yourself?' [Show card used]. For the taxation versus spending scale the question was: 'On a scale from 0 to 10, where 0 means government should cut taxes a lot and spend much less on health and social services, and 10 means government should raise taxes a lot and spend much more on health and social services, where would you put yourself?' [Show card used]. Note that additional scales were included in the self-completion questionnaire, but the N's on this a significantly smaller than on the main face-to-face questionnaire.

7 Thus the measure is:

$$\text{Proximity} = \Sigma(X_i - L_i)^2 + \Sigma(X_i - C_i)^2 + \Sigma(X_i - LD_i)^2$$

where X_i is the respondents self-assigned position on the left–right scale, L_i is the respondents assigned position of the Labour party, C_i is the respondents assigned position of the Conservative party, LD_i is the respondents assigned position of the Liberal Democrats.

8 This is the change in the probability of voting caused by varying the predictor from its minimum to its maximum value while holding other predictors at their means. This is done using Gary King's clarify programme in Stata 8. See Tomz *et al.* (1999).

9 Note that election interest, policy dissatisfaction, political knowledge and attention to the campaign on TV are all indicators of the cognitive engagement model. Efficacy time benefits, perceived costs, individual benefits, system benefits and social norms are all indicators of the general incentive model. Social capital is represented by trust in others; civic voluntarism by social class and party mobilisation; and equity-fairness by personal economic expectations and perceived relative deprivation. A detailed coding of these measures can be found in Clarke *et al.* (2004).

10 This refers to the zone around a gravitational black hole which if crossed prevents any matter or energy escaping from the black hole. See Mills (1994: 197–199).

References

Adams, J. and S. Merrill (1999) 'Modeling Party Strategies and Policy Representation in Multiparty Elections: Why are Strategies So Extreme?', *American Journal of Political Science* 43: 765–791.

Aldrich, J.H. (1995) *Why Parties?: The Origin and Transformation of Party Politics in America* (Chicago: University of Chicago Press).

Alesina, Alberto and Howard Rosenthal (1995) *Partisan Politics, Divided Government, and the Economy* (Cambridge: Cambridge University Press).

Alvarez, M., J. Nagler and S. Bowler (2000) 'Issues, Economics, and the Dynamics of Multiparty Elections: The 1997 British General Election', *American Political Science Review* 94: 131–150.

Ansolabehere, S. and J. Synder (2000) 'Valence Politics and Equilibrium in Spatial Election Models', *Public Choice* 103: 327–336.

Banks, J., J. Duggan and M. Le Breton (2002) 'Bounds for Mixed Strategy Equilibria and the Spatial Model of Elections', *Journal of Economic Theory*, 103: 88–105.

Black,.D. (1948) 'On the Rationale of Group Decision Making', *Journal of Political Economy* 56: 23–34.

Black, D. (1958) *The Theory of Committees and Elections* (Cambridge: Cambridge University Press).

Budge, I. and D. Farlie (1977) *Voting and Party Competition* (London and New York: Wiley).

Budge, I., D. Robertson and D. Hearl (1984) (eds) *Ideology, Strategy and Party Change: Spatial Analysis of Post-War Election Programmes in 19 Democracies* (Cambridge: Cambridge University Press).

Budge, I. and D. Robertson (1987) 'Do Parties Differ and How? Comparative Discriminant and Factor Analysis', in Ian Budge, David Robertson and Derek Hearl (eds). *Ideology, Strategy and Party Change: Spatial Analyses of Post-War Election Programmes in 19 Democracies* (Cambridge: Cambridge University Press).

Budge, I. and H. Keman (1990) *Parties and Democracy: Coalition Formation and Government Functioning in Twenty States* (Oxford: Oxford University Press).

Budge, I., H.-D. Klingemann, A. Volkens, J. Bara and E. Tanenbaum (eds) (2001) *Mapping Policy Preferences: Estimates for Parties, Electors and Governments 1945–1998* (Oxford: Oxford University Press).

Budge, I. and H.-D. Klingemann (2001) 'Finally! Comparative over-time mapping of party policy movement', in Ian Budge, Hans-Dieter Klingemann, Andrea Volkens, Judith Bara and Eric Tanenbaum (eds) *Mapping Policy Preferences: Estimates for Parties, Electors and Governments 1945–1998*. (Oxford: Oxford University Press), pp. 19–50.

Calvert, R. (1985) 'Robustness of the Multidimensional Voting Model: Candidates, Motivations, Uncertainty and Convergence', *American Journal of Political Science* 29: 69–85.

Clarke, H., D. Sanders, M. Stewart and P. Whiteley (2004) *Political Choice in Britain* (Oxford: Oxford University Press).

Dalton, R. (1985) 'Political Parties and Political Representation', *Comparative Political Studies* 17: 267–299.

Dalton, R. (2002) *Citizen Politics: Public Opinion and Parties in Advanced Industrial Democracies* (New York: Chatham House).

Davis, O., M. Hinich and P. Ordeshook (1970) 'An Expository Development of a Mathematical Model of the Electoral Process', *American Political Science Review* 64: 426–448.

Denzau, A. and K. Greer (1984) 'Determinants of Local School Spending: Some Consistent Estimates', *Public Choice* 44: 375–383.

Downs, A. (1957) *An Economic Theory of Democracy* (New York: Harper and Row).

Duverger, Maurice, (1954) *Political Parties* (London: Methuen).

Enelow, J.M. and M. Hinich (1984) *The Spatial Theory of Voting* (Cambridge: Cambridge University Press).

Groseclose, T. (2001) 'A Model of Candidate Location When One Candidate Has a Valence Advantage', *American Journal of Political Science* 45: 862–886.

Hinich, M.J. (1977) 'Equilibrium in Spatial Voting: The Median Voter Theorem is an Artifact', *Journal of Economic Theory* 16: 208–219.

Holmberg, Soren (1989) 'Political Representation in Sweden', *Scandinavian Political Studies* 12: 1–35.

Hotelling, Harold (1929) 'Stability in Competition', *Economic Journal* 39: 41–57.

Iversen, Torben (1994) 'Political Leadership and Representation in Western European Democracies: A Test of Three Models of Voting', *American Journal of Political Science* 38: 45–74.

Laver, M. and I. Budge (1992) *Party Policy and Governmental Coalitions* (London: Macmillan).

Lin, T.-M., J.M. Enelow and H. Dorussen (1999) 'Equilibrium in Multicandidate Probabilistic Spatial Voting', *Public Choice* 98: 59–82.

Macdonald, S.E. and G. Rabinowitz (1993) 'Direction and Uncertainty in a Model of Issue Voting', *Journal of Theoretical Politics* 5: 61–87.

Macdonald, S.E. and G. Rabinowitz (1998) 'Solving the Paradox of Nonconvergence: Valence, Position and Direction in Democratic Politics', *Electoral Studies* 17: 281–300.

McKelvey, R.D. and P.C. Ordeshook (1990) 'A Decade of Experimental Research on Spatial Models of Elections and Committees', in J. Enelow and M.J. Hinich (eds) *Advances in the Spatial Theory of Voting* (Cambridge: Cambridge University Press).

May, J. (1973) 'Opinion Structure of Political Parties: The Special Law of Curvilinear Disparity', *Political Studies* 21: 135–151.

Merrill, S. and B. Grofman (1999) *A Unified Theory of Voting* (Cambridge: Cambridge University Press).

Mills, R. (1994) *Space, Time and Quanta: An Introduction to Contemporary Physics* (Oxford: W. H. Freeman and Co).

Mueller, E.N. (1979) *Aggressive Political Participation* (Princeton, NJ: Princeton University Press).

Pommerehne, W. and B.S. Frey (1976) 'Two Approaches to Estimating Public Expenditures', *Public Finance Quarterly* 4: 395–407.

Poole, K. and H. Rosenthal (1984) 'The Polarization of American Politics', *Journal of Politics* 46: 1061–1079.

Putnam, R. (1993) *Making Democracy Work: Civic Traditions in Modern Italy* (Princeton, NJ: Princeton University Press).

Putnam, R. (2000) *Bowling Alone: The Collapse and Revival of American Community* (New York: Simon and Schuster).

Riker, W. and P. Ordeshook (1968) 'A Theory of the Calculus of Voting', *American Political Science Review* 62: 25–42.

Riker, W.H. and P. Ordeshook (1973) *An Introduction to Positive Political Theory* (Englewood Cliffs, NJ: Prentice-Hall).

Rabinowitz, George and Stuart Elaine Macdonald (1989) 'A Directional Theory of Issue Voting', *American Political Science Review* 83: 93–121.

Runciman, W.G. 1966. *Relative Deprivation and Social Justice* (Berkeley, CA: University of California Press).

Schofield, N. (2003) 'Valence Competition in the Spatial Stochastic Model', *Journal of Theoretical Politics* 15, pp. 371–383.

Schofield, N. and I. Sened (2006) *Multiparty Parliaments* (Cambridge: Cambridge University Press).

Schofield, N., G. Miller and A. Martin (2003) 'Critical Elections and Political Realignment in the US: 1860–2000', *Political Studies* 51: 217–240.

Schofield, N., A. Martin, K. Quinn and A. Whitford (1998) 'Multiparty Electoral Competition in the Netherlands and Germany: a Model Based on Multinomial Probit', *Public Choice* 97: 257–293.

Seyd, P. and P. Whiteley (1992) *Labour's Grassroots: The Politics of Party Membership* (Oxford: Oxford University Press).

Seyd, P. and P. Whiteley (2002) *New Labour's Grassroots: The Transformation of the Party Membership* (London: Palgrave-Macmillan).

Tomz, M., J. Wittenberg and G. King (1999) *CLARIFY: Software for Interpreting and Presenting Statistical Results* (Cambridge, MA: Harvard University: Department of Government).

Verba, S., K. Lehman Schlozman, H. Brady (1995) *Voice and Equality: Civic Voluntarism in American Politics* (Cambridge, MA: Harvard University Press).

Walker, I. and H. Smith (eds) (2002) *Relative Deprivation: Specification, Development and Integration* (Cambridge: Cambridge University Press).

Whiteley, P. and P. Seyd (2002) *High Intensity Participation: The Dynamics of Party Activism in Britain* (Ann Arbor, MI: University of Michigan Press).

Wittman, D. (1977) 'Candidates with Policy Preferences: A Dynamic Model', *Journal of Economic Theory* 14: 180–189.

Wittman, D. (1983) 'Candidate Motivation: A synthesis of Alternative Theories', *American Political Science Review* 77: 142–57.

12 Preference shaping and party competition

Some empirical and theoretical arguments

Hugh Ward

Introduction

> Winning an election is a splendid thing, but it is only the prologue to the vital business of government . . .. We have to move this country in a new direction, to change the way we look at things, to create a wholly new attitude of mind. Can it be done? . . . Yes, the Conservative party can do it. And we will do it. But it will take time.
>
> (reprinted in Harris, 1997: 97)

This quotation from Margaret Thatcher's speech to the Tory Party Conference shortly after her 1979 election victory suggests that some politicians believe that in time governments can shift the electorate in their direction. As natural as this view might seem to a leader like Thatcher, it is capable of creating shock-waves among rational choice theorists seeking to model party competition in the 'Downsian' tradition. Following neo-classical economics' assumption that consumer preferences are exogenous to competition between firms, voter preferences are typically treated as exogenous to political competition. As usual, Downs' view is more complex and nuanced: 'though parties will move ideologically to adjust to the [voter] distribution under some circumstances, they will also attempt to move voters towards their own location, thus altering it' (1957: 140). Although some have also recognised this possibility (Dunleavy and Ward, 1981; Przeworski and Sprague, 1986: 125–126; Gerber and Jackson, 1993; Grofman and Withers, 1995: 56; Jackson, 2003), it has largely been lost sight of in the formal literature, and many remain sceptical about the empirical case for preference shaping.

Data from the Manifestos Project opens up new possibilities for empirically testing preference shaping. At first sight some of the patterns observed strongly suggest that preference shaping does occur. In Figure 12.1, I map data on the positions of the Republican and Democrat parties, covering the period November 1948 to November 1996, the last US presidential election coded (Budge *et al.*, 2001: 25). Faced with the problem of a set of multiple indicators of the left-to-right views of the US electorate, with the set of indicators and wording of questions changing over time and with large numbers of missing observations, Stimson uses a complex algorithm to calculate 'policy mood' (1999: 47–55). Figure 12.1 shows quarterly data on policy mood from the fourth quarter of 1958, when Stimson's reported series starts. A movement upwards of any of the variables indicates a shift to the political right. Visual inspection of trends and turning points strongly suggests that when the Republicans move to the right so does the electorate, though with a substantial lag of around two presidential terms.[1] I bring this out in Figure 12.2, which maps the values of *policy mood* standardised around mean value and the position of the Republican Party lagged 28 quarters. The fit could be a coincidence. Certainly more sophisticated data analysis is needed before anything can be concluded; and some will be suspicious of an effect operating with such a long lag. But a correlation of this sort should be a wake-up call for political scientists whose belief that voters' preferences are exogenous is firmly entrenched.

In the first section I show that the literature strongly supports the idea of opinion leadership through information transfer and is not inconsistent with Dunleavy and Ward's (1981, 1991) idea of structural preference shaping by shifting voters between socio-structural positions. In the next section I use data on UK party positions drawn from the Manifestos Project to examine the reciprocal links between parties' left–right positions and voters' positions, using vector autoregression. Dunleavy and

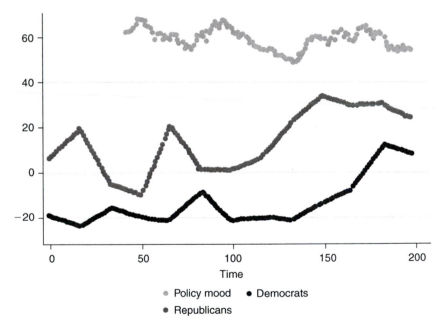

Figure 12. 1 Party positions and policy mood in the US, 1948 to 1996.

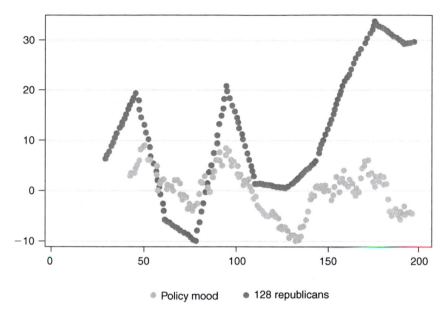

Figure 12.2 Policy mood standardised to mean value and the position of the republican party lagged 28 quarters.

Ward argue on theoretical grounds that the governing party should be more influential, and I find evidence for this. Finally I summarise my own formal model (Ward, 2001) which is designed to investigate the effects of such power differentials.

Parties' influence over voter positions

Citizens' policy preferences may be pictured as deriving from: (i) beliefs about causal links between policies and end-states; (ii) fixed underlying preferences over end states, deriving from their social location and (iii) personal idiosyncracies. First, to treat policy preferences as exogenous to political competition is to ignore the ability of parties to shape voters' beliefs (Przeworski, 1998: 143). Although it is not rational for most voters to be well informed about issues (Downs, 1957), they have a number of avenues open to cast a vote in a boundedly rational way, using low-cost information (Fiorina, 1990; Ottati and Wyer, 1990: 201–214; Grofman and Withers, 1995; Popkin, 1995). Among the sources of information are: party leaders, especially popular leaders (Page and Shapiro, 1992: 348–350; Cohen, 1997: 124–125; cf. Miller and Shanks, 1982); prominent and trusted policy specialists, such as key opinion formers in the US Congress (Carmines and Kuklinski, 1990); and party activists in voters' social circles (Stimson, 1990). Of course parties' ability to shape attitudes is constrained by voters' political awareness, predispositions to receive or reject messages, tendency to utilise messages that are prominent in their minds (Zaller, 1992) and relative unreceptiveness to messages that do not 'resonate' with their concerns and with events (Ansolabehere *et al.*, 1997; Petrocik, 1997).

In an uncertain world voters need to fit together information by using an ideology (Downs, 1957) or cognitive paradigm (Ottati and Wyer, 1990) to make sense of it. Parties are important and active forces in creating these structures (Przeworski and Sprague, 1986: 143–144; Zaller, 1992; Przeworski, 1998). Parties can also generate issues (Riker, 1986) or change voters' issue priorities (Robertson, 1976). For instance Cohen shows that presidential state of the union addresses in the US are both influenced by and influence the issue priorities of voters (1997: 49–59). In summary, there is convincing evidence that parties can influence voters' views through provision of information and conceptual tools for structuring it.

Especially in systems like the UK in which the executive predominates, the judiciary is weak and there is little decentralisation of power, the governing party is relatively free to use state power for structural preference shaping (Dunleavy and Ward, 1981, 1991). By developing policies that move voters into new social locations in which their interests are different, the governing party may hope to increase its support; and governing parties can create or make more prominent social cleavages that structure the vote in advantageous ways (Garrett, 1992). For instance, after 1979 some argue that the Conservative Party was able to create new Tory voters by squeezing the number of public-sector jobs through privatisations. Beside building their support, this was more in line with their policy preferences than centrist policies, and it freed up financial resources for tax breaks (Dunleavy and Ward, 1991; Garrett, 1992; Garrett, 1993).

This argument, partly based on the electoral significance of non-class based production and consumption cleavages in the UK (Dunleavy and Husbands, 1985), has been contested. Crewe and Searing (1988: 375) see no obvious trend in a Thatcherite direction in public opinion between 1974 and 1987. Heath *et al.* (1991: chapters 6, 7, 8) see confusion over causality e.g. those predisposed to vote Tory were more likely to buy their council houses. However, controlling for partisan identity, Garrett (1992) found that there were significant effects on the probability of Tory vote from buying a council house, first-time share purchases and ceasing to be a union member. Bartle (1998) confirms that some production and consumption cleavages had significant direct and indirect causal effects in the 1992 election. Clarke *et al.* (2004: 109) find homeownership to have been a factor in the 2001 election. In a sophisticated study using non-recursive structural equation modelling of individual panel data, Stubager (2003) found effects from council house purchase to vote intention but he did find purchase of shares in privatised industries to be significant.

These studies focus on privatisation and council house sales, ignoring other potential causal pathways and longer-term effects. If voters care about their relative well-being, policies that affect income and wealth differentials will affect the government's support.[2] Voters give most attention to issues and information that feature prominently in the media in the run-up to elections (Iyengar, 1990). The executive's ability to manage the political agenda and news coverage may be significant, then.[3] The executive can also use its ability to manage international crises (Dunleavy and Ward, 1991). Garrett (1993) points out that it takes time to shift structural features of society and there may be short-term electoral costs. Opportunities for successful structural preference shaping are relatively rare. Despite its methodological sophistication Stubager's study (2003) fails to control for shifts in the macro-economy and in personal economic circumstances. It is quite possible that increasing unemployment over the first Thatcher term influenced individuals' economic attitudes. Indeed Alcoe (2001; cf. Studlar *et al.*, 1990) shows that there was a shift away from using current unemployment and inflation as the basis for personal economic expectations towards the use of house prices and stock-market indices, consistent with the idea that the British electorate moved away from a 'Keynesian' viewpoint.

The relevant empirical question is whether the position of the median voter is in a more favourable position for a party than it would have been in the absence of preference shaping, given other developments – notably in the macro-economy. Individual-level data is certainly better for examination of particular causal pathways and mechanisms. But to study the overall picture that might arise as a result of the operation of a range of mechanisms, while controlling for economic circumstances, and to answer the key question of whether preference shaping operates controlling for other trends, aggregate-level time-series data on public opinion together with time-series data on party positions has considerable advantages.

A VAR analysis of aggregate UK data

VAR is a method of analysing a set of several variables through time when it is believed that each of the variables might influence the other, so that none is exogenous (Greene, 2003: 586–607). It is particularly suitable when there are no strong theoretical grounds on which to place restrictions on which variables influence others and the lags with which influence occurs. Each variable is regressed on its own lagged values and the lagged values of all other variables in the system. This makes it easy to test for 'Granger causality'. Variable x is said to Granger cause y when the lagged values of x have explanatory power in a regression of y on its lagged values together with the lagged values of any control variables, z i.e. prediction of y is enhanced by x. Some dispute whether Granger causality has any relationship to causality as it has generally been understood in the social sciences, but many econometricians believe that the existence of a statistical relationship can never establish anything about the direction of causality: even when changes in x precede those in y, this could be due to anticipation of changes in y, rather than being a cause of them (e.g. Kennedy, 1992: 68). My central focus in this section will be on whether party positions Granger cause forms of opinion at the aggregate level that might be related to voters' positions on the left–right spectrum. To put it another way, I test for the strong exogeneity of the aggregate voter distribution.

VAR is a data-hungry technique. Few questions asked with any regularity by opinion pollsters are plausible indicators of public opinion of the left–right spectrum. From 1979 to 2001 Gallup has asked whether respondents' own views come closest to tax cuts, on the one hand, or expansion of services, even if it means tax increases, on the other hand (King *et al.*, 2001, 238), but the question has been asked irregularly and often only once in a given year. Similar problems arise with questions about spending priorities (King *et al.*, 2001: 240). [4] On the other hand, in most months from 1961 to 2001 Gallup asked some variant on the question of what is the most urgent or important problem facing the country, allowing respondents to answer 'cost of living' or 'unemployment', amongst other possibilities. (King *et al.*, 2001: 266). Although this does vary, in most months by far the majority of respondents have either answered 'cost of living' or 'unemployment'.

I took the percentage of respondents who said unemployment was the most important problem, *unprob*, and the percentage who said inflation was the most important problem, *infprob*, as proxies for the left–right position of the median voter. This is based on the hypothesis that the probability with which a respondent will see unemployment as an urgent problem is a function of their ideology, represented in Downs' sense by position of the left–right spectrum, and how high unemployment actually is. Specifically the further to the right a respondent self-places and the lower the rate of unemployment the less likely they are to see unemployment as an urgent problem. Holding unemployment constant, if *unprob* falls, this could be accounted for by a shift of some voters to the right, although this inference is not a firm one as it moves from the aggregate to the individual level. Although it is possible that a shift of some voters to the right would not mean that the position of the median voter moved to the right, conversely this change is not logically compatible with the median voter moving to the left, and is most plausibly linked with a rightward shift of the median. Recognising the problems with this indicator, the mean level of concern for unemployment conditional on actual unemployment seems as reasonable an indicator as any available of the median. A similar case can be made out for the mean level of concern for inflation, conditional on actual inflation, although this time increased concern indicates a rightward shift, controlling for the actual level of inflation.

Concern for consistency of question wording over the 'urgent problem question' meant that my analysis could not start before January 1978. In fact I started it June 1979, with Margaret Thatcher's election to office, and ran it up to the June 2001 election. When occasionally Gallup did not ask the relevant question, I averaged the preceding and succeeding month, based on the fact that short-term variation is relatively low, to get continuous monthly time series, *unprobi* and *infprobi*, with the *i* indicating interpolation. Because my indicators of the median voter position are conditional on the levels of unemployment and inflation respectively, the set of variables I analysed included monthly data on the rate of unemployment, *un*, and change in the consumer price index, *inf*.[5]

The Manifestos Project provides widely accepted measures of the left–right positions of UK parties for the 1979, 1983, 1987, 1992 and 2001 elections (Budge *et al.*, 2001). These derive from content analysis of manifestos, being the percentage of quasi-sentences that contain right-emphases minus the percentage of quasi-sentences that contain left-emphases (Budge and Klingemann, 2001: 20–21). It would be a step too far to say that these measures fully capture the *actual* positions of the parties between elections. Supporters of mandate theory find evidence that what parties do in office does correlate with these positions (Budge and Hofferbert 1990; cf. King and Laver, 1993), but it is entirely plausible that there is some policy drift between elections. Also there are numerous reasons why the perceived positions of parties could vary from their official ones. The variable *rcons* takes on the value of the Conservative Party's left–right score in the previous election for every month until one month before the next election, then it changes to the value of the left–right score in the next election. The variable *rlabs* is the analogous measure for the Labour Party. Because of uncertainty about what happens between elections, these variables can only capture the effects of shifts in the 'official positions' of parties on the aggregate voter distribution. Positions are taken to shift just one month before the election, because manifestos are generally *officially* launched between the dissolution of Parliament and the election – a period of around six weeks. *Rcons* and *rlabs* do not vary much. But this has the methodological virtue of providing a very stringent test of preference shaping: if these variables can be shown to Granger cause *unprobi* and/or *infprobi* despite their low variance, we can be more assured about the empirical grounds for preference shaping.[6]

Theory is ambiguous about whether parties respond to each other's position, partly because the focus has been on predicting equilibria, where they exist, not on out-of-equilibrium dynamics. Nonetheless it is plausible that adaptive parties, subject to bounded rationality, might copy the other party if they think that movements this party made have proven popular (cf. Kollman *et al.*, 1992).

Finally I included the percentage of Gallup respondents who approved the government's record *govapp* (King *et al.*, 2001: 172–178) and the percentage of respondents who believe the leader of the opposition is proving a good leader of his/her party, *oppapp* (King *et al.*, 2001: 210). First, as we have already seen, the literature suggests that whether parties' messages are heeded depends partly on whether they are popular. Second, whether the government (and possibly the opposition) are likely to change their left–right position in response to public opinion on issues like unemployment is likely to depend on these variables e.g. if the government thinks it has solid support it will be less inclined to respond when this goes against its policy goals (cf. Wittman, 1983).

Augmented Dickey-Fuller tests suggested that the null-hypothesis of the existence of a unit root could not be rejected for any of the variables in the set I analyse. So as to avoid spurious correlation between trending variables and also problems with violating the assumption of no autocorrelation in the disturbances necessary for inference in VAR, I took the first difference of each variable. Thus *dunprobi = unprobi(t) – unprobi(-1)*, and so on for the other differenced variables, denoted by the prefix *d*. The results here refer, then, to the effects of changes in variables, not levels.

One of the problems with VAR is selecting the number of lags to be used in the models. Different tests gave contradictory advice: while the Likelihood-Ratio test suggested models with 12 lags, the Akaike Information Criterion (AIC) test suggests just two lags. Some argue that if the aim of the research is to make accurate forecasts, the AIC test gives better advice with monthly data (Ivanov and Kilian, 2000), but my primary aim here is to examine Granger causality, which hardly recommends leaving out significant effects at longer lags. Preliminary modelling suggested that the main effects of party positions on public perceptions of economic problems took place at lags of around eight months. Ultimatately I estimated models with 12 lags, but results did not seem sensitive to this so long as the number of lags does not drop below nine.

The results reported are VAR estimates of models of each variable on 12 lags of its own values and 12 lags of each of the other variables in the system. So long as the residuals suggest that the stability condition of error structure covariance stationarity holds, and so long as there is no evidence for autocorrelation of disturbances from the residuals, inferential statistics derived from VAR can be used. The overall estimated model passes the stability test (Stata Corp, 2003: 324–328) and a residual autocorrelation test for first- and second-order autocorrelation (Stata Corp, 2003: 308–310).

It is a tedious and space-consuming business to present the full results, so I will cut straight to the Granger causality tests.[7] After VAR estimation a Wald test of the null hypothesis that in the model for y the coefficients on the lags of x are jointly zero can be performed. If the null hypothesis can be rejected, the conclusion is that x does Granger cause y (Greene, 2003: 592). Table 12.1 shows the results. There is much that could receive comment here, but I will focus largely on the interaction between party positions and my indicators of the voter distribution.

Table 12.1 Granger causality Wald tests

Equation	Excluded	chi2	df	Prob > chi2
dinfprobi	dunprobi	9.6527	12	0.6464
dinfprobi	drcons	13.8697	12	0.3091
dinfprobi	drlabs	6.2119	12	0.9050
dinfprobi	dgovapp	10.7193	12	0.5531
dinfprobi	doppapp	8.7694	12	0.7225
dinfprobi	dinf	36.0510	12	0.0003
dinfprobi	dun	11.0647	12	0.5234
dinfprobi	ALL	141.5621	84	0.0001
dunprobi	dinfprobi	23.4743	12	0.0240
dunprobi	drcons	20.1757	12	0.0638
dunprobi	drlabs	22.9727	12	0.0280
dunprobi	dgovapp	22.8526	12	0.0290
dunprobi	doppapp	36.9071	12	0.0002
dunprobi	dinf	33.9144	12	0.0007
dunprobi	dun	38.1631	12	0.0001
dunprobi	ALL	239.3788	84	0.0000
drcons	dinfprobi	6.5616	12	0.8852
drcons	dunprobi	12.2043	12	0.4294
drcons	drlabs	5.2864	12	0.9477
drcons	dgovapp	49.2600	12	0.0000
drcons	doppapp	6.8559	12	0.8670
drcons	dinf	12.0621	12	0.4407
drcons	dun	20.2914	12	0.0618
drcons	ALL	94.8058	84	0.1973
drlabs	dinfprobi	8.6892	12	0.7292
drlabs	dunprobi	24.0982	12	0.0197
drlabs	drcons	9.6448	12	0.6471
drlabs	dgovapp	19.4956	12	0.0772
drlabs	doppapp	15.9884	12	0.1918
drlabs	dinf	14.5359	12	0.2678
drlabs	dun	23.6356	12	0.0228
drlabs	ALL	117.7211	84	0.0090
dgovapp	dinfprobi	6.9593	12	0.8603
dgovapp	dunprobi	36.6531	12	0.0003
dgovapp	drcons	18.3998	12	0.1041
dgovapp	drlabs	49.2626	12	0.0000
dgovapp	doppapp	37.6139	12	0.0002
dgovapp	dinf	23.4686	12	0.0240
dgovapp	dun	15.2007	12	0.2306
dgovapp	ALL	163.4953	84	0.0000
doppapp	dinfprobi	13.3085	12	0.3470
doppapp	dunprobi	32.0725	12	0.0013
doppapp	drcons	197.7508	12	0.0000

continued

Table 12.1 continued

Equation	Excluded	chi2	df	Prob > chi2
doppapp	drlabs	78.8137	12	0.0000
doppapp	dgovapp	12.4395	12	0.4111
doppapp	dinf	8.1534	12	0.7730
doppapp	dun	17.6861	12	0.1256
doppapp	ALL	425.2551	84	0.0000
dinf	dinfprobi	45.4787	12	0.0000
dinf	dunprobi	15.7413	12	0.2034
dinf	drcons	13.8110	12	0.3129
dinf	drlabs	9.2267	12	0.6835
dinf	dgovapp	39.7805	12	0.0001
dinf	doppapp	25.7984	12	0.0115
dinf	dun	24.5701	12	0.0170
dinf	ALL	213.1505	84	0.0000
dun	dinfprobi	23.0641	12	0.0272
dun	dunprobi	14.1879	12	0.2889
dun	drcons	33.8269	12	0.0007
dun	drlabs	13.3753	12	0.3424
dun	dgovapp	21.3575	12	0.0454
dun	doppapp	19.9826	12	0.0674
dun	dinf	35.1116	12	0.0004
dun	ALL	178.6875	84	0.0000

At conventional levels of significance we cannot reject the null-hypothesis that the coefficients on the lags of *drcons* are all zero in the model for *dinfprobi* (prob > chi2 = 0.3091). Neither *drcons* nor *drlabs* Granger causes *dinfprobi*. On the other hand, both *drcons* (prob > chi2 = 0.0638) and *drlabs* (prob > chi2 = 0.0280) Granger cause *dunprobi* at close to or above the 95 per cent significance level. So at least for one of the two indicators, concern about unemployment, there is evidence that shifts in party position shift the voter distribution. Although we will have to worry about the direction of these effects shortly, this suggests that preference shaping does occur in the UK.

Evidence for the 'Downsian' link from public opinion to party position is somewhat ambiguous. Neither *dinfprobi* nor *dunprobi* Granger cause *drcons*, although *dun* does so at close to the 95 per cent level (prob > chi2 = 0.0618). In contrast, *dunprobi* does Granger cause *drlabs* (prob > chi2 = 0.0197), as does *dun* (prob > chi2 = 0.0228).[8] While changes in the government's approval rating, *dgovapp*, do Granger cause *drlabs* at close to the 95 per cent level (prob > chi2 = 0.0772), *drcons* does not Granger cause *drlabs*. Neither *drlabs* nor *doppapp* Granger cause *drcons*, although *dgovapp* does so (prob > chi2 = 0.0000). The picture here seems to be one where the opposition, Labour for most of the period being studied here, is more responsive to changes in public opinion than the government, in line with the view that the party with state power is in a better position to preference shape.

VAR allows us to simulate the effects through time of changes in variable x on another variable y, using impulse response functions (irf). Inferring whether a change in x has a negative or a positive effect on y is not a simple matter of reading the signs of regression coefficients for the lagged values of x in the model for y. Over time such shifts impact on *all* other variables in the system and, thus, have complex second-order effects. These are allowed for in calculating impulse response functions.[9] In Figures 12.3 and 12.4, I report cumulative impulse response functions for *drcons* and *drlabs* on *dunprobi*. Over a 20 month period these track what would happen to concern for unemployment if there was a *sustained month-on-month movement* of the parties to the right of one unit per month. The time trends show how concern for unemployment settles to a new equilibrium. When either the Conservative Party or the Labour Party continue to shift to the right, the central forecast estimate is that concern for unemployment diminishes.[10] If reduction in concern for unemployment is a reasonable proxy for a shift to the right in the aggregate voter distribution, as preference shaping theory suggests, the electorate moves in the same direction as the parties.

Careful scrutiny of the scales of the vertical axis suggests that the impact of a shift to the right by the Conservatives is greater than that of a shift to the right by Labour: whereas concern for unemployment eventually falls by under 1 per cent as a consequence of a sustained shift to the right by Labour, it eventually falls by around 5 per cent as a consequence of a sustained shift by the Conservatives.

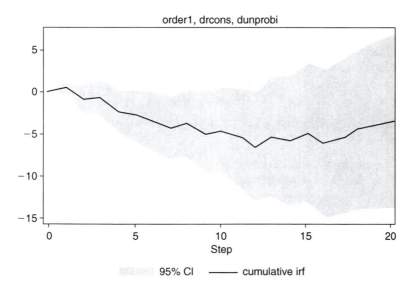

Figure 12.3 Cumulative impulse response function for the impact of shifts in Conservative Party to the right on perceptions of the importance of unemployment.

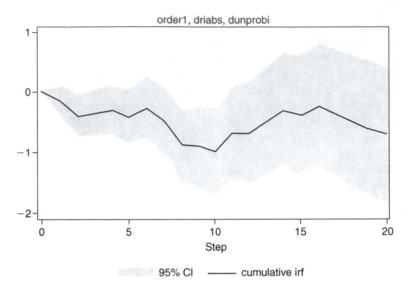

Figure 12.4 Cumulative impulse response function for the impact of shifts in Labour Party to the right on perceptions of the importance of unemployment.

To summarise, although caution is advisable when interpreting what VAR techniques actually tell us about causality, and although doubts must exist about the way that the position of the median voter and that of the parties between elections is proxied here, there are indications that key elements of preference shaping theory are empirically supported: (i) the aggregate voter distribution is endogenous to party competition; (ii) it shifts in the same direction as the main parties (iii) it is more responsive to shifts in the position of the party of government.[11]

Formal models of party competition and endogenous voter preferences

While some authors have attempted to endogenise the voter distribution in formal models of party competition (see the survey in Ward, 2001), they have largely failed to acknowledge differentials in the power of parties of the sort suggested by evidence and argument. One possible explanation is that holding the executive confers less power in the US context, because of division of powers and frequent failure of the executive's party to control both houses, and this informally shapes the way the literature frames the problem.

The most significant recent attempt to develop a fully-specified model of electoral competition in which preferences are endogenous is Jackson's computational model (2003; see also Gerber and Jackson, 1993). Here the probability that a voter casts her vote for a party is a function of her partisan identification and the parties' positions on the left–right spectrum compared to her policy ideal point. Voters' ideal points shift from their past value in the direction of the party they identify with and away from the party they do not identify with, with strong identifiers shifting furthest and larger shifts to the extent that parties' positions have altered since the last election, providing new information. Partisanship is a running tally of past evaluation of parties relative to policy positions, including current evaluation of parties' positions, with less weight on the past. Hence partisanship and policy positions are codetermining at any time, t. Parties have policy preferences and maximise a weighted function of the probability of winning and losses due to departing from their policy ideal point.

Jackson allows for differences in parties' influence that derive from the different numbers of partisans they have. But this is, at most, one source of differential influence: parties' access to the media and ability to influence news coverage differs (e.g. Sanders *et al.*, 1993); the credibility, perceived competence and personality of their candidates differs (Zaller, 1992; Popkin, 1995: 29–33; Alvarez, 1998); past shifts in positions, may lead voters to question parties credibility (Downs, 1957: 103–109); parties' influence varies with the nature of the perceived problems that face society and social 'shocks' (Garrett, 1992, 1993);[12] and incumbents control state power (Dunleavy and Ward, 1981).

Jackson's view, that voter's positions are positively influenced by that of their own party and negatively influenced by that of the other party, is not particularly plausible. Some do argue that voters with a strong and stable party identification but weakly developed attitudes on issues are the most likely to be influenced by their party's positions (Campbell *et al.*, 1960: 141; cf. Zaller, 1992), but this hardly applies to the large number of people in countries like the UK who express no, or only weak, partisan identity (Clarke *et al.*, 2004: 176–181). The media and interest groups can identify politicians who lie, so there are reputational incentives for politicians to convey reliable information even to those who do not identify with their party (Austen-Smith, 1990, 1992; Grofman and Norrander, 1990; Carmines and Kuklinski, 1990: 266; Lupia and McCubbins, 1998; Popkin, 1995: 19–28).

A model of party competition with endogenous voter preferences and differentials in party power

Analysis of manifestos (Robertson, 1976; Budge *et al.*, 2001) as well as evidence on policies (reviewed in Ward, 2001) strongly suggests that persistent and politically significant differences exist between parties on the main dimension of competititon. Each of the major assumptions of the 'Downsian' model can be changed in such a way that convergence is no longer necessarily predicted (Grofman, 1995a). This chapter is a development from models that drop the assumptions of pure office-seeking and certainty over the voter distribution, both of which are empirically implausible (Lewin, 1991, chpt. 3; Przeworski and Sprague, 1986, chpt. 4; Budge, 1994; Strøm and Müller, 1999; Jackson 2003).[13] Such models generally predict divergence (e.g. Wittman 1983; Hansson and Stuart, 1984; Wittman, 1990; Roemer, 2001), but the degree of divergence tends to be slight except for very high degrees of uncertainty over the voter distribution or for parties that care very little for office per se (Calvert, 1985).[14] By introducing the extra assumption that parties can influence the voter distribution, it is possible to get highly divergent equilibria, even when there is little uncertainty and parties care a lot about winning office. Existing spatial models are unable plausibly to explain why parties sometimes choose leaders or candidates with views more extreme, compared to the expected position of the median voter, than the median members of the 'selectorate' that chooses the leader.[15] This failure is empirically significant, as Crewe and Searing (1988) argue in relation to the selection of Margaret Thatcher as leader of the Conservative party in 1975. I show that influential parties may benefit from adopting extreme platforms, because this drives up their chances of electoral success more than enough to compensate for having to implement policies more extreme than the selectorate ideally wants.

The model

First, parties choose a position on the dimension of competition to campaign on and second they chose a package of 'instruments' to move the voter distribution and a level of effort to apply using these instruments. The information parties provide to the electorate and party policies that might influence the position of voters are assumed to be consistent with the position they adopt. This is to make a strong assumption about credibility losses from inconsistency. I assume that efficient choices of instruments are made relative to the parties' positions, and my model starts with an influence function giving the expected position of the median voter as a function of where parties locate. The influence function summarises the power of the parties in different contingencies.[16] I assume that each party shares a common perception of the influence function and neither holds private information about the way that the electorate can be influenced.

Two parties X and Y compete on a single issue dimension represented by the real line, $\Re$. X and Y have continuous, differentiable, strictly concave utility functions over the issue dimension, denoted by $u_X(.)$ and $u_Y(.)$, with maxima at the parties' ideal points, x^* and y^*. These utility functions represent policy pay-offs – parties' preferences over policy outcomes, abstracting from any implications policies have for their electoral support. Assume that the parties do not have the same policy ideal point – specifically $x^* < y^*$.

The party obtaining the greatest number of votes wins the election; and if parties obtain the same number of votes, a coin is tossed to see which of them will hold office. As well as policy pay-offs, parties may also get pay-offs from holding office per se, for example from the rents that they can earn in office. X and Y's office pay-offs are denoted by $\Omega_X \geq 0$ and $\Omega_Y \geq 0$ respectively.

There is a prior aggregate voter distribution before the parties announce their positions. Then there is a posterior voter distribution after the parties have announced their positions. The posterior distribution shifts as a function of where the parties locate. Underlying this shift is a shift in some voters' ideal points and/or utility functions. Citizens vote on the basis of their posterior utility functions.

Voters have a single-peaked utility function over the issue dimension, symmetric about the ideal point. Assume voters know x and y, for certain (cf. Alvarez, 1998). The set of voters that turn out is independent of the positions adopted by the parties and contains an odd number of voters. Each voter votes for the party yielding the highest pay-off, on the basis of their utility function after the parties have announced their positions. Indifferent voters toss a coin to decide how to vote.

Neither party knows for sure the prior and posterior locations of the median voter. A continuous probability distribution $M(m)$ over the prior position of the median voter, such that $M(m) > 0$ for all m, is common knowledge for the parties. The mean of this distribution is $\mu_m = 0$. $M'(m)$ is the posterior distribution over the position of the median voter. For any m, $M'(m) = M(m - \pi(x,y))$. $\pi(x,y)$ is the influence function, representing parties' influence over the median voter's position. Notice that $M'(m)$ is simply a translation of $M(m)$ to the left or to the right, with a different mean but the same higher moments. The mean of $M'(m)$ is $\mu'_m = \pi(x,y)$.

It is assumed $\pi(x,y)$ to be continuous in x and y. Its first partial derivatives are also assumed to be continuous in x and y. $\pi(0, 0) = 0$, i.e. if the parties both locate at the expected prior position of the median voter, the posterior position is not shifted. For all x and y, $\partial\pi/\partial x > 0$ and $\partial\pi/\partial y > 0$, i.e. for a given location of the other party, the further to the right a party locates, the further to the right the expected posterior position of the median voter is.[17] It seems plausible that $\partial\pi/\partial x < 1$ and $\partial\pi/\partial y < 1$ i.e. for a given move by a party, the expected position of the median voter does not move as far. Although this additional assumption makes no difference to the results reported below, it makes their interpretation in terms of party influence more natural.

It is convenient to work with a transformation of points on the real line which subtracts $\pi(x, y)$ from their values, under which: μ'_m becomes the new origin; X's position becomes $x - \pi(x, y)$ and Y's position becomes $y - \pi(x,y)$. The point $z = (x+y)/2 - \pi(x,y)$ is half way between X and Y's positions under the transformation. Let $\Phi(.)$ be the cumulative distribution function for the posterior distribution for the position of the median voter, under the transformed axes. Note that $\Phi(.)$ is always the same no matter where X and Y locate, for their positions only alter the mean, not the higher moments, of the distribution over the median voter. As $\Phi(.)$ is the cumulative distribution function over the median voter, $\Phi(z)$ is the posterior probability that the median voter is at or to the left of z. Notice that because $M(m) > 0$ for all m, $d\Phi/dz > 0$, i.e. the higher the mid-point between the parties' transformed positions, the higher the probability that the median is at or to the left of the mid-point. Denote the probability that X wins the election when the parties locate at x and y by $p_X(x, y)$. Suppose, first, that $x < y$. Then $p_X(x, y) = \Phi(z)$. First the members of the set of voters with ideal points to the left of z, $L(z)$, will vote for the nearer of the two parties, X. Suppose z is to the left of the median voter. Then $L(z)$ cannot form a majority because the median voter and those voters located to the right of her constitute a majority and will vote for the nearer party, Y. So the probability that X wins is the probability that z is at or to the right of the median voter, i.e. the probability that the median voter is at or to the left of z. As already stated, this probability is equal to $\Phi(z)$. If $x > y$, by a similar argument, $p_X(x, y) = 1 - \Phi(z)$. If $x = y$, $p_X(x, y) = 1/2$, because the expectation is that half the time X will get a majority if voters toss a coin when X and Y locate in the same place. Denote the probability that Y wins the election by $p_Y(x, y)$. Then $p_Y(x, y) = 1 - p_X(x, y)$. Notice that $\Phi(z) > 0$ for all z; so $p_X(x, y) > 0$ and $p_Y(x, y) > 0$ for all x and y. Notice that unless $\Phi(w) = 1/2$, $p_X(x, w)$ is discontinuous in x at $x = w$ and X's expected pay-off is also discontinuous in x.

Here I work with a 'short-term' view of how parties influence voter positions and of their objective functions, although I have shown that the results still hold under a 'longer-term' view designed better to capture possibilities of structural preference shaping (Ward, 2001). This 'short-term' model is based on the notion of a campaigning period in which informational flows from the parties' manifestos, policy statements and pledges, influence voter positions. The parties just care about their utilities *after* the election is held. I assume that reputational effects ensure that parties implement whatever policy they run on, if they get into office; so whichever party wins implements its strategy. The time line is that parties simultaneously announce their strategies. Voters observe these strategies, and some voters may alter their ideal points as a consequence. Voters then vote for one of the two candidates. Whichever party wins office then implements a policy corresponding to the strategy it has run on. Then X's expected pay-off during the next electoral term is:

$$U_X(x,y) = p_X(x, y).(u_X(x) + \Omega_X) + p_Y(x, y).u_X(y)$$

where $(u_X(x) + \Omega_X)$ is X's pay-off if it wins, composed of the policy pay-off from its platform plus its office pay-off, and $u_X(y)$ is X's pay-off if it loses – its policy pay-off from Y's platform. Similarly Y's expected payoff is:

$$U_Y(x,y) = p_X(x, y).u_Y(x) + p_Y(x, y)(u_Y(y) + \Omega_Y))$$

Forces acting on parties

Here I define what it means for a party to be influential and relate this to the pressures on parties to converge or to diverge generated by their desire to win. Parties balance these pressures against their desire to run on platforms as close as possible to their policy ideals when making locational choices. Uninfluential parties get better odds to the extent to which they *replicate* their opponent's messages about the good society and desirable policies. In contrast influential parties increase their chances of being elected by diverging, because they take enough of the electorate with them as they move. They gain better electoral odds by *contrast* rather than by reinforcement of messages.

a A party is influential to the extent that voters are highly responsive to shifts in its position. Recall that the expected posterior position of the median voter is $\mu'_m = \pi(x,y)$. Let $S \subseteq \mathfrak{R}^2$ be a subspace of pure strategy space. Say X is influential on S if $\partial\pi/\partial x > 1/2$ for all x, y: $\in$ S. (X is globally influential if $S = \mathfrak{R}^2$.)

It is intuitively obvious that this condition implies that X increases its chances of winning the election by diverging from Y's position, although a little care needs to be exercised about what happens when the parties start out in a convergent position. If $x < y$, $p_X(x, y) = \Phi(z)$. As $\partial\pi/\partial x$ is assumed to be continuous in x, there is an open interval around the value of x concerned in which $\partial\pi/\partial x > 1/2$. On this interval, treating y as fixed,

$$dp_X/dx = d\Phi/dz. \, dz/dx = d\Phi/dz \, (1/2 - d\pi/dx)$$

Because $d\Phi/dz > 0$ (as noted above), $dp_X/dx < 0$ when $(1/2 - d\pi/dx) < 0$. X increases its chances of being elected by moving to the left in the interval, further away from Y's position. What happens is that the expected position of the median voter changes faster than the point halfway between the parties, so X increases its chances of winning. If $y < x$, $p_X(x, y) = 1 - \Phi(z)$. As $\partial\pi/\partial x$ is assumed to be continuous in x, there is an open interval around the value of x concerned in which $\partial\pi/\partial x > 1/2$. On this interval treating y as fixed,

$$dp_X/dx = -d\Phi/dz. \, dz/dx = -d\Phi/dz \, (1/2 - d\pi/dx)$$

so $dp_X/dx > 0$ i.e. X increases its chances of winning by diverging from Y's position further to the right on the interval. Finally suppose that $x = y = w$. Then $p_X(x, y) = 1/2$. If $\Phi(w) \neq 1/2$, $p_X(x, w)$ is discontinuous in x at $x = w$. As $p_X(x, w)$ is continuous in x for $x < w$ and $x > w$, X can increase its chances of winning by moving either just to the left or just to the right of w, depending on whether $\Phi(w) > 1/2$ or not. If $\Phi(w) = 1/2$, $p_X(x, w)$ is continuous in x at $x = w$, but not differentiable at that point. Nevertheless as $\partial\pi/\partial x$ is assumed to be continuous in x, there is an open interval around $x = w$ in which $\partial\pi/\partial x > 1/2$, implying $p_X(x, w)$ increases as X moves away from w in either direction on the interval.

b　If $\partial\pi/\partial x < 1/2$ for $(x, y) \in S \subseteq \Re^2$, say X is uninfluential in S. (X is globally uninfluential if $S = \Re^2$.) Under this condition X's chances of winning are increased by converging on Y's position, the proof being similar to that in the last paragraph.[18]

c　If $\partial\pi/\partial x = 1/2$ for $(x, y) \in S \subseteq \Re^2$, say X has a neutral influence in S.

d　Similarly Y is influential, uninfluential or has neutral influence depending on whether $\partial\pi/\partial y$ is greater, less than, or equal to $1/2$.

Summing up:

Proposition 1. *If a party is influential at some point in strategy space {x, y}, it increases its chances of winning by diverging from its opponent's position; if it is uninfluential, it increases its chances of winning by converging when x ≠ y.*

Convergent equilibrium

My concern is largely to set out *necessary conditions* for pure strategy pairs to be Nash equilibria and to rule out certain possibilities.[19] Parties that are globally uninfluential always increase their chances of winning by converging, like parties in the standard 'Downsian' model. To the extent that parties predominantly care about office pay-offs, they also meet the standard 'Downsian' assumption. Under these assumptions it is not surprising that my model predicts full convergence, for this maximises parties' chances of being elected. Moreover, I show that they converge on the expected prior position of the median voter.

Proposition 2. *If both parties are globally uninfluential and Ω_X and Ω_Y are sufficiently greater than zero, then {μ_m, μ_m} is the unique pure-strategy Nash equilibrium.*[20]

On the other hand if parties care little enough about office per se they will never fully converge in equilibrium: moving towards their policy ideal point would increase their expected pay-off when this was dominated by terms reflecting policy considerations, even if this lowered their chances of winning. Thus:

Proposition 3. *If Ω_X and Ω_Y are sufficiently small, then there are no convergent equilibrium.*[21]

It is possible to get convergence in equilibrium, including convergence at points other than {μ_m, μ_m}.[22] However, this is ruled out under the following condition:

Proposition 4. *Suppose that at each point of convergence, {w, w}, there exists an influential party with a strictly positive office pay-off. Then no such point is an equilibrium.*

For values of w that are 'extreme' relative to μ_m, it is plausible that a move to moderation would appeal to enough voters to ensure that it would increase a party's electoral chances, even if the move had little impact on the position of the median voter. On the other hand, if w were a moderate position, there would typically be advantages in offering a distinct platform rather than a fully convergent one, because the message sent would be more noticeable for voters, and be more likely to receive media attention, when it was contrasting. Especially for the more influential party, it is plausible that moving away from a moderate, fully-convergent platform would bring gains. The condition in Proposition 4 is likely to be met empirically.

Divergent equilibria

I start by considering the case where both parties are globally uninfluential:

Proposition 5. *Suppose X and Y are globally uninfluential. Then {x, y} is a divergent pure-strategy Nash equilibrium only if $x^* < x < y < y^*$.*

Here centripetal forces push parties together to increase their chances of winning, as would be expected. When both parties have low credibility, for instance, we would expect platforms more convergent than party activists desired.

It is worth considering the case where both parties are globally influential, although this is empirically implausible:

Proposition 6. *Suppose X and Y are globally influential. If {x, y} is a divergent pure strategy Nash equilibrium: (i) when x < y, then $x < x^*$ and $y^* < y$; (ii) when y < x, it cannot be the case that either $y < x < x^*$ or $y^* < y < x$.*

Proposition 6 does not rule out all equilibria in which y < x, where the parties occupy positions that are 'perverse' in the sense that the platforms are not ordered in the same way as the ideal points. It turns out that such equilibria are ruled out by a plausible restriction on the influence function, though:

Proposition 7. *Suppose that both parties are influential whenever x < y and are uninfluential whenever x > y. Then{x, y} is a divergent pure-strategy Nash equilibrium only if $x < x^* < y^* < y$.*

If the electorate knows the parties' policy ideal points, it is implausible that they would be influential when their messages were inconsistent in the sense that 'the party of the left' was running on a more right-wing platform. This may help to explain why we seldom observe perverse platforms empirically (e.g. Budge and Klingemann, 2001: 19–50).

Proposition 7 show that highly divergent equilibria can occur even when parties care a lot about office per se and there is a high degree of certainty about the prior position of the median voter. Next I address the issues of extreme candidates and divergent equilibria under conditions where only one party is influential:

Proposition 8. *Suppose that X is uninfluential everywhere and Y is influential so long as $x < y$ and uninfluential if $y < x$. Then if $\{x, y\}$ is divergent Nash equilibrium, $x^* < x < y$ and $y^* < y$.*

If there is an equilibrium, under the conditions of Proposition 8, Y locates to the right of its ideal point. In the most likely case empirically, in which the expected prior position of the median voter lies between the parties' policy ideal points, Y moves to a more 'extreme' position than its ideal point. This is 'ideological exaggeration for effect': it pays Y to move *beyond* its ideal because it expects to be able to drag enough voters far enough to the right by doing so to more than compensate any losses of policy pay-off by increasing its chances of office pay-offs. At the party's ideal point it is still better to move further to the right, for expected losses of policy pay-off are 'small' compared to the gains through better electoral odds that can be made.

Conclusion

We should no longer take seriously models of party competition that assume that the distribution of voters is fixed. Simplicity is being bought at the cost not only of assumptional implausibility but also of empirical invalidity. There is ample empirical support for the view that voters' beliefs derive from party positions, and moderately strong empirical case can be made out for structural preference shaping. Not only do models allowing for preference shaping fit the stylised facts about non-convergence, but they can also help us understand what at first sight seem incomprehensible choices of extreme leaders – once differentials in parties' power is allowed for. While my model of party competition certainly needs extending to the multidimensional case, which is certainly feasible technically (Ward, 2001), it represents an advance over existing models that endogenise preferences, because it generates hypotheses about the effects of power differentials.

Allowing for the way that parties can shape opinion reconnects rational choice theory with normative democratic theory, which has seldom neglected the idea that political leaders should shape opinion for the public good. If some have doubts about whether politicians attempt to sway the electorate in ways that serve the public interest, it is doubly the case that structural preference shaping requires close scrutiny from a normative perspective.

Notes

1 Also the Democrat's position is highly correlated with that of the Republicans lagged around 12 to 16 quarters.
2 Glazer (1995) considers relative deprivation effects within the context of an expressive model of voting. Plausibly the government would hit the comparitor groups, likely to vote for the opposition, of those whose vote might go either way.
3 In the US the range of issues over which such effects occur may be surprisingly limited, with causality running both ways from the executive to the media (Edwards and Wood, 1999).
4 Estimates of the position of the median voter based on party positions and known electoral support, made as part of the Manifestos Project (Kim and Fording, 2001) are too infrequent to be useful here. A promising approach for future research would be to calculate Stimson policy mood (1999) for the UK.
5 There is a case from economic theory for treating *un* as exogenous in this exercise, since under the rational expectations hypothesis governments can do little to affect changes in real variables. Empirical evidence does suggest small, and relatively temporary effects associated with the partisan and rational expectations version of opportunistic business cycle (e.g. Alesina and Roubini, 1997).
6 I repeated the analysis here using various ad hoc interpolations of the party position variables with similar results. I have omitted the related measure of Liberal/Social Democrat/Liberal Democrat position from the analysis reported here. Initial exploration suggests that the results are not greatly affected by this.
7 Full results, and the data set in Stata 8 format, can be obtained from the author on request.
8 Examination of impulse response functions suggests, somewhat inexplicably, that increased concern for unemployment shifts Labour to the right while actual increases in unemployment shift it to the left.
9 Here the effect of a 'shock' to x is on y holding all other variables, z, constant at time t. This is controversial. Some say that this conflicts with the foundational philosophy of VAR, that 'nothing is exogenous and we don't know anything much about causality from theory'. An alternative is to calculate 'orthoganilized impulse response functions' (Sims, 1980). Here the residuals from the model are used to estimate an error term covariance matrix, which then allows the use of a mathematical transformation to define shocks to a set of variables, including the one at issue, without disturbing anything else. It makes little difference to the picture whether we use simple or orthoganilised impulse response functions here. Also many no longer recommend this procedure, because the transformation arbitrarily depends on the way that the equations in the model are ordered. Structural VAR involves using what we already know from theory to place restrictions on the model, bringing VAR closer to structural equation modelling. My problem is we lack such theory.
10 Figures 12.1 and 12.2 show 95 per cent confidence bands for the forecast. As the confidence interval at most time points includes zero, the sceptic could conclude that it has not been established that any effect occurs. At first sight this seems to conflict with the results of Granger causality tests, but the calculated confidence intervals (CI) in impulse response functions (irf) also allow for uncertainty in relation to the impact of indirect change through other variables.
11 It could be objected that the Labour Party was in office from mid-1997 to mid-2001. Repeating the analysis for the period up to the 1997 election, so that the Conservatives were in office throughout, makes no substantive difference to

the results. One structural advantage the Tories did possess that was not associated with control of the state was favourable press coverage of the economy
near elections (Sanders *et al.*, 1993).

12 The contentious idea of critical elections, punctuating the existing equilibrium
of party competition, has been related to such shocks (e.g. Krasner, 1993).

13 The plausibility of pure office-seeking may vary depending on the electoral
system and the institutional structure of parties (Strøm, 1990). There are likely
to be intra-party conflicts over the trade-offs between electoral success and
policy, too (Strøm and Müller, 1999).

14 Chappell and Keech (1986) come to a different conclusion on the basis of
their model of sequential elections, allowing for voter uncertainty as well as
party policy goals.

15 Rabinowitz and Macdonald's (1989) directional model has the implication of
'wild' divergence of candidates unless their idea of a 'circle of acceptability' is
introduced, but this seems ad hoc (Merrill and Grofman, 1999: 32).

16 John Roemer's state-space approach (2001: 39–45) is a promising one for providing micro-foundations for the influence function: (i) individuals can occupy
one of a set of states (informational and/or related to their position in the
social structure); (ii) the positions of the parties on the left–right spectrum
influences the distribution of voters over these states; (iii) the state that a voter
belongs to influences their position on the left–right spectrum, up to a random
error; (iv) votes are cast for the nearest party. The influence function amounts
to a reduced form of this set of mappings. While I will not attempt to model
them in more detail here, this might be a key to fuller understanding of the
influence function.

17 An alternative assumption is that $\pi(x,y)$ is concave in x and y in both directions, so that if a party moves to 'extreme enough' positions the expected prior
position of the median voter actually starts moving in the *opposite* direction,
other things being equal. As long as negative effects occur outside the interval
bounded by the parties' policy ideal points, this makes no difference here.

18 Again $p_X(x, w)$ may not be continuous in x at x = w, implying that if X was at w
it would increase its chances of winning by moving 'a little' one way; but it
could always increase its chances of winning *still further* by moving even closer
to w.

19 Discontinuity in the pay-off functions at points of convergence cause difficulties with applying general existence results about equilibria, but in some
cases discussed below it would to sufficient to restrict the influence function
and the voter distribution function to ensure that parties' expected pay-offs are
concave in their own strategies in the region where any equilibria must occur.

20 Full proofs of subsequent propositions appear in Ward (2001).

21 Cf. Theorem 5, Calvert (1985).

22 This cannot occur if both parties are globally influential or if one of them is
'highly influential', so long as the other has 'some influence'.

References

Alcoe, G. (2001) 'Economic Theories of Voting and the Political Business Cycle: A
Cross-National Comparative Analysis' (PhD thesis, University of Essex).

Alesina, A. (1988) 'Credibility and Policy Convergence in a Two-Party System with
Rational Voters', *American Economic Review* 78: 796–806.

Alesina, A. and N. Roubini (with G.D. Cohen) (1997) *Politic Cycles and Macro-
economy* (Cambridge, MA: MIT Press).

Alvarez, R.M. (1998) *Information and Elections* (revised edn) (Ann Arbor, MI: University of Michigan Press).

Ansolabehere, S., S. Iyengar and A. Simon (1997) 'Shifting Perspectives on the Effects of Campaign Communication', in S. Iyengar and R. Reeves (eds) *Do The Media Govern: Politicians, Voters and Reporters in America* (Thousand Oaks. CA: Sage), pp. 149–155.

Austen-Smith, D. (1990) 'Information Transmission in Debate', *American Journal of Political Science* 34: 897–918.

Austen-Smith, D. (1992) 'Strategic Models of Talk in Political Decision Making', *International Political Science Review* 16: 45–58.

Bailey, M. (2003) 'A Computational Analysis of Publicly Financed Campaigns', in K. Kollman, J.H. Miller and S.E. Page (eds) *Computational Models in Political Economy* (Cambridge MA: MIT Press), pp. 157–185.

Bartle, J. (1998) 'Left-Right Position Matters, But So Does Social Class: Causal Models of the 1992 British Election', *British Journal of Political Science* 28: 501–529.

Budge, I. (1994) 'A New Spatial Theory of Party Competition: Uncertainty, Ideology and Policy Equilibria Viewed Comparatively and Spatially', *British Journal of Political Science* 24: 443–467.

Budge, I. and R.I. Hafferbert (1990) 'Mandates and policy outputs: U.S. party platforms and federal expenditures', *American Political Science Review* 84:1, 111–131.

Budge, I. and H.-D. Klingemann (2001) 'Finally: Comparative Over-Time Mappings of Party Policy Movement', in I. Budge, H.-D. Klingemann, A. Volkens, J. Bara and E. Tanenbaum (eds) *Mapping Policy Preferences: Estimates for Parties, Electors and Governments 1945–1998* (Oxford: Oxford University Press).

Budge, I., H.-D. Klingemann, A. Volkens, J. Bara and E. Tanenbaum (2001) *Mapping Policy Preferences: Estimates for Parties, Electors and Governments 1945–1998* (Oxford: Oxford University Press).

Calvert, R. (1985) 'Robustness of the Multidimensional Voting Model: Candidate Motivations, Uncertainty and Convergence', *American Journal of Political Science* 29: 69–95.

Cambell, A., P.E. Converse, W.E. Miller and D.E. Stokes (1960) *The American Voter* (New York: Wiley).

Carmines, E.G. and J.H. Kuklinski (1990) 'Incentives, Opportunities, and the Logic of Public Opinion in American Political Representation', in J.A. Ferejohn and J.H. Kuklinski (eds) *Information and Democratic Processes* (Urbana, IL University of Illinois Press), pp. 240–268.

Chappell, H.W. and W.R. Keech (1986) 'Policy Motivation and Party Differences in a Dynamic Spatial Model of Party Competition', *American Political Science Review* 80: 881–899.

Clarke, H.D., D. Sanders, M.C. Stewart and P. Whiteley (2004) *Political Choice in Britain* (Oxford: Oxford University Press).

Cohen, J.E. (1997) *Presidential Responsiveness and Public Policy Making: The Public and the Policies that Presidents Choose* (Ann Arbor, MI: University of Michigan Press).

Crewe, I. and D. Searing (1988) 'Ideological Change in the British Conservative Party', *American Political Science Review* 82: 361–384.

Downs, A. (1957) *An Economic Theory of Democracy* (New York: Harper and Row).

Dunleavy, P. and H. Ward (1981) 'Exogenous Voter Preferences and Parties With

State Power: Some Internal Problems of Economic Models of Party Competition', *British Journal of Political Science* 11: 351–380.

Dunleavy, P. and C. Husbands (1985) *British Democracy at the Crossroads: Voting and Party Competition in the 1980s* (London: Allen and Unwin).

Dunleavy, P. and H. Ward (1991) 'Party Competition: The Preference Shaping Model', in P. Dunleavy, *Democracy, Bureaucracy and Public Choice* (Harvester Wheatsheaf: London), pp. 112–128.

Edwards, G.C. and B.D. Wood (1999) 'Who Influences Whom?: The President, Congress, and the Media', *American Journal of Political Science* 93: 327–344.

Enelow, J.M. and M.J. Hinich (eds) (1990) *Advances in the Spatial Theory of Voting* (Cambridge: Cambridge University Press).

Ferejohn, J.A. and J.H. Kuklinski (eds) (1990) *Information and Democratic Processes* (Urbana: University of Illinois Press).

Fiorina, M.P. (1990) 'Information and Rationality in Elections', in J.A. Ferejohn and J.H. Kuklinski (eds) *Information and Democratic Processes, Information and Democratic Processes* (Urbana, IL: University of Illinois Press), pp. 329–44.

Garrett, G. (1992) 'The Political Consequences of Thatcherism', *Political Behaviour* 14: 361–382.

Garrett, G. (1993) 'The Politics of Structural Change: Swedish Social Democracy and Thatcherism in Comparative Perspective', *Comparative Political Studies* 25: 521–547.

Garrett, G. (1998) *Partisan Politics in the Global Economy* (Cambridge: Cambridge University Press).

Gerber, E.R. and J.E. Jackson (1993) 'Endogenous Preferences and the Study of Institutions', *American Political Science Review* 87: 639–656.

Greene, W.H. (2003) *Econometric Analysis* 5th edn (Upper Saddle River, NJ: Prentice-Hall).

Grofman, B. (1995a) 'Towards an Institution-Rich Theory of Political Competition with a Supply-side Constraint' in B. Grofman, (ed.) *Information, Participation and Choice* (Ann Arbor, MI: University of Michigan Press), pp. 179–196.

Grofman, B. (ed.) (1995b) *Information, Participation and Choice* (Ann Arbor, MI: University of Michigan Press).

Grofman, B. and B. Norrander (1990) 'Efficient Use of Reference Group Cues in a Single Dimension', *Public Choice* 64: 213–227.

Grofman, B. and J. Withers (1995) 'Information Pooling Models of Electoral Politics', in B. Grofman (ed.) *Information, Participation and Choice* (Ann Arbor, MI: University of Michigan Press), pp. 55–66.

Hansson, I. and C. Stuart (1984) 'Voting Competition With Interested Politicians: Platforms Do Not Converge to the Preferences of the Median Voter', *Public Choice* 44: 431–444.

Harris, R. (ed.) (1977) *The Collected Speeches of Margaret Thatcher* (London: Harper Collins).

Heath, A.F., G. Evans, J. Field and S. Witherspoon (1991) *Understanding Political Change* (Oxford: Pergamon Press).

Ivanov, V. and Kilian, L. (2000) 'A Practioners's Guide to Lag-Order Selection for Vector Autoregressions', mimeo.

Iyengar, S. (1990) 'Shortcuts to Political Knowledge', in J.A. Ferejohn and J.H. Kuklinski (eds) *Information and Democratic Processes* (Urbana, IL: University of Illinois Press), pp. 160–186.

Iyengar, S. and R. Reeves (eds) (1997) *Do The Media Govern?: Politicians, Voters and Reporters in America* (Thousand Oaks, CA: Sage).

Jackson, J.E. (2003) 'A Computational Theory of Electoral Competititon', in K. Kollman, J.H. Miller, and S.E. Page (eds) *Computational Models in Political Economy* (Cambridge MA: MIT Press), pp. 109–142.

Kennedy, P. (1992) *A Guide to Econometrics* 3rd edn (Cambridge MA: MIT Press).

Kim, H.-M. and R.C. Fording, (2001) 'Extending Party Estimates to Governments and Electors', in I. Budge, H.-D. Klingemann, A. Volkens, J. Bara and E. Tanenbaum (eds) *Mapping Policy Preferences: Estimates for Parties, Electors and Governments 1945–1998* (Oxford: Oxford University Press).

King, A., R.J. Wybrow and A. Gallup (2001) *British Political Opinion 1937–2000* (London: Politicos).

King, G. and M. Laver (1993) 'Party platforms, mandates, and government spending', *American Political Science Review* 87:3, 744–747.

Kollman, K., J.H. Miller and S.E. Page (1992) 'Adaptive Parties in Spatial Elections', *American Political Science Review* 86: 929–937.

Kollman, K., J.H. Miller and S.E. Page (eds) (2003) *Computational Models in Political Economy* (Cambridge MA: MIT Press).

Krasner, S. (1993) 'Approaches to the State: Alternative Conceptions and Historical Dynamics', *Comparative Politics* 16: 223–246.

Lewin, L. (1991) *Self-Interest and Public Interest in Western Politics* (Oxford: Oxford University Press).

Lupia, A. and M.D. McCubbins (1998) *The Democratic Dilemma: Can Citizens Learn What They Need to Know?* (Cambridge: Cambridge University Press).

Macdonald, S.E. and G. Rabinowitz (1998) 'Solving the Paradox of Nonconvergence: Valence, Position and Direction in Democratic Politics', *Electoral Studies* 17: 281–300.

Merrill, S. and B. Grofman, (1999) *A Unified Theory of Voting: Directional and Proximity Spatial Models* (Cambridge: Cambridge University Press).

Miller, W.E. and J.M. Shanks (1982) 'Policy Direction and Presidential Leadership', *British Journal of Political Science* 12: 299–356.

Ottati, V.C. and R.S. Wyer Jr (1990) 'The Cognitive Mediators of Political Information Processing', in J.A. Ferejohn and J.H. Kuklinski (eds) *Information and Democratic Processes* (Urbana, IL: University of Illinois Press), pp. 186–218.

Page, B.I. and R.Y. Shapiro (1992) *The Rational Public: Fifty Years of Trends in American's Policy Preferences* (Chicago: University of Chicago Press).

Petrocik, J.R. (1997) 'Campaigning and the Press: The Influence of the Candidates', in S. Iyengar and R. Reeves (eds) *Do The Media Govern?: Politicians, Voters and Reporters in America* (Thousand Oaks: Sage).

Popkin, S. L., (1995) 'Information Shortcuts and the Reasoning Voter', in Grofman (ed.) *Information, Participation and Choice* (Ann Arbor, MI: University of Michigan Press), pp. 17–36.

Przeworski, A. (1998) 'Deliberation and Ideological Domination' in J. Elster (ed.) *Deliberative Democracy* (Cambridge: Cambridge University Press).

Przeworski, A. and J. Sprague (1986) *Paper Stones: A History of Electoral Socialism* (Chicago: University of Chicago Press).

Rabinowitz, G. and S.E. Macdonald (1989) 'A Directional Theory of Issue Voting', *American Political Science Review* 83:. 93–121.

Riker, W.H. (1986) *The Art of Political Manipulation* (New Haven: Yale University Press).

Robertson, D. (1976) *A Theory of Party Competition* (New York: Wiley).

Roemer, J.E. (2001) *Political Competition: Theory and Applications* (Cambridge MA: Harvard University Press).

Sanders, D., D. Marsh and H. Ward (1993) 'The Electoral Impact of Press Coverage of the UK Economy, 1979–87', *British Journal of Political Science* 23: 175–210.

Sims, C.A. (1980) 'Macroeconomics and Reality', *Econometrica* 48: 1–48.

Stata Corp. (2003) *Stata Time Series Reference Manual Release 8* (College Station Texas: Stata)

Stimson, J.A. (1990) 'A Macro-Theory of Information Flow', in J.A. Ferejohn and J.H. Kuklinski (eds) *Information and Democratic Processes* (Urbana, IL: University of Illinois Press), pp. 345–368.

Stimson, J.A. (1999) *Public Opinion in America: Moods, Cycles and Swings* (Boulder, CO: Westview).

Strøm, K. (1990) 'A Behavioral Theory of Competitive Political Parties', *American Journal of Political Science* 34: 565–598.

Strøm, K. and W.C. Muller (1999) 'Political Parties and Hard Choices' in W.C. Muller and K. Strom (eds) *Policy Office or Votes? How Parties in Europe Make Hard Decisions* (Cambridge: Cambridge University Press).

Stubager, R. (2003) 'Preference-Shaping: An Empirical Test', *Political Studies* 51: 241–261.

Studlar, D.T., I. McAllister and A. Ascui (1990) 'Privatisation and the British Electorate: Microeconomic Policies, Macroeconomic Evaluations, and Party Support', *American Journal of Political Science* 34: 1077–1101.

Ward, H. and P. John (1999) 'Targeting Benefits for Electoral Gain: Constituency Marginality and the Distribution of Grants to English Local Authorities', *Political Studies* 47: 32–52.

Ward, H. (2001) '"If the Party won't go to the Median Voter, then the Median Voter must come to the Party": A Spatial Model of Two-Party Competition with Endogenous Voter Preferences', Essex Papers in Politics and Government, no. 141.

Wittman, D. (1983) 'Candidate Motivations: A Synthesis of Alternative Theories', *American Political Science Review* 77: 142–157.

Wittman, D. (1990) 'Spatial Strategies When Candidates Have Policy Preferences', in J.M. Enelow and M.J. Hinich (eds) *Advances in the Spatial Theory of Voting* (Cambridge: Cambridge University Press) pp. 66–98.

Zaller, J.R. (1992) *The Nature and Origins of Mass Opinion* (Cambridge: Cambridge University Press).

13 Party competition and deliberative democracy

Albert Weale

Introduction

Party competition in open elections is the principal institutional device used in modern political systems to implement the ideals of democracy and to secure representative government. Of course, there is nothing in the history of elections, let alone party competition, that associates them uniquely with democratic values. Indeed, as Manin (1997) has shown, selection by lot was the classical democratic device for choosing those to hold political office, and elections were seen over many centuries as aristocratic devices. Rousseau (1762: book 3, chapter 15) notoriously asserted that the British people thought they were free, but were only really so at the moment at which they chose their government. Between elections, not directly governing themselves, they were slaves. So, there is no simple inference from the ideals of democracy to the practice of representative government chosen by election. Yet, since the emergence of modern democracy in the late eighteenth and early nineteenth centuries, elections have been viewed as the means by which governments could be rendered accountable and responsible to those whom they governed. James Mill's (1822) account of the incentives that elections gave to governors to pay attention to the interests of the governed is an early, influential and paradigmatic statement of what is now orthodoxy among most political commentators, political scientists and political theorists of democracy.

In a compact, yet remarkably fertile, discussion in *The New Challenge of Direct Democracy*, Ian Budge (1996: 7) makes his own contribution to democratic theory and its account of elections. He argues that elections record 'popular judgements about what is generally needed'. Underlying such an account is an anti-paternalist principle to the effect that people are the best judges of their own interests, both individually and collectively. By providing a mechanism through which preferences can be measured, elections provide the opportunity for people to articulate their legitimate interests. They also allow for freedom of expression. These two aspects of democracy – interest articulation and free expression – should be seen as complementary rather than rival on Budge's view. Interests are not something that we can take as ready-made. They have to be discovered and developed in discussion. Conversely, having freedom is part of one's interests. In Ian Budge's democratic pantheon, both James Mill and Jean-Jacques Rousseau are properly accorded high status.

In outlining a justification of democracy Budge offers a teleological account, as the following passage shows:

> the various democratic freedoms – of speech, association and voting – find their main justification in allowing for the safeguarding and identification of interests. They permit citizens to protect themselves against their individual and collective interests being ignored; they allow decision-makers to identify popular interests through these preferences which are expressed, and to check whether they are stable through their resistance to change in the midst of discussion and debate.
>
> (Budge, 1996: 8)

The structure of the argument here is clear. We have a set of political freedoms that form the core political rights of a democracy. A system of government that embodies these rights is a practice justified by its tendency to promote individual and collective interests. If the practice did not serve these purposes then it could not be justified.

Within this account, there are two distinct motifs that are worth identifying and distinguishing. The first is the theme of democracy as a protective device, the central argument of James Mill. Competitive elections safeguard citizens and prevent their interests being ignored. This turns on the claim that the process of competition forces political leaders to pay attention to citizens' interests, whatever their personal motives. Just as the profit motive provides an incentive for business to supply goods that citizens want, so the motive of political office provides an incentive for parties to provide policies that citizens want. In both cases the existence of genuine competition is crucial. The second theme is a discursive one. It stresses the extent to which interests have to be identified before they can be protected or advanced. For example, the choice between guns and butter is likely to be a relatively easy one for farmers and armaments manufacturers, but for citizens at large it may be much more difficult to decide. The priority to be given to defence depends upon assessments of threats and the posture that one's country ought to be taking in the international system. Finding the right balance between competing considerations is not easy and requires the discussion and debate of which Ian Budge speaks. Thus, alongside the incentive component of democracy, we also need to consider its deliberative component.

In recent years this deliberative component of democracy has received a great deal of attention from normative theorists. In some cases, the thrust of the deliberative turn has been to downplay the role of party competition and to favour alternative non-competitive decision procedures. However, the question of the role of party competition in elections cannot so easily be dismissed, if the electoral mechanism does play the central role in accountability that Budge (and I suspect the majority of political scientists who study these things) think that it does. For example, someone who stresses the important role of deliberation in public policy may well end up favouring the delegation of a large number of decisions to courts or to technocratic bodies (to cite just two of the canvassed alternatives). But this is not just to draw an implication; it is also to make a serious political choice, which if implemented might well turn out (for familiar reasons associated with path-dependency) to be irreversible. So, in this chapter, I shall take the model of political representation based on party competition and confront it with ideals and norms drawn from deliberative theories of democracy. How well do competitive party democracies perform when judged against deliberative ideals?

A model of political representation

One important achievement of Ian Budge and his colleagues in the Comparative Manifestos Project (CMP) is to provide an empirically informed account of how political representation is secured across the full range of liberal democracies. The CMP account shares the assumption of economic theories of democracy, like those of Schumpeter (1954) and Downs (1957), that parties compete with one another in elections in order to win votes. However, by contrast with such accounts, parties are not seen as pure office-seekers, who set their agendas competitively and are willing to shift their policy positions purely in response to the prospect of electoral advantage. Rather, according to the CMP view, parties maintain distinct, ideologically informed policy positions, seeking support from the electorate by stressing the extent to which their own policy stance accords with widely shared values. Thus, in the choice between guns and butter, the proponents of guns will stress the importance of national defence and security in the international order, whereas the proponents of butter will stress peace, prosperity and plenty.

The fundamental methodological insight of the CMP is to devise a means by which these relative emphases can be interpreted as position taking by political parties. This is done by counting the quasi-sentences in which such terms appear, inferring the positions of parties within a policy dimension by counting the relative frequency of particular assertions. For example, if a party stresses the need to maintain military expenditure, modernise the armed forces and uphold treaty obligations, a pro-defence position is inferred. Conversely, if a party frequently mentions the importance of peaceful means of resolving international disputes or the desirability of countries joining in negotiations with hostile countries, an anti-defence position is inferred (Budge *et al.*, 2001: 222). The same approach can be repeated across all dimensions of public policy. By the alchemy of the code book, policies discussed in valence terms are transmuted into an estimate of the positions of political parties.

Manifestos are general statements of a political position, and must, in the nature of the case, cover a wide variety of policy questions. Although party competition in liberal democracies is often spoken of in terms primarily of left and right and the left–right ideological spectrum was central to Downs's exposition of his economic theory, there is no reason in principle why the CMP technique cannot be applied more widely or to a specific set of issues. (Together with others, for example, I have used it myself to explore party competition in six European democracies on the productivist-environment dimension of public policy, Weale *et al.*, 2000: 246–256.) Yet, a central claim from the CMP is that, although there is no logical necessity for party competition to take left–right form, in practice it does take this form. Inferred positions across a range of issues are correlated with one another, and in accounting for party movements over time, a one-dimensional representation of positions does as well as a 20-dimensional representation (Budge *et al.*, 2001: 59).

Let us accept, even if only temporarily, this first move in the argument. The system of party competition would still not perform the function of political representation, if there were no correspondence between the expressed preferences of voters and the governments that were formed after the election. However, as McDonald *et al.* (2004) have shown, there is such a correspondence. There is a high degree of correspondence between median voters and median parties in parliaments, and also a high degree of correspondence between median parties and participation in government. To be sure, the degree of correspondence varies across political systems, and PR systems do a better job than those based on first-past-the-post in translating popular preferences into political representation. But the main result is that elected governments do typically contain parties whose policy positions coincide with those of the median voter on the left–right spectrum. In that sense, at least, such governments are representative. They have a median mandate bestowed upon them.

Governments may also be representative in their actions as well as their composition. Although the findings have not met with universal agreement, it has been argued that the implementation of manifesto commitments, as measured by public expenditure changes, tracks the changing emphases of party manifestos in the US (Budge and Hofferbert, 1990) and Britain (Hofferbert and Budge, 1992). (For the controversy, see King and Laver, 1993 and Hofferbert *et al.*, 1993.) Parties not only say in their manifestos what they are going to do in government, but when in government they do what they say. From this point of view, the electoral connection is a relatively efficient instrument of citizens' choice over the priorities of the public budget.

As other contributors to this volume have pointed out, it is possible to weaken the links in the chain of reasoning just described at various points. Both McLean and Nagel highlight the problems associated with using a single left–right scale for the measurement of party competition. McLean points out that there may be controversial judgements made in coding some items, for example free trade, such that the position of parties on a general left–right scale is an artefact of the coding procedure rather than an empirically based assessment. Similarly, Nagel highlights the difference in substantive political terms between explaining variance and explaining outcomes, where the latter may turn on the role that particular issues play in moving pivotal voters. Finally, as Ward points out, governments can engage in practices of preference shaping, and for that reason the legitimacy of the democratic mandate may be questioned. It is, of course, a matter for judgement how far these problems are fundamental to the enterprise and how far they are merely qualifications that need to be borne in mind when conducting any particular analysis. For the rest of this chapter, however, I shall leave these methodological issues to one side, in part because they have been dealt with in these other chapters. Instead, I shall focus on the normative issues.

Properly to understand the normative issues, we need examine the concept of representation, the modern account of which begins with Pitkin's (1967) *The Concept of Representation.* Pitkin explicitly identified five different senses in which we can meaningfully talk about representation: authorisation, accountability, descriptive, symbolic and substantive. In addition, she also mentions a principle of responsiveness, which she associated with accountability, but which is clearly logically distinct. Adding that sense, we can identify six types of representation.

If we take these logical distinctions and apply them to the CMP description of political parties, what is the sense in which political parties represent? Clearly, political parties in government are authorised by virtue of election, since elections are the institutional device for selecting those who are to hold public office. Similarly, the process of putting oneself up for elections on a platform is an instance of accountability. Indeed, if it were not, the presupposition of the work of CMP would not make sense. Manifestos have meaning precisely because they record what parties set themselves to do upon election. Finally, if the incentive part of the story is correct, party competition provides a reason for parties to act in the interests of their constituents, at least in the sense that the expressed wishes of citizens can be said to constitute their interests. So, applying Pitkin's distinctions to the CMP account of electoral competition, the story runs something like this: political parties are authorised to enter into office, subject the demands of accountability created by the electoral system and in the expectation that by being accountable they will act in and be responsive to the interests of citizens. Competitive party elections therefore provide a form of preference aggregation that exemplifies political representation in a number of the central senses that Pitkin has identified. But is a satisfactory account of preference aggregation what we should be looking for in a democracy?

Deliberative democratic ideals

In setting down the outlines of Ian Budge's own account of democracy, I drew attention to the importance he placed on practices like free expression and free association that enabled citizens to discover and develop an account of their own interests. This highlights the deliberative component of democracy, a topic on which there are many people writing at present. Among those advocating deliberative democracy, there are subtle and important differences of view. For this reason, we cannot speak of a single deliberative theory of democracy, and it would not be fair nor reasonable to present a simple amalgam of all the claims that have been made under the heading of deliberative democracy. However, there are a number of themes that recur regularly among those who identify themselves as deliberative democrats. So, without pretending to any spurious comprehensiveness, it is possible to pick out some particular propositions.

If we were looking for a single slogan to summarise the basic contention of deliberative democrats, it would probably be Dryzek's claim that deliberative democracy holds 'that outcomes are legitimate to the extent they receive assent through participation by all those subject to the decision in question' (Dryzek, 2001: 651). There are a number of ways in which this claim might be motivated, but one important strand of thinking has been to link the search for political legitimacy with the ideal of government by consent. Richardson (2002: 62–65), for example, links the idea of government through public discussion to the liberal demand that persons be treated as autonomous, which gives rise to three requirements. The first of these is 'that the political process publicly address each citizen as someone capable of joining in discussion'. The second is 'that the political process solicit the participation of each citizen as a potential agent of political decision', which is tied, third, to the idea that each person is to be treated as a self-originating source of claims.

If we think, along with Rawls (1996: 4), that moral and religious pluralism is the inevitable result of the powers of human reason at work in the context of free institutions, then it seems natural to say that common political decisions need to reflect the inevitable differences of viewpoint to which moral pluralism gives rise. In these circumstances, legitimacy through discussion and public reasoning involves a conception of political association in which citizens are disposed to seek for fair terms of cooperation with one another (Gutmann and Thompson, 1996: 53). This in turn suggests a principle of reciprocity, according to which political legitimacy rests upon decisions that derive from mutually acceptable reasons among citizens who nonetheless differ in their moral and religious views. Thus, respecting autonomy or reciprocity, deliberative theorists aspire to found political legitimacy upon the principle of consent. As Cohen (1989: 22) has put it, political outcomes are legitimate, according to deliberative democracy, if they could be the object of free and reasoned agreement among equals.

What is the relationship between political deliberation as the basis for political legitimacy and legitimate decision making through voting? At one time, it was common to advocate deliberative democracy by contrasting it with a (somewhat ill-defined) model of aggregative democracy, with the implication that these were opposing modes of political organisation. Since the CMP view of representation stresses the importance of voting and party competition, it would seem that it would provide a natural foil for deliberative democrats who wished to stress the distinctiveness (and superiority) of deliberation.

However, since the early heady days, many deliberative theorists have recognised that in the absence of complete consensus, and perhaps even in the presence of deep disagreements, voting and other aggregative methods will continue to be necessary (Bohman, 1998). There are at least two responses that are possible along these lines. The first encapsulates a more radical abandonment of the deliberative ideal. It suggests that there is nothing intrinsically undesirable about aggregation, merely that what is aggregated should be reasoned and reflective preferences, rather than raw or uninformed preferences. The problem is not with aggregation as such but with what Goodin (2003: 12) calls the 'mechanistic and meat-grinder aspect of the aggregation of votes into collective decisions'. I have already drawn attention to the way in which in the CMP account, as expounded in Budge's own account, brings out the element of debate or discussion in democratic politics. The political freedoms of speech and association enable citizens and political parties not only to express their interests but also to identify them. If we allow deliberation at the pre-decision stage and aggregation at the decision stage, we do not have a contest between the two models of democracy, merely different aspects of a not very complex story. When we vote we do not reason, but if we cast reasoned votes our aggregation scheme will be improved.

This is clearly a possible move within one version of deliberative democracy and it is difficult to see logically what there is to stop someone going down this route, if that was thought attractive. However, I am inclined to think that the original contrast between deliberative and aggregative accounts of democracy was not only an expository device but also marked a distinct view about what was involved in a good decision process. Perhaps one way of describing an ideal decision procedure is to recall Barry's (1965: 87–88) account from some years ago of decision through 'discussion on merits'. I quote:

> As an 'ideal type' this involves the complete absence of threats and inducements; the parties to the dispute set out ... to reach an agreement on what is the morally right division, what policy is in the interests of all of them or will produce the most want-satisfaction, and so on.

> (Barry, 1965: 87)

I cite from this because, though written sometime before the emergence of deliberative theories of democracy, Barry's account of decision through discussion on merits states a core idea to be found in deliberative thinkers. For example, Bessette (1994: 46) writes: 'The deliberation that lies at the heart of the kind of democracy established by the American constitutional system can be defined most simply as reasoning on the merits of public policy.'

The idea of taking decisions through discussion on merits might therefore suggest that there is a deeper issue at work here about the relationship between public deliberation and public choice. And if one wants some confirmation of the thought that to stress deliberation makes one sceptical of aggregation and voting, one might recall Habermas's view that 'the decision reached by the majority only represents a caesura in an ongoing discussion; the decision records so to speak, the interim result of a discursive opinion-forming process' (Habermas, 1996: 179). In short, whilst majority rule may have certain practical benefits, it cannot substitute as a source of legitimacy for consensus brought about through the power of reason.

So, rather than take the easy way and simply assume that there is a complementarity between deliberation and aggregation, I want in the rest of this chapter to explore the continuing tension between the two. In post-industrial societies governments have little choice but to use deliberative devices of policy making particularly in matters like environmental regulation and risk-management (Weale, 2002). On the other hand, I simply do not share Habermas's downgrading of the principle of majority rule and the competitive party process that goes with it. Losing the vote is not the same as losing the argument, and to suppose that a majority decision is the interim result of a continuing deliberative process is to collapse that important distinction.

Party competition and deliberative ideals

Deliberation versus party competiton?

I have already noted that a central finding of Ian Budge and his colleagues is a median correspondence result. If we plot party competition on a left–right spectrum then, across most developed democracies, parties in government have policy preferences that correspond to those of the median voter. This finding is central to the claim that party competition serves the values of democracy. In the absence of unanimity, the argument runs, majority opinion must be the authoritative guide to public policy. Median correspondence is an operationalisation of this idea within the framework of representative democracy. Within a broadly aggregative view of democracy, therefore, the median correspondence finding plays a key role. Such median correspondence provides for both authorisation and responsiveness, and this is central to democratic legitimacy. The demo-cratic account of political authorisation, it may be argued, is founded on the idea that governments should be responsive to public opinion.

How does this claim comport with deliberative ideals? This idea of government as responsive to public opinion being constitutive of demo-cracy is developed within the deliberative tradition by Richardson (2002: 56–72), in his claim that any democracy must in some qualified sense be populist. By contrast, there are strands of thinking among deliberative democrats for whom the tests of responsiveness and deliberation are not easily reconciled. For example, Joshua Cohen (1989: 22) writes that 'the deliberative conception emphasizes that collective choices should be *made in a deliberative way*, and not only that those choices should have a desir-able fit with the preferences of citizens'. A median correspondence is, of course, only one sort of 'desirable fit' and other forms of correspondence (for example with modal preferences) may be advanced. However, to the extent to which any form of fit is interpreted as being partial or inade-quate by the deliberative conception, it follows that median correspon-dence will be judged as inappropriate.

Taken literally, Cohen's argument seems to suggest that whilst the fit of median correspondence cannot be a sufficient condition for legitimate democratic choice, it could be a necessary condition, as implied by the claim that it is 'not only' that choices should have a desirable fit with the preferences of citizens. Read in this way, the argument might be taken to assert that both fit and deliberation may be necessary (and possibly jointly sufficient) for democratic legitimacy. But are we entitled to assume that the two tests can so easily be rendered consistent with one another? To say that preferences must be deliberated is to point to a desirable feature of the processes by which preferences are arrived at; to insist on median correspondence is to point to the way in which preferences should mesh with public choices. Suppose, however, that there are unequal patterns of deliberation across different members of society, so that some groups have well-reasoned opinions and others only ill-considered views. The median position will not be the median of the deliberated preferences but of all preferences. In these circumstances, does the deliberative criterion trump the aggregative criterion or vice versa?

Moreover, if the underlying justification of deliberative democracy is based upon ideals of political legitimacy through consent, it is difficult to see what status the median position has. The requirement of general consent would seem to suggest a super-majoritarian criterion of choice, not the median one that is a version of the majoritarian view. Even if one gives up on the idea of unanimous consent as being hopelessly utopian, one might still think that it was worth taking the trouble to secure as large a consensus as possible before making serious public decisions and so end up at a super-majoritarian position. Indeed, critics of majoritarian demo-cracy, like Lijphart (1984), base part of their case on the need to ensure that the institutional and political conditions are in place to ensure that discussion can take place in a politics of accommodation.

From this point of view, it seems that one of the central empirical results of the CMP approach, a result that seemed to carry a number of implications for the theory of democratic legitimacy and the evaluation of functioning political systems, is shown to be less important. If deliberation is really important, then why should so much emphasis be placed upon median correspondence, when the undeliberated and possibly partial preferences of the median voter are suspect? However, this is to move the argument rather too quickly. Critics of the super-majoritarian account of democracy have pointed to the way in which institutionalising the require-ment to secure extensive consent in effect can bestow disproportionate veto power on minority groups and entrench the status quo, even when change would be generally beneficial (Barry, 1965: 237–285). From this point of view, majoritarian arrangements provide an incentive from polit-ical groups to compromise with others in their views, by contrast with a situation in which they could just hold out knowing that the bias of the status quo could work in their favour.

The central problem here, I suggest, is that there is an inevitable tension between the concern for fair procedures of aggregation, given that actors have political views, and a concern for the quality of reasoning by which those views are formed and evaluated. These concerns relate to different domains of political democracy, and it is simply implausible to think that deliberative ideals can be applied to the processes of party competition without attenuation. It is equally implausible to think that the deliberative ideals lead to a valid critique of the practices of party competi-tion, given a concern for fair preference aggregation. However, this is only to look at one feature of competitive political democracy. What of the ways in which the CMP model raises questions about the way in which political discussion is institutionalised through party programmes?

Party competition and the burdens of judgement

One premiss that is important in underwriting a deliberative conception of democracy is that, what Rawls calls the burdens of judgement, will produce a variety of opinions and views among citizens. This assumption can be used to support what Rawls then terms 'the fact of pluralism' by which he means the existence of a legitimate variety of views about the character of the good life (Rawls, 1996: 58). It can also be used to under-line the extent to which any political decision has to rest on premises or invoke forms of evidence that are not self-evident, so providing a direct ground for the need for deliberation in matters of collective choice. Inter-ests have first to be defined before they can be aggregated.

From this perspective, party competition contributes to a reduction in the burdens of judgement. The principal way in which this occurs is by parties defining the public agenda and simplifying the choice of alternatives. By organising the agenda of politics in terms of broad choices of political value and party position, electoral competition presents citizens with a relatively straightforward set of choices. Voting for a party, rather than having to make a specific choice on each and every set of issues, enables voters to rely upon the available heuristic of party commitment. Instead of inferring one's party choice from one's views about the issues, one can infer one's view about the issues from one's party choice.

As Nagel has pointed out in his chapter, the CMP view of the dominance of the left–right dimension over-simplifies the character of the choices that need to be made in politics. However, to say that there is a danger from over-simplification is not to say that one can dispense with simplification completely. Suppose that there are five main domains or dimensions of public policy as envisaged by the CMP coding frame (external relations, freedom and democracy, the political system, the economy and welfare and the quality of life). Suppose also that attitudes in each of these domains are binary so that it is possible to take just one of two positions in relation to each (for example, hawk or dove in the domain of external affairs or libertarian or authoritarian in the domain of freedom). Then over five dimensions there would be 32 logically possible positions that one could hold. Notionally, each of these possibilities could be translated into distinct political parties, each resting upon different combinations of attitudes, a possibility that Sidgwick (1891: 563–577) anticipated many years ago. So, with just five domains and a binary set of attitudes in each domain, we rapidly arrive at a situation in which there is a plethora of alternatives – too many for voters to process easily or intelligibly – and the possibility of a large number of political parties based upon the multiplication of policy and political alternatives.

Clearly, in practice we do not find this. Even if we think that the CMP reduction of party competition to just one principal dimension is sometimes too great an oversimplification, the effective choice that is offered to voters in modern democracies falls far short of what could be offered. No doubt there are important institutional and historical constraints that limit the range of alternatives on offer. Thus, in political systems in which the public budget is centralised, interconnections between domains become rapidly apparent, since more spent on guns means less butter. Equally, however, it is going to be difficult to understand the observed range of choice without taking into account the practice of many political parties (parties that aspire to be something more than merely catch-all or vote-winning parties) to justify their policy stances by reference to a core set of political values. In this vein, parties seek to explicate and develop their policy stances through programmes, ideological statements and narratives the purpose of which is to provide an account of a political position that shapes commitments across wide domains of policy. Fundamental ideas on equality versus personal freedom or international cooperation versus the assertion of national sovereignty will help explicate and some-times explain why parties adopt the positions that they do. For these reasons, manifestos are the tip of considerable intellectual and ideological icebergs.

From the viewpoint of deliberative democracy, this process of simplifi-cation through party competition is somewhat ambiguous. On the one hand, it facilitates public discussion. If there were no structuring of public discussion in this way, the process of public reasoning would be formless. In place of discussion about established party political positions one would find either the rise of personality politics, as voters struggled to find some available heuristic to deal with the large number of alternatives, or a pro-liferation of specialised policy networks, the price of entry to which would be the acceptance of certain premises and assumptions in terms of which issues were to be discussed. Neither of these alternatives could be said to foster a community of free and reasoning equals.

On the other hand, the structuring of public discussion through the competition of political parties can be seen as one more demonstration of the extent to which politics in the 'mobilisation of bias' (Schattschneider, 1960). Simplification brings with it exclusion. Probably the best example of this is to be found in the politics of liberal democracies in the 1950s and 1960s. Because so much of the political discourse was organised around the struggle between labour and capital, growing out of the depression of the 1930s, ecological concerns were marginalised until the 1970s, when party systems began to change under the influence of the environment and related social movements. This cartelisation instanced a closing down of the space of public reasoning.

Systems of party competition do not lend themselves easily to institu-tional design or redesign, and therefore it is difficult to see what institu-tional changes might be thought to flow from a concern with deliberative openness. In any case, particular circumstances are likely to be important when considering how to ensure that party competition performs the job of structuring the public discourse without cartelising it. One obvious thought is that PR systems with low thresholds make it easier for new issues and minority concerns to be expressed within the system of party competition. From this point of view, principles of deliberative democracy might be thought to justify reforms of systems towards this pattern. However, even this inference is ambiguous, for the same conditions that make party systems open to a wide range of concerns are also the same conditions that enable flash parties to emerge, and such effects can easily distort the political agenda by focusing attention excessively upon the con-cerns of those parties to the detriment of wider and more long-lasting con-cerns. Deliberative theory is thus suggestive rather than definitive in these respects.

The quality of political debate

Deliberative democrats have been critical of the quality of political campaigning in functioning democracies. Gutmann and Thompson (1996: 124) for example, in noting the way that salacious personal details of politicians' lives are introduced into campaigns, assert that a political version of Gresham's law operates in American democracy, so that cheap talk drives out quality talk. It may well be that there are substantial cross-national differences in the tendency towards negative campaigning, since we might expect that in party systems in which personality plays a less prominent role in campaigning, the returns to personal invective are lower. Nevertheless, it is not difficult to see why deliberative democrats would be critical of cheap talk in politics wherever it occurs.

However, it is possible also to argue that deliberative democrats should also be critical of the sort of saliency campaigning upon which the CMP has built its analysis of party competition. The CMP account of campaigning, it will be remembered, rests upon the assumption that parties do not directly confront one another over domains of public policy. Instead, they distinguish themselves from their opponents by stressing those themes that they think will be to their advantage. From this point of view, party competition does not resemble a democratic debate in which common topics are addressed and examined, but rather a market in which stallholders call out the attractiveness of their wares on offer to the public.

If we are concerned about the quality of public discussion, this stallholders conception of party competition is hardly going to be satisfactory. If we consider the conditions that need to be in place if sound public choices are to be made, then there are at least two that party competition seems ill-equipped to provide. The first of these is to facilitate the examination of decision premises, the assumptions and conjectures upon which policy choices have to be based. All policies involve decision makers holding to causal accounts of how policy instruments are related to policy goals, and what the effects of acting are going to be in terms of policy outputs and outcomes. Studies of implementation failure have typically shown, for example, that mistaken understandings of causal relationships lead to policy failures, producing outcomes that may be at odds with the intentions of policy makers (Pressman and Wildavsky, 1973). Without the possibility of examining the premises that decision makers use in coming to policy decisions, the possibility of implementation failure increases. Examining decision premises, however, requires those advocating policies to expose the reasoning upon which they have come to their conclusions, and it requires opponents to meet one another on a common set of issues. However, if the saliency theory of party campaigning is correct, neither of these forms of engagement is something that we should expect in party competition.

The second condition that is needed for sound decisions is an articulation of the opportunities forgone in making one decision rather than another. Policy making is always a choice among alternatives. For example, tax cuts will imply deteriorations in public services or an increase in problems like poverty. Tax increases may well reduce investment or economic growth. For these reasons, policy making is a matter of nicely calculated less or more, seeking to find a balance between competing objectives. However, if the saliency theory of campaigning is correct, politicians and political parties have little incentive to confront the full implications of their decisions. Instead, the rhetoric will be one of costless choices, large efficiency gains without pain and the complementarity of competing values.

However, even if these lines of argument do offer valid criticisms of party competition from a deliberative point of view, it does not follow that the best way of dealing with them is to think of ways in which party competition should be reformed. In some ways, the strength of the CMP analysis is to show how deeply rooted are the incentives to shy away from engaged discussion on decision premises and implications. It may simply be that party competition, whatever its other merits, is simply too crude a device for thinking about choices of policies seriously. To suppose otherwise is to suppose that election campaigns can be forums of policy analysis, and they cannot. The implication is that other devices are needed to supplement party competition if policy making is to be successful. Paul Sabatier (1987: 679–680) for example has suggested that one condition for successful policy learning is the existence of neutral, apolitical forums within which advocates of competing policy advocacy coalitions can be forced to confront one another. If there is any merit in this suggestion (and for myself I think there is, see Weale, 1992), then one would not expect election campaigns to be the principal venue for policy discussion. Instead, forums within which those with an understanding of specific areas of policy would be more productive. In short, whereas elections necessarily take us wide to broad confrontations of political principle, policy development is about the accumulation of minute particulars, examined in ways that do not allow advocates to avoid the implications and presuppositions of their favoured policies.

Conclusion

What then are we to conclude from applying the principles of deliberative democracy to the understanding of political democracy associated with Ian Budge and the CMP? Ian Budge is surely right to locate the practice of electoral competition in the context of a broader justification of democratic freedoms. Even if elections are successful in representing the preferences of the median voter and providing an incentive for political parties to put into practice what they promise in campaigns, it does not follow that these are the sole criteria by which we should judge the performance of democracy. Deliberative theorists have done much work in examining what exactly is involved in the articulation of interests and indeed in the way that interests are defined and constituted through dialogue and debate. But it does not follow from the fact that a full account of democracy requires us to look at deliberation as well as aggregation that these two components of democracy cohere, either institutionally or intellectually. The methodological achievement of the CMP is to bring out the ways in which behind voting lies talk and that both talk and voting are essential ingredients in any coherent account of democratic political representation. But, as deliberative theorists have reminded us, it is talk with defects. The next challenge is to move beyond manifestos. Meanwhile, the debate between the heirs of James Mill and those of Jean-Jacques Rousseau continues.

References

Barry, B. (1965) *Political Argument* (London: Routledge and Kegan Paul).

Bessette, J.M. (1994) *The Mild Voice of Reason: Deliberative Democracy and American National Government* (Chicago: University of Chicago Press).

Bohman, J. (1998) 'Survey Article: The Coming of Age of Deliberative Democracy', *Journal of Political Philosophy* 6:4, 400–425.

Budge, I. (1996) *The New Challenge of Direct Democracy* (Cambridge: Polity Press).

Budge, I. and R.I. Hofferbert (1990) 'Mandates and Policy Outputs: U.S. Party Platforms and Federal Expenditures', *American Political Science Review* 84:1, 111–131.

Budge, I., H.-D. Klingemann, A. Volkens, J. Bara and E. Tanenbaum (eds) (2001) *Mapping Policy Preferences: Estimates for Parties, Electors, and Governments 1945–1998* (Oxford: Oxford University Press).

Cohen, J. (1989) 'Deliberation and Democratic Legitimacy' in A. Hamlin and P. Pettit (eds) *The Good Polity* (Oxford: Basil Blackwell), pp. 17–34.

Downs, A. (1957) *An Economic Theory of Democracy* (New York: Harper and Row).

Dryzek, J. (2001) 'Legitimacy and Economy in Deliberative Democracy', *Political Theory* 29:5, 651–669.

Goodin, R.E. (2003) *Reflective Democracy* (Oxford: Oxford University Press).

Gutmann, A. and D. Thompson (1996) *Democracy and Disagreement* (Cambridge, MA: Harvard University Press).

Habermas, J. (1996) *Between Facts and Norms* (Cambridge: Polity Press).

Hofferbert, R.I. and I. Budge (1992) 'The Party Mandate and the Westminster Model: Election Programmes and Government Spending in Britain, 1948–85', *British Journal of Political Science* 22:2, 151–182.

Hofferbert, R.I., I. Budge and M.D. McDonald (1993) 'Party Platforms, Mandates, and Government Spending', *American Political Science Review* 87:3, 747–750.

King, G. and M. Laver (1993) 'Party Platforms, Mandates, and Government Spending', *American Political Science Review* 87:3, 744–747.

Lijphart, A. (1984) *Democracies* (New Haven and London: Yale University Press).

McDonald, M.D., S.M. Mendes and I. Budge (2004) 'What Are Elections For? Conferring the Median Mandate', *British Journal of Political Science* 34:1, 1–26.

Manin, B. (1997) *The Principles of Representative Government* (Cambridge: Cambridge University Press).

Mill, J. (1822) 'Government' reprinted in T. Ball (ed.) (1992) *James Mill: Political Writings* (Cambridge: Cambridge University Press).

Pitkin, H. (1967) *The Concept of Representation* (Berkeley: University of California Press).

Pressman, J. and A. Wildavsky (1973) *Implementation* (Berkeley: University of California Press).

Rawls, J. (1996) *Political Liberalism* (New York: Columbia University Press, paperback edition).

Richardson, H.S. (2002) *Democratic Autonomy: Public Reasoning about the Ends of Policy* (Oxford: Oxford University Press).

Rousseau, J.-J. (1762) *The Social Contract* translated G.D.H. Cole (1973) (London: J. M. Dent and Sons).

Sabatier, P.A. (1987) 'Knowledge, Policy-Oriented Learning and Policy Change', *Knowledge: Creation, Diffusion, Utilization* 8:4, 649–692.

Schattschneider, E.E. (1960) *The Semi-Sovereign People: A Realistic View of Democracy in America* (New York: Holt, Rinehart and Winston).

Schumpeter, J.A. (1954) *Capitalism, Socialism and Democracy* (London: Allen and Unwin, first edition 1943).

Sidgwick, H. (1891) *The Elements of Politics* (London: Macmillan).

Weale, A. (1992) 'Close Encounters of the Third Sector Kind' in S. Hargreaves Heap and A. Ross (eds) *Understanding the Enterprise Culture: Themes in the Work of Mary Douglas* (Edinburgh: Edinburgh University Press), pp. 203–217.

Weale, A. (ed.) (2002) *Risk, Democratic Citizenship and Public Policy* (Oxford: Oxford University Press).

Weale, A., G. Pridham, M. Cini, D. Konstadakopulos, M. Porter and B. Flynn (2000) *Environmental Governance in Europe* (Oxford: Oxford University Press).

14 Political tolerance

Meaning, measurement and context

Donald D. Searing, Ivor Crewe and
Pamela Johnston Conover

Ian Budge's research programmes are framed by a democratic, utilitarian and interest aggregating perspective that is widely shared among his colleagues who study comparative political behavior and institutions. He departs from many of these colleagues, however, in his strong support for direct democracy as an alternative to our present representational regimes.

In direct democracies, citizens would vote on the most important political decisions, and their votes would determine public policy. Much of the skepticism directed at this regime type concerns its feasibility and its presumed intolerance. Budge wrote *The New Challenge of Direct Democracy* (1996) to address such criticisms with logic and empirical data. Using these tools, he constructs an institutionally sophisticated and compelling case for the feasibility of electronically-based direct democracy in the twenty-first century. It is difficult to read his book and not be persuaded that direct democracy should be taken very seriously as a program for institutional reform, and that it deserves much more attention and study than it has been given by the profession of political science.

By contrast, Budge's case against the fears of direct democracy's presumed intolerance is somewhat less convincing. It is less convincing in part because it rests on propitious data about referendums and policy initiatives which are difficult to interpret because those who vote on these matters tend to be high in education (one of tolerance's strongest correlates) and quite poorly informed about the issues involved. But the case is less convincing mainly because it runs up against the consistent findings of survey research since the 1950s that, in most modern liberal democracies, the majority of citizens are often disturbingly intolerant. It is difficult not to worry that an electronically-based direct democracy would open the door to even more intolerance than we have now. Budge's analysis of the data on referendums and policy initiatives shows that there is less to fear than direct democracy's critics claim – but that may nevertheless leave much to fear, despite the constitutional and institutional safeguards he would keep in place.

Yet, just as the optimistic data on referendums and policy initiatives are difficult to interpret, so the pessimistic data from survey research that skeptics use to justify their skepticism is not so clear and convincing either. To assess the critics' fears systematically, we need to know much more than we do about tolerance in liberal democratic regimes and how it might best be investigated. As a modest step in this direction, our chapter uses surveys, focus groups and in-depth interviews to analyze comparatively the attitudes of tolerance held by citizens in Great Britain and the United States. We proceed as follows. First we review focus group data on the frames of reference that citizens use to understand tolerance. Then we turn to survey data to assess relative degrees of tolerance and to analyze important correlates of these orientations. Finally we use qualitative materials from focus groups and in-depth interviews to examine justifications for tolerance found in the political cultures of these two nations. Our goal is to explain tolerance by exploring its meaning.

The quintessential liberal practice of political tolerance is also the historical condition from which liberalism itself first emerged during the Protestant Reformation and its aftermath (Rawls, 1993: xxiv ff.). Since then, tolerance has evolved under the guidance of the ideas of John Locke, the principal architect of both tolerance and liberalism, and, more recently, of John Stuart Mill, who carried these conceptions into the modern age.

In Great Britain and the United States today, tolerance is highly valued by many citizens, but it is imperfectly understood, and it is therefore an unstable and sometimes unsuccessful liberal "practice." A practice is an institutionalized pattern that includes a set of formal and informal rules, a mode of conduct, and associated attitudes (see Frazer and Lacey, 1994). The formal rules of tolerance are legal and constitutional; the informal rules are social norms. The mode of conduct, toleration, is what liberalism wishes to achieve. But the attitudes of tolerance are the key. Where they are not firmly established, intolerant attitudes will make intolerant behavior more likely, and their communication to others will promote intolerance in the culture and thereby undermine the entire practice (Williams, 1996).

Our attitudinal data are drawn from interviews conducted in Great Britain and the United States to study a wide range of topics concerning citizenship and the making of citizens. The project employed a quasi-experimental research design, a variation of a "non-equivalent comparison group" design, (see Cook and Campbell, 1979) which integrated a macro-comparative case study design at national and community levels with a variable-oriented design at the individual level. The principal virtue of these data for analyzing comparatively the meaning of a concept like tolerance is their cross-national cultural and linguistic commonality. This should facilitate the cross-national reliability and validity of our psychological measures. The design's basic element is the local community, where citizens learn, experience and talk about their citizenship (cf. Huckfeldt and Sprague, 1995: 8). Thus, the data are not national samples but are instead drawn from demographically matched research sites: small, stable market/farming communities in Lincolnshire and Minnesota; urban, predominantly working class communities in Manchester and Philadelphia; and, upper middle class suburban communities in Essex and North Carolina.

In each of these communities, we assembled accounts of local history, participant observation information, aggregate data, transcribed interviews with focus group and community leaders, and face-to-face survey interviews with secondary school students and their parents and teachers, as well as with random samples of adult citizens – approximately 3,000 interviews in all.[1] The analysis in this chapter employs the surveys with random samples of adults and the transcribed focus group data and in-depth elite interviews.[2]

The concept of tolerance: focus groups

Philosophers find tolerance peculiar, paradoxical and equivocal (Heyd, 1996). It is peculiar, they say, in that it is liked neither by those who practice it (who would prefer to meddle) nor by those to whom it is applied (who would prefer approval) (see Fletcher, 1996). Tolerance is paradoxical because it characterizes as virtuous putting up with things that one believes are wrong (see Horton, 1996). And it is equivocal, for its liberal prescriptions frequently contravene democracy's majority rule, public order, civility and community; and there is little agreement on what its proper limits should be. Our citizens find tolerance equally problematic, but less for its abstract philosophical conundrums than for its applications in particular cases. Thus, most of our American respondents accept tolerance as a desirable part of their constitution, while most Britons understand it as a desirable part of their national character. But what puzzles them both nonetheless is how exactly they should react to the Ku Klux Klan (KKK) organizers, Moonies, National Front members or New Age Travelers who appear in their communities.

The paradoxical aspect of tolerance's prescriptions – putting up with things that one believes wrong – gives everyone the greatest difficulty. This becomes especially troubling when opposition to a group is rooted more in moral reasoning than in prejudice, more in *disapproval* of New Age Travelers, for example, than in plain *dislike*. Raphael (1988: 139) formulates the dilemma as follows: "to disapprove of something is to judge it to be wrong. Such a judgement does not express a purely subjective preference. It claims universality . . . .. [Therefore] the content of the judgement, that something is wrong, implies that the something may properly be prevented." This paradox troubled discussants in the British and American focus groups, who tended to confound disapproval and dislike. If we feel that a group is wrong or, worse, positively evil, they said, why should it be "allowed?" What are the uses of a tolerance that permits what we believe should be condemned?

To impress, such uses must seem important. And they do. The first utility of tolerance is to promote freedom by increasing choice. The second is to ensure civic peace by "making room" for beliefs and ways of life that others wish to pursue. "Constitutional" and "civic" are important frames of reference that our citizens use to incorporate these two utilities as they seek to understand the problem.[3] The constitutional frame is political, public and official, whereas the civic frame is social, moral and informal.[4]

Constitutional and civic frames

Political scientists have carefully studied constitutional tolerance, which is associated with political freedom – freedom from government control – for it enables citizens to pursue political ideas and programs and thereby enriches democracy. There is a long, cumulative tradition of empirical research in this area, and as a result we know a good deal about the subject. By protecting minorities, and particularly extreme minorities (e.g. KKK), constitutional tolerance is said to protect all citizens. This constitutional frame of reference focuses upon the electoral arena to warn against formal interference (typically by government) with freedom of speech, association or participation in elections. It is driven by respect for constitutional rules of the game. This is what most political scientists have studied and what we ourselves have investigated with our quantitative survey data.

But for most citizens, the concept of "tolerance" calls up instead narratives about intolerance toward cultural minorities in their communities. This is what they discuss first in our focus groups. Thus they are more likely to lead with civic than with constitutional frames of reference, even when a discussion of tolerance is introduced (as ours was) with a constitutionally-oriented question. Civic tolerance facilitates coexistence among groups in pluralistic societies. It concentrates on conduct in the community, on inhibiting dispositions to shun, demean, exclude, manipulate, censor or stifle fellow citizens.[5] And it is driven by the moral belief that toleration is the right response to difference.

Although few of our British or American citizens readily think in constitutional frames, when these frames of reference enter their discussions they take them up and – particularly in the United States – acknowledge their importance and talk seriously about the principles involved. Constitutional frames of reference occasionally appear in the British transcripts too. But since the British constitution is unwritten, and since most of its doctrines are unfamiliar to most British citizens (Searing, 1982), the principles that tolerance calls to mind are much more likely to be moral than constitutional, legal or political.

If constitutional and civic concerns commingle in our Americans' discussions of tolerance,[6] these Americans nevertheless join their British counterparts in treating civic contexts as the place where the most difficult problems and temptations arise. This is where they say the most intransigent intolerance exists. Even those who gave tolerant answers to our explicitly constitutionally-oriented questions, knew that, outside this legal framework, they themselves would be able to find effective means of being intolerant if they wished. That was the chief implication they drew out of their discussions of the contrast between official, constitutional tolerance and unofficial civic intolerance, between public and formal compliance with the law and private and informal action designed to undermine unpopular groups. "A community can have laws without legislation," they said. And those laws are often intolerant.

Negative tolerance and positive tolerance

The British focus group discussions of tolerance mainly address negative tolerance, which like negative freedom, refers simply to an absence of interference. American discussions, by contrast, are more likely to address positive tolerance which, like positive freedom, asks citizens to respect one another. These divergent understandings reflect the divergent paths that Locke's prescriptions have taken in Britain, which still sees itself as a relatively homogeneous nation state, and in the United States, which has come to see itself as a heterogeneous society of immigrants. And these contrasting interpretations are captured in the leading definitions of tolerance found in each nation's dictionaries:

Tolerance, n:

Great Britain.   1. The *action* or practice of bearing pain or hardship; the power or ability *to endure* something. 2. The action of allowing something or granting permission. 3. The disposition to accept without protest or adopt a liberal attitude toward the opinion of others; forbearance.

The New Shorter Oxford English Dictionary

United States   1. A *fair and objective attitude* toward those whose opinions, practices, race, religion, nationality, etc., differ from one's own; *freedom from bigotry.* 2. Interest in and concern for ideas, opinions, practices, etc., foreign to one's own; a liberal, *undogmatic* viewpoint.

The Random House Dictionary of the English Language

Some American dictionaries go further still:

United States.   1. Recognition of and *respect for* the opinions, practices, or behavior of others.

Webster's II New Riverside University Dictionary

British definitions stress actions more than attitudes and concentrate on enduring things that one dislikes. The emphasis on "enduring" is central to these traditional definitions. It derives from the concept's English roots in religious conflicts and the Act of Toleration by which the authorities granted freedom of religious worship, on certain conditions, to dissenting Protestants whose opinions and practices they detested. This is negative tolerance. The closest that British dictionary definitions come to anything like respect is "forbearance," which suggests patience and leniency. This traditional definition, which exhorts us "to endure" beliefs and practices that we may detest, has historically been of the greatest importance. Today it continues to serve as a powerful deterrent to violations of basic human rights.

The more recent American understandings of tolerance promise members of minority groups something more: a positive tolerance of respect to help them maintain the essentials of their identities and ways of life, and to help them to feel welcome and comfortable in the societies where they live (Walzer, 1997). Positive tolerance asks citizens to be open-minded and empathetic toward "difference;" it asks them to work sympathetically to build institutional and cultural arrangements that will accommodate different ways of life (Mendus, 1987).

Positive tolerance extends the baseline from endurance to empathy, from disapproval to open-mindedness, from non-interference to respect. But even positive tolerance stops short of "approval," for it would make no sense at all to say that one is tolerant of those whom one anyway supports. A neo-Nazi who expresses approval of racist agitation on street corners is expressing support, not tolerance negative or positive. If support is one bookend to tolerance, then "neutrality" is the other, not because prejudices have been overcome but rather because with neutrality there are no prejudices there. Putting up with the political campaigns of groups about which one knows little and cares less is being indifferent, not tolerant. So for tolerance to exist, it must have something to overcome, some prejudice strong or mild, some discomfort, distance or awkwardness in the face of difference.

Although positive tolerance loses coherence as it approaches approval, its spirit of open-mindedness is nevertheless needed to address very real inconsistencies in the traditional logic of negative tolerance (Sniderman, 1993). Without open-mindedness: (a) the most prejudiced people count as the most tolerant because they have the most to endure; (b) the most tolerant person of all is the most narrow-minded (albeit self-restrained) bigot in the community (Horton, 1996); and, (c) citizens become more tolerant by becoming more prejudiced, so long as they still restrain their behavior. This is not what most citizens today mean by a tolerant person. What is missing is the empathy, open-mindedness and respect that positive tolerance brings to the subject.

Traditional tolerance was originally formulated as "endurance" because at the time much blood was flowing from religious and ethnic hatreds, and no one took seriously the feasibility and significance of open-mindedness (Laslett, 1971). For centuries, "endurance," seemed to press the limits of the possible and seemed sufficient. It is one thing to ask people not to interfere with the expression of views they detest, quite another to ask them to listen sympathetically. Open-mindedness is a tall order for most citizens, one that neither Locke nor Mill required. "To endure" will always be central to the concept of tolerance. For if the most tolerant citizens today are those who also show "a willingness to listen and learn," (Walzer, 1997: 11), this is a willingness more appropriate for resolving difficulties of civic multiculturalism than battles over fundamental rights for those whose points of view the majority detests.[7]

Constitutional tolerance: measurement and meaning

Over the past half-century, political scientists have created a body of cumulative survey research on attitudes toward traditional, negative constitutional tolerance. This work has been theoretically rich, methodologically intriguing and policy relevant. But it has not yet told us enough about the meaning of these attitudes to the citizens surveyed. To better understand how they understand tolerance, we need to visit the worlds where their views develop. This is what we have sought to do with our community-based research design, focus groups and in-depth interviews. These qualitative data have already drawn out the concept of positive tolerance and, in the analyses below, they will suggest some new interpretations of responses to established survey instruments.

Much survey research on constitutional tolerance has been conducted in the United States, where it has consistently produced disturbing results and debates about measures. The first such study, directed by Samuel Stouffer (1955) in the early 1950s, found that the American public was prepared to deny basic civil rights to unpopular minorities: a majority would deny American citizens who were atheists, communists or socialists the right to speak in public, run for office or even work as a clerk in a store and would condone tapping their phones. Stouffer's results probably reflected the era's McCarthyte hysteria; but even after this hysteria had subsided, Prothro and Grigg (1960) found similar patterns. Although a large majority of rank and file American citizens endorsed the abstract principles of minority rights, much smaller proportions were prepared to apply these principles in concrete cases. A similar discrepancy between principle and practice was found by McClosky (1964).

The support from ordinary Americans for constitutional tolerance seemed decidedly shaky. Public opinion apparently threatened individual liberty, much as John Stuart Mill had worried it would do in democratic regimes. How then was constitutional tolerance successfully maintained in the United States? One answer suggested that it wasn't, that there were more cases of intolerance than people cared to admit. Another answer provided the foundation for "the elitist theory of democracy" – it was the country's leaders who, despite intolerant publics, upheld America's regime of constitutional tolerance. This view was encouraged by survey evidence that found local notables and politicians comparatively tolerant and disposed to practice what they preached. Similar results were subsequently reported for national politicians too, as well as for British Members of Parliament (Sullivan *et al.*, 1993).[8]

Sullivan *et al.* (1982) identified several weaknesses in these early investigations. By concentrating on attitudes towards communists,[9] the early studies may have *under*-estimated the true level of intolerance. Respondents who were counted as tolerant because of their tolerant attitudes toward communists on the far left might, if given the chance, have revealed intolerant attitudes to groups on the far right. Moreover, when Nunn *et al.* (1978) replicated Stouffer's study 20 years later, their finding that intolerance had declined substantially was suspect because Americans' fear of communists had declined during the same period. Had Stouffer's survey instrument, which was also used by Nunn *et al.*, measured citizens' attitudes toward tolerance, or, had it measured their attitudes toward communists? If Nunn *et al.*' 1970s citizens had been asked not about communists but rather about political groups they despised as much as their predecessors had despised communists during the 1950s, perhaps they would have reacted with equally intolerant attitudes.

Sullivan and his colleagues therefore advocated two changes in the way tolerance was gauged. First, it should not be measured in terms of citizens' declarations of support for abstract principles because these are disconnected from actual political groups and situations. Second, although tolerance must be assessed with reference to actual political groups, the measure should not be standardized by focusing on only one group (e.g. communists) which investigators preselect. Instead it would be preferable, (a) to use a self-anchoring measure that would allow each respondent to identify the political group that she most strongly opposes, and then (b) ask her about the appropriateness of "absence of interference" with members of this group acting in public contexts as equal citizens. Accordingly, Sullivan *et al.* (1982) asked respondents to identify, from a list of controversial political and campaigning groups, the one they most disliked, and then asked them whether or not they would approve of their "least-liked" group engaging in, or being prevented from engaging in, a range of activities that included freedom of speech, press, association and other legal and peaceful public activities. Using new survey questions based on these considerations, they found that intolerance had probably not declined since the 1950s, although the principal targets of intolerance might have changed. A large majority of the public still wanted to ban their most disliked group from running for President, or teaching in schools; in fact, they wanted to outlaw it altogether.[10] Sullivan *et al.*'s least-liked measure of constitutional tolerance

has become the standard approach.[11] With only minor and contextual variations, it has been applied in a wide range of nations, to both publics and
leaders.[12] Our survey measure closely resembles theirs. And our focus group
discussions suggest that respondents do not distinguish very much between
disapproval and dislike. Thus, citizens were shown a list of ten controversial
political groups and asked to identify, in two steps, the group they disapproved most of all.[13]

As Table 14.1 shows, in each country there were two groups which
together attracted most disapproval: white supremacist groups like the
KKK (37 percent) and the American Nazi Party (30 percent) in the
United States, and Provisional Sinn Fein (the political wing of the IRA)
(47 percent) and the neo-Nazi National Front (30 percent) in Britain.
Here is the first common pattern from our American and British survey
data. The distribution of disapproval varied only slightly among
communities.[14] Each country's communist party, toothless and virtually

Table 14.1 Least liked group by country

Political group	US (%)	GB (%)
1 Provisional Sinn Fein	n.a.	47
2 White supremacist groups (e.g. KKK)	37	n.a.
3 American Nazi Party/National Front	30	30
4 American/British Communist Party	10	06
5 Gay rights groups	09	06
6 Pro-choice groups	07	05
7 Pro-life groups	02	03
8 Black rights groups	02	01
9 Right-wing fundamentalist groups (e.g. Moral Majority)	02	00
10 Feminist groups	00	00
11 Animal rights groups	00	02
12 Campaign for Nuclear Disarmament	n.a.	01
	100	100
(n)	(375)	(375)

Notes
Categories of political groups are spelled out in more detail in the question where they are
also listed in a different order than in this table.

defunct by this time, is far behind. And, these four extremist groups are the ones that, in each country, are most often associated with serious violence and intimidation.[15] Together they will constitute, in the measure's next stage, the key reference groups for two-thirds of the Americans and three-quarters of the British. The remainder of the respondents will be asked about the appropriateness of toleration for another group in the table, the group of which they said they disapproved even more than of Sinn Fein or the KKK. This is clearly the foundation for a measure of negative tolerance, of the disposition not to interfere with citizens whose beliefs and practices one strongly disapproves or detests.

Thus, respondents were asked whether or not a member of the group they disapproved most should be allowed to: (1) teach in a local school or college; (2) form a local branch of the organization; (3) run for the local town council; and (4) organize and speak at a local public meeting. They were also asked whether they would (5) support a campaign to ban from the local library a book favoring the organization. Responses were coded as "yes," "no," "don't know" and "no answer." The list of groups, and its administration in the interview, differs from Sullivan *et al.* (1982)' instrument in minor respects and was also varied slightly between the American and British samples to take account of the different political conditions in the two countries.[16] Respondents were given one point for a tolerant response to each of these five items, and the points were summed to form a scale (range zero to five) where high scores signify high tolerance.[17]

This is a measure of negative constitutional tolerance toward a political group that each respondent strongly dislikes. It is a measure of the respondent's willingness to accept, at least formally and minimally, members of this group as equal citizens. It is by design not a direct measure of tolerance as a simple, general moral principle, for it has been context-grounded by making it group specific. Still, our focus group discussions of similar items support the view that it nonetheless functions as an indirect measure of a general disposition "to endure," to put up with the public activities of citizens who are members of groups whose practices the respondent detests or disapproves.[18] The generalization of this context-grounded measure is based on two related assumptions. One is that a reasonably valid assessment of a general disposition toward constitutional negative tolerance is the reluctance to interfere with public activities of members of political groups that one thoroughly detests. The second spells this out: citizens who are willing to endure the communists, Nazis, or vivisectionists they detest will be disposed to endure as well the beliefs and practices of groups they merely dislike.

The psychology of toleration

Negative constitutional tolerance is a demanding virtue, because it requires responses that are far from obvious. It is a difficult disposition to learn, because it seems to depend on hypothetical reasoning and on the inculcation of counter-intuitive habits. It also relies on context.

A context-dependent disposition

Negative constitutional tolerance is embedded in quite particular contexts. This frustrates our efforts to construct measures that "travel well" across places and times. The centers of gravity that ground it are community situations and group characteristics. Given all the contextual baggage that burdens this notion, the least-liked measure nevertheless appears to capture remarkably well the concept's central ideas. It identifies effectively the most constitutionally tolerant citizens in the community. And if some of these tolerant citizens are also narrow-minded (albeit self-restrained), this muddle has more to do with the concept of negative constitutional tolerance than with the standard least-liked measure, which has produced the results reported in Table 14.2.

In Table 14.2 we report tolerance scores by nation and by type of community. Respondents were given one point for willingness to endure the participation of their least-liked group in each of the measure's five public activities, e.g. speaking at a local public meeting or running/standing for the town council. Hence, their highest possible tolerance score is five and the lowest zero.

First of all, and most strikingly, Table 14.2 suggests that our citizens' experience of tolerance is indeed rooted in their local communities: their

Table 14.2 Tolerance scores by country and type of community

Number of tolerant responses	US (%)	GB (%)	Suburban (%)	Urban (%)	Rural (%)
0	19	27	13	34	22
1	19	19	14	24	19
2	12	17	13	15	15
3	12	11	12	09	14
4	16	13	20	09	15
5	22	14	29	09	15
	100	100	100	100	100
(n)	375	375	250	250	250
Mean score	2.5	2.1	3.0	1.6	2.3

dispositions towards negative constitutional tolerance vary more across the different types of communities than they do between the two nations. This seems strong support for the contextual claims about tolerance, which in this case, apparently depends a good deal on the local community experience.

The pattern across different types of communities (suburban most tolerant, urban least tolerant, and rural in between) is the same in both the United States and Great Britain. This constitutes a second pattern shared by our American and British citizens, the first being the types of groups that they liked least (Table 14.1). Yet our participant observations in these communities suggest to us that this pattern may reflect a still further example of context dependency. Urban communities are surely not the least tolerant in all places and times. They may be so here because many citizens in each felt threatened by disadvantaged minorities in adjacent high-crime neighborhoods. Initially, we expected to find the least tolerance in our rural settings, both of which are relatively homogeneous, closed and isolated and possess a strong sense of community and common values. But our mainly white, mainly working-class, urban Manchester community is adjacent to a crime-ridden West Indian and Asian neighborhood, while our mainly white, mainly working-class urban Philadelphia community is an island that extends out westwards into a depressed African-American area with burned-out houses and drug dealers.[19]

Third, and again similarly, those citizens who strongly support constitutional tolerance for the groups they detest (tolerance scores of four or five) are very much in the minority in both the United States (38 per cent) and Great Britain (27 per cent). Approximately two-thirds of our respondents are unwilling to treat as equal citizens members of a group whose beliefs or practices they very strongly disapprove. They are disposed to exclude them from employment and political activities which, as citizens, they have the right to pursue. "A community can have laws without legislation." And those laws are often intolerant. This is what they told us in the focus groups. And this is what they tell us in the surveys. They would bar members of their most disapproved group from teaching in a local school or forming a local branch in the community. Under half would allow them to run/stand for the town council. The only toleration that a majority would extend to such organizations is the right to speak at a local public meeting and the right of the local library to stock books favoring the group's aims. Thus our data support the sobering conclusions of the early surveys of the 1950s and 1960s. Low as the proportions of tolerant citizens among our respondents are, they are actually somewhat higher than those found in subsequent surveys for the United States by Sullivan *et al.* (1982) and Gibson (1989) and for Britain by Barnum and Sullivan (1989). This may reflect the fact that our samples are community-based rather than national like these other surveys or, perhaps the effects of presenting the tolerance items in the middle of our long face-to-face interview on citizenship, which may have brought forward respondents' civic dispositions. But it may also reflect differences in the groups included in our least-liked measure and theirs, which takes us to the other principal source of context dependency.

As can be seen in Table 14.2, levels of tolerance are higher among our American than among our British respondents, a result also at variance with Barnham and Sullivan's (1989) study, which found very similar levels of tolerance in these two nations, and with Davis's (1986) study which likewise reported similar attitudes on civil liberties. Part of the explanation is the choice of Sinn Fein as the most disapproved group by almost half (47 per cent) of the British respondents and, in consequence, their focus on whether or not Sinn Fein should be permitted to participate in the designated five public activities. There is no established political party in the United States with anything like an equivalent record of support or responsibility for domestic violence and terror.[20] To assess Sinn Fein's part in pushing British levels of tolerance below those of the Americans, we removed from the analysis the British respondents whose least-liked group was Sinn Fein and balanced this by removing on the American side the respondents whose least-liked group was the KKK. Although this did not change the level of tolerance in the US data (it declined by only 2 per cent), the level of tolerance in the British data increased (by 12 per cent) to exceed the American scores.

This exercise draws our attention to the likelihood that negative constitutional tolerance depends not only on the situation of the particular community but also on the character of the disliked group, on its conduct and on the reactions that the conduct elicits. When the conduct of different types of disliked groups is incommensurable across countries (e.g. Sinn Fein and the KKK), this distorts comparative assessments. When disliked groups act up (e.g. the National Front in Manchester) or move into particular communities (e.g. the KKK in Philadelphia), this too distorts comparative results. And when disliked groups change their conduct over time (e.g. Sinn Fein), so will the outcomes in the data. Moreover, citizens' reactions to disliked groups may range from a brittle fear for their own physical safety, to moral revulsion at programs of violence against others, to bigoted racism, homophobia or sexism, or to distaste for self-righteous, intolerant Christians. Differences among these feelings, and among cognitive assessments of the groups and their conduct, affect citizens' judgements about the types of local public activities in which they are willing "to endure" a particular group's participation.

All this context dependency makes it very difficult to construct standardized measures that compare precisely levels of tolerance across countries and communities and over time. Is the United States more tolerant than Britain, or is Britain more tolerant than the United States? Since we are talking about relatively small differences in the survey data, these measures cannot tell us.[21] For there is no such thing as a meaningful abstract, universal attitude of tolerance, levels of which can be measured and compared precisely across different places and times. Comparative political psychologists are always challenged, whatever concept they are studying, by the fact that there are no context-free thinking processes. But tolerance is especially intractable. Context dependency defines it. The older context-free measures, which treated tolerance as an abstract, universal principle failed (Prothro and Grigg, 1960; McClosky, 1964). Sullivan *et al.* (1982)' least-liked measure is an ingenious attempt to introduce the missing contexts while rescuing something of the notion of a general psychological disposition "to endure." It introduces the missing contexts by introducing specific disliked groups. It rescues the elusive generality by standardizing citizens' feelings about the groups (all "least-liked"). This produces a measure that has been used successfully to investigate the dynamics of tolerance, the correlates of tolerance and how tolerance is learned. But these groups are quite different, as are the community contexts in which citizens react to them, not different enough to undermine the entire scientific enterprise, but different enough to create fundamental difficulties for precise descriptive work within that enterprise.

Furthermore, although our survey measure of tolerance suggests important information about levels and distributions, it cannot tell us anything about the reasoning behind respondents' answers. The tolerant say that they would allow a group of which they thoroughly disapprove to exercise its rights. Why? What persuades them to overcome the natural inclination to interfere? To understand the reasoning of the tolerant, we turn to the focus group discussions and in-depth interviews with community leaders where tolerance was explored in a semi-structured but free-ranging format.

Our qualitative measures of tolerance, both in the focus groups and in the interviews with the leaders, began with hypothetical references to a local branch of a neo-Nazi or Communist party. This scenario was chosen because it paralleled the survey question and because substantial proportions of survey respondents, particularly the Americans, identified a neo-Nazi, white supremacist or communist group as the one they disapproved most. Hence we asked the following questions about tolerance:

> Suppose that the vast majority of this community did *not* want a controversial group such as the National Front (U.S.: American Nazi Party) or the Communist Party (U.S.: American Communist Party) to establish a local branch and organize public meetings here in (Name of Community). Should these groups be allowed to do so anyway? What makes you say that? Anything else?

The first thing that we learn from the focus groups and in-depth interviews is that the quantitative survey measure seems have considerable validity – many respondents appear to understand and react to it in the constitutional frame of reference that was intended. Yet these discussions also suggest that the question strikes them as rather abstract, hypothetical and odd. Although they accepted and discussed the question, it became clear that the constitutional rights of such extreme groups were for them not a serious concern. They knew about such groups because of what they had read or seen on television, and in two instances from incidents in their communities. Nevertheless, in nearly every case they shifted the discussion quickly to the context of civic tolerance in order to discuss other groups of which their community had recently disapproved; and these groups were less often political than ethnic, religious or cultural: Mexican-Americans, Asian Britons, Moonies, Scientologists, Jehovah's Witnesses, Gypsies, New Age Travelers. Thus although the "least-liked" format of our survey question may "standardize" target groups in the constitutional context, it may not be connecting respondents with what are for them the most salient groups and contexts with which they experience and discuss tolerance.

Correlates of tolerance

We now turn our investigation of the meaning of tolerance toward two empirical issues. First, is tolerance associated with particular conceptions of good citizenship? Second, is there a trade-off between tolerance and other forms of good citizenship?

We preface our answers by reporting one startling negative finding. Among the citizen duties assessed in our survey is the duty "to be tolerant of people you disagree with." Respondents were asked whether they considered this a legal duty, a moral duty, not a duty but a good thing for citizens to do, or neither a duty nor a good thing for citizens to do. We expected that citizens who scored high on our constitutional tolerance scale would be more likely to regard "being tolerant of people you disagree with" as a legal or moral duty than would citizens who scored low on that scale. But, in fact, there is no significant correlation at the 0.05 level between these variables in either the American sample or the British sample. Perhaps this duty question taps dispositions toward civic tolerance that are not related to constitutional tolerance. Or, perhaps people who score high on the constitutional tolerance scale understand the legal–constitutional situation, but do not understand it as tolerance. In any case, the two indicators evidently measure different things.

Liberal and communitarian orientations

Table 14.3 presents the significant bivariate correlates of tolerance for the United States, Great Britain, and the two countries combined. It shows that, apart from type of community, the strongest correlates of tolerance are education (0.32), political knowledge (0.30) and political participation (0.24).

Table 14.3 Correlates of tolerance: US and GB

Variables	US/GB	US	GB
Background			
Education	0.32**	0.39*	0.25**
Suburban	0.26**	0.25**	0.29**
Urban	−0.24**	−0.25**	−0.27**
Social Class	0.17**	0.14**	0.22**
Political behavior			
Political Knowledge	0.30**	0.37**	0.23**
Political Participation	0.24**	0.26**	0.16**
Citizen predispositions			
Emphasizes Social Rights	−0.24**	−0.28**	−0.12*
Emphasizes Political Rights	0.21**	0.25**	0.16**
Emphasizes Contested Civil Rights	0.18**	0.20**	0.12**
Patriotism	−0.18**	−0.28**	−0.22**
Emphasizes Legal Duties	0.13**	0.23**	0.02
Emphasizes Civil Rights	0.11**	0.10	0.07
Emphasizes Liberal Duties	0.11**	0.13*	0.01
Emphasizes National Duty	−0.12**	−0.17**	−0.19**
Local Community Identification	−0.10**	−0.12**	−0.13**
Feminism	0.09**	0.14**	0.04
Specific rights and duties emphasizes duty to:			
Respect the Rights of Others	0.15**	0.17**	0.08
Respect the Flag	−0.13**	−0.23**	−0.14**
Being Loyal to Your Country	−0.11**	−0.13**	−0.17**
Defend Rights of Minorities	0.10	0.14**	−0.02
Protest Bad Laws	0.06	0.13**	0.03
Tolerate People You Disagree With	−0.04	−0.10	0.02
Emphasizes right to:			
Demonstrate Against Government	0.21**	0.25**	0.16**
Be Homosexual	0.10**	0.14**	0.04
Read Anything, inclu. Pornography	0.10**	0.14**	0.07

Notes
** = sig. <0.01 (2 tailed) * = sig. <0.05 (2-tailed)

These results echo those of earlier studies and lend broad support to the traditional idea that tolerance is more widespread among the politically informed and active. Table 14.3 also reveals that constitutional tolerance correlates with a range of measures of liberal and communitarian orientations, albeit less strongly but in the expected directions. The tolerant tend to give a high priority to politically-defined rights (the right to vote and to demonstrate) and to consensual civil rights such as freedom of speech and religion and the right to a fair trial, to privacy and to the protection of property. But there is a particularly strong association between tolerance and an emphasis on contested individual rights such as the right to an abortion, to be homosexual, to read pornography, to own a gun. By contrast, our most tolerant citizens are particularly unlikely to give priority to social rights – health care, education, housing and welfare – rights of a kind that people with relatively communitarian conceptions of citizenship might stress. The tolerant also tend to give high priority to specifically "political" duties – voting, protest, political discussion and education and defending minority rights, including the duty to "respect the rights of others." In other words, those citizens who are most likely to tolerate groups of which they disapprove have a heightened sense of their own individual civic and political rights, including their individual right to engage in unpopular or controversial acts. They are "liberal" democratic citizens with an understanding of citizenship that is relatively political, individualistic and contractarian.

This profile of the tolerant is sharpened by an examination of the intolerant. Their most pronounced characteristic is their identification with and loyalty to the nation and its symbols. Thus, they score high on the patriotism scale, which measures emotive attachments to nationalistic and patriotic symbols such as the American flag and the national anthem, and on the "national duty" scale, which measures the perceived importance of military service, respecting the flag and supporting the Prime Minister/President at times of crisis. The intolerant also express stronger than average identification with their local communities. In short, the high value that the intolerant put on national and local solidarity is difficult to convincingly reconcile with making room for minority groups of which they disapprove. This does not confirm a link between communitarian orientations and intolerance, but it is certainly consistent with it.

Tolerance and good citizenship

The simple correlates of tolerance also help us address the second empirical issue: is there a trade-off between tolerance and other forms of good citizenship, such as patriotism, participation and law-abidingness? The answer is mixed. We have already established that constitutionally tolerant citizens tend to place a low value on national solidarity. On the other hand, they are not politically indifferent – as the high positive correlations with political participation and political knowledge show. Nor do the tolerant undervalue law-abidingness, as might have been expected of those with permissive attitudes to groups with a reputation for law breaking. On the contrary, the tolerant give high priority to specifically legal duties – the duty to obey minor as well as major laws, to pay taxes, to report serious crimes, appear as witnesses in trials and serve on juries. Nor is there any evidence that their disapproval of the groups to which they concede rights is grounded in social prejudice. For example, there was no significant correlation between tolerance and sympathy for stigmatized groups such as Blacks, people with AIDS, immigrants, or people on welfare.

Our analysis has so far focused on the combined American and British samples. But an important difference between these samples needs to be underlined. Although the pattern of correlations is very similar for the two nations (in terms of direction and significance) the correlations are generally stronger among the American than among the British respondents. In particular, the association of tolerance with political knowledge and participation, and with a belief in the importance of individual rights and the duty to respect and protect those rights, is much stronger in the United States than in Britain. Given what we have already learned about the constitutional frame of reference within which people interpret the measure of constitutional tolerance, we interpret this difference as follows. In the United States, constitutional tolerance may be part of a constitutionalist ideology, which emphasizes individual political and civil rights,[22] and which is particularly strong among the politically involved; whereas in Britain tolerance is much less firmly embedded in any crystal-lized ideology or value-set. In the United States, a predisposition to be constitutionally tolerant is part of a wider consciousness of the rights of citizens. In Britain, where such consciousness is much weaker, tolerance is a free-floating value largely detached from others. This impression is rein-forced by our analysis of the third empirical issue: the grounds on which tolerant citizens justify their positions.

Justifications for tolerance

The tolerant say that they would allow groups of which they thoroughly disapprove to exercise their rights. Why? What persuades them to over-come the natural inclination to shut such groups down? To understand the reasoning of the tolerant, we return to our in-depth interviews with community leaders and focus groups.

The "trigger" question on tolerance, both in the focus groups and in the interviews with community leaders, was about the rights of a hypotheti-cal neo-Nazi or Communist Party to establish a local branch and organize public meetings in the community. The responses showed that most of our discussants believed that these groups had a reputation for violent confrontation and the disparaging of liberal and democratic institutions. And many assumed that the local presence of such groups would indeed lead to violence. Moreover, those citizens who gave the intolerant responses usually justified them on precisely those grounds.

The majority of American community leaders gave a tolerant answer to the trigger question. Still, there were marked differences in their under-standings and motives. When asked, "What makes you say that?" the Amer-icans (having confirmed that the groups should be allowed to set up a local branch) invariably referred to rights under the Constitution, often in their opening sentences: "they are protected under the First Amend-ment;" "I feel very strongly about First Amendment rights;" freedom of

speech, freedom of assembly;" "because they are protected under the Constitution." Indeed, it was striking how many American community leaders
began with a confident, crisp three or four word reply ("It's their right;"
"Freedom of Speech;" "First Amendment") as if they were answering a
technical or factual question rather than addressing a complex moral
issue. Even the small minority of intolerant leaders framed their answers
in terms of the Constitution, feeling the need to justify a departure from it
in favor of other overriding principles

The responses of the British community leaders were, by contrast,
notably more hesitant and discursive. They sought to avoid the issue by
speculating about whether such a group could make any headway in their
community (although this also reflected the hypothetical nature of the
question) and tended not to answer analytically or in terms of general
principles. They lacked a conceptual framework of rights in which to fit an
answer. Although the rights of the group were sometimes mentioned, it
was usually as an afterthought, or as only one consideration, to be weighed
against others such as the impact on local ethnic minorities. For the
majority, the scales came to tilt in favor of tolerance, but it was evident
that a minor change in circumstances could make them tilt the other way.
They saw the issue as one of contingency and political judgement, not
principle, and therefore said in effect, "It depends." For American leaders
the absolutistic discourse of constitutional rights was natural, almost
instinctive; whereas British community leaders sought to balance the costs
and benefits suggested by the preferences of those involved.

These very different routes of reasoning to tolerance taken by the
American and British community leaders were repeated by the focus
groups in both countries. In the United States the dominant response to
the trigger question was couched in terms of individual rights, rights given
by the Constitution, not by a wider principle of equal respect for persons
or equal liberties. The tone was often resigned. The law gave little option:
"Actually, if we want to abide by the Constitution, yes;" "As difficult as it is,
they have the right." Indeed, the American focus groups justified granting
rights to unpopular groups in terms of protecting their own rights: "the
tables could reverse;" "Who decides they're undesirable? I mean someone
could all of a sudden decide I'm undesirable."

By contrast, the British focus groups replace the language of individual
rights with a practical utilitarian language of community values and benefits. These discussants are much readier to give majorities in the local
community the right to determine whether or not unpopular groups
should be allowed entry. We have shown elsewhere (Conover *et al.*, 1991)
that in Britain conceptions of national identity and citizenship are not
constitutional or legal but "organic," a matter of gradually acquired
characteristics and shared experiences that enable people to "belong."
Thus, the emphasis highlights the duty to "fit in" rather than the "right to
dissent." This was particularly noticeable when the discussion moved away

from the Communist Party or National Front and into the civic frame with minorities like Gypsies or the homeless. Minority groups had the right to pursue their own way of life but only if they "conformed to the majority" (thereby undermining the principal function of tolerance according to J.S. Mill), or "did not adversely affect the community." Tolerance was predicated on judgments about whether a group was likely to conform in the future, even if it was currently unpopular; and much of the focus group discussion was, in fact, constructing a narrative about the degree to which the minority in question did or would conform. Information, impression and anecdote were traded, rumors were repeated and contradicted, in an attempt to reach a consensus about the acceptability of the minority. Whether or not to tolerate therefore became a matter of judgment, not about the applicability of principles to particular cases but rather about the acceptability of minorities to the local community.

Conclusion

Tolerance is one of the foremost values associated with citizenship. Good citizens are expected to be tolerant, and healthy liberal democracies are expected to produce a tolerant citizenry. But surveys of the public in the United States and Great Britain have consistently found that a majority of citizens are intolerant. We have considered this well-known finding from a number of perspectives. First, we have argued that the idea of tolerance has an ambiguous relationship with conceptions of good citizenship. The purpose of tolerance is to promote freedom and civic peace. But people can be tolerant for reasons that contradict our common understandings of good citizenship, and intolerant for reasons that are consistent with them. Second, we have argued strongly that the relationship of tolerance to citizenship depends on the understandings that people have both of tolerance and of citizenship, and that these understandings will be shaped by the national and community contexts in which people live.

Because American conceptions of tolerance incorporate ideas from the English political philosophers John Locke and John Stuart Mill, it may not seem surprising to find in the United States and Great Britain similar response patterns to equivalent survey items (e.g. Barnham and Sullivan, 1989). But it should be surprising, because the liberal political cultures of tolerance in these nations have evolved over 300 years in response to quite different demographic, political, social and economic challenges. Hence, when Americans and Britons express in surveys similar conclusions about the desirability of tolerating similar activities of similar groups, they are likely to have come to these conclusions by way of rather different understandings and justifications. The focus groups and in-depth interviews suggest that tolerance today means quite different things to citizens in these two liberal democracies, and that these different meanings structure the different practices of toleration that are recorded in their history books and daily newspapers.

Context matters so much because citizens' understandings of the concept of tolerance are structured by particular systemic, institutional and cultural factors, including controversies about intolerance in their local communities. Citizens store information about such events as narratives, which they process through their culture's frames of reference in order to work out their own feelings and views about the subject. Tolerance is a topic about which many of them have quite crystallized, if intolerant, attitudes, because hardly a month goes by without dramatic tolerance issues becoming topics for public discussion. What then are desirable aims for civic education in this area? The negative tolerance of "enduring" fellow citizens whose ways of life one detests does not sound at all as attractive as does the positive tolerance of open-mindedness and respect. Yet it is clearly the more critical of the two, and must be vigorously taught, for it prevents serious harm and secures equal rights, whereas the other protects identities and ameliorates second-class citizenship. Surely both must be promoted by liberal democratic states, but the mix and the particular formulations will vary according to the circumstances of international, national and local contexts.

British and American citizens have been educated to be tolerant and can be educated to be more tolerant still. But 100 years of public instruction and voting has not yet created publics anything like as tolerant as John Stuart Mill hoped to see. Survey data on the subject are not convincing because it is so difficult to measure precise levels of tolerance across communities and countries. It is clear enough, however, that citizens who strongly support constitutional tolerance for groups they detest are very much in the minority in both the United States and Great Britain. Specific plans for more effective education in the liberal virtue of toleration, including plans for learning through the democratic discussion that Ian Budge advocates, is required to put to rest the sceptics' fears of majority tyranny and to strengthen the case for electronically-based direct democracy.

Notes

1 These tape-recorded interviews with focus groups, community leaders and teachers were conducted by the principal investigators between 1991 and 1993. In all three communities in Great Britain, professional survey organizations conducted the face-to-face interviews with the adult random samples, parents and pupils. Corresponding interviews in the suburban and rural communities in the United States were carried out by interviewers who were recruited, trained and supervised by the principal investigators. Since the number of respondents in the adult random samples, parent samples and student samples varies somewhat between communities, each of these samples has been weighted to produce equal Ns for each community.

2 The random samples of adult citizens included approximately 125 respondents per community. The focus groups include 11 from British communities and 12 from American communities. Each was composed of eight to ten members

recruited as "quota samples" stratified to reflect community composition by gender, social class, ethnicity and age. We excluded respondents who had been interviewed in the surveys but, to facilitate interaction, included acquaintances as well as strangers (see Bloor *et al.*, 2001: 22–24). All the groups were chaired by a principal investigator. The elite interviewees (15 per community) were chosen according to a positional sample that included leaders from the following sectors of each community: political (e.g. mayor, city council members), business (e.g. CEO of major local employer), religious (e.g. minister), media (e.g. newspaper editor), education (e.g. head local secondary school).

3 Contemporary philosophers recognize this distinction too, although they are concerned that it is not so clear cut. (Heyd, 1996). Scanlon (1996), for example, characterizes the distinction as one between *institutional* politics, which involves fundamental legal and political rights (including voting, running/standing for election, and organizing and propagandizing to shape public policy), and *informal* politics, which involves attitudes, communications and relationships among individuals and groups in the political community.

4 Political scientists often characterize as "political tolerance" what we will call here "constitutional tolerance." We prefer the adjective "constitutional" to avoid falling into the habit of treating this electorally-focused arena as more genuinely "political" than the civic side of tolerance, or citizenship for that matter.

5 Civic tolerance directs attention more to persons than to their ideas, because the ways of life in question are typically embodied in the identities of the persons themselves (see Horton, 1996).

6 In the same vein, Sullivan *et al.* (1982: 111–112) asked their respondents about ten intolerant acts, six of which were "political" (e.g. free speech) and three of which were "social" (e.g. moving in next door). In a factor analysis, these items loaded consistently on two separate factors; but the factors were strongly correlated with each other.

7 Nonetheless, something like open-mindedness apparently helps in the constitutional arena too. Sullivan *et al.* (1982: 155) have found that, in the United States, dogmatism has a very strong negative relationship to their measure of constitutional tolerance. In their model, they introduce dogmatism as one of the important independent variables associated with tolerance. It makes sense to treat open-mindedness/dogmatism as a distinct independent variable when we are discussing extremist political groups like the KKK, with whom we would not expect even the most tolerant citizens to adopt a sympathetic listening orientation. But it doesn't make as much sense to treat it as a separate independent variable in the civic context, because here the most tolerant citizen is the most open-minded citizen. Here, open-mindedness is part of the *definition* of tolerance itself.

8 British commentators were, characteristically, neither startled by the "discovery" of illiberal publics in the United States and Britain, nor particularly worried about it. And, as for the elitist theory of democracy, that seemed old hat too, for it had long been embedded in the prevailing liberal interpretation of the British constitution.

9 Stouffer's study also explored public attitudes to the rights of socialists and atheists. But it is evident that for many respondents these terms were almost synonymous with "communist."

10 Subsequent studies have found somewhat more sanguine results (Sniderman *et al.*, 1989; Page and Shapiro, 1992). Still, as Kinder (1998) observes, the record isn't inspiring.

11 Cf. Sniderman *et al.* (1989); Gibson (1992).

12 See, for example, Gibson *et al.* (1992) on Russia, Shamir (1991) on Israel, and

Barnum and Sullivan (1989) on Britain, who report a level and distribution of political intolerance very similar to that in the United States.

13 Now I'm going to read out the names of various political groups one at a time. For each one, please tell me how much you approve or disapprove of this group using the numbers on this card. If you very strongly disapprove of the group, you should give it a score of "0." If you very strongly approve of the group, you should give it a score of "10." If you neither disapprove nor approve of the group, you should give it a "5." If your views are somewhat in between, you should read out the number that comes closest to how you feel." From what you have told me, you particularly disapprove of *Read Names of R's Two Lowest-Rated Groups (or All Groups Tied For the Lowest rating)*. Which group do you disapprove of the most?

14 Still, the patterns reflect how local contexts shape thinking about tolerance. The American suburban community was more likely to choose the KKK (there had recently been a march), and the British suburban community was more likely to choose the National Front (there had recently been trouble in the nearby East End, from which many of them came). Gay rights groups were more likely to be chosen in the rural communities of both countries. Pro-choice groups were more likely to be chosen in the American rural community (where Protestant churches are very active) and in the British urban community (where there is a large Catholic minority).

15 This survey was conducted before Sinn Fein transformed itself into a legitimate political force pursuing a peaceful settlement of the conflict in Northern Ireland.

16 Sullivan *et al.* list was read out whereas ours was shown on a card. Sullivan *et al.* gave short labels to their groups ("socialists," fascists," etc.) whereas our card spelled out the type of organization in slightly more detail and gave specific examples. Groups included in their list but not in ours were: socialists, atheists and the Symbionese Liberation Army. Groups included in our list but not in theirs included feminist groups, gay rights groups, animal rights groups and, in Great Britain, Provisional Sinn Fein and the Campaign for Nuclear Disarmament. Sullivan *et al.* asked their respondents whether the disliked group should be outlawed, banned for running for the Presidency, and subject to wiretaps, whereas our survey did not.

17 Reliabilities: sample 1 (0.6500), sample 2 (0.6946).

18 It is the universality of tolerance as a general principle or rule that is most problematic, for tolerance is a virtue that is pragmatic and contextual. That is why Americans have found it so difficult to construct universally applicable laws in this area, laws that will constrain the activities of neo-Nazis but not civil rights groups. There always seem to be limits, which always seem to be defined in the context of the character of particular groups and situations. Tolerance is a psychological disposition and a practice, not a general principle. Tolerance is always case-specific; as a "principle," it is always wrapped in "It depends."

19 The particular character of these two urban contexts may trigger what Walzer (1997: 38–39), revising Sidgwick, suggests may be an inverse relationship between heterogeneity outside the local community and intolerance within it, or what Sullivan *et al.* (1982) characterize as the powerful influence of "threat perceptions."

20 The impact of Sinn Fein on the results is suggested by the particularly wide gap between American and British respondents in the proportions who would tolerate their most-disapproved group running for office.

21 We might learn more about *this* question by collecting comparative data on laws and intolerant activities, on the rules and conduct that constitute, along-

side the attitude, the *practice* of tolerance. The problem lies not in our measures but instead in the equivocal nature of the attitude that drives this practice,
the attitude that considers toleration desirable and motivates it.
22 Sullivan *et al.* (1982) find in their American model a strong relationship
between constitutional tolerance and support for constitutional principles.

References

Barnum, D.G. and J.L. Sullivan, (1989) "Attitudinal Tolerance and Political
Freedom in Britain", *British Journal of Political Science* 19: 136–145.

Bloor, M., J. Frankland, M. Thomas and K. Stuart, (2001) *Focus Groups in Social
Research* (London: Sage).

Budge, I. (1996) *The New Challenge of Direct Democracy* (Cambridge: Polity Press).

Conover, P.J., I. Crewe and D.D. Searing (1991) "The Nature of Citizenship in the
United States and Great Britain: Empirical Comments on Theoretical Themes",
Journal of Politics 53: 800–832.

Cook, T.D. and D.T. Campbell (1979) *Quasi-Experimentation: Design and Analysis
Issues* (Boston: Houghton Mifflin).

Davis, J.A. (1986) "'British and American Attitudes: Similarities and Contrasts", in
R. Jowell, S. Witherspoon and L. Brook (eds, *British Social Attitudes: The 1986
Report* (Aldershot: Gower).

Fletcher, G.P. (1996) "The Instability of Tolerance", in D. Heyd (ed.) *Toleration;
An Elusive Virtue* (Princeton: Princeton University Press).

Frazer, E. and N. Lacey (1994) "MacIntyre, Feminism and the Concept of Practice" in J. Horton and S. Mendus (eds) *After MacIntyre: Critical Perspectives on the
Work of Alasdair MacIntyre* (Notre Dame: University of Notre Dame Press).

Gibson, J.L. (1989) "The Structure of Attitudinal Tolerance in the United States",
British Journal of Political Science 19: 562–570.

Gibson, J.L. (1992a) "Alternative Measures of Political Tolerance: Must Tolerance
Be 'Least Liked'", *American Journal of Political Science* 36: 560–577.

Gibson, J.L., R.M. Duch and K. Tedin (1992) "Democratic Values and the Transformation of the Soviet Union", *Journal of Politics* 54: 329–371.

Heyd, D. (1996) "Introduction", in D. Heyd (ed., *Toleration; An Elusive Virtue*
(Princeton: Princeton University Press).

Horton, J. (1996) "Tolerance as a Virtue", in D. Heyd (ed.) *Toleration; An Elusive
Virtue* (Princeton: Princeton University Press).

Huckfeldt, R. and J. Sprague (1995) *Citizens, Politics and Social Communication* (New
York: Cambridge University Press).

Kinder, D.R. (1998) "Opinion and Action in the Realm of Politics", in D.T.
Gilbert, S.T. Fiske and G. Lindzey (eds) *The Handbook of Social Pschology* (New
York: McGraw Hill).

Laslett, P. (1971) "Political Theory and Scientific Research", *Government and
Opposition* 6: 219–223.

McClosky, H. (1964) "Consensus and Ideology in American Politics", *American
Political Science Review* 58: 361–382.

Mendus, S. (1987) "Introduction", in S. Mendus and D. Edwards (eds) *On Toleration* (Oxford: Oxford University Press).

Nunn, C., H.J. Crockett Jr and J.A. Williams Jr (1978) *Tolerance for Non-Conformity*
(San Francisco: Jossey-Bass).

Page, B. and R. Shapiro (1992) *The Rational Public* (Chicago: University of Chicago Press).

Prothro, J.W. and C.W. Grigg (1960) "Fundamental Principles of Democracy: Bases of Agreement and Disagreement", *Journal of Politics* 22: 276–294.

Raphael, D.D. (1971) "Toleration, Choice and Liberty", *Government and Opposition* 6: 229–234.

Raphael, D.D. (1988) "The Intollerable", in S. Mendus (ed.) *Justifying Toleration: Conceptual and Historical Perspectives* (Cambridge: Cambridge University Press).

Rawls, J. (1993) *Political Liberalism* (New York: Columbia University Press).

Scanlon, T.M. (1996) "The Difficulty of Tolerance", in D. Heyd (ed.) *Toleration; An Elusive Virtue* (Princeton: Princeton University Press).

Searing, D.D. (1982) "Rules of the Game in Britain: Can the Politicians Be Trusted?", *American Political Science Review* 76: 239–258.

Shamir, M. (1991) "Political Intolerance Among Masses and Elites in Israel: A Reevaluation of the Elitist Theory of Democracy", *Journal of Politics* 53: 1010–1043.

Sniderman, P.M. (1993) "The New Look in Public Opinion Research", in A.W. Finifter (ed.) *Political Science: The State of the Discipline II* (Washington DC: The American Political Science Association).

Sniderman, P.M., P. Tetlock, J.M. Glaser, D.P. Green and Michael Hout (1989) "Principled Tolerance and the American Mass Public", *British Journal of Political Science* 19: 25–46.

Stouffer, S.A. (1955) *Communism, Conformity and Civil Liberties* (Garden City, NY: Doubleday).

Sullivan, J.L., J. Piereson and G.E. Marcus (1982) *Political Tolerance and American Democracy* (Chicago: University of Chicago Press).

Sullivan, J.L., P. Walsh, M. Shamir, D. Barnum, and J.L. Gibson (1993) "Why Politicians Are More Tolerant: Selective Recruitment and Socialization Among Political Elites in Britain, Israel, New Zealand and the United States", *British Journal of Political Science*, 23: 51–76.

Walzer, M (1997) *On Toleration* (New Haven: Yale University Press).

Williams, B. (1996) "Toleration: An Impossible Virtue?", in D. Heyd (ed.) *Toleration; An Elusive Virtue* (Princeton: Princeton University Press).

Bibliography of the works of Ian Budge

Published books

1   Patterns of Democratic Agreement PhD Thesis 1966 (Ann Arbor, MI, University Micro-films, USA).
2   (with D.W. Urwin) (1966) *Scottish Political Behaviour*, (London, Longman).
3   (1970) *Agreement and the Stability of Democracy*, (Chicago, Markham), (Spanish edition, Buenos Aires, 1971).
4   (with J. Brand, M. Margolis and A.L.M. Smith) (1972) *Political Stratification and Democracy*, (London, Macmillan).
5   (with C. O'Leary) (1973) *Belfast: Approach to Crisis*, (London, Macmillan)
6   (with Ivor Crewe, D.J. Farlie) (1976) *Party Identification and Beyond*, (London and New York, Wiley).
7   (with D.J. Farlie) (1977) *Voting and Party Competition*, (London and New York, Wiley).
8   (with D.J. Farlie) (1983) *Explaining and Predicting Elections*, (London, Allen and Unwin) (Spanish edition, Centre for Constitutional Studies, Madrid, (1986) *Pronosticos Eletorales*).
9   (with David McKay, Ivor Crewe and Kenneth Newton) (1983) *The New British Political System*, (London, Longman). Second edition *The Changing British Political System, (1987)*. Third edition *The Developing British Political System: the 1990s*, (1993).
10 (with D. Robertson, D.J. Hearl, eds) (1987) *Ideology, Strategy and Party Movement*, (Cambridge, CUP).
11 (with Hans E. Keman) (1990) *Parties and Democracy: Coalition Formation and Government Functioning in 22 Democracies*, (Oxford, OUP) Paperback 1993
12 (with M.J Laver, ed.) (1992) *Party Policy and Government Coalitions*, (London, Sage)
13 (with J. Woldendorp, Hans E. Keman) (1993) *Handbook of Democratic Government*, (Dordrecht, Kluwer). Also published as special issue of *European Journal of Political Research*, (1993).
14 (with David McKay (eds)) (1994) *Developing Democracy*, (London, Sage), (with two editorial chapters).
15 (with H.D. Klingemann, R.I. Hofferbert) (1994) *Parties, Policies and Democracy* (Boulder CO, Westview)
16 *The New Challenge of Direct Democracy*, (1996) (Cambridge, Polity) Japanese edition, (2001).

17   (with K. Newton) (1997) *The Politics of the New Europe*, (London, Longman) Polish, Spanish and Korean editions.

18   (with Ivor Crewe, David McKay, Kenneth Newton) (1998) *The New British Politics*, (London, Addison Wesley Longman). Revised edition 2000, second edition 2002, third edition 2004.

19   (with Jaap Woldendorp, Hans Keman) (2000) *Party Governments in 48 Democracies*, (1945–1998) (Dordrecht, Kluwer).

20   (with H.D. Klingemann, Andrea Volkens, Judith Bara) (2001) *Mapping Policy Preferences, Estimates for Parties, Governments and Electors 1945–1998*, (Oxford, OUP). Reprinted 2004: Winner, APSA Comparative Data-Set Prize, 2003.

21   (with Michael McDonald) (2005) *Elections, Parties, Democracy: Conferring the Median Mandate*, (Oxford, OUP5).

Index

eBooks

eBooks – at www.eBookstore.tandf.co.uk

A library at your fingertips!

eBooks are electronic versions of printed books. You can store them on your PC/laptop or browse them online.

They have advantages for anyone needing rapid access to a wide variety of published, copyright information.

eBooks can help your research by enabling you to bookmark chapters, annotate text and use instant searches to find specific words or phrases. Several eBook files would fit on even a small laptop or PDA.

NEW: Save money by eSubscribing: cheap, online access to any eBook for as long as you need it.

Annual subscription packages

We now offer special low-cost bulk subscriptions to packages of eBooks in certain subject areas. These are available to libraries or to individuals.

For more information please contact webmaster.ebooks@tandf.co.uk

We're continually developing the eBook concept, so keep up to date by visiting the website.

www.eBookstore.tandf.co.uk